UNDER THE
BLOODY
FLAG

UNDER THE BLOODY FLAG

Pirates of the Tudor Age

JOHN C. APPLEBY

First published 2009

The History Press
The Mill, Brimscombe Port
Stroud, Gloucestershire, GL5 2QG
www.thehistorypress.co.uk

British Library Cataloguing in Publication Data.
A catalogue record for this book is available from the British Library.

ISBN 978 0 7524 4851 0

Typesetting and origination by The History Press
Printed in Great Britain

Contents

Acknowledgements

Many thanks to Jonathan Reeve of The History Press for commissioning the book, to Simon Hamlet and Robin Harries for seeing it through to publication, and to Sandra Mather of the University of Liverpool for preparing the maps with such skill. Although this work draws on my own research among the records of the High Court of the Admiralty in The National Archives at Kew, which was originally undertaken under the supervision of Professsor Kenneth Andrews, it makes extensive use of the contributions of other scholars. In particular, I would like to acknowledge my debt to the works of K.R. Andrews, D. Loades, D.B. Quinn and N.A.M. Rodger on maritime and naval history, and the works of Peter Earle and Marcus Rediker on the history of piracy. In addition, I thank the staff of The National Archives and The British Library for their assistance, and the archivists of local record offices who responded promptly to my enquiries.

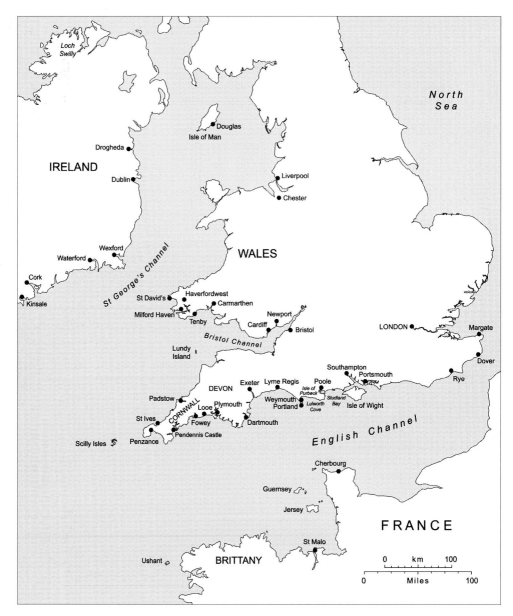

Map 1: Southern England, Wales and Ireland.

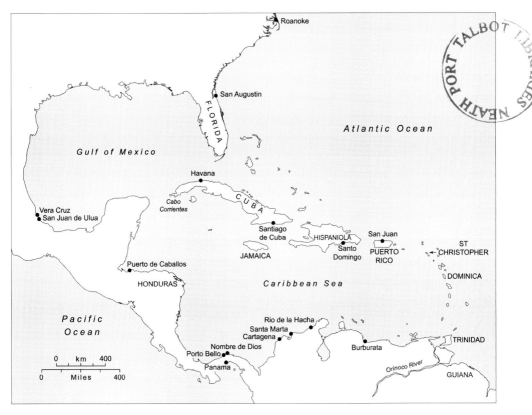

Map 2: The Spanish Caribbean.

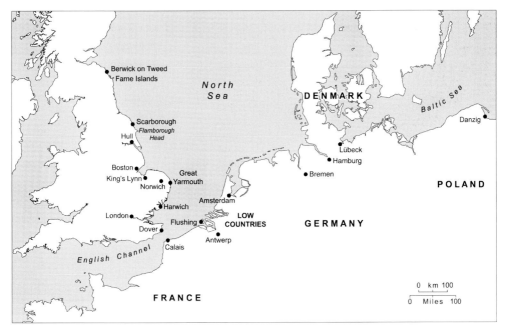

Map 3: Eastern England and the North Sea.

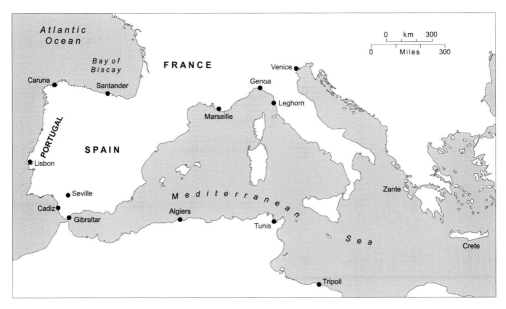

Map 4: Spain, Portugal and the Mediterranean.

Introduction

By the later Middle Ages maritime depredation was a long-standing and widespread problem. The voyages of traders and fishermen were threatened by sea robbers of varying description, though the intensity of activity ebbed and flowed like the seas on which they sailed. At times, the prevalence of such predators contributed to a deep-seated aversion of the sea, particularly as an unsettling and unknowable place of danger and chaos.[1]

Yet maritime robbery and spoil assumed varied forms. Although legal definitions were blurred by practice, which at times eroded the boundary between trade and plunder, a distinction can be drawn between piracy, reprisal venturing and privateering, and corsair enterprise. Piracy had a protean and prosaic quality, enabling it to develop and flourish almost unchecked. In theory, pirates were criminals, the enemies of all mankind who faced execution if caught; in practice, they were often maintained by seafaring communities and protected by local officials or rulers. Within some regions piracy flourished as a community crime. Organized as a small-scale business, it provided employment and profit, while serving as an outlet for adventurous or violent men and boys. Ports and havens along the south coast of England, including Rye, Fowey or Dartmouth, acquired notorious reputations as nests of pirates who plundered unwary shipping in the Channel. According to the law and custom of the sea, reprisal venturing and what was later to be known as privateering were distinguished from piracy by their legal character and status. Although a clear distinction was to emerge between these lawful forms of seaborne plunder, acknowledged in the separate use of letters of reprisal and letters of marque, both were hopelessly confused during the sixteenth and early seventeenth centuries. Authorizing reprisals was a widely accepted means of allowing merchants and shipowners to recover losses from the subjects of a foreign state, and it was subject to strict control and regulation. During times of war, however, when reprisal venturing was encouraged for strategic and economic purposes, through the indiscriminate issue of commissions, it assumed the characteristics of privateering. As a form of war it might be compared with the tradition of corsair activity within the Mediterranean, though this encompassed plunder, brigandage and slave raiding.[2]

There was, of course, a degree of overlap between these different forms of plunder and spoil. Recruits from various backgrounds, including a large number of seafarers, served aboard pirate and reprisal vessels. The companies of some ships might resort to piratical spoil and lawful plunder during the course of the same voyage. While the law did not recognize the nuances of such fractured voyages or life cycles, they were overtly acknowledged in the language of seamen, notably in the widespread use of the term 'sea roving' to describe an enterprise which seemed to fall between piracy and privateering. Whether justified as a means of

A nineteenth-century illustration of a pirate ship being careened. Islands such as the Scilly Isles provided secure locations for the repair and maintenance of pirate ships during the sixteenth century. (*Authentic Memoirs of the Lives and Exploits of English Highwaymen, Pirates and Robbers*)

unauthorized retaliation or reprisals, sea roving represented blurred boundaries at sea, reflecting the way in which piracy was also a contested crime, thriving on ambiguity and uncertainty.

The difficulty in maintaining the distinction between lawful and unlawful depredation was a direct consequence of the nature of the early modern state and of sea power in general. In the absence of professional navies, and with small royal fleets made up of ships which could still be challenged by well-armed private vessels, maritime power was essentially fragmented. In addition it was marked by an inescapable intermingling of public and private interests. Under these conditions it has been argued that 'private, commercial warfare was the normal form of warfare in the open sea'.[3] In England during the fourteenth and fifteenth centuries it became common practice for monarchs to sanction what were effectively private wars of reprisal, unintentionally encouraging the spread of disorder and lawlessness at sea. While this expedient mobilized and exploited private resources, it also drew on a shadowy tradition of piracy and piratical enterprise which persisted throughout the sixteenth and early seventeenth centuries. It allowed arch-pirates, such as Henry Strangeways or John Callice, to redeem their misdeeds through royal service at sea, and enabled more renowned pirate leaders, like Francis Drake or Martin Frobisher, to serve as officers in the Queen's Navy. It is no coincidence that the development of an effective state navy during the second half of the seventeenth century was followed by a sustained, and largely successful, effort to eradicate organized piracy.[4]

Past experience demonstrated that piracy and other forms of irregular depredation flourished at times of weak rule or in remote regions. In south-west England it may have served as a safety valve for aristocratic and gentry disorder or violence, which successive monarchs found difficult to contain. Within a distant, maritime borderland, however, resorting to piracy was almost a way of life, especially for itinerant seafarers subject to occasional and disjointed patterns of employment. Favoured by geography and well-established commercial links, pirates and sea rovers from the south-west ranged across the Channel and into the Irish Sea, disposing of their booty in favoured haunts which served as unofficial markets and provisioning centres. The importance of Ireland to the maintenance of this pattern of venturing was recognized in 1521 by Henry VIII's lieutenant in Dublin. In the face of a growing problem, he requested a commission 'to put to death all rovers of the sea taken in this land', warning that Ireland was 'the very land of refuge that English pirates most resort unto'.[5]

Piracy and other forms of depredation flourished throughout the sixteenth century. As a result, the Tudor regime was faced with an intractable problem which grew progressively worse. To some extent this was self-inflicted, particularly given the apparent decline in lawlessness at sea during the 1480s and 1490s. Thereafter war bred piracy and maritime disorder. Conditions at sea were reinforced by the unsettling consequences of social and economic change, including population growth, which were increasingly influenced by religious rivalries and hostility.

A nineteenth-century illustration of a clash between two men-of-war. Most conflicts at sea involving pirates were fought with small ordnance and hand weapons, including bows and arrows and stones, though more serious clashes could occur, especially on longer voyages. (*Authentic Memoirs of the Lives and Exploits of English Highwaymen, Pirates and Robbers*)

But the growth of disorderly plunder merged with aggressive commercial ambitions and ventures, especially in new, long-distance enterprises to west Africa and America. The competition with Spain and Portugal which accompanied such schemes helped to re-direct and re-structure piracy and privateering, opening up profitable opportunities which were eagerly seized by Drake and his successors.

The adventurous and aggressive foreign policy of Henry VIII from the 1520s to the 1540s thus witnessed a resurgence of seaborne spoil which initiated a long-term upward trend in depredation, punctuated by short-term fluctuations. The official encouragement of privateering during the wars with France led to the spread of disorderly venturing within, and occasionally beyond, the Channel. Flemish and Iberian shipping became a target for adventurers such as Robert Reneger of Southampton, whose activities along the coast of Spain during the early 1540s paved the way for others to follow. Much of this enterprise was based in ports and

A nineteenth-century illustration of a conflict at sea between a pirate ship and a naval vessel. Though such sea fights were unusual during the sixteenth century, royal ships occasionally caught pirates in the Channel or the Irish Sea. Many more escaped. (*Authentic Memoirs of the Lives and Exploits of English Highwaymen, Pirates and Robbers*)

harbours along the coast of south and south-west England, though it spread rapidly to southern Ireland. The difficult mid-Tudor period provided an opportunity for the consolidation of the disorder at sea. It also favoured the anti-Spanish direction of English plunder. The persistence of piracy and piratical activity during the 1560s and 1570s contributed to the growth of Anglo-Spanish tension; mutual resentment and antagonism drew a growing number of predators into the eastern Atlantic. At the same time, the later 1560s and 1570s experienced a dramatic increase in the scale and intensity of local piracy around the British Isles.[6]

These conditions encouraged the emergence of deep-sea depredation, exacerbating a crisis in Anglo-Spanish relations. Such was the nature of the problem, that the revival of diplomacy during the mid-1570s saw little decline in the lawlessness at sea. Alongside the activities of local pirate groups, led by Callice and others, in 1577 Drake embarked on a voyage that dramatically revealed the oceanic range

A sixteenth-century vessel, well armed with ordnance for protection against pirates or for use in the spoil of trading vessels. (*Buccaneers of the Pacific*)

A Dutch illustration of pirates or sea rovers in the North Sea. During the 1560s and 1570s English pirates were very active in the North Sea. Under the leadership of captains such as William Johnson of Boston, who operated in a variety of small craft, they inflicted significant damage on fishing fleets from the Low Countries. (*The Scourge of the Indies*)

of English rovers. His return, three years later, after circumnavigating the globe, also demonstrated the rich rewards from preying on vulnerable trade and shipping in weakly defended regions of Spain's empire. Furthermore, the support of the monarchy for this venture underlined the ambiguous response of successive rulers to the problem of piracy.

In these circumstances the outbreak of hostilities with Spain during 1585, followed by the promotion of reprisal venturing as a means of waging war at sea, served to channel much of the maritime disorder into a legitimate form of enterprise. But the Elizabethan regime failed to control the rapid growth of a disorderly business. The loosely regulated expansion of privateering was followed by piratical attacks on the shipping of friends and allies which grew in scale and range as the war progressed. The experience of the 1580s and 1590s affirmed the striking power and profitability of private maritime enterprise. But it was based on such lax control that it confused the boundary between lawful reprisal voyages and piracy. From the perspective of friends as well as enemies, indeed, the later stages of the war seemed to confirm a widespread suspicion that piracy was a peculiar English addiction.

If the experience of the sixteenth century served to confuse the relationship between piracy and privateering, at the same time it demonstrated the growing variety and vitality of seaborne robbery. In terms of its operation and organization, it ranged from highly opportunistic, almost accidental spoil, by small numbers of poorly armed men and boys, to more effectively structured and planned entrepreneurial plunder, undertaken by large groups of well-armed rovers who were usually promoted and protected by shore-based supporters. Between these two extremes there was a great variety of practice, which included river piracy along the Thames. This varied pattern was manifest in the differences between coastal, offshore and deep-sea piracy and roving. Coastal and offshore spoil was a well-established activity which flourished with renewed vigour during the sixteenth century. Although it was particularly concentrated within the Channel and its approaches, it easily grew into a widespread and endemic problem. By contrast, deep-sea piracy was a new form of depredation which appeared after 1550. Its emergence had far-reaching consequences for the development of piracy, especially in the use of overseas bases and markets. This was the result of a centrifugal tendency within English depredation, reinforced by hostility towards Spain, which encouraged pirates and rovers into the eastern Atlantic, the Caribbean and the Mediterranean seas. Though it was still undeveloped in 1603, the resort to ports and harbours in north Africa by disorderly men-of-war and pirates during the later years of the war with Spain foreshadowed a weakening in the link between sea rovers and their home communities.[7]

While the growing dependence of pirates on overseas bases after 1604 facilitated their social and cultural labelling as outcasts, throughout the period covered by this study they remained attached to local communities, retaining links with family, friends or neighbours. An impressive body of evidence testifies to the importance of these connections for the maintenance of piracy as a business venture. Without widespread assistance from land-based dealers, including the connivance of officials, robbery at sea would not have developed as a vigorous commercial enterprise or become such a serious problem. The case of John Piers, a notorious pirate from Padstow, who haunted the coasts of south-west England during the 1570s and early 1580s, with the aid of his mother, Ann, a reputed witch, was an unusual example of the commonplace relations between sea and shore.

By various means pirate booty was re-distributed and widely dispersed in commercial and gift exchanges. During periods of intense activity pirate companies effectively organized their own shipboard markets, attracting large groups of potential purchasers eager to acquire cheap commodities, free of customs duties. In terms of the damage inflicted by pirates on trade and shipping, the circulation of plundered cargoes may have helped to limit the cost to the wider economy. Although this was no comfort to the victims of piracy or privateering, some of whom were faced with bankruptcy or worse, the traffic in stolen goods undoubtedly promoted community tolerance of organized crime, especially if it was focused on overseas targets. Nonetheless, maritime depredation inflicted widespread disruption and damage to trade, fishing and shipping, provoking allegations of commercial decay from ports such as Southampton during the 1570s, as well as a growing volume of international complaint.

The characteristics of piracy during the sixteenth century influenced or informed the tactics, life cycles and emerging culture of pirate groups. At the same time, they shaped the response of the Tudor regime to a crime which was also a social problem and a means of employment for a growing number of recruits.

Pirates operated at various locations at sea, along the coast and rivers, adopting tactics which drew on a tradition of past practice and knowledge. For those who wore masks, it was intended as an anonymous crime, comparable to the activities of poachers and robbers on land.[8] For others, it was a very public execution of robbery by men who were often widely known ashore, and whose leaders earned notoriety or renown as arch-pirates. Driven by the grinding pressures of poverty and lack of work, and attracted by the prospect of booty at sea, pirates exploited and employed a repertoire of tactics to achieve their aims. Depending on the size and armament of vessels, success often depended on surprise and surreptitious enterprise. Although few pirate groups publicly proclaimed their identity, during the later sixteenth century a growing number of captains and companies were prepared to adopt bolder, aggressive and occasionally defiant methods. At sea the use of red and black flags appeared among men-of-war or privateering vessels during the war with Spain. Both were meant to intimidate victims and opponents. While Drake employed black flags and streamers in the Caribbean during 1585, three years later one of the Queen's ships, the *Elizabeth Bonaventure*, had 'a bluddey flagge' and two flags of St George, for use during the Armada campaign.[9]

Intimidation, violence and even torture were part of the tactics employed by pirates and other rovers. It is difficult to determine the extent of the violence at sea. It may have been used more against overseas, rather than domestic, victims, especially during times of war and international crisis. While religious rivalries inflamed violent behaviour, anti-Catholicism should not be confused with long-standing enmity towards France, though it certainly affected the behaviour of some groups of maritime robbers, while influencing the emergence of hostility towards Spain. Depending on conditions and context, the use of violence ranged from the symbolic to the pathological. Although a functional purpose is indicated by reports that some pirate groups only used violent methods if they met resistance, this does not account for the horrific, and apparently arbitrary, catalogue of injuries which were inflicted on seafarers and others during the period covered by this book. In the North Sea some Flemish fishermen were badly beaten and treated like dogs, while others were unharmed and even granted a share of the booty. Across the Atlantic, within the competitive and contested arena of the Caribbean, pirates handled some of their victims with courtesy, while inflicting cruel and barbaric punishments on others. The undercurrent of violence which was an inescapable characteristic of piracy and sea roving appeared to grow stronger during the second half of the sixteenth century.

Living with danger was an unavoidable fact of life for seafarers, though its exaggerated significance aboard pirate ships may have powerfully contributed to the development of pirate culture, especially during the 1560s and 1570s. If piracy for many of its practitioners was a part-time employment, from the 1540s onwards conditions favoured prolonged participation in the business for a growing number of recruits. In an unusual, though far from unprecedented development, what might be termed 'career pirates' emerged. They survived partly by exploiting the uncertain boundary between piracy and privateering; many of those who were caught, and put on trial before the High Court of Admiralty, defended their actions as legitimate, but unauthorized, reprisals. Some of these recruits enjoyed lengthy careers, serving as links between different generations of pirates, in a way that encouraged the inheritance of past custom. Under these conditions patterns of behaviour and conduct coalesced in the formation of a loose pirate brotherhood during the 1570s, whose leading figures were Callice and his associate, Robert Hicks.

Although they were neither as independent nor as coherent as subsequent pirate communities, the groups of pirates who operated during the 1570s were bound together by similar life cycles and backgrounds. Their sense of community was articulated through common practices, including an unwritten and informal code of conduct which was reinforced by a hierarchical structure, publicly acknowledged by the loyalty of pirate companies to their leaders. Loyalty and community were promoted by shipboard life. Both were recognized in the division of booty into shares, with captains and other officers receiving more than other members of the company. While the ownership of pirate ships remains obscure, vessels were

granted by captains to loyal officers, spawning new groups as well as encouraging
solidarity and bonds of association. Companionship and hospitality were deliberately promoted in pirate haunts along the coast, where crowds of men and women
gathered for purposes of business and entertainment, or to secure employment.
William Baylye, a sailor of Barnstaple, recounted how he was hired by the pirate
captain, Stephen Haynes, in Studland Bay during October 1582, when he was
unemployed and 'in greate extreamitye for wante of raymente and moneye'.[10] He
was given a suit of clothing of green cotton by Haynes, whose company of about
thirty wore a similar outfit.

Nevertheless, piracy was a serious crime which provoked a firm but uneven
response from the Tudor regime. As a crime it was dealt with by the Lord Admiral
and the High Court of Admiralty. Because of its potentially damaging international consequences, however, monarchs and their councillors retained a close
interest in the problem. From the 1540s onwards the Privy Council was heavily
involved in dealing with overseas complaints against English piracy and disorderly
spoil. But this was a problem which taxed the resources and efficiency of Tudor
rule. Although it encouraged administrative innovation during the 1560s and
1570s, with the appointment of commissioners for piracy in the maritime shires
of England and Wales, the scale and nature of the problem encouraged an uneasy
combination of coercion and compromise. The result was a fluctuating pattern of
punishment and pardon, and the survival of lawlessness and violence at sea which
flourished under the cover of ambivalent public attitudes and responses.[11]

By drawing upon a wealth of evidence, including the rich resources of the
High Court of Admiralty, this book aims to provide a narrative of English piracy
and sea roving from *c.*1485 to 1603. Because of the inherent ambiguity of the
subject, it encompasses reprisal venturing and privateering, though its main focus
is on charting the contours of illegal and disorderly enterprise. While examining
the structure and organization of maritime plunder, it also surveys the changing character of piracy, at a time when the state was prepared to sanction, or to
tolerate, certain forms of robbery at sea. As such, it provides a perspective on the
broader development of English seafaring activity, and of the wider response to
the growth of maritime lawlessness and disorder.

War and Maritime Plunder from the 1480s to the 1540s

Like the trade off which it fed, piracy within the British Isles fluctuated widely in scale and intensity. Random and opportunistic spoil occurred almost anywhere and at any time during this period; however, more organized and business-like enterprise was closely associated with war and linked with lawful reprisals or privateering. Although rarely used by Henry VII, the exploitation of reprisal venturing for economic or strategic purposes became a feature of war at sea under the early Tudor monarchy. Henry VIII's wars with France created a fertile breeding ground for the growth of maritime plunder in various guises. Indeed, the period from the 1520s to the 1540s was a transitional stage in the expansion of English seaborne plunder, during which well-established methods of depredation were revitalized and renovated by the opportunities presented by Anglo-French rivalry and conflict. The resurgence of piracy during these years drew on a long tradition of cross-Channel raiding, heavily focused on French targets, which also led to the increasing spoil of Spanish trade and shipping. In confusing and chaotic conditions, English depredation began to develop a pattern of activity that would profoundly influence its subsequent character and direction.

Later medieval traditions and contexts

The development of English piracy and other forms of depredation during this period grew out of varied traditions of maritime plunder which were main-

tained during the later Middle Ages. From an early date piracy was supported
by members of local communities, including merchants and mariners as well as
landowners, and sustained by aristocratic warlords or chieftains who possessed
private fleets that were used for a variety of purposes. Furthermore, in exploiting
and exposing the limitations of the medieval state, the growth of maritime depredation was assisted by conflicting and ambiguous attitudes, which continued to
undermine attempts to deal with the problem of piracy well into the seventeenth
century. Crucially such limitations were reflected in a lack of continuity in the
development of a royal navy, and in an uncertain appreciation of its use at sea,
reinforced by concern at the cost of deploying large numbers of warships. During
the 1420s and 1430s, for example, Henry VI effectively sold off his navy at a time
when the author of the *Libel of English Policy* was urging the King to secure lordship over the sea.[1]

In these circumstances two distinct traditions of depredation evolved within
the British Isles, reflecting differences in geography and socio-economic structures that were mediated through local or regional political systems. Thus a crude,
though fundamental distinction can be drawn between the commercialized
seaborne plunder which was characteristic of much of England, Wales, lowland
Scotland and the pale of Ireland, and the subsistence sea raiding that flourished in
the north-west Gaelic regions of Scotland and Ireland.

Despite some superficial similarities, there were profound differences between
these traditions. Within the maritime economy of Gaelic Scotland and Ireland
piracy was part of a wider, regular and socially accepted form of raiding. In
the western highlands the Halloween raid was seen as an appropriate time to
acquire additional provisions to get through the winter. Among poor highland
and island communities, where economic opportunity was restricted by the
barrenness of the environment, raiding may have been an inherent feature of the
life cycle for most males. It was undertaken in fleets of galleys, small vessels with
sails and oars, which grew out of the Viking longboat tradition of shipbuilding;
and it was endemic in parts of the western islands, and northern and western Ireland. Under the leadership of clan chiefs, sea raids resembled subsistence
expeditions, during which much-needed supplies of cattle or clothing were
plundered from rival groups or from vulnerable ships sailing along the coast or
crossing the Irish Sea. These economic purposes reflected the needs of remote
and isolated regions. But raiding also fulfilled various social and cultural functions. It provided the opportunity for leaders to win glory and renown, while
maintaining loyalty among followers through feasting and the re-distribution
of booty as gifts. At the same time it provided an outlet for male aggression and
revenge among feuding clans. The violence was sanctioned by Gaelic rulers, and
its leading protagonists were subsequently celebrated in stories and verse. Gaelic
sea raiding persisted into the sixteenth century. In 1545, for example, Donald
Dubh reportedly led an expedition to Ireland made up of 180 galleys which
were manned with 4,000 men from the Hebrides.[2] But its continued survival

was threatened by the centralizing and civilizing ambitions of the English and Scottish monarchies, which came to identify its participants and supporters as outlaws and rebels, as well as pirates.

Elsewhere in the British Isles a different tradition of plunder developed, as expressed in the growth of piracy and legitimate reprisals. Although there were local differences of emphasis in the scale and structure of such enterprise, and wide fluctuations in its intensity over time, it tended to be commercialized in nature, becoming more so partly as a result of international rivalry and conflict. Much of it was small scale, short distance and often highly localized, based on opportunistic depredation in the Channel by heavily manned small sailing ships, operating alone or in association with another vessel. At its most basic, it resembled indiscriminate petty robbery by loosely organized bands of thugs. While war encouraged an increase in lawlessness at sea, it also generated more organized forms of enterprise. At times of intense activity, nonetheless, widespread confusion prevailed: cross-Channel hostility cut across local feuds along the south coast, in both cases initiating disputes that could last for generations. In the south-west, Plymouth and Dartmouth built up a mixed reputation for their promotion of maritime plunder; Fowey earned notoriety as a pirate haven, while the harbour of Helford was widely known as Stealford as a result of local involvement in maritime robbery. But across the south coast, ports and havens were heavily involved in the spoil of shipping in the Channel. As well as the seizure of ships at sea,

St Mawes Castle and Falmouth Bay, Cornwall. Favoured by geography and local tradition, Falmouth and its neighbouring ports were notorious havens for pirates and rovers. The distant harbour of Helford was known as Stealford for its reputation in supporting piracy. (Author's collection)

moreover, this activity included the robbery of vessels within English harbours, the cargoes of which were often disposed locally.[3]

Medieval monarchs met with limited success as they struggled to control maritime plunder and violence. Lacking the means, if not the will, to maintain the law and custom of the sea, rulers tended to adopt inconsistent, short-term policies that were qualified by an overt recognition of the value of sea rovers during periods of war. As a result maritime plunder and policy were increasingly entangled. Officially-sanctioned depredation was, in any case, a long-standing and widely acknowledged practice through the use of reprisals, which enabled merchants and shipowners to recoup losses or damages suffered at the hands of foreigners. The issue of commissions by sovereigns or their representatives, authorizing voyages of reprisal, was an accepted means of redress, which may have contained potentially aggressive commercial disputes. But without strict regulation, which was beyond the means of medieval monarchies, it was also open to abuse. During the Hundred Years' War between England and France, monarchs repeatedly authorized private venturing of this nature, with little or no control, as a way of damaging enemy trade and shipping.

The blurring of legal distinctions, especially during periods of conflict, created opportunities that adventurers in the south-west readily seized. During the late fourteenth and early fifteenth centuries merchants like John Hawley of Dartmouth turned maritime depredation into a profitable and patriotic business. The attraction of earning profit and honour at sea encouraged the participation of gentry and aristocratic adventurers, notably among those who were owners or part-owners of shipping. The scale of activity, and the basis for mutual cooperation between commercial and landed interests, increased dramatically during the civil wars of the 1450s and 1460s. Political crisis, the decay of good lordship and the collapse of sea-keeping led to widespread and endemic disorder. Powerful magnates and aristocratic families pursued rivalries and vendettas at sea, creating a cover for indiscriminate plunder and piracy. The successes of experienced rovers, including John Mixtow of Fowey or William Kyd of Exmouth, attracted the attention of prominent members of the Cornish gentry. Men such as Thomas Bodulgate or Richard Penpons, who were deeply implicated in piracy, used their local power and influence to shelter themselves from investigation or legal proceedings. Members of the Courtenay family, the head of which was the Earl of Devon, were also regularly involved in piratical venturing from bases in the south-west. With a fleet of men-of-war operating from Calais under the auspices of Richard Neville, Earl of Warwick, the Channel became dangerously infested with pirates and rovers of uncertain legality.[4]

Despite the recovery of royal authority and the revival of the King's Navy, varied forms of maritime depredation persisted into the later fifteenth century. The records of the central government, though based on cases which provoked complaint, indicate that English, Welsh and Irish pirates were operating during the 1470s and 1480s at locations in southern Ireland, Devon, Cornwall, Sussex,

Hampshire and Essex. In February 1479 the Crown ordered an investigation into complaints that a Breton vessel had been seized by pirates at the entrance to the River Thames and subsequently taken north. Although much of this activity appears to be irregular, and random in its targets, some ports, such as Fowey, were repeatedly engaged in more purposeful piratical enterprise. The persistence of what seems to have been an unofficial little war of plunder against Breton and Iberian vessels was sustained by small-scale entrepreneurs, including ship masters and owners, who probably combined commerce with plunder in short voyages into the Channel. During 1483 John Davy and Stephen Bull, with a company of pirates aboard the *Nicholas* of Fowey, seized several Iberian vessels. The following year Captain Tege Smale, in the *Kateryne* of Fowey, captured a French ship, and in 1485 John Morys, master and part-owner of the *Little Anne*, described as a ship-of-war of Fowey, seized a Breton vessel laden with wines and salt in the port of Southampton.[5]

The social and economic dimensions of piratical enterprise were equally varied. The essential concern of most sea rovers was all too evident from their behaviour: captured ships and crews were ransacked of their possessions. An English vessel seized off Bearhaven in Ireland during 1477 was spoiled of goods worth £60. The pirates, led by one Pykerd from Minehead, stripped the company 'and put them naked ashore at Kinsale'.[6] During the 1470s the *Mary London*, a large vessel of 320 tons which had transported a large party of 400 pilgrims from Ross in Ireland to Santiago in northern Spain, to celebrate the jubilee of St James, was seized on its return voyage by three ships owned by Nicholas Devereux and others of Waterford, which were reportedly manned with a force of 800 men. The *Mary London* and its passengers were taken into Youghal and plundered. The owner of the vessel was robbed of 140 marks and allegedly imprisoned for three years. As this unusual case suggests, pirates and other sea rovers were prepared to use extortion and ransoming when it served their purpose. In May 1483 Mathew Cradock of Swansea, captain of a ship-of-war, seized a Breton vessel off Ilfracombe with the assistance of local pirates. The vessel and its cargo were then put to ransom for £50. Collectively these cases demonstrate the localized and opportunistic nature of piratical activity which was encouraged by the prospect of securing profitable captures, such as the Spanish ship laden with a cargo of cloth valued at 40,000 crowns, seized along the coast of Hampshire during 1483 by Sir John Arundell.[7]

The monarchy attempted to take firm action against pirates and sea rovers during these years. Commissions of inquiry were issued to investigate complaints of spoil and plunder. The Crown ordered the arrest and imprisonment of men accused of piracy, and the restitution of plundered cargoes. In some cases offenders were commanded to appear before the King and council. At times compensation was awarded to foreign merchants who were the victims of English pirates. In 1484 the sheriffs were ordered to publish a proclamation concerning the regulation of ships-of-war, which were not to put to sea without their owners 'first

Fowey harbour, Cornwall. During the later Middle Ages Fowey acquired notoriety as a pirate refuge. Like other ports and havens in the region, it continued to be visited by pirates in search of recruits and provisions. In the later 1530s the companies of some rovers even went ashore to attend mass in local churches. (Author's collection)

making oath and finding surety for good bearing towards the King's subjects, friends and confederates and all under the King's safeguard or safe-conduct'.[8]

But royal regulation met with mixed success. Incidents such as the plunder of a Breton vessel, carrying letters of safe conduct from the Admiral of England, by three ships from Topsham, starkly revealed the limitations of the late medieval monarchy in trying to curb the piratical tendencies of seafaring and seashore communities.[9] The inability of the Crown to deal with the piracies of its subjects at sea was linked with the coastal plunder of vessels cast ashore by bad weather. In many parts of England landowners appear to have seen such vessels as legitimate casualties of the sea, though the use of violence against the surviving companies of wrecks sometimes looks like a form of land piracy. Despite recent improvements to the King's Navy, it proved difficult to provide for the regular patrolling of the coasts. Although the navy was restored to a total of sixteen vessels under Edward IV, the financial and physical problems in maintaining it were reflected in its subsequent decline. Thus, in 1485 Henry VII inherited a force of seven ships.[10] Under these conditions the monarchy could do little more than attempt to contain, rather than eradicate, the problem of piracy. Nor was this a problem limited to England. Political and diplomatic relations in north-west Europe, combined with the rudimentary development of international law, constituted a favourable environment for the widespread maintenance of maritime depredation of varying shades of legality.

The safety of the seas during peace and war from the 1480s to the 1520s

During the early decades of Tudor rule the Crown's growing concern with the safety of the seas was reinforced by the demands of domestic and dynastic security. Henry VII's cautious foreign policy and support for naval development were accompanied by a firm approach towards piracy. This was reinforced by the careful control of the issue of letters of reprisal, which helped to contain the potential for disorder at sea. Furthermore, the continued expansion of overseas trade, despite short-term fluctuations, may have limited the economic and social pressures that encouraged maritime depredation. By the 1520s, however, these conditions were beginning to change as a result of the problems and opportunities presented by Henry VIII's aggressive diplomacy and overseas ambitions. The onset of Anglo-French hostilities was accompanied by a resurgence of cross-Channel plunder and raiding by Scottish sea rovers, which paved the way for widespread disorder at sea.

The persistence of piracy during the 1480s and Henry VII's handling of it were demonstrated by the prompt response to overseas complaints against English depredation. During February 1486 the new King issued two commissions concerning attacks on foreign shipping. The first concerned the seizure of a French vessel by two English men-of-war. The crew of the French prize were put ashore in Normandy, and the vessel was taken to the Isle of Wight where its cargo was divided up and distributed among the captors. Sir Edward Woodville, captain of the Isle, was instructed to arrest those involved and to ensure that the plunder was restored; if the latter refused to cooperate, they were to be brought before the King and council. Several weeks later the bishop of Exeter and other commissioners were ordered to investigate complaints from several Hanseatic merchants about the seizure of two vessels from Hamburg, off the coast of Cornwall, by a group of rovers from Fowey led by John Gaye and William Bruer. The commissioners were commanded to arrest the vessels and their cargoes, which had been brought into the Cornish port. Moreover, Gaye, Bruer and their followers were to be imprisoned until either restitution or compensation was made. In an effort to contain the spread of piracy, Henry issued a proclamation in November 1490 which ordered the punishment of pirates who spoiled Spanish and Imperial shipping. In addition the purchasers of plundered commodities were warned that they faced the forfeiture of property and imprisonment at the King's will.[11]

As in the past, piracy provoked retaliation and reprisals at sea. Henry, however, was unwilling to sanction the widespread or indiscriminate use of letters of reprisal, preferring to rely on diplomacy and other means of seeking redress. The treaty between the King and Ferdinand of Aragon in 1489 thus revoked all letters of reprisal; in future, if justice was denied, the 'King of the injured party must twice demand redress from the sovereign of the party which has done the damage before he deliver letters of marque and reprisal.'[12] Commissions of reprisal were issued only after careful consideration, and usually under strict conditions, especially when compared with later practice. Thus in October 1495 Richard Wele and others of King's Lynn were authorized to seize ships of Dieppe, following their inability to obtain satisfaction from the Admiral of France for the capture of their vessel off the coast of Norfolk by two ships from the French port. The following year two London merchants received a letter of reprisal after they were unable to gain compensation for the loss of goods laden aboard a ship in Falmouth, which was plundered by a French vessel. Unwilling to act precipitately, Henry postponed the issue of the commission until diplomatic efforts to gain redress were exhausted. After long delay and deliberation, the King granted a commission, authorizing the recipients to recover the amount of £700 from the French. The proclamation announcing the peace treaty with France of August 1498 sought to reduce such lengthy delays by establishing a new and speedier procedure for dealing with cases of spoil and robbery between the two countries.[13] Though the initiative was not developed, it was a further indication of Henry VII's concern to use letters of reprisal as a last resort. For most of his reign, indeed, there was neither the opportunity nor the need to promote large-scale reprisals at sea or other forms of licensed plunder.

Although these conditions limited the growth of organized piracy, the ability of the early Tudor regime to tackle the problem rested on an uncertain combination of naval power and patrolling with the support and cooperation of local officials and communities. None of these could be taken for granted. Outrageous cases of spoil continued to take place on the Thames, exposing serious weaknesses in the policing and internal security of the river. In March 1502 a commission of oyer and terminer was issued to the Lord Admiral, for the investigation of an attack on a vessel anchored between Ratcliffe and St Katherine's by William Palmer, Richard Bray and others, who reportedly 'threw the mariners in the river and so drowned them and plundered the ship'.[14] River piracy was a long-standing problem which was nurtured by the growing size and commercial significance of the port of London. The vulnerability of shipping along the Thames attracted organized gangs and opportunist thieves who provided a potential recruiting ground for more ambitious piratical enterprise.

The gradual improvement in the security of the sea, which appears to have reflected changes in the level and intensity of maritime depredation during the later fifteenth century, was not sustained. It may appear paradoxical that the reign of Henry VIII, which witnessed impressive naval development, should also experience a striking increase in piracy and maritime spoil. But the roots of both lay in the rapidly changing international environment. The new King's aggressive foreign policy revived Anglo-French rivalry and conflict. Hostilities from 1512 to 1514, followed by renewed conflict between 1522 and 1525, led to widespread disorder at sea.

During the early decades of the reign, English enterprise was heavily overshadowed by the activities of French and Flemish men-of-war in the Channel, as well as by the raiding of Scottish rovers sailing with commissions from James IV. In 1512 Henry VIII was reported to be deeply perplexed and annoyed at the actions of the Scots. Despite the peace between the two countries, Scottish adventurers, including close associates of James, such as David Falconer or the Barton brothers, supported the French in the spoil of English shipping. To the anger of Henry, moreover, when 'James's subjects attack Henry's, they call themselves the French King's servants, when taken as pirates, in company of Frenchmen, they are James's subjects'.[15] The English responded by seizing Scottish ships. In July 1512 James complained about attacks on his subjects' shipping and the capture of Scottish merchants, some of whom were dubbed 'the Pape's men' and sent to London for trial. The prisoners included Falconer, though James persuaded Henry to defer his execution, 'notwithstanding his manifold piracies, for which he well deserved to die'.[16]

The confusion between Scottish and French depredation posed serious problems for the English. During 1515 Henry VIII was faced with growing complaints from English merchants against French pirates and rovers who were masquerading as Scots. In reality the French were operating with Scottish commissions. Nonetheless, by August 1515 Henry was prepared to issue letters of reprisal if his subjects were unable to obtain redress in France. At the same time attempts were made to deal with the issue by diplomatic means. This included the appointment of English and French commissioners, who met at Calais and Boulogne during 1517, to resolve disputes over piracy and disorderly plunder. The English also proposed an exchange of pirates and other rovers, probably because of the cost of maintaining foreign prisoners. However, negotiations between the commissioners were hindered by 'their ignorance of the language, and the absence of necessary documents'.[17] Nor did the subsequent treaty with France, of 1518, end the attacks on English shipping. Continued complaints against French raiding were accompanied by reports that the Chancellor of France objected to the restoration of English property. In such circumstances Henry issued a proclamation, proffering compensation to the victims of French piracy if proof was provided.[18]

The disorderly activities of men-of-war at sea were accompanied, if not sustained, by localized spoil and pillage. Much of this was opportunistic and random in nature. It was also disorganized and often amateurish, as indicated by an abortive attempt by a group of stowaways to persuade the owner and master of a vessel, sailing down the Thames, to turn to piracy. According to William Bochether, one of the ship's company, the owner found four mariners, who had been secretly taken aboard by other members of the crew, hiding in the hold. The stowaways urged the owner to abandon the voyage in favour of robbery along the river or at sea: 'We are good fellows that will strike a hand', they declared, 'if you will consent with us'.[19] When he refused, they appealed to Bochether for assistance. But the latter replied that 'he had a good occupation [and was] able to get his living with truth'. Thereafter the owner put the four men ashore. Bochether, who was apparently sick, appears to have followed them. During the night the four mariners used the vessel's boat to take a Breton ship, with which they put to sea. Bochether recovered and returned aboard the vessel; however, when it arrived at Harwich, he was arrested and imprisoned in Colchester Castle, for complicity in the seizure of the Breton ship. From prison, 'laden with irons, lying on the bare ground without meat and drink', he begged relief from the Lord Admiral and constable of the castle.[20]

The attraction of robbery at sea, at a time of such disorder, may have been widespread and capable of wider development. A carefully prepared, though abortive, pioneering expedition to North America, led by John Rastell in 1517, was partly sabotaged by the mariners' overriding interest in the prospect of piracy. Shortly after putting to sea Rastell was urged to seize an Irish pirate, Henry Mongham, in order to take a Portuguese ship which the pirate had captured. At least one of Rastell's officers also advised him to turn to robbery at sea.[21] In fact the venture was abandoned at Waterford, in a manner that foreshadowed the predilection for piracy or illicit plunder among English mariners engaged in long-distance voyages beyond Europe.

The regime tried to respond swiftly, and in a varied manner, to the threat of sporadic piracy. In March 1515 a commission of oyer and terminer was issued to the Lord Admiral and his deputy to investigate the alleged piracies of John

Baker, John Brigenden and their followers. Several years later, during 1519, the King granted another commission to the Lord Admiral and others, to determine all civil cases of spoil between England and France in accordance with the recent treaty. The navy was also employed to combat pirates and rovers, though with mixed results. In 1519 Thomas Howard, Earl of Surrey, captured a group of Scottish pirates. But successful expeditions against pirates in the seas around the British Isles required small, speedy and specialized vessels which did not always meet the vision or requirements of the King's fleet. During 1523, for example, Sir Anthony Poyntz, the commander of a naval force patrolling the sea between Wales and Ireland, hired a ship for £1 to reconnoitre the coasts of the Isle of Man and Scotland.[22]

The presence of foreign men-of-war in English waters increased during the 1520s, despite an agreement between the King and Charles V for more naval patrols against pirates and enemies. At varying times Spanish, French and Flemish predators haunted the coasts of southern England and Ireland, seeking prizes or disposing of plundered cargoes. The confusion and disorder at sea presented opportunities for a diverse collection of adventurers, whose activities undermined the pretensions of rulers to defend maritime jurisdictions against the danger of legal and illegal raiding. To some extent the increase in depredation during these years may have been more apparent than real, reflecting growing concern among monarchs, such as Henry VIII, with their rights and responsibilities as sovereigns over vaguely defined home waters. Under tense international conditions, efforts to assert such rights, without adequate coastal and naval defences, ran the risk of inviting retaliation.

Growing complaints about piracy thus occurred against a background of confused competition and cooperation. In November 1525 Queen Margaret of Scotland complained about the seizure of a ship belonging to Robert Barton by one Flemish and two English vessels. Two years later local officials in Southampton were powerless to prevent three large Flemish vessels entering the port and seizing a merchant ship. As the Channel became crowded with men-of-war during the later 1520s, the threat to peaceful commerce and shipping intensified. During April 1528 an English naval patrol daily met with French and Flemish ships-of-war seeking prizes. According to a subsequent report from the Low Countries, if war broke out, there were 10,000 mariners ready to rig out vessels, at their own charge, against the English. Concerned at the dangers of renewed conflict, Henry attempted to maintain English neutrality, in an effort to limit the threat of French and Imperial coastal raiding. But there was little that the King could do to keep overseas spoil at arm's length. By December 1528 the Spanish were complaining of attacks on their vessels, in English waters, by the French. Allegations of English complicity fuelled demands for the issue of letters of reprisal against France and England.[23] The ensuing disruption to trade and shipping encouraged the growth of maritime depredation at an acutely sensitive time for England's relations with the rest of Europe.

Peace and plunder: disorder at sea during the 1530s

During the 1530s, against a threatening international background, piracy and disorderly plunder became a more menacing problem in the seas around the British Isles. To some extent the nature of the problem, and the response to it, were influenced by a shifting concern with domestic and international security. Unavoidably both were linked with Henry VIII's divorce from Katherine of Aragon and the subsequent break with Rome. The anxiety of the regime about the danger of internal disorder and rebellion was thus reflected in its handling of the problem of maritime depredation. Pirates and rebels could be easily identified as a common threat to Henrician rule, particularly at a time when the risk of foreign invasion seemed to be growing. It is possible, therefore, that the striking increase in the volume of evidence concerning piracy may be partly the result of the greater seriousness with which it was viewed by an insecure and embattled regime. In such circumstances new legislation to deal with piracy was passed by Parliament in 1536, in order to strengthen and clarify the existing law.

It was in Ireland that the prospect of rebellious subjects taking to the seas emerged as a danger. In the later 1520s James Fitzgerald, 11th Earl of Desmond, who was reported to be at sea with certain English vessels, appealed to Emperor Charles V for assistance against his enemies, including the English. In exchange, he offered to attack the Emperor's rivals, while expelling them from Ireland. Regardless of the Emperor's response, the death of Desmond effectively neutralized the prospect of organized maritime action against the English in Ireland. Nonetheless, the dangers of discontented and feuding magnates resorting to continental intrigues alarmed the Tudor monarchy. Only a few years later, two Spanish ships laden with munitions of war were reported to have reached Ireland.[24] At a time when the Tudor regime was trying to extend its authority over Ireland, it may have been particularly prone to confuse piracy and rebellion, creating a climate of fear and expectation that was to recur with the raiding of the O'Malleys and O'Flahertys along the west coast during the later sixteenth century.

The widespread activities of pirates, especially within the Channel and the Irish Sea, underlined the continuing insecurity of the seas during the 1530s. In 1531 Lord Lisle, the Vice Admiral of England, and others were authorized to investigate and determine cases of piracy. Later in the year it was reported that Kilmanton, a sea rover, intended to seize Sir William Skeffington, the Lord Deputy of Ireland, during his passage to England, and hold him to ransom for the King's pardon. Kilmanton was captured in the Isle of Man, though other members of his company managed to escape aboard a vessel bound for Grimsby. The following year a group of Bretons claimed to have been robbed at sea by English rovers, some of whom came from Plymouth. But the Channel was infested with French and Scottish, as well as English, rovers. In March 1532 John Chapman, master of a London vessel, reported continually sighting men-of-war in search of prey.

He encountered two Breton vessels coming from the west, one of which surrendered after he prepared to board it. According to Chapman the vessel was of 150 tons burden, full of ordnance and manned with a mixed company of 'Frenchmen, Bretons, Portingales, Black Moors, and others'.[25]

Equally alarming were the activities of the Scots. A merchant of Fowey informed Chapman about the seizure of fourteen English vessels, and one Scottish ship laden with English commodities, by four Scottish rovers. To the consternation of the English, the Scots refused to offer any of their prisoners for ransom, breaking with a well-established custom of the sea. In these conditions Chapman complained that he had 'much ado to keep ... [his] company together, for they ... [were] not inclined to go further, except for war'.[26] By February 1533 Scottish rovers were operating along the east coast, ranging as far south as the River Humber, and disrupting the supply of Berwick. According to the emperor's representative in London, the English were 'astonished at the number of ships the Scots have, and suspect they receive help elsewhere'.[27] But the King was so concerned with his marital affairs, that he showed little interest in dealing with the problem.

Companies of English pirates, usually acting independently of each other, were heavily engaged in coastal plunder during the 1530s. In October 1533 the King and council expressed great displeasure at the seizure of a Biscayan

Bardsey Island and Bardsey Sound, Gwynedd. This island off the Llyn peninsula has many legendary and real associations with pirates. It was regularly visited by pirates during the 1560s and 1570s, when it may have served as a convenient haven for the disposal of booty to local landowners, including the Wynn family. According to tradition the celebrated Welsh pirate and poet, Tomos Prys, built a house on the island on the site of a derelict monastery. (Author's collection)

St Tudwal's Road, Gwynedd. This remote region served as a resort for pirates and other rovers who preyed on shipping in the Irish Sea and the Channel. During the later 1590s it was a base for Hugh Griffiths, who was involved in the disorderly plunder of foreign vessels. On one occasion he brought in a French prize, laden with canvas and a great chest of treasure. But when the chest was brought ashore, possibly to the house of Griffiths' father, it provoked a tumult among Griffiths' company. (Author's collection)

ship by pirates off the west coast of Ireland. About the same time a French vessel was robbed, while anchored off Pevensey, by pirates who seized a trunk and parcel containing cloth, jewellery and other wares valued at £24 1s 4d. By its very nature this kind of petty scavenging, which commonly depended more on surprise than superiority in numbers or armaments, was not always a success. In March 1534 Michael James confessed to a local Admiralty official in Southampton that Henry Holland and others had seized a ship of St Jean de Luz anchored at Calshot. The robbers put the crew below deck, under the hatches, but they broke out, regained control of the ship and carried it off to Brest. Swift action by officials could also be an effective response to small-scale piracy. During 1534 Skeffington encountered a pirate company, led by Broode, as he crossed the Irish Sea. Broode's vessel was driven ashore near Drogheda, and he and his men were taken by the mayor of the town. By February 1535 the pirate leader and other members of his company had been hanged, drawn and quartered.[28]

Much of this small-scale coastal and Channel plunder depended on wide-spread community support, which enabled pirates and rovers to operate from secure land bases and to dispose of booty in safe markets among buyers who were unconcerned with their provenance. In 1534 the King's chief minister, Thomas Cromwell, was informed of a pirate based in the Isle of Wight, whose recent captures included an English vessel returning from Guernsey and a French ship sailing out of Portsmouth. The remote coastal regions of Wales, which were haunted by rovers attacking Breton and other vessels, provided an opportunity for pirates to dispose of plunder, though sometimes in ambiguous circumstances. During 1535 members of the local community in the lordship of St David's purchased salt and wine from the pirate Thomas Carter, 'thinking him to be a true man'.[29] Carter and his men were subsequently arrested in north Wales, but they refused to confess to the disposal of the goods. Though placed in the custody of the constable of Caernarvon Castle, five of the pirates managed to escape. Two years later the chanter of St David's was indicted as an accessory to piracy, in a case that exposed the rivalry and potential conflict between the jurisdiction of the bishop and the deputy justice.[30]

These conditions increased the difficulties of the regime in dealing with localized piratical activity. But it was impossible for the early Tudor state to eradicate piracy, particularly given its social roots. For many it was part of a way of life, adopted by necessitous members of seafaring communities, as well as by some of the more resourceful or adventurous representatives of the poor in general. The confession of Adams, a pirate operating during the early 1530s, illuminates the economic and social context of piracy, demonstrating its opportunistic character. Adams admitted that he and seven other mariners took a small boat at St Katherine's which they rowed down the Thames until they were within two miles of Gravesend, where they seized a vessel of 30 tons with only one man and three boys aboard. The pirates sailed their new vessel along the coast to Southampton. At Portsmouth and Southampton the company was joined by a master, several mariners and servants. Somewhere off the Isle of Wight they anchored close to a group of five vessels of Spanish, French and English ownership. During the night one of the Breton vessels, laden with salt and parchment, was boarded and taken. Sailing west, the pirate company was forced by wind into Portland Bay. When two Breton vessels also sought sanctuary in the bay, the pirates seized 'the lesser as being the better sailer'.[31] Lacking sufficient men to handle their new prize, they gave the Bretons the ship taken off the Isle of Wight with its cargo of salt, retaining the more valuable and less bulky parchment. Bad weather subsequently forced the pirates into Brixham. The sale of one of the ships aroused local suspicions. As a result several of the pirates were arrested ashore. Adams escaped with four others. He later reached Newcastle, where he sold the Breton ship, since which time he had 'been where as pleased God'.

Adams' activities at sea formed part of an unsettled career of petty, part-time criminality which spanned sea and shore. Prior to turning to piracy, he was a member of a gang of thieves who operated along the Thames and its hinterland. Under the leadership of Reynolde, a draper of London, and in company with four other men, he admitted to robbing a house in Essex. Allegedly, he was persuaded to take part in the robbery by a well-chosen appeal from

Reynolde: '"Adams ... I know thou art in necessity and thou art in great debt. ... And", saith he, "if thou wilt do as we do it will be worth to thee a 100 mark; and if thou wilt not meddle, stand by and look upon us". And with that one of them burst open a wall and went in', although Adams claimed he 'tarried still without and one other'.[32] The robbers got £24, of which Adams received £4, though this was some way short of what he had been promised to take part in the venture. Adams struggled to defend his actions at sea, insisting that he 'thought never to rob Englishmen', claiming instead that he was enticed into piracy by another member of the company. But the successes of this small band of rovers and thieves, who took at least four vessels during a brief spell of river and coastal plunder, revealed the availability of easy prey, within sight of the shore, which a growing number of seafarers and others found difficult to resist.

In an effort to improve the law regarding piracy, during 1536 Parliament passed legislation which was intended to remedy shortcomings in the legal procedure of the High Court of Admiralty. According to civil law, under which pirates were tried, it was only possible to impose the death penalty on offenders either through their own confession or by the testimony of witnesses, who were difficult to find. Consequently the act placed the criminal jurisdiction of the court, including 'treasons, felonies, robberies, murders and confederacies', in the hands of specially appointed commissions, 'in like form and conditions as if any such offence' had been committed on land.[33] By these means criminal offences committed within the jurisdiction of the Admiralty were transferred to commissions of oyer and terminer, operating in accord with the common law of the realm. At the same time the act denied all offenders, including pirates, the use of benefit of clergy or sanctuary.

On paper the new legislation demonstrated the resolve of the Henrician regime to improve the law concerning piracy. In the short term, at least, it seems to have led to an upsurge in condemnations for piracy. Nonetheless, the law was unable to tackle the root cause of the problem or the political expediency which it was occasionally subject to. In March 1537 the regime was embarrassed by complaints of the seizure of a Portuguese vessel off the coast of Wales by a band of thirty-five pirates. The captured vessel was taken to Cork where it was sold to the mayor and others. The case coincided with other complaints concerning the disposal of pirate goods in the lordship of St David's, and may have provoked the Lord Admiral into a very public assertion of his legal responsibilities and jurisdiction later in the year, when he condemned eleven mariners for piracy in the Guildhall of London. Within weeks, however, and in the same surroundings, the Lord Admiral pardoned Thomas Skye, a yeoman of Brompton in Norfolk, and four others, for piracy on a Scottish ship off Sunderland. The attack was justified as retaliation for the previous spoil of the Scots, though Skye also claimed that it was undertaken against his will, at the command of the master, Giles Carre, who warned him 'to be contentyd or ellys he wold caste hym into the Sea'.[34]

Skye's pardon was followed in July 1537 by another for Edward Foster of London, alias John Gryffyn of East Smithfield, mariner, and others, for committing piracy on a vessel at Tilbury, along the Thames.

To some extent this apparent inconsistency may have been a reaction to the persistent threat from overseas raiders in English waters. While many of these rovers were lawfully commissioned men-of-war, their search for plunder easily spilled over into piratical attacks on vulnerable English trading ships. Faced with increasing complaints from his subjects, and angered by the infringement of the Crown's maritime jurisdiction, Henry VIII resorted to a combination of public and private methods to protect trade and shipping. In effect, the strict implementation of the new legislation against piracy was qualified by wider considerations of policy and practicality.

Both the scale and intensity of overseas depredation in English waters increased during the later 1530s as a result of international rivalry and conflict between the Holy Roman Empire and France. During 1536 Flemish vessels seized several Breton ships off Southampton. The following year Breton and French vessels were reported to be haunting the coast of Wales, 'robbing all the English ships they could, and coming on land to steal sheep'.[35] Among the vessels attacked was the *Mary Fortune* of Hull, the master of which, John Crowne, claimed to have been badly handled by his captors. The French compelled Crowne to admit, falsely, that his vessel was laden with Flemish goods. To combat such disorder the Vice Admiral was sent out with instructions to take any French or Imperial vessels suspected of spoiling English shipping. But it was difficult to contain the spread of coastal raiding by either side, especially as it was occasionally supported by the King's own subjects. In October 1537 Henry was informed of the activities of various French ships which were plundering in English waters without commissions; one of them carried the red cross of England and included English pilots and mariners among its company, 'the rather to train men into their danger'.[36] In addition to the depredations of the French and Flemish, Spanish Biscayners were reported to have attacked several English vessels and tortured one of the masters.

Under these conditions the distinction between friend and enemy threatened to dissolve. Henry saw the attack on shipping in English harbours by French and Imperial raiders as a matter that touched on his honour. He authorized private ships-of-war to defend English shipping, with permission for their owners or masters to retain pirate plunder. In March 1538 Lord Lisle was informed that if any of his ships took a pirate in the Channel who had 'no merchants' goods on board to bear the charge, the King will bear the burden of it'.[37] Indeed, Lisle's rescue of an English vessel, and seizure of its French captor, earned him much respect and renown at court.

Although these initiatives met with some success, they also encouraged piratical enterprise under cover of legitimate retaliation against the French. The seizure of a Breton vessel by the *Clement* of London during 1538 was justified on the grounds of reprisal, although at least one of the company was reported to have spoken out against the plunder of the vessel. Much of this small-scale scavenging was care-fully planned, organized and deliberately targeted on French shipping. The *Mary Thomas* of 30 tons, for example, was sent out with the purpose of seeking recom-pense from the French for losses sustained by Henry Davy and others of London, in a venture which appeared to be a form of unauthorized privateering or repris-als. John Broke, a member of the company, was recruited by Thomas Lyllye, the master, 'to goe on Rovyng with hym upon the Sea'.[38] Broke subsequently related that he attended a dinner, organized by Davy at a tavern, the Goat in Cheapside, after which Lyllye and William Scarlett, the purser, 'shewyd ther mynds from one to one, that they purposyd to goe to the Sea, and theruppon dyvers of them brake bred and dyd ete it, promesyng therby that they wold be trewe'. Sailing down the Thames, additional recruits came aboard the vessel; with several others joining at Rye, the company amounted to about twenty men. Broke, however, left the ship at the Isle of Wight to seek treatment for an infection which he had acquired from a woman before leaving London. The *Mary Thomas* went on to seize a Breton ship near Guernsey, the cargo of which was disposed in Looe, Falmouth and neigh-bouring havens. Following the sale of the goods, Scarlett assembled the company, and presented each member with a share of twenty shillings, and thirty shillings for the master and officers. Although six of the company were able to go ashore to hear mass, near Falmouth the rovers fled when a large group of about 100 countrymen came down towards the ship. Scarlett returned home to his wife and children, but was taken, with £10 in money and household stuff, after seeking sanctuary in St Michael's Church, Cornhill.

The official response to the disorder at sea demonstrated that small-scale plunder and piracy were a widespread problem. During 1538 the Lord Admiral ordered the judge of the Admiralty court to investigate French complaints against Walter Soly of the West Country, concerning a piratical attack on the *Mary* of St Malo. The French ship, of 28 tons burden and with a crew of twelve mariners, was returning home from Carlingford with a lading of hides and herrings, when it was forced to seek shelter along the coast near Dublin. The ship was seized about midnight by Soly and his company, 'in a greate shippe with [two] tops', who resorted to casting stones and using swords on their victims.[39] The French crew were kept as prisoners under the hatches for ten days, after which they were set ashore on the Isle of Man.

Cromwell also continued to be concerned with cases of piracy and spoil. During 1538 he urged Bishop Rowland Lee to apprehend a group of pirates from south Wales. Later in the year he was informed of an attack by pirates on an English or Flemish vessel returning from Ireland. Although the pirates escaped to the Isle of Wight and then into the West Country, by the middle of September they had been captured. In April 1539 a Breton ship was brought into Dartmouth with only two men and a boy aboard; although the circumstances were obscure, the case aroused such concern that the pirates were ordered to London so that either Cromwell or the Lord Admiral could investigate and determine it.

The Smugglers Cott, Looe, Cornwall. The building dates from the fifteenth century, when men from Looe were regularly engaged in piracy. It was evidently restored with timber from a Spanish fleet which reached the coast of Cornwall in 1595. (Author's collection)

Several weeks later, Cromwell was investigating complaints of piracy against Will Swadell, a servant of Sir William Godolphin, the sheriff of Cornwall. In his correspondence with Cromwell the latter was compelled to deny any involvement in the activities of Swadell, rebutting rumours that he received the goods of an Irishman, allegedly worth £500.[40]

Piracy and spoil were endemic problems in English waters throughout the 1530s. While the Bretons regularly raided the exposed entrance to the River Severn, and inflicted widespread damage on Irish Sea trades, the Scots plundered shipping along the east coast and in the North Sea. At the same time, the Channel swarmed with sea robbers of varying nationalities, including a growing number of English pirates and rovers, who ranged along the south coast and into the Irish Sea. The Thames also remained a favoured haunt for river thieves and petty piracy. One group of men, who were intending to rob a vicarage in Essex close to the river, boarded a small boat manned with four men, 'with ther weapons drawen, and sayd good fellows be of good chere, we will do you no harme, but take parte of your goods'.[41] Two of the company informed the robbers that 'their money was in a barrel standing upon the hatches'. The robbers departed with £12 in cash, a loaf of sugar and a new cap, though they stayed long enough to drink with their victims, while leaving them forty shillings. Such was the nature of the problem that, on occasion, officials may have been forewarned about, but still ill-equipped to deal with, the menace. In February 1539 Lisle warned one of his officers at Calais about the departure of an English pirate from the Thames, who intended to pillage the friends and allies of the King. The pirate ship, described as a galleon of 35 tons with a company of thirty men, was 'an entirely new ship and hath long time been maintained in areadiness and equipped as for war'.[42]

Many of these pirate companies were composed of small groups of mariners, operating in ambiguous circumstances over short distances, and in vessels which were often weakly armed. Thomas Skye was at sea in the *Mary Walsingham* of 55 tons, with twelve mariners and one boy, six of whom were concealed under the hatches. The company was armed with two hand guns, four or five bows, twenty-four sheaves of arrows, two or three rusty bills, three swords and three cases of wild fire.[43] Yet the activities of these rovers posed a serious threat to trade and shipping. During the later 1530s the Merchant Adventurers requested the use of one of the King's ships to convoy their vessels across the Channel. The request was reinforced by a report from Sir Thomas Wriothesley to Cromwell, concerning the fears of English merchants about pirate attack. Although Wriothesley suggested that three or four of the King's ships be sent out to scour the seas, another of Cromwell's correspondents, while noting that small trading vessels were 'fatt booty', informed the merchants that 'they should provide for themselves against pirates'.[44]

The prolonged nature of the disorder at sea encouraged more ruthless and violent methods among some pirates and rovers. William Swadell and his followers captured two small prizes off the Scilly Isles, the companies of which were thrown overboard with their hands bound behind their backs. In May 1539 the representative of the French King in London complained of the seizure of a Breton ship by English pirates, who drowned all of the company except one, 'who, as if by a miracle, swam six miles to shore'.[45] Within two weeks of the complaint, the pirates were captured and condemned: six were executed immediately, while another eight were kept in custody to be confronted by their alleged accomplices who had been recently arrested. The violence may have been the product of long-standing feuds and grievances across the Channel, but in some cases it was inflamed by incipient religious rivalry. Robert Reneger, a Southampton merchant who was to be heavily involved in privateering during the 1540s, complained of the spoil of one of his ships, returning from Spain, by a French man-of-war, claiming that his factors were cruelly treated and libelled, with the rest of the company, as 'erronyouse lutheryans'.[46]

The demands of war: privateering and piracy during the 1540s

Endemic piracy and sea roving during the 1530s were superseded by the growth of organized privateering enterprise during the Anglo-French war from 1542 to 1545. Royal encouragement of private plunder on this scale represented a new departure for the early Tudor monarchy, though it was part of a wider re-shaping of English maritime enterprise in which the predatory dynamism of the seafaring community became more focused on Iberian trade and shipping. It was no accident that this shift was accompanied by radical religious change. During the 1540s and 1550s traditional cross-Channel competition was overlaid by inflammatory religious rivalries. In a deeply divided Europe, the combination of Protestantism and patriotism served to mobilize powerful forces in the pursuit of plunder. Under the cover of legitimate privateering against France, some English adventurers launched a piratical campaign against Spain, laying the foundations for a new pattern of maritime predation which ranged beyond the Channel into the eastern Atlantic.

Hostility towards Spain was manifest in the uneasy relationship between transatlantic trade and piracy, even though the English were only finding their way in a difficult and dangerous enterprise. The disorderly voyage of the *Barbara* of London in 1540, which was intended as a peaceful venture to Brazil to lade dyewood, ended with the seizure of a Spanish vessel off Santo Domingo in the Caribbean. The London merchants who promoted the venture instructed the company of the *Barbara* that 'they shulde do no robbery but folowe ther voyage like honeste men'.[47] Off Cape St Vincent, nonetheless, several vessels were spoiled, while another was plundered near the Canary Islands. Although the company acquired small amounts of dyewood and cotton wool, as well as parrots and monkeys, along the coast of Brazil, they faced hostility from rival French traders and the native inhabitants. The trading venture was abandoned following an attack by a group of natives, when at least one member of the company was killed, cut up, cooked and eaten. Many others died from sickness or a lack of provisions. The *Barbara* returned with thirteen healthy men, out of an original complement of ninety four, who were arrested to face charges of piracy before the High Court of Admiralty. The voyage may have discouraged and delayed interest in transatlantic depredation, at least until the later 1560s and 1570s. In any case, during the 1540s Anglo-French rivalry and conflict provided more secure prospects of plunder within the Channel.

The war with France was preceded by a spate of cross-Channel disputes over spoil and plunder, which to some extent both justified and shaped the maritime conflict. English complaints of rough and cruel justice in France were offset by French grievances over delays in securing relief or compensation in England. According to a report of 1540 one Breton merchant had spent six or seven years vainly suing for assistance across the Channel; his appeal for a commission of reprisal was rebuffed, apparently because the French King did not wish to antagonize Henry.

Such complaints and experiences were widespread, reflecting the deterioration in international relations within western Europe during these years. In September 1540 the council of Spain demanded compensation from Henry for the seizure of a Spanish carvel by an English rover. Spanish officials also warned that the owners of the vessel, a group of merchants of Seville, requested the right to recover their losses by reprisals on the English. About the same time, the Emperor demanded justice from the Scottish King, James V, for the piracies

A group of pirates hunting for turtles off Santo Domingo. As the voyages of Drake indicate, within the Caribbean pirates and rovers adapted to conditions, exploiting local resources in a variety of ways in order to stay in the region over extended periods. (*Scourge of the Indies*)

of Robert Fogo on fishermen of Ostend. He also complained bitterly about the activities of other Scottish rovers who were operating with letters of reprisal, demanding that James 'put an end to these illicit and piratical exploits'.[48] The Scottish King disowned Fogo's actions, arresting him when he returned to Scotland, though he had already sold his booty in England. Several weeks later, James revived a long-standing complaint of the Barton family against the Portuguese, concerning a case of spoil that was more than fifty years old. Although the Bartons had been awarded a commission of reprisal, previous monarchs had suspended its execution. At the request of the family descendants, however, James intended to ratify the old commission, to the concern of the King of Portugal. James was likewise requesting justice from the Emperor, in a case of piracy on a Scottish vessel that occurred more than twenty years previously.[49] By the early 1540s it seemed that rulers in north-west Europe were lining up to issue letters of reprisal on behalf of their subjects.

The activities of pirates and rovers thus intensified the international tension and insecurity at sea, provoking grievances that rival monarchs made use of for diplomatic or political purposes. As war between France and the Empire loomed, in August 1542 Henry prepared to send out ships-of-war to deal with the danger of French raiding in English waters. The French complained about the lack of English neutrality, claiming that the Flemish were able to use English ports at will. But the King's actions were partly a response to the plunder of English shipping by French rovers, which included the recent seizure of a London vessel at the mouth of the Thames. By September 1542 the Emperor's agent in London reported that Henry's ships had almost cleared the coast of French men-of-war. For their part the French complained angrily about the ill-treatment of their mariners at the hands of the English, alleging that lawful men-of-war were treated like pirates, while objecting to the way in which Francis I was derided as a Turk by unruly crews of piratical Englishmen.[50]

The Anglo-French conflict coincided with widespread maritime disorder, and in circumstances which encouraged the Henrician regime to rely on private enterprise for supporting the war at sea. Even so, the war was a very costly business, involving large-scale expeditions to Scotland in 1542 and to France in 1544. It was also risky, exposing England to the dilemma of fighting on two fronts. The dangers were starkly revealed by the seizure of seven English vessels off the coast of Normandy, early in 1542, by Scottish warships manned with French seamen. Given the experience of the 1530s the combatants resorted to reprisals, licensing private adventurers to plunder the trade and shipping of the enemy. In England the regime sought to channel the indiscriminate predatory activities of sea rovers into more effective and targeted raiding, with the intention of alleviating the pressure on the King's Navy while weakening its opponents. The Privy Council noted during a meeting in 1544 that it was 'over burdensome that the King should set ships to defend all parts of the realm, and keep the Narrow Seas'.[51] Consequently, it was prepared to sanction a private war of plunder, which was to serve as an important precedent for the subsequent development of organized privateering.

Although this strategy needed no justification, it raised questions regarding the control and direction of private enterprise. During the early stages of the war the regime attempted to regulate the issue of letters of reprisal, though in a manner which betrayed uncertainty or inexperience. While the Lord Admiral issued commissions to adventurers who claimed losses at the hands of the French or Scots, it was the council which took recognizances or bonds for good behaviour at sea. In April 1543, for example, Thomas Guillett, vintner, and George Doddes, fishmonger, acted as sureties for a group of adventurers in Rye, on condition that they would only plunder French or Scottish vessels. However, there appears to have been no attempt to restrict such seizures to a specified amount. Robert Borough was awarded a commission in March 1543 in response to the injuries he had received from the French, which allowed him to take as many French ships as he could. These regulations were relaxed further by a proclamation of December 1544 which authorized any of Henry's subjects to send out vessels against the enemy. Officials in port towns were enjoined to ensure that it met with a favourable response.[52]

It is impossible to gauge the scale of English privateering from 1543 to 1546, though a cautious estimate for the annual number of vessels at sea on legitimate reprisal ventures probably lies between thirty and sixty. The number may have increased significantly after December 1544. The development of privateering during these years was facilitated by the strong tradition of predatory enterprise in the south and south-west. It was within this region, moreover, that the commercial consequences of the war with France were most damaging. Though the evidence is scrappy, it suggests that merchants and shipowners in provincial ports, such as Rye, Southampton and Plymouth, were prominent among those who received letters of reprisal prior to their replacement by the proclamation of December 1544.

Between 28 March and 28 April 1543 at least eleven or twelve commissions were issued to adventurers authorizing them to seize the ships of France or Scotland. They included John Ball of Winchilsea; John Fletcher, John Reynolds and Thomas Fugler of the neighbouring port of Rye; Robert Reneger of Southampton; and John Burgh of Devon.[53] The most notable adventurer was Sir John Russell, 1st Earl of Bedford, a leading courtier who was appointed Lord Admiral in 1540 and Lord Privy Seal in 1542. Russell possessed considerable landed property in the West Country, which included 30,000 acres formerly owned by the monastery at Tavistock. He was also a shipowner with varied commercial interests. In this capacity he seems to have acted as a representative for a group of promoters in Plymouth and other ports, who were known as the adventurers in the west. Traders and shipowners in London and east-coast ports, particularly Hull, which were exposed to raids by Scottish rovers, were also among the recipients of commissions. During April 1543 the craft guilds of

London were reported to be sending out several ships with a licence from the King. Later in the year Miles Myddleton, a yeoman of the guard, was authorized to go to sea with two vessels from Hull, to annoy the enemy and take prizes.[54]

The opening months of the war thus met with an encouraging response from private adventurers, though most of the vessels sent out were probably small, if heavily manned, non-specialized craft. The four vessels of Rye, which John Ball and John Reynolds intended to send out in April 1543, were of 20 tons burden. To a considerable extent, the tonnage of such shipping dictated tactics at sea, restricting most adventurers to hit-and-run raids over short distances. As Russell informed the council later in the conflict, most of the vessels from the south-west were 'too small to encounter men-of-war, their usage being to keep along the shore and meddle only with merchants'.[55] The bulk of the ships sent to Portsmouth in July 1545 by the adventurers in the west were between 30 and 40 tons; ten shallops from the West Country, employed in patrolling the Channel in March 1546, amounted to 450 tons burden, though they carried a total complement of 400 men.

Among merchants and shipowners, privateering was a business which developed a commercial infrastructure that was designed to share the cost of fitting out ships-of-war among a group of adventurers, while reducing the risks of an uncertain and dangerous enterprise. The uncertainty was also qualified by limiting the investment to a specific voyage, after which any captured prizes were shared out among the adventurers. Although it became commonplace for this to include shipowners, victuallers and crew, who usually served on the understanding that their wages were dependent on prizes taken during the voyage, there was room for flexibility. An agreement for a privateering voyage, based on a formal indenture of January 1544, between William Bulley (owner of the *Martin Bulley* of London), Sir John Gresham (merchant and alderman), and William More and William Hollande (the captain and master of the vessel respectively), demonstrates the structure of these ventures. According to the terms of the indenture, it was agreed that 'with the fyrste good wynde and wether … [the ship] shall dyrectlie saile into the seas there to have warre of the Kinge's enemyes at the onely adventure of … William Bulley'.[56] The charge for victuals, powder and munitions was shared between Gresham (who was responsible for one-third of the total), More and Hollande (who were responsible for one-quarter), and Bulley (who accounted for the remainder). All prizes were to be divided between the adventurers in accordance with their investment in the voyage. Before the division of the prizes, however, the gunners were to receive a special reward of eighteen shares. Furthermore, the adventurers agreed that if any mariners were unwilling to serve for a share in the voyage, they were to be paid wages as in the King's fleet.

Under the guise of such ventures the adventurers in the west, including William Hawkins, an enterprising merchant of Plymouth, seized the opportunity to conduct a private war of plunder at sea. This combined depredation with other duties. In September 1544 the council issued a commission to Hawkins and others, to send out between four and eight vessels at their own charge, to annoy the enemy and to assist in the defence of the realm. The adventurers were also authorized to levy mariners and soldiers, and to take up victuals and artillery in Devon, Cornwall, Somerset and Dorset.[57]

As a result of such arrangements the maritime conflict was characterized by an uneasy partnership between the regime and private enterprise. But the results were striking. In November 1544 the council reported that during the year the ports of the south-west had between twelve and sixteen ships-of-war at sea, which seized prizes worth at least £10,000. At the same time, adventurers in Rye had three or four vessels at sea 'and gained much by it'.[58] John Stow subsequently reported that 300 French prizes were taken during 1544. It seemed, therefore, that for a modest investment, the business of plunder was capable of yielding a profitable return.

The reliance on private enterprise by the state was as much defensive as it was offensive. In part it was intended to meet the twin threat of French and Scottish raiding in English waters. On the one hand, Scottish rovers were a serious menace to trade and fishing along the east coast. On the other hand, the presence of French men-of-war on the coast of Ireland provoked concern that the Bretons 'will be lords between Brittany and Scotland', without an adequate defensive force at sea.[59] Although the regime managed to shift some of the costs of defence onto the shoulders of private adventurers in the south and south-west, it met with less success in the port towns of the east coast. In November 1544 the council rebuked Newcastle for not sending out vessels to defend its trade. Local leaders claimed that there were insufficient mariners in the port to send out ships; most were either employed in the King's service or had fled to Norfolk and Suffolk to avoid a recent outbreak of sickness. Prominent northern magnates, such as Francis Talbot, 5th Earl of Shrewsbury, were also used to put pressure on port towns to support the war at sea. In response to promptings from Shrewsbury, who served on the Anglo-Scottish border during 1544 and 1545, officials in Hull insisted that most of their principal shipping was unavailable for service. Local merchants and shipowners had 'been at importunate costs in manning three ships of war' during the year.[60] Two had guarded the north coast until they were driven off by a fleet of Scottish vessels, the third was forced into Dover by bad weather. Nonetheless, the Hull men offered to send out two ships if Shrewsbury granted them a commission to take prizes. Their neighbours in Scarborough agreed to send out two small vessels if they were supplied with guns, powder and shot. Further north, Whitby was in no position to respond to the urgings of Shrewsbury: following the decay of the harbour, local traders and shipowners had sold their vessels.

The proclamation of December 1544 was an attempt to deal with local recalcitrance by authorizing privateering without the need for letters of reprisal. This was a gamble, resting on the effectiveness of self-regulation among promoters, whose overriding concern with prize taking generated potential conflicts of interest in the conduct of the war at sea between their own priorities and the objectives of the regime. The dangers of disorderly activity at sea, by naval officers as much as by private adventurers, were self-evident. The previous year the council had been forced to reprimand a captain in the King's Navy for stopping friendly vessels at sea. The King's anger at this practice provoked a sharp letter from the council, with instructions to the captain to behave in such a way 'as itt might nott appere that his Grace were in hostilitie wyth all the worlde'.[61] But the proclamation of 1544 encouraged the growth of maritime disorder, including the spoil of neutral trade and shipping, which led to a storm of diplomatic protest. Within months of its publication, Henry was reported to be so annoyed at the English seizure of Spanish ships that he intended to recall all men-of-war.

Although the growth of privateering drew on the strength of localized piracy, it was shaped by deeper undercurrents which linked predatory overseas commercial expansion with anti-Spanish hostility. Commercial and religious rivalries lent new direction to seaborne depredation, with far-reaching consequences for the development of piracy and privateering. Merchants and shipowners in the provincial ports of the south and south-west played a key role in what was to become a prolonged, intermittent assault on Spanish trade and shipping. The leading figures in this rising tide of organized plunder during the 1540s included William Hawkins of Plymouth and Robert Reneger of Southampton, both of whom had extensive trading interests in the Iberian Peninsula. Hawkins was one of the pioneers of English commercial enterprise in the Atlantic, developing interests in the Brazil and Guinea trades during the 1530s. Reneger was also involved in the Brazil trade. The character of this expansion was inherently aggressive, attracting not just prominent provincial traders but also ambitious adventurers of dubious reputation, such as Thomas Wyndham, who were tempted into the illicit spoil of Iberian shipping during the 1540s. Wyndham was a naval commander with experience of serving aboard private ships-of-war, including one owned by Lord Russell. The anti-Spanish interests of these adventurers were shared by a younger generation of courtiers, particularly Sir Thomas Seymour, who were part of an increasingly powerful group of evangelical, if not Protestant sympathisers.[62] Several of Seymour's captains came to the attention of the council during these years for their attacks on ships belonging to the Emperor's subjects, Flemish as well as Spanish.

The prospect of richer Iberian prizes, laden with cargoes of American treasure, lured English raiders into the Atlantic, laying the foundations for the emergence of long-distance plunder. Reneger's seizure of the *San Salvador*, off Cape St Vincent, laden with gold, sugar and pearls valued at 19,315 ducats, provoked a crisis in relations with Spain, but it also demonstrated the attraction of this kind of enterprise. On his return to England, Reneger informed the Privy Council of the incident and placed some of the plunder in the Tower of London. In June 1545 the Imperial ambassador in London complained

Drake's Island and Plymouth Sound, Devon. Formerly known as St Nicholas' Island, it
acquired the name of Drake's Island during the later sixteenth century. The island was fortified
in 1549 to defend the port against overseas attack. As well as the link with Drake, Plymouth
was the home of the Hawkins family. (Author's collection)

that Reneger, instead of 'being punished like a pirate, was treated like a hero'.
Furthermore, he warned that 'the English mean to seize everything they meet
at sea as French and then refer claimants to the Admiralty'.[63] Within weeks
Reneger was reported to have seized a French vessel laden with Spanish commodities, returning from the Levant.

Although reports that the King intended to recall privateers and halt the issue
of commissions of reprisal were premature, the council tried to limit the danger
of indiscriminate plunder by instructing officials in provincial ports, like Bristol,
to take bonds of adventurers not to attack the subjects of the Emperor. However,
these instructions did little to reduce the volume of complaint to the council
from Spanish and Flemish merchants whose vessels continued to be seized by
English raiders of varying legality. Early in July 1545 the council issued orders for
the release of three Spanish vessels brought into Plymouth by the King's ships.
Later in the month, William Hawkins was imprisoned at the council's command
during the course of a bitterly contested dispute over the ownership of plundered
commodities, which were eventually restored to their Spanish owners.[64]

The problem of disorderly depredation, while showing no sign of abating
during 1545, was an inescapable consequence of the conduct of the war at sea.
Faced with fighting an expensive conflict on two fronts, the regime was compelled to rely on private adventurers to undertake various duties at sea which
were subsidized by the returns from plunder. But the difficulty in implementing
this strategy was underlined by the lukewarm, if not indifferent, response from

the east-coast ports to the council's persuasions in 1544. After further negotiations, by February 1545 Shrewsbury informed the council that the port of Hull
was prepared to send out six vessels at its own charge. According to Shrewsbury
the ships would perform a combination of public and private duties, enabling
the Hull men to keep open their trade while frustrating the enemy. Their success
might also encourage others. Indeed, within a few weeks officials in Newcastle
indicated that they were willing to send out two ships.[65]

Though these arrangements were intended to alleviate the pressure on the
King's Navy, the main priority of private adventurers was profit. During April
and May 1545 ships of Hull seized neutral vessels from the Low Countries
and elsewhere on the grounds that they were carrying Scottish cargoes.
John Dove, one of the leading adventurers in Hull, plundered several vessels
from Pomerania and Denmark, as well as a Flemish ship reportedly carrying
Scottish goods and a passenger bearing letters from the Pope. Several weeks
later a vessel of Bremen was forced into Newcastle by bad weather, where it
was plundered of provisions and tackling by John Iven of Hull. The plunder
amounted to less than £10 in total, but it included a range of useful accessories
such as an anchor and cable; a compass and lead line; eight bow staves, five axes
and a sword; ten hats and two caps; four pairs of shoes and one pair of boots; a
doublet and a pair of hose. Yet the actions of men-of-war along the east coast
failed to contain the spread of Scottish depredation. By April 1545 Scottish
privateers, who were using bases in Normandy and Brittany, were reported
to have taken plunder from the English, valued at between 30,000 and 40,000
crowns.[66]

In a further attempt to encourage and organize private enterprise at sea,
the King issued a proclamation in April 1545, appointing 'John of Calais' as
the captain of 'Ships of Marque', with the power to levy recruits on both sides
of the Channel 'as shall offer themselves to serve at their own adventure'.[67]
Soldiers, servants and apprentices were ineligible for service without a special
licence from their masters or captains. But the proclamation had a limited
impact. Shortly after its publication the Lord Deputy of Ireland, Sir Anthony
St Leger, informed the council that John Hill seized two French prizes off
the Irish coast; however, like many others he seems to have been operating
independently of government control, though he was seeking a commission
to levy men and provisions. His request was supported by St Leger whose
brother, Robert, had a ship furnished for war which he intended to send out
in consort with Hill.[68]

The uneasy relationship between the early Tudor regime and private adventurers encouraged the growth of aggressive spoil at sea, blurring the distinction
between legal and illegal plunder. At the same time it contained inherent weaknesses which were demonstrated during the crisis of July 1545, when a French
naval force sailed into the Solent after raiding Portsmouth and the Isle of Wight.
The regime struggled throughout the summer to assemble a fleet off Portsmouth.

Orders were sent to the ports of the south-west recalling adventurers from the sea and for a press of all mariners, but they met with a tardy response. A varied force of vessels from the region reached Portsmouth by early August; nonetheless, there were complaints that many had failed to respond to demands from London. Moreover, some of those already at Portsmouth abandoned the service. The Lord Admiral complained that many were 'wholly given to pillage and robbery'.[69]

Although the King came under pressure from the council to make peace with France, the war lingered on until June 1546, becoming increasingly disorderly at sea during its closing stages. The seizure of Spanish and Flemish ships persisted, despite the concern of Henry and his diplomatic representatives. Scattered reports and complaints to the council demonstrate the extent of these attacks. Despite the emphasis of such evidence on the unruly and uncontrolled nature of the war at sea, privateering, loosely defined and regulated, was an organized business based on extensive networks of suppliers for the provisioning and fitting out of men-of-war. It was heavily concentrated in the port towns of the south and south-west, and Calais on the other side of the Channel. While provincial ship-owners and traders were deeply involved in the business, it attracted the interest of some London merchants as well as officials and courtiers, including the Lord Admiral, John Dudley, Viscount Lisle, who had extensive interests in shipping. Under the shadow of the wars with France and Scotland, the regime had called into being a voluntary force of seaborne predators which it could neither control nor direct effectively.

During 1545 the council instructed privateers to use the Emperor's subjects in a 'gentle sort', but shipping from the Low Countries and Spain continued to bear the brunt of English aggression at sea.[70] Throughout the summer the council was forced to intervene in cases of spoil, in response to complaints from Flemish, Iberian and other neutral traders. Early in June it ordered the return of a lading of canvas plundered by Freeman of Calais out of a ship bound for Flanders; later in the month it issued orders for the restoration of the *Mary* of Dunkirk which had been brought into Plymouth. Despite this, and other interventions, the council was unable to stop the seizure of neutral shipping at sea.

The persistence of such unruly depredation invited retaliation. In September 1545 the council heard complaints concerning the detention of a Chester ship in Spain. Several months later it received a petition from Robert Thorne of Bristol on behalf of Walter Roberts, the captain of a local ship, who had been driven by bad weather into San Sebastián with five French prizes, where he was arrested and imprisoned by officials of the inquisition. The arrest of English ships in Spanish ports complicated the council's efforts to prevent attacks on Iberian vessels. In any case the disciplining of disorderly captains was occasionally tempered by public and private circumstances. In December 1545 George Butshed was freed from a long spell of imprisonment, for unruly spoil at sea, after 'shewing himself very repentant for his lewdness committed by rage of youth without due consideracion, and promising to be hereafter of honest behaviour'.[71]

During the later stages of the conflict the council was faced with a growing number of cases concerning irregular spoil which were essentially piratical in nature. In January 1546 it established an inquiry into the seizure of a Flemish ship, taken by English adventurers and reportedly sold in Ireland. A few weeks later it faced complaints about the plunder of a Spanish ship off Plymouth. In this case the council acknowledged that the attack was piracy; those involved, who had been taken, were to be handed over to the deputy of the Lord Admiral for punishment. At the end of March it ordered the arrest of John Thompson follow-ing complaints of the plunder of several Flemish vessels laden with pepper and other goods valued at 40,000 ducats. Several weeks later it investigated reports of the robbery of two Spanish ships by a Falmouth vessel, the captain of which 'was said to keep an inn there and to be blemished in one eye'.[72] According to the governor of Calais, 'every Spaniard, Portugall or Fleming that comes from the South is robbed by our adventurers, some calling themselves Scots and some with vizers'.[73]

In response to the growing volume of complaint, in April 1546 the council issued instructions to officials in the Cinque Ports and in the south-west to detain men-of-war in port and to recall those at sea. It also ordered the arrest of several of the leaders involved in the spoil of neutral shipping in the Channel, includ-ing William Trymel of Rye and John Thompson, one of the western adventurers based in Calais. In May, Trymel was committed to the Tower, under instructions from the council that he was to be denied any visitors. But the regime found it difficult to apply an effective remedy to the problem of illicit plunder and piracy, not least because of the increasing number of 'wandering freebooters' of varying nationalities who were operating in the Channel.[74]

As the activities of Trymel and Thompson indicated, English rovers used local ports as bases for their raids, exploiting the potential of Calais as a cross-Channel haven, while disposing of plunder in markets scattered across the coastal regions of southern England and Ireland. As during the 1450s and 1460s there was a lively, informal trade in plundered cargoes which supported piracy and privateering. Plunder brought into Ilfracombe and Barnstaple by Thompson and Trymel was purchased by local merchants, including Roger Worthe, John Hollond, Henry Cade, Robert Cade and John Shapter (alias Butler), who re-sold part of it to 'sundry other gentilmen and others farre under the just valewe of the same'.[75] On investigating the case, the council ordered the restoration of the stolen goods. It also commanded those purchasers who had acquired the goods below their market value, to pay an additional sum of two shillings for every pound of pepper, cloves or sugar to the owners, partly to dissuade men of their status from dealing in pirates' plunder.

Despite the order recalling men-of-war, the regime continued to allow adven-turers to put to sea on lawful voyages of reprisal. In May 1546 the King licensed John Frencheman of Rye to set out for the North Sea with two small vessels and a row boat on condition that he 'behave well towards the King's subjects and friends and … register all prizes at the first English port'.[76] Later in the month the council issued a licence to Henry Golding, captain of the *Bark Ager*, for a similar voyage with two pinnaces of Plymouth manned with eighty men. Yet the inability of the regime to control the activities of such vessels was exposed by the disorderly depredations committed by ships-of-war sent out by members of Henry's increasingly divided and factionalized court, including the Lord Admiral and the Seymour brothers who were uncles of the King's son and heir. One of the Lord Admiral's vessels, under Captain Richard Gray, seized a Flemish prize laden with sugar and wines off the coast of Barbary, with the assistance of a ship of Sir Thomas Seymour, under the command of Richard Hore, an experienced sea captain. Hore led an expedition across the Atlantic in 1536, apparently with the purpose of exploring the region beyond Newfoundland. According to a later account, however, the expedition ran out of provisions, leading some of the company to resort to cannibalism; in harrowing circumstances, Hore and the survivors returned to England aboard a French vessel which they seized in exchange for their own ship. Another of Seymour's captains, Robert Bruse, came to the attention of the council for his attacks on neutral shipping in the Channel. Following the plunder of a merchant of Antwerp, the council issued orders for Bruse's arrest in June 1546. In addition Seymour's brother, Edward, 1st Earl of Hertford, was also involved in cross-Channel raiding and pillaging. During May 1546 he informed the King that one of his vessels had brought in three small prizes laden with victuals, after a brief cruise along the coast of France.[77]

As Lisle predicted, the attack on neutral trade and shipping provoked angry protests from the Emperor's subjects. However, it was the council, not the ageing King, which increasingly had to deal with the problem. Although some cases of spoil were passed on to the High Court of Admiralty, the diplomatic and political implications of the plunder of neutral traders compelled the council to take a leading role in handling complaints and resolving disputes, in an effort to limit the damage of English excesses at sea. Thus it sought to restore illegally plundered cargoes; it issued orders for the arrest of unruly captains, such as Bruse; and it ordered the investigation of suspected cases of piracy.

The pressure of such business consumed more of the council's time during the final months of the war. Towards the end of May 1546 it instructed the Lord Admiral to recall two adventurers, Robert and John Bellyne, who were allegedly attacking vessels of Flushing. At the same time it dealt with complaints against John Malyne of Calais, who was ordered to appear before the council on charges of piracy and spoil following the disposal of plundered commodities in Ireland. Several days later it issued letters of assistance for the recovery of goods taken by English adventurers out of a Spanish vessel. The following month it issued orders for the arrest of various rovers or pirates who had seized a vessel of Lübeck off the coast of Cornwall, and set the master and company adrift in the ship's boat. By mid-June it was investigating complaints against an English captain who was accused of selling booty in Cork with the connivance of the mayor.[78]

Much of this maritime activity was in the form of petty marauding by small vessels carrying a variety of armaments, which produced modest returns from the plunder of shipping in local waters, as is suggested by several cases dealt with by the High Court of Admiralty during the latter part of the war. In April 1546, for example, a small man-of-war, the *Mary Anne*, plundered a Spanish ship off Dursey Head of wines and other goods which were owned by Frenchmen. According to the master of the *Mary Anne*, the proceeds of the spoil amounted to £100. Out of this total the purser retained £18 for the owners of the ship to purchase victuals; the remainder was divided among the ship's company. The master's own share amounted to 13s 4d in cash, and included a sword, crossbow and a pair of horns. A few months later another Spanish vessel, the *Sancta Maria del Guadeloupe*, laden with iron and woad for various merchants of Chester, was attacked by a small ship under the command of Michael James. The English assaulted the Spanish 'very fiercely with guns and arrows', plundered the cargo and left the ship four leagues from land.[79] Though the Spanish sailed on to Waterford, within sight of the harbour they were approached by another small vessel, manned by a group of rovers led by Leonard Sumpter. When the latter got within gun shot of the *Sancta Maria* the crew apparently fled in fear for their lives, taking with them some of the iron. Sumpter seized the abandoned ship, carried it off to Penarth in south Wales and subsequently claimed it as a casualty of the sea.

The restoration of peace during the summer of 1546 failed to halt the disorder at sea, which continued to claim the attention of the council. In July it ordered the return of a French prize taken since the peace by John Frencheman of Rye. In August John Donne of Rye, captain of the *Dooe*, was imprisoned in the Marshalsea for seizing cloth out of a Spanish vessel. Later in the year John Thompson was still reportedly robbing Spanish ships in the Channel. Early the following year the accomplices of Cornelius Bellyne of Calais were executed for plundering Flemish vessels. Bellyne remained at sea, and was reported to be robbing the Flemish daily.[80]

The disorganization of the war at sea created profound difficulties for the Henrician regime. But they were a consequence of the military weaknesses of the early Tudor state which led it to promote privateering as a means of sharing the cost of the maritime conflict with private enterprise. The confusion between public and private interests that followed from this strategy was compounded with the spread of illegal and legal depredation. In effect the war at sea produced a varied pattern of indiscriminate and disorderly spoil. Small-scale, opportunistic raiding, involving short-distance voyages into the Channel and its approaches, including the North Sea and the Irish Sea, remained a characteristic feature of the conflict. But it was accompanied by the emergence of longer-distance venturing into the eastern Atlantic, which was larger in scale and ambition. Inevitably the emergence of Atlantic privateering and piracy was focused on the spoil of Iberian trade. The vulnerability of Spanish and Portuguese commerce during these years was underlined by the plunder of four Portuguese vessels in the harbour of Munguia by English adventurers during March 1546. The English seized a rich haul of sugar, and carried off one vessel laden with oil, ivory, pepper and other commodities of great value. However, the boldness of the attack provoked unease and disunity among the raiders. The master of the *John* of Kingswear was derided by some of the company as a coward who was more suited to keep sheep than to be a master of a man-of-war.[81]

Although these private actions of plunder provoked widespread complaint, they were supported by leading officials and courtiers in a way that served to sanction the activities of men such as Reneger and Wyndham. Under these conditions the predatory activities and ambitions of the English were re-shaped and re-directed during the 1540s with profound consequences for their subsequent development. The scale and intensity of the disorder at sea unavoidably confused the distinction between piracy and privateering. Although piracy was overshadowed, if not obscured, by the spread of disorderly plunder, it did not disappear from the waters of the British Isles. But the kind of opportunistic and localized piracy which flourished during the 1530s, and which persisted in some regions, seems to have been displaced by competing forms of licensed and unlicensed privateering. In some cases the change was little more than cosmetic. The war created more opportunities for small-scale rovers to exploit, as demonstrated by the attack on the *John* of Middelburg in the harbour of St Aubin, in Jersey, during July 1546. At the same time, the economic potential of privateering provided an opportunity for larger-scale venturing to flourish, organized in a more business-like fashion by merchants and shipowners. Moreover, some of this venturing was sustained by an extensive and illicit commerce in plundered commodities. Shore-based networks of supporters were essential to the maintenance and elaboration of English depredation during these years. Merchants such as Thomas Edmunds of Scarborough, who purchased goods 'under very suspicious circumstances … for much less and smaller sums and prices than they were worth', provided markets for rovers, in concealed transactions that took place in unusual conditions, sometimes at night and usually involving a rapid re-sale to hinder detection.[82] By these and other means the appeal of maritime depredation was widely and deeply scattered during the 1540s.

Pirates and Rebellious Rovers during the 1540s and 1550s

English piracy and disorderly depredation remained a persistent problem during the period from the end of Henry VIII's war with France to the closing years of the reign of his daughter, Mary I, when renewed conflict with the French led to the loss of Calais. The intervening years were a profoundly difficult period for the Tudor regime, which was marked by weak royal rule, religious rivalries and mounting economic and social tension. International conflict, social unrest and rebellion created a fertile environment for seaborne plunder in many parts of north-west Europe, undermining the ability of rulers to deal with the threat of lawlessness at sea, while commercial crisis and change, including the decline and disruption of the fishing trades in England, helped to expand the recruiting grounds for piracy and privateering. To a considerable degree the maintenance of English plunder during these years was an elaboration of patterns of activity that were established during the 1520s and 1530s. Consequently piracy and other forms of maritime depredation varied in intensity and scale. Casual, opportunistic and locally based spoil remained a widespread and persistent menace, but it was overlaid by more organized enterprise, especially within a region linking the West Country and south Wales with southern Ireland. The combination of domestic weakness and external threat encouraged the spread of disorderly plunder, but in a way which reflected a broader shift in English overseas relations. The rapid growth of anti-Spanish hostility promoted predatory venturing to the coasts of Spain and Portugal, where richer prizes were readily available. At the same time, the activities of an ill-assorted group of rebellious rovers and privateers, operating from bases in France against the Marian regime, indicated that under certain conditions piratical enterprise could acquire a political purpose that was also patriotic and popular.

Piracy, sea roving and privateering during the later 1540s and 1550s

The mid-Tudor regimes struggled to contain the spread of maritime disorder during the later 1540s and 1550s. Although Henry VIII had created one of the largest navies in Europe, it struggled to deal with the spread of small-scale depredation. For much of the period English, Scottish and French rovers remained active in the Channel, indulging in indiscriminate petty spoil. The haphazard and apparently erratic nature of such activity conceals subtle distinctions between different types of sea roving, which ranged across a spectrum of dubious legality. Although piracy and privateering continued to be confused, officially the state sought to maintain a clear distinction between legitimate and illegitimate plunder, partly in response to overseas complaint, but also in order to retain a lawful means of redress and reprisal. Nonetheless, privateering was becoming an established expedient for waging war at sea, though it was difficult to regulate effectively. As the experience of the 1540s indicated, inexorably it led to the growth of disorderly plunder and piracy.

Undercover, or in the guise, of lawful depredation, piratical activity grew increasingly organized and purposeful. One of the most striking developments of the later 1540s and 1550s was the emergence of a group of pirate captains who appear to have made a career out of plunder. Such men, including John Thompson, Henry Strangeways and Richard Coole (or Cole), formed a loose network of rovers and pirates, though they were as much potential competitors as partners. These groups of rovers operated in fairly well-defined hunting grounds, supported by an informal exchange economy, that is almost hidden from view, in markets on either side of the Irish Sea, encouraging the use of temporary bases in southern Ireland. Though publicly proclaimed as notorious pirates, men like Thompson were capable of skirting the boundaries between illegal and legal enterprise, serving as captains of pirate ships and men-of-war. While the activities of these 'head pirates' were sustained by a favourable social and economic environment, their survival also owed much to the weaknesses of the mid-Tudor monarchy.[1]

Among the most pressing problems facing the new regime of Henry's successor, the boy-king Edward VI, was the persistence of lawlessness in the Channel and the western approaches, and along the east coast. In addition the regency government inherited protracted disputes concerning the spoil of the Emperor's subjects during the 1540s, which were costly and diplomatically damaging. In an important gesture of goodwill, at the end of 1547 the booty which Robert Reneger had seized and placed in the Tower was returned to the Spanish. Reneger, a leading member of the merchant community of Southampton, was awarded £250 by the council towards the cost of resolving the dispute.[2]

In response to growing complaints against the piracies of Thompson and other English rovers, during September 1547 the council tried to regulate the activities of private men-of-war. It prohibited the sending out of such vessels without a special licence from the Lord Admiral. The owners were also required to take out bonds for the good behaviour of their ships at sea. Furthermore, at the direction of the Lord Admiral and the Lord Warden of the Cinque Ports, local officials were to take similar bonds from the owners of all vessels engaged in trading and other voyages. The council expected that bonds would be taken in every port and creek by local officials, in 'suche summes of money as they shall think' necessary, though there is little evidence for the implementation of this unusual and possibly unworkable scheme to tackle maritime disorder.[3]

The need for more effective regulation at sea grew urgent during the later 1540s as the regime faced increasing complaints against the activities of English pirates and rovers. These included the plunder of a Lübeck vessel by the servants of Robert St Leger, and the spoil of several French vessels in the Channel, as well as a case of piracy and murder near Deal Castle. Along the east coast the plunder of shipping provoked conflicting claims to prizes taken by English and Scottish rovers. Complaints of English piracy continued into 1548. In May the Lord Admiral issued sweeping instructions for the examination of all vessels entering the realm, following the spoil of French ships in the Channel which were freighted with merchandise by a group of London merchants. Greater vigilance in some regions may have persuaded pirate groups to resort to more remote bases in Ireland. In July, for example, officials in southern Irish ports, including Youghal, Cork and Kinsale, reported the growing presence of English pirates, who were attacking French, Spanish and local vessels.[4]

Yet the regime was so alarmed at the rival dangers of Scots and French raiding that in August 1548 the council authorized the Lord Admiral to send out armed vessels from Devon and Cornwall, against 'the Scots, pirates and the King's other enemies'.[5] This revival of the western adventurers was partly in response to the growing attack on English shipping by the French which included the recent seizure of five vessels, three of which were burnt and their crews committed to the galleys. The victims of such plunder also complained that they were unable to obtain justice in France. As during the 1520s, French men-of-war claimed to be operating with Scottish commissions. When Pietro Strozzi, the Italian adventurer in the employ of the French King, was challenged by one of his English victims, he replied, 'that he and the rest were, for the time of their stay there, Scots'.[6]

In an effort to control the activities of the western adventurers, the council issued the Lord Admiral with orders for their regulation. They included provision for taking bonds from shipowners and captains, and for a record to be kept of all vessels that were licensed to go to sea, a copy of which was to be sent to the council.

While publicly acknowledging peace with France, however, the council's orders
gave warrant to the adventurers in the south-west for a private war at sea. Thus the
owners of men-of-war, their captains and masters, were 'to be told secretly that,
besides Scots and pirates, they may stay the French fleet with the Newfoundland
fish and any other French ships, saying that they have previously been spoiled by
Frenchmen and could have no justice, or pretending that victuals or munitions
in any such French ships were sent to aid the Scots'.[7] All captured prizes were
to be returned to an English port, where inventories and valuations were to be
made of them, so that if the peace continued and the French offered redress for
English claims, they might be restored. The administration of these regulations was
left in the hands of the Lord Admiral, his Vice Admirals, Sir Peter Carew and John
Grenefeld, and other officials in Devon and Cornwall.

These secret instructions demonstrated an early appreciation of the strategic
value of private enterprise in disrupting the transatlantic trade of a rival and
potential enemy. They also anticipated the outbreak of war with France during
August 1549. The conflict witnessed a short-lived revival of privateering which
drew on the experience of the Henrician wars with France. In the south-west
a wide range of promoters, including shipowners, traders and lesser landowners,
were involved in sending out vessels from ports such as Dartmouth, Exmouth
and Plymouth. They included Thomas Winter, mariner and shipowner, of
Stonehouse near Plymouth, and a varied group of adventurers from Exmouth
and the neighbouring region, such as Gregory Cary, a local Admiralty official
who was involved in several ventures with Walter Ralegh and his sons, John
and George. Elsewhere, armed vessels were sent out from ports along the south
coast, particularly Rye, as well as from Calais across the Channel. London and
some of the east-coast ports were also involved in the sea war. In addition, vessels
operating from Irish ports participated in the spread of opportunistic privateering and plunder.[8]

Although the sea war with France was too short for the sustained development
of private maritime enterprise, which may have been disrupted in parts of the
south-west by the outbreak of popular rebellion against religious change, it was
unruly and piratical in nature. Alarmed at the increase in piracy the regime issued
a proclamation early in 1549 which extended the death penalty to the supporters
of pirates, though there is no evidence that it was ever implemented. In any case,
the underlying problem was disorderly plunder by lawful men-of-war. Walter
Ralegh and Gilbert Drake were partners in victualling a vessel which illegally
seized a Spanish ship of San Sebastián. It was ransacked of much of its cargo of
wine, by the wives of the mariners, after its return to Exmouth. Following Spanish
complaints, the vessel was restored. Later in the year two small men-of-war, of
about 30 or 35 tons, from Plymouth and Waterford, brought a Biscayan prize
laden with wine into Youghal. The Plymouth vessel was reportedly owned by
John Ellyot, merchant, though he later claimed to have sold it to Griffith Vaughan
of south Wales. The Irish vessel, under the command of James Gough, was owned

by David Power and James Fitzgerald, 14th Earl of Desmond. The captors claimed that the prize was found at sea 'with no creature aboard her'.[9] However, several Biscayan mariners, who were in Youghal on a trading voyage, while noting the absence of Spaniards either aboard the prize or the men-of-war, recognized it as a vessel from Plasencia which had been involved in a fishing expedition off Baltimore, further along the coast, in the year previously.

Flemish vessels in the Channel were also the target of disorderly depredation. Towards the end of 1549 a variety of Flemish-owned commodities, taken by an adventurer known as Irish George of Calais, were recovered by one of the King's ships. At the same time French trade and shipping were legitimate prey for men-of-war. During the year French prizes laden with varied cargoes such as fish and salt were brought into Rye and other ports along the south coast. But the limitations of this short-range, and low-cost, form of plunder are suggested by the need of Thomas Woddman, captain of the *Falcon Grey*, set out by Sir Thomas Grey, to borrow money in Youghal to re-victual his ship.[10]

The confusion between legitimate and disorderly depredation, particularly in the south-west, encouraged the spread of piratical activity across the Irish Sea. The problem grew more severe during the 1540s. Although local officials complained repeatedly about the threat to trade and shipping, pirates and rovers were supported by coastal communities which benefited from a vigorous trade in plundered cargoes. Within a region where the authority of the Tudor regime was demonstrably weak, Irish Sea trades, undertaken in small, often unarmed and poorly manned vessels, were acutely vulnerable to the pirate menace. The local maritime conditions and environment, with open and remote coastlines and islands, also favoured the growth of piracy. Islands such as Caldey, off south-west Wales, may have played a crucial role in the operation of this kind of scattered roving, not least in providing cover for surprise attacks. The Isle of Man, which lay beyond the jurisdiction of the Lord Admiral, was frequently visited by pirates of varied backgrounds. The spread of English piracy widened the hinterland for the disposal of plunder, within a dangerously exposed maritime region that was irregularly patrolled by the King's ships, while potentially directing the attention of pirates and rovers towards the Atlantic.

Reports from officials in Irish ports reveal the growing importance of Ireland for the expanding range of English depredation. In April 1549 the mayor of Waterford informed the Lord Deputy, Edward Bellingham, of the activities of pirates during the previous three years. Much of this was small scale and casual in nature, involving petty plunder by groups of rovers whose identity was occasionally known to their victims. During 1547, for example, a vessel bound from Kinsale to Dungarvan, with a lading of wheat and malt for Thomas and Robert Hyat, was attacked by a small English ship with a crew of ten or eleven mariners under the command of Thomas Fyshebill. One member of the company of the Irish vessel, Robert Lovedaye, was taken aboard the pinnace. He recognised at least six of Fyshebill's men, and urged them 'not to meddle with Hyat's goods

Caldey Island, Pembrokeshire. According to the *Description of Penbrokshire* by George Owen, written during 1602 and 1603, the inhabitants of the island were afraid to keep oxen because of the threat from pirates or their purveyors, who regularly raided for provisions. (Author's collection)

for that he was his neighbour and a man that he knew well'.[11] Against the wishes of Fyshebill, evidently Lovedaye and other members of the company, including Robert Hyat, were sent ashore in a boat with a chest of their possessions and three or four bags of wheat. Before reaching land, Lovedaye was forcibly taken out of the boat by a small group of pursuing rovers, concerned that 'he should not go ashore to be their confession'.[12] About one year later, indeed, Lovedaye was a leading witness in a case heard by the High Court of Admiralty, during which he identified six of Fyshebill's company, who were being tried for piracy.

It was difficult to guard against this kind of opportunistic robbery at sea, though the size of some groups of rovers exposed them to the risk of capture. In July 1548 officials in Youghal informed the Lord Deputy of their seizure of a pirate, operating under the name of Smith, and his followers, who had plundered local fishing boats. But this success was offset by a report from Kinsale of a recent outbreak of pestilence which killed most of the male inhabitants, leaving an empty town 'with few men and naughty neighbours', including several groups of pirates who were threatening to blockade entry into the port.[13] One of them, Richard Coole, had married the aunt of a local landowner, Barry Oge, and resided in his castle, which he used as a base to pillage visiting vessels. About the same time the mayor of Cork complained that English pirates were boldly haunting the mouth of the haven. They were accompanied or followed by groups of Scottish, French and Spanish rovers. Later in the year a Scots pirate was cruising off Lambay Island and the Head of Howth, within easy reach of Dublin.

The inability of the regime to combat the spread of piracy across the Irish Sea was starkly underlined by the activities of Thompson and Coole off Waterford during the summer of 1548. Towards the end of July the mayor announced Thompson's arrival to the Lord Deputy, adding that he threatened 'to do them mischief for the taking of his boy by Watkin Apowell'.[14] Thompson was captured, but within a month he was set at liberty by a powerful lord, O'Sullivan Beare, on the payment of a large ransom. In response to Coole's seizure of a Portuguese vessel which was brought into the port during August, the Lord Admiral sent one of his servants to Waterford to ensure that it was restored to the original owners. But the action invited retaliation from the pirates, who demonstrated their local power by plundering and seizing shipping. Although some of the pirates were captured, in September the mayor requested their speedy discharge, partly because of the cost of maintaining them, but also on the grounds that they 'behaved very ill in gaol'.[15] The problems facing Waterford seemed to get worse during October, with the arrival of more pirates or rovers led by David Power and James Gough. When they were denied the opportunity to re-victual, Power and his associates plundered a Portuguese vessel in the harbour. As a result, the mayor complained that other foreign shipping refused to visit the port.

Local responses to the spread of piracy across the Irish Sea were uncertain and deeply ambivalent. Faced with an increase in the number of pirates and rovers operating along the coast, in November 1548 the mayor of Cork requested advice from the Lord Deputy as to whether they should be apprehended or killed. Several weeks later, officials reported the arrival of Thompson and Richard Stephenson, who had served under Robert St Leger, on Christmas Day with a ship laden with a cargo of wine, figs and sugar. The Lord Deputy authorized the inhabitants of the port to trade with Thompson and Stephenson, as it seemed that their goods were not stolen, and they had recently received pardons. At least part of this was misleading or based on misinformation. In 1549 the council instructed the Lord Deputy to publish a proclamation offering rewards for the capture of notorious pirates, who included Thompson. But such inducements appear to have made little difference to the situation in and around Cork, where the mayor admitted that 'the people of the adjacent country have long traded for [the] … wares' of Thompson and Stephenson.[16]

Officers acting on behalf of the Lord Admiral struggled to deal with the problem. In January 1549 the mayor of Cork noted that some of the port's neighbours had been compelled to restore goods purchased from pirates as a result of recent inquisitions by Admiralty officials. About the same time, another of the Admiral's officers, Thomas Wodloke, requested the mayor to arrest Henry Strangeways and fifteen other members of Thompson's company. Wodloke complained, however, that the mayor 'was loth to make variance between Cork and the pirates without special commandment'.[17] Indeed, the inhabitants were reported to be making ordnance for the pirates as well as supplying them with provisions. Weeks after his arrival, Thompson was still trading in the port, possibly in competition with another English rover who brought in a Flemish prize. Competition between rival groups of pirates or rovers could easily become hostile. In February 1549 a Danzig ship was brought in by the *Mary Winter*, owned and sent out by Thomas Winter, apparently on the grounds that it was sailing for Scotland with a cargo of wine. But it was tempting and easy prey for Thompson, Coole and Freeman, who recaptured the prize and claimed it as their own.

In order to deal with the pirate threat, in 1549 Walter Cowley, the Solicitor-General in Dublin, proposed to the Lord Admiral that some of the King's ships should be sent to Ireland. The proposal was linked with more ambitious measures for the defence and security of English interests, which included the reduction of Ireland through the construction of forts and the establishment of presidencies and councils in the provinces of Munster, Ulster and Connacht. The activities of pirates and rovers during the wars with Scotland and France thus raised wider concern about the vulnerability of Ireland to external threat. In March 1549 rumours circulated that the French and Scots intended to expel the English from Ireland. An earlier report had warned of the exposure of Skerries, a favourite haunt of pirates near Dublin, to a French landing, particularly as it was the 'only road in those seas for them betwixt Brittany and Scotland, being in their direct trade into the Frith of Dumbarton'.[18]

Lacking the resources for the effective defence of Ireland or the Irish Sea, the regime adopted improvised tactics which included the employment of pirates for military purposes. In 1549 the council authorized the Lord Deputy to use pirates against the MacDonnells, who had renewed their raiding from the Western Isles across the North Channel during the 1540s, either in conflict or cooperation with Gaelic leaders in the north. One of those employed was Richard Coole, whose testimony illustrates the adaptable and criss-crossing careers of many of the pirates and rovers operating during these years. Coole was a mariner from Minehead in Somerset. By his own admission, he served as a pirate for one year, during which time he took several prizes, including one taken off Caldey Island in December 1548. After petitioning the Lord Deputy for a pardon, he took part in an expedition to recover Strangford Castle from the Scots. Thereafter, he was involved in action against an Irish rebel. Although Bellingham promised him a pardon, it is not clear if the bargain was fulfilled. Coole subsequently sailed to the Isle of Man, 'landed his mate as a pledge' and was captured 'of his own good will'.[19] In May 1549 Rice ap Morgan and two associates received £100 as a reward for his capture. He was imprisoned in the Tower, where his fellow prisoners included the rebel leader Robert Kett and his brother William. He was still in custody at the end of October, awaiting examination by the officers of the Lord Admiral, though his career of sea roving was far from over.

The increase in piracy and maritime disorder during the later 1540s had serious consequences for the Lord Admiral. Within a divided and faction-ridden regime, it presented his rivals with an opportunity that they exploited to engineer his downfall and execution during 1549 on the grounds of high treason.

Although the main charges against Seymour concerned his alleged scheme for an 'alteration in the state', it was supported by damaging accusations concerning his dealings with pirates.[20] These included claims that he cultivated relations with pirates, ignoring orders from the council and his brother, the Lord Protector, for the restitution of plunder which was concealed for his own profit. While the captors of pirates were imprisoned, moreover, pirate leaders were freed, as if the Lord Admiral was 'authorized to be the chief pirate, and to have had all thadvantage thei coulde bring'.[21] Allegedly, the Lord Admiral's purchase of the Scilly Isles, and his plan to acquire Lundy Island, both well-established haunts for pirates, were seen as a sinister attempt to provide a safe refuge, where he could conspire with the pirates against his rivals. These accusations, which lacked corroborating evidence, were intended to destroy an ambitious and powerful competitor at court by equally ambitious and self-seeking rivals. Nonetheless, they suggest that the spread of piracy was facilitated by vested political interests within a weak and self-interested regime. Such conditions created opportunities for officials and others to manipulate the porous boundary between piracy and public service for private gain.

The end of the war with France in 1550, followed by peace with Scotland in 1551, brought little respite to the problem of disorderly plunder and piracy. English, Scottish and French rovers continued to be active, provoking widespread complaints about the extent of illegal spoil. The council was forced to take repeated action to ensure that ships and goods belonging to the subjects of the King of France or the Emperor, captured since the peace, were restored, while also seeking the return of English vessels taken by the Scots or French. Scottish rovers continued to plague the east coast. Some were able to use Ipswich as a base to spoil Flemish shipping; others raided in the Irish Sea or ranged into the Channel, visiting long-standing pirate hunting grounds. In October and November 1550 the council ordered the arrest of a Scots pirate, who had robbed a Spanish vessel and seized a Breton ship off the Isle of Wight, but with little effect. French rovers of varying legality also remained active in the Channel and the western approaches, where they preyed on English and Irish shipping, occasionally seizing Iberian vessels. In November 1551 the council ordered the release of a French man-of-war and two Portuguese prizes which had been seized by the mayor of Tenby.[22]

Yet the volume of complaint against the French and Scots appears to have been outweighed by the clamour against the activities of English rovers. In response to an appeal from the French ambassador about the cost and delay in pursuing cases of spoil and piracy before the High Court of Admiralty, during 1550 the council revived a previous practice of appointing commissioners for depredations, with the authority to provide speedy justice for French claimants. Their appointment failed to appease the ambassador. Nor did it reduce the level of complaint reaching the council, although it provided an opportunity for the latter to pass contested cases of depredation to another agency. The commissioners were involved in hearing

A Tudor merchant's house in Tenby, Pembrokeshire. Pirates and rovers occasionally visited this small, but busy port, to dispose of plunder and take on supplies. In 1562 a Scottish pirate, Alexander Hogg, was arrested in the port. (Author's collection)

such cases intermittently, and sometimes in association with the High Court of Admiralty, through to the 1570s. But their use met with limited success.[23]

Alongside the widening range of English piratical venturing, localized spoil and pillage flourished. Many of those involved in this form of depredation continued to haunt the Channel as well as the entrance to the Thames, operating from bases along the south coast, which included Calais. Local support and maintenance for such activity meant that it was rarely an anonymous crime: pirate captains and their leading associates were well known to local officials and increasingly to the council. But attempts to apprehend such men were frustrated by delays in the investigation and administration of complaints about spoil, which gave pirates and rovers time to go into hiding or return to the sea. In October 1550 the council dealt with allegations of piracy against Henry Stafforde dating back to May 1547. It took another three months for the council to instruct Robert Reneger to seek and arrest Stafforde and one of his accomplices, William Piers of Southampton, who was reportedly a servant of the Lord Protector.[24]

The deterioration of relations with France and the Empire during the early 1550s led to a resurgence of Flemish and French raiding in English waters. During the last years of Edward VI's reign the council dealt with growing complaints against the depredations of foreign men-of-war, some of whom included English recruits among their companies. In 1552 an Irish ship was attacked and sunk off Rye by two French rovers, who were manned with several Englishmen. French raiding led to diplomatic demands for redress; in June 1552, however, the council reported that 'no reformation followeth'.[25] But conditions at sea led to complex and contested cases of spoil which were difficult to resolve. In April 1553, for example, the council sought the advice of the judge of the High Court of Admiralty, concerning the ownership of a French ship which had been taken by Flemings, re-taken by Scots and subsequently sold to an Englishman in the Isle of Wight.

The raiding of foreign rovers provoked retaliation of varying kinds which was difficult to distinguish from the persistence of piracy in the West Country or southern Ireland. The confused disorder at sea was reflected in the activities of the *Bark Aucher*, owned and sent out by Sir Anthony Aucher, the marshal of Calais. Aucher's man-of-war piratically attacked a vessel of Denmark, shortly after the plunder of various other Danish ships by Thomas Wyndham while in the service of the King, provoking angry complaints in May 1552. Later in the year the *Bark* rescued the *Little Bark Aucher* from attack by two of the French King's vessels. Thereafter it appears to have ranged the Channel, challenging and engaging in conflict with French vessels, and taking prizes which were subsequently restored. The voyaging of the *Bark Aucher* was part of a wider pattern of Channel plunder that remained focused on the shipping of France. In May 1553 the Lord Admiral ordered the punishment of a group of English rovers, in prison at Milton, for the seizure of a French vessel, the crew of which were killed. Later in the year the council decreed the restoration of the vessel to the widows of the French mariners. Under these conditions, as the activities of Wyndham demonstrated, English rovers became increasingly indiscriminate in their spoil of shipping.[26]

Piracy and disorderly sea roving continued despite the damage to trade and fishing. Coole's survival illustrates the erratic and limited success of the regime in dealing with disorder at sea. Despite his imprisonment in the Tower, he returned to Ireland and his career of petty depredation. According to reports among merchants and mariners in Dublin he was involved in the capture of a French vessel within Carlingford Lough during 1553, though in his defence it was claimed that he purchased the vessel as lawful prize from a Flemish man-of-war. Thereafter, with the assistance of eight men armed with swords and daggers, he seized the *Eugenius*, a fishing vessel which had been converted into a small man-of-war, in the harbour of Youghal. Formerly the *Katherine* of Calais, it was renamed, rebuilt and 'made ready for the wars', for John Challenor who intended sending it out from the island of Lambay.[27] As described by one of its company, the vessel was armed with two brass pieces of ordnance, carried a main, fore and mizen mast, and 'was made low with netting above, with a fair cabin of wainscot, and a nose like a pinnace'.[28] It was later recovered by William Tyrell during a naval patrol to apprehend Coole and other pirates in Ireland.

Indeed, during the early 1550s the regime met with some success in the arrest of pirates. Henry Machyn, a London draper, recorded that 100 mariners were arraigned at the Guildhall in March 1551 for robbing on the sea, and the captain, a Scot, was taken to Newgate on the same day and hanged.[29] During 1552 sessions of oyer and terminer were scheduled to determine cases of piracy in the Cinque Ports. Pirates were executed in Calais and Dover, while the council issued instructions for pirates in the West Country to be dealt with according to the law. In February 1553 the council in Ireland was ordered to apprehend Strangeways, whose reputation as a pirate captain was growing on either side of the Irish Sea. The Earl of Desmond was requested to assist in his capture. The following month two of the King's ships were sent out to hunt down Strangeways, Killigrew and their associates in Ireland. Strangeways was captured about this time.[30]

Rebellious pirates and privateers during the 1550s

Under Mary, who became Queen following the unexpected death of Edward during 1553, vigorous action was taken against piracy and disorderly plunder. The new monarch's religious and dynastic policies, as reflected in the restoration of Catholicism and the marriage alliance with Prince Philip, soon to be King of Spain, reinforced the need to combat the growing assault on Imperial and Iberian shipping by English rovers. The diplomatic interests and priorities of the new regime thus led to a sustained attempt to deal with the pirate menace. Inadvertently, however, its successes were undermined by the increasing intensity of anti-Spanish hostility, especially in south-west England, where seaborne depredation was becoming linked with evangelical Protestantism. Hostility towards Spain and the Marian regime was expressed in the activities of rebellious rovers and privateers, operating from bases across the Channel under the loose protection of the King of France. Against a background of deepening religious and political division, the experience of Mary's reign hastened the re-direction of English depredation into the spoil of Iberian trade and shipping.

The early years of the reign witnessed intense activity by the council to apprehend and bring pirate leaders and their followers to trial. In July 1554 it sent out a fleet to capture the pirate Lightmaker. The following month it ordered the execution of pirates in Dartmouth and in Dorset, in an effort to reinforce the authority of the Lord Admiral. Shortly after, Patrick Colqhon, a Scot, was imprisoned at its command, on suspicion of piracy and counterfeiting the coinage. About the same time it instructed two merchants to appear before the recorder of Bristol on the grounds that they were in possession of the goods of Robert Vaughan, a pirate. In February 1555 it despatched three officers to seize Strangeways, who was reported to be in hiding in Suffolk. In March it issued instructions for the arrest of another pirate or rover, Woodman, who claimed to have a licence to serve against France, under the authority of which he was robbing French and other shipping. Nicholas Thomas, one of Woodman's associates, was subsequently arrested in Bristol, while other members of his company were taken in Portsmouth. These successes were followed by the capture of Stephenson, by the Earl of Desmond, in Ireland.[31]

With the benefit of unidentified reports and information, the council kept up its campaign against piracy. During June 1555 it ordered the sheriff of Norfolk to search for the pirate, Jones, 'who shifteth himself from place to place in the said countie'.[32] Jones was reportedly lurking at the house of Sir Nicholas Straunge, though the latter apparently ignored a request to apprehend him. In July, however, the council congratulated those involved in the arrest of one of the Killigrews, who had been involved in the plunder of Spanish ships. Several months later, it authorised Sir Edmund Rouse and others to apprehend Coole and his followers, with the offer of a share in the pirates' plunder. The determination of the council to tackle the problem of maritime disorder was further illustrated by its instructions to officials in Dover to seize Sir Anthony Aucher's vessel, the *Bark Aucher*, following reports of its recent arrival 'with certayne maryners that are stollen out to go fourthe a robbing'.[33] With a growing number of pirates, including Strangeways, in custody, by January 1556 it was working with the High Court of Admiralty on the issue of commissions of oyer and terminer for their trial and punishment.

To some extent the council's response to piracy and lawlessness at sea was a continuation of the practices established during the closing months of the previous reign. But it was also motivated by the diplomatic requirements of the Queen, who was seeking closer relations with Spain. The plunder of Flemish and Spanish vessels threatened to cast a shadow over Mary's marriage to Philip in July 1554, particularly as it was fuelled by anti-Spanish feeling. Popular hostility towards the Spanish appears to have provoked widespread unease. Rumours of a 'stir in Devon', early in 1554, were accompanied by reports that 'there was like to be a mad world in that county shortly'.[34] Sir Ralph Hopton, a Protestant landowner in the West Country, made clear his views of the Spanish by asking 'his workmen how they liked them who will occupy their wives before their faces'.[35] In response, one worker claimed 'he would rather cut off the king of Spain's head himself'. Such hostility was accompanied by the intimidation of local Catholic loyalists. According to one report, 'if any man would not withstand the King of Spain's entry, because they would ravish their wives and daughters and rob and spoil the commons, their throats should be cut'.

In these tense circumstances plans for a rebellion against the new regime attracted support not only from local landowners in Devon, but also from opportunistic maritime adventurers and pirates in the south-west. Piracy and rebellion thus became uneasily yoked together, but in a way that anticipated French support against the spread of Spanish influence in England. In December 1553 it was reported that an English adventurer, possibly one of the Killigrews, offered to serve the King of France, Henry II, with eight or nine ships, which would almost certainly have been used to attack Spanish vessels in the Channel. Indeed, the Killigrews may have served as intermediaries between leading supporters of the rising in Devon, such as Sir Peter Carew, and the French. According to rumour, Carew was also linked with Strangeways, in a plan to seize control of Exeter.[36]

In reality the rebellion failed to proceed as planned. Early in February 1554 Carew and others were reported to have fled from Weymouth with the assistance of Walter Ralegh. The rebel leaders and their associates went into exile in France, where they established bases in northern and western ports for raiding in the Channel, with the support of the French King and sympathizers, such as Jean Ribault, the maritime adventurer whose castle at Dieppe became a hotbed for plots and piracy or privateering.

Although relations among this motley collection of pirates and rebels varied, and were based on a superficial coincidence of interests, their activities from 1554 to 1556 demonstrated the dangers of English adventurers seeking employment with a rival, and potentially hostile, monarch. In addition to the Carews and Killigrews, the leading figures in these overlapping groups included Andrew and Nicholas Tremayne, Henry Dudley, Christopher Ashton and Edward and Francis Horsey. But a clear distinction appears to have existed between the aims of the rebels, such as the Carews, for whom piracy was a subsidiary, if attractive concern, and those of pirate leaders, like the Killigrews, who were essentially interested in the pursuit of plunder rather than in a change of regime across the Channel. The backgrounds of such men, indeed, suggest that they were tempted into piracy and conspiracy by socio-economic pressures as much as by political ambition. Most of the leading figures among the exiles in France have been aptly described as 'minor gentry who lived by their swords'.[37] Some were in difficult economic circumstances. Dudley fled to France because 'he was outlawed for debt', though before departing he informed an associate of his determination to return, with ten or twelve ships, to drive out the 'vile nation of Spaniards'.[38]

By 1556 the exiles in France were capable of sending out a small fleet of at least six men-of-war, possibly manned with between 300 and 500 recruits, to attack Spanish and other shipping. Little is known of the composition or character of this irregular force of maritime adventurers, although the two vessels under the command of the Killigrews had a combined company of 180 men 'of all nations', including French, Dutch, Scots as well as English.[39] Moreover, they were reportedly all willing volunteers. Following his capture in July 1556, Peter Killigrew insisted that he 'forced no man, neither did his brother'.[40]

These groups of pirates and rovers were involved in the plunder of trade and shipping within the confines of the Channel. In June 1556 the council informed Philip II 'that English pirates had spoiled various ships in the west. Although they seem to treat the English more favourably than foreigners, they spare no nationality, and especially plundered the French'.[41] Within a few days, their reported number had grown from three ships to seven or eight. In response the Queen sent out seven royal ships from Portsmouth, under the command of Tyrrell, the Vice Admiral, 'since it did not seem fit for the Admiral of England to pursue these pirates'.[42] During July the royal fleet met the pirates off Plymouth and seized six of their vessels. One small ship escaped, but, with only one of their leaders still active across the Channel, the threat from rebel rovers in France seemed to have been checked.

A detailed account by Peter Killigrew, who operated at sea in partnership with his brothers, Thomas and Henry, sheds light on the character and conduct of this piratical venturing. Shortly after their arrival in France, the Killigrews acquired the *Sacret*, one of Henry II's vessels, either as a gift or on loan for two years. In addition they purchased the *Francis* from a French merchant, who owed them 300 crowns. As the ship was valued at 600 crowns, half of the cost was covered by the debt; the other half was to be paid within six months, out of the proceeds from plunder. Like other exiles in France, the Killigrews lived in impoverished, hand-to-mouth circumstances, seeking assistance wherever it could be found. On one occasion Peter Killigrew was arrested for debt in Le Havre, though he was released through the help of several French captains. These economic difficulties were reinforced by the psychological discomforts of exile. Thus the Tremaynes informed Killigrew at La Hogue that 'they did not like France and desired to go to sea', while Dudley 'wished … that all were well at home, [and] to be there with one of his legs broken'.[43] Henry Killigrew also urged his brother that if they had good fortune at sea, they would be able to pay off their debts and seek a pardon in England. Although they lacked the political ideology of their more celebrated Dutch successors, who operated from English bases during the early 1570s, this collection of adventurers appeared to be genuine sea beggars, for whom plunder was more a stratagem for survival than for political change.

Killigrew's account indicates that he and his brothers made five voyages from bases in France, which met with mixed success. Lacking victuals on the first voyage, they spoiled an Irish vessel returning from Flanders, and seized another ship laden with salt and wine. During the second voyage they captured an English ship laden with wood belonging to a Flemish merchant; when the prize was brought into Le Havre, however, one of the brothers was imprisoned until compensation was made to the Fleming. The third voyage was more successful. In consortship with one of Henry II's ships, three prizes were taken, laden with wine and salt. In company with the same ship, on the fourth voyage they 'did nothing but fought with a carrack and drew her into Dartmouth'.[44] During the last voyage, in June 1556, sailing in the *Sacret* and the *Falcon*, they took at least three prizes, including two Spanish ships laden with wool and iron. Returning to La Hogue, they sold most of the wool, nearly 400 bales, which were worth fifteen or sixteen crowns each, to pay off their debts.

At the end of these voyages Henry Killigrew proposed an expedition to South America. As recounted by his brother, this was an ill-conceived, wayward and confusing project for plunder, though it may have grown out of conversations with French seafarers who had experience of preying on the Spanish in the Caribbean. Thus 'they minded not to take wares with them meet for Peru or Guinea, or any other place, but to go thither and there get some prize, they cared not of whom, and therewith come into the Straits, set to shore, sell their ships and go to Italy, and there live and rid themselves of this misery wherein they have long lived'.[45] Such a curious scheme suggests the ambition of needy and necessitous adventurers, though it rested on very weak foundations. Indeed, the opportunism that characterized the activities of the Killigrews and their associates was matched by their exploitation as pawns in a game of international rivalry by Henry II.

The activities of the Killigrews in France came to a messy and untidy end during the summer of 1556. Peter Killigrew was captured during 1556, though he avoided trial for treason. In September twenty-four of his men were hanged for piracy; according to the Venetian ambassador in London, they died in a godly manner. The attempts of Henry II to recover the *Sacret*, which he claimed had been loaned to the Killigrews, did little to ease Anglo-French relations. With war looming, by 1557 Killigrew had been sufficiently rehabilitated to be placed in charge of one of the Queen's ships.[46]

To some extent the raiding of the Killigrews and their associates diverted attention away from the persistence of widespread local piracy which continued to be a serious problem, despite the early successes of the regime. During the opening months of 1556 the council handled complaints concerning the robbery of a Flemish vessel off Tilbury, the spoil of a Spanish ship by pirates allegedly from Liverpool and Chester, and the plunder of various vessels along the east coast. Pirates and rovers continued to operate in the Irish Sea and off the Scilly Isles. Consequently, the council resorted to a variety of expedients to deal with a problem that was growing in complexity. During June 1556, in response to Spanish complaints, John Killigrew the elder and younger were bound to appear before the court, following which they were imprisoned separately in the Fleet.[47] They were released under a recognizance of £2,000 to answer an Admiralty action brought by a Spanish merchant. Later in the month John Bourchier, 2nd Earl of Bath, was instructed to issue orders prohibiting mariners and others in the West Country from associating with pirates cruising in the Irish Sea. Similar instructions were sent to the mayor and aldermen of Bristol, and to the Lord Deputy and council in Ireland.

The following month the council appointed commissioners for the trial of pirates at Portsmouth. Proceedings were stayed against those who had been 'taken and kepte against their willes or otherwise brought to this lewde doings by force', the rest were to be executed along the coast in Portsmouth, Southampton and the Isle of Wight, while the captains were to be hanged in chains.[48] In August a similar commission was issued to proceed against pirates imprisoned at Southampton. Local officials also continued to send pirates to the council, though like Giles Graylocke, they were usually handed over to the Lord Admiral to be dealt with. At the end of July, Leonard Marshall, an Irish pirate, was despatched to the council by the mayor of Rye on suspicion that he was an accomplice of Dudley and Aston. Although Marshall provided no evidence of contact with the exiles, during his examination he confessed that he knew the pirate, Stephenson, who he saw at the house of Robert St John in Ireland.[49]

But the regime's attempt to combat piracy remained heavily dependent on the cooperation of local communities and officials, with uncertain and variable results. In September 1556 a Breton vessel was seized by English pirates and brought into Tenby. Although the pirates were apprehended, the French complained that their goods were sold by Sir John Wogan, a local Admiralty official. Later in the month the council reprimanded Sir William Godolphin, one of the Vice Admirals in Cornwall, over the recent trial of Thompson and his company. Thompson was captured shortly after reports that he was cruising off the Scilly Isles with three ships. The council was surprised, however, that only Thompson and four other pirates were condemned by a local jury. The acquittal of the rest could only be explained either by 'parcialitie of the jurye or negligence in giving the evidence'.[50]

The interest of the council in the local implementation of justice betrayed a deeper concern with the trial and punishment of pirates. The law, even when used in a discretionary fashion, was intended to punish pirates and deter potential recruits, while providing the opportunity for victims to recover property or seek compensation. Increasingly the spectacle of punishment sought to place pirates beyond the pale of civil society, with their execution at locations along the sea shore, where bodies were left, sometimes in chains, in denial of a Christian burial. The Venetian ambassador in London reported during 1551 that the 'punishment inflicted on corsairs is to hang them in such a way that their toes well nigh touch the water; so they are generally hanged on the banks of rivers and on the sea shore'.[51] It was a well-established practice that Machyn regularly noted during Mary's reign. On 31 July 1556 a group of six pirates were arraigned at the Guildhall, 'and the morrow after they were hangyd at Wapping at the low-water marke'.[52] Seven more robbers at sea were likewise executed the following year, in April 1557. About the same time, as part of a wider initiative, local officials in Southampton were instructed to hang in chains Captain John Jones and two others. The body of Jones was to remain hanging by the seaside, 'for the terror and example of others'.[53] These occasions might represent the ritual expulsion of social outcasts and criminal deviants, uneasily suspended between land and sea, but they appeared to lack either the public confessions or the moral condemnation which were subsequently demanded by the agencies of state and church.

Maritime disorder continued to be a problem for the remainder of Mary's reign. The persistence of piracy was complicated by the renewal of war between France and Spain, in which England was reluctantly embroiled. By February 1557 French men-of-war were reportedly haunting the coast of England. Several spoiled three Flemish ships in the Thames. Another Flemish vessel on the river was seized by a group of French and English rovers. As in the past the conflict at sea provoked retaliation and unofficial reprisals, threatening the apparent neutrality of the regime. In March, for example, a cargo of wheat aboard a French prize, which was brought into Plymouth by a Flemish rover, was unladen for the relief of the town on the dubious authority of old custom.[54]

Conditions at sea were aggravated by the unruly activities of adventurers in England and Ireland, and the indiscriminate attack on shipping by rival groups of men-of-war operating in increasingly crowded hunting grounds. The voyage of the *Anne* of Dublin, and its seizure by the *Moon* of London, led to a prolonged case before the High Court of Admiralty which illustrates the dangers of unlicensed venturing during these years. The *Anne* was owned by Thomas Borrowe and John Marshe, who purchased it from a group of Spaniards for £50 after it was cast away at Drogheda. The vessel was repaired and sent out during 1557, with a company of sixty soldiers and mariners and provisions for one month. The soldiers, who made up half of the company, were each armed with a sword and dagger. In May the vessel was sailing off Land's End in search of plunder when it encountered the *Moon*, sent out by Lord Paget, the Lord Privy Seal, reportedly with a royal commission. According to members of the company of the *Moon*, Borrowe and Marshe approached in the *Anne* 'with force, might and main … their tops having armed men in them, with swords waving, crying "Amain, Amain, Amain, villains Amain".'[55] This was contradicted by some of the *Anne*'s company, who claimed that the ensuing conflict was initiated by the *Moon*. After a brief fight, during which there were several casualties, one of whom subsequently died from his wounds, the *Anne* was seized and brought into Plymouth, where Borrowe and Marshe were apprehended as pirates. It became evident during legal proceedings that they had no commission for the voyage of the *Anne*. In their defence, however, it was claimed that the vessel was sent out at the command of the Lord Deputy in Dublin, in response to the presence of French and Scots rovers off the coast of Ireland, and with the promise of a commission to follow. Paget did not press the case; on his orders the *Anne* was restored, though it was later captured by a French rover and carried off to St Malo as prize.

The disorder at sea was intensified by the revival of English privateering, following the outbreak of Anglo-French hostilities during 1557. The plunder of enemy trade and shipping was authorized by a proclamation of 9 June. It was modelled on the decree of December 1544 and was evidently intended to encourage private depredation. Adventurers who sent out vessels to attack the French did not need a licence or commission from the High Court of Admiralty, nor were they required to put in bonds for good behaviour at sea. In addition there was no requirement for adventurers to make any account of the proceeds of prizes, which they were to enjoy without surrendering any part thereof either to the Lord Admiral or the Lord Warden of the Cinque Ports.[56] Armed vessels sent out under these loose provisions were enjoined not to spoil the Queen's subjects of friends, though it was almost impossible to enforce such conditions.

Scotland was excluded from the proclamation in the hope that conflict with France's traditional ally might be averted. However, Scottish incursions across the border led to the outbreak of hostilities at the start of August. The change in Anglo-Scottish relations was reflected in the council's policy towards the seizure of Scottish ships. Days before the outbreak of war, on 29 July, it ordered that two Scottish vessels laden with salt and wine, taken by a group of West Country adventurers, including Walter Ralegh, were to be restored if there was 'only a pretence of warre' between the two countries.[57] By 2 August the Scots were enemies. Consequently their vessels, including Ralegh's seizures, were lawful prizes.

Despite official encouragement, the initial response to the proclamation, particularly in London where the war was very unpopular among city merchants, appears to have been disappointing. In June 1557 the Lord Admiral, William Howard, informed the Queen of a recent cruise in the Channel, during which he noted that there were no French ships at sea between Brittany and Boulogne, though he was informed that they were 'making ready ten or twelve out of Dieppe on the charge of the burgesses of the town. I wish', he added, 'London merchants would do so much for your highness with their ships'.[58] Yet the Lord Admiral was also acutely aware of the potentially damaging competition for recruits between private adventurers and royal service. Shortly after returning from his expedition in the Channel, he was doubtful about 'equipping any more ships presently to sea because the mariners to be pressed will claim the liberty of the last proclamation for annoying the enemy'.[59]

The difficulty in mobilizing private enterprise during an unpopular war was also apparent in Rye, where local adventurers were reported to be discouraged by the levy of dues on prizes by officials, against the terms of the proclamation. As a result, the council complained 'the coast is the worse defended, the enemy encouraged and their majesties worse served'.[60] In July, therefore, the council instructed the mayor and other officers to 'suffer them that are disposed to go at their adventure, to enjoy such prizes as they take, and assist them in their doings'. The ambiguous but potentially rewarding relationship between public and private enterprise was underlined by the despatch of two royal fleets during July 1557, complemented by twenty-two private ships 'appointed for war' on condition that their owners received a share of all prizes 'according to ancient custom'.[61] The captains of the royal ships included Peter Killigrew and several of his associates.

Although the French war was short lived, the 'free licence' offered to adventurers to send out armed vessels against the enemy led to a resurgence of privateering.[62] While the scale of activity is difficult to gauge, it appears to have been similar in character and organization to private enterprise during the 1540s. The surviving evidence suggests that more than twenty men-of-war were operating from ports in Devon during 1557 and 1558. If the prevailing pattern of activity was similar to that during the closing years of the reign of Henry VIII, this would indicate that between forty and sixty ships may have been engaged in privateering during the war. But its impact, at least in terms of prize taking, is even more difficult to estimate, and was offset by the seizure of English vessels by the French. As during earlier conflicts, moreover, the sea war was marked by the rapid growth of disorderly plunder, including attacks on neutral and friendly shipping.

Ports and havens in the south and south-west, which had long-standing interests in maritime depredation, played a leading role in sending out men-of-war. In May 1558 Rye was described as 'such a scourge to the French as the like is not in this realm'.[63] Further west, Dartmouth, Plymouth and neighbouring havens were heavily involved in the business of plunder. London seems to have played a modest part in the sea war. Along the east coast Newcastle also participated in sending out men-of-war. The promoters of such ventures included traders and shipowners, such as Richard Fletcher of Rye, or William and John Hawkins of Plymouth, and Hugh Offley of London. Lesser members of the gentry, including the Raleghs in the West Country, whose landed interests were complemented to some extent by interests in shipowning, were also involved in sending out armed vessels against the enemy.[64]

The activities of these men-of-war were heavily concentrated in the Channel and the western approaches, and usually took the form of short-distance raiding which spilled over into the spoil of vessels of varied origin. The war thus provoked widespread complaints from the victims of indiscriminate attacks, who included the subjects of Philip II. In July 1557 a Flemish adventurer complained that his ship and a French prize had been taken by the Raleghs and their associates. At the prompting of the council, both were returned with compensation for the owners. In the following month the council dealt with complaints concerning the disorderly plunder of Spanish merchants by Strangeways, and the piratical seizure of another Flemish vessel. The Lord Warden of the Cinque Ports was also involved in investigating similar allegations against adventurers based in Rye.[65]

The house of John Davis, Dartmouth, Devon. Conveniently located, this modest residence was the home of one of the leading navigators and explorers of Elizabethan England, who appears to have had little interest in plunder. By contrast, Drake was able to purchase Buckland Abbey with the booty he acquired from his voyage of 1577 to 1580. (Author's collection)

The disorder at sea appears to have intensified during 1558. The men of Rye, especially, pursued a form of enterprise that repeatedly confused the distinction between legitimate privateering and piracy. In February 1558 Richard Fletcher and his partner came to the attention of the council for the seizure of a vessel laden with a cargo from France, which was claimed as lawful prize, though the owner was an alderman of London. In March the council ordered the restoration of the *Job* of Antwerp, which had been taken by Fletcher. Towards the end of May it ordered the imprisonment of various local seamen for their disorderly conduct in a ship of the port.[66] The following month, in a case which may have been connected, Thomas Wait, shipowner, was sent by local officers to appear before the council for an offence committed at sea by one of his vessels. Despite employing spies in Rye and neighbouring ports to arrest Wait's men, the officers informed the council that '[neither] ship nor any of the mariners came here since'.[67]

With the war going badly, the regime faced a difficult situation at sea. The loss of Calais early in 1558 was a profound blow to the status of the Tudor monarchy. But it reflected the growing disorganization and disorder of the maritime conflict. In March the council intervened in an Admiralty case to assert that a Scottish vessel, taken by a group of adventurers in Newcastle, was lawful prize. Several weeks later, it ordered the appearance of John Asshe, gentleman and captain of the *John* of Chepstow, and John Ellyzaunder, the master of the vessel, to answer a charge of piracy for sinking a ship of Lübeck. In May it issued similar orders for the appearance of Strangeways and Thomas Stukeley. The survival of pirates such as Strangeways was accompanied by the appearance of a new group of adventurers, including Stukeley and Thomas Phetiplace who was taking French prizes off Alderney during August 1558.[68]

Despite a determined effort to deal with piracy and unruly spoil, the closing months of Mary's reign witnessed widespread complaints against the piratical activities of English men-of-war. With the war still going on, these problems were part of Mary's legacy to her successor. In 1559, for example, John Ralegh, who was at sea in a ship owned by Hugh Wright, seized the *Hawk* of Danzig off the Scilly Isles.[69] The plunder of neutral shipping was the product of a prolonged period of disorder at sea which grew out of conflict with France during the 1540s. Weak royal rule provided greater opportunity for piratical activity to flourish. But if the later 1540s and 1550s demonstrated the inability of the mid-Tudor regime to eradicate piracy or lawlessness at sea, the period also underlined the difficulties it faced in trying to deal with an increasingly complex activity that was sustained by forces beyond its control.

The persistent disorder at sea enabled a growing number of men to earn renown or notoriety, or a mix of both, as pirates. The activities of Strangeways, one of the most notorious pirate captains operating during these years, to some extent mirrors the development of piracy, while demonstrating the challenge it presented to the mid-Tudor monarchy. In 1549 Strangeways, who probably came from Dorset, was one of Thompson's company at Cork. By 1553 he was known to the council as the 'Irish pirate', though he operated on either side of the Irish Sea, plundering vessels and disposing of their cargoes locally.[70] He fled to France to avoid arrest, but in March 1554 he returned with two vessels laden with munitions and mail shirts, arriving at court in search of a pardon from the Queen. After a short spell of imprisonment, during which his portrait was evidently painted by a fellow prisoner, the German artist Gerlach Flicke, he was released, allegedly through purchasing the favours of one of the Queen's ladies-in-waiting. Undeterred, he resumed his piratical activities, provoking Spanish complaints and claims in the High Court of Admiralty. He seems to have established contact with leading figures among the rebel rovers in France, though it is possible that he was acting as an informer. In March 1556 Thomas White recounted the troubling experiences of the Tremaynes, who were arrested for piracy and accused by Strangeways of being involved in a conspiracy against the Queen. Despite 'being but little men in person', White reported that they reviled Strangeways so convincingly, and in the face of either the threat or use of torture, that he 'was ready to weep and think he had accused them wrongfully'.[71] The Tremaynes were released, and Strangeways was roundly rebuked by the council. By the later 1550s the pirate captain was in straitened circumstances. Following an Admiralty case of 1557, involving Spanish claims of £4,000, he served as one of the captains of the vessels assembled at Portsmouth for service in the Channel. The following year he was living in Dorchester, apparently poor and in great debt, though he was planning an expedition to seize the Portuguese fort at Elmina in Guinea, with the backing of a group of London merchants and the Lord Admiral.[72]

Strangeways's volatile career encapsulates the changing character of English depredation, which laid the groundwork for the emergence of more ambitious and far-reaching schemes for plunder during the 1560s and beyond. The survival of other members of his company reinforced the link between succeeding generations of pirates. In September 1559, when Strangeways was arraigned at Southwark, his accomplices included William Cheston, described as an old pirate, who had served with Coole, Thompson and Stephenson.[73] At a time of severe social and economic tension, the careers of such men suggest that the attraction of piracy and sea roving was growing, particularly among seafaring communities. With the benefit of favourable attitudes ashore, the rapid growth of hostility towards Spain during the 1550s, reinforced by commercial grievances among merchants in the south-west and London, laid out the prospect of piracy becoming a patriotic, popular and profitable enterprise.

Pirates, Privateers and Slave Traders from the later 1550s to the later 1560s

English depredation grew more varied and wide-ranging during the opening decade of the Elizabethan regime. Small-scale, sporadic spoil remained a problem within the waters of the British Isles, but it was accompanied by the development of more purposeful and systematic piracy and sea roving. The activities of English raiders provoked widespread complaint from Spain and Portugal, as well as from France and the Low Countries, but they were not the only threat to peaceful commerce in north-west Europe. A wide range of maritime predators, of varied backgrounds, operated during these years, creating opportunities for cooperation and competition among unruly groups of pirates and privateers that rival monarchies struggled either to repress or re-direct against their enemies. The disorder at sea was reinforced by international rivalries, civil wars and rebellion. The outbreak of the French wars of religion, followed by the Dutch revolt against the Spanish monarchy, led to inflammatory political and religious conflicts which intensified maritime lawlessness and violence, particularly as rebel leaders in the Low Countries and France issued commissions, justifying the plunder of their enemies. The confusion between religious hostility and pre-existing commercial rivalries served as a driving force for the striking expansion of piracy and privateering along the coasts of Spain and Portugal. During the 1560s this was accompanied by the aggressive development of English trade with Guinea, linked with speculative schemes for breaking into the transatlantic slave trade. Though supported by the Queen and leading courtiers, these ventures were inherently predatory. From the perspective of the Portuguese and Spanish, indeed, they were an alarming, piratical challenge to vulnerable commercial and imperial interests. The relationship between commercial grievances and political and religious enmities thus created the conditions for a dramatic shift in the range of English depredation that laid the basis for the emergence of transatlantic armed trade and plunder during the 1560s and early 1570s.

Piracy and plunder around the British Isles during the later 1550s and early 1560s

The new Queen inherited an unpopular and unsuccessful war with France which was marked by widespread disorder and illegal plunder at sea. The restoration of peace in 1559 failed to ease Anglo-French tension, or to prevent the outbreak of another brief conflict during 1562. In these circumstances disorderly plunder and piracy threatened to become a serious problem, though initially it remained concentrated in the Channel, and focused on the spoil of French trade and shipping. But the Elizabethan regime was soon faced with the danger of the spread of unruly privateering and piracy. English men-of-war continued to seize neutral vessels, despite the risk of retaliation. During 1558 a ship of Hamburg was captured and taken to Ireland. Attacks on Flemish vessels provoked complaints in December about injustice and delay in the High Court of Admiralty. In January 1559 Philip II expressed outrage at the plunder of Flemish ships which carried his safe conduct, complaining to his ambassador in London that 'although the Queen and council are well aware of the justice of the case no retribution can be obtained'.[1] The problem of English depredation thus cast a shadow over relations between the new regime and its European neighbours, at a time of unsettling religious and political change.

From the outset, overseas complaints were aggravated by uncertainty concerning the recovery of pirate booty, which damaged the international reputation of the High Court of Admiralty. Scottish merchants, who claimed losses of £2,300 to local pirates operating along the coast of Northumberland in 1559, struggled for more than seven years to receive compensation awarded by the court. But piracy cases raised genuine difficulties that were not easily resolved by legal process, especially when the rights of the Lord Admiral were involved. The uncertainty and confusion in the application of the law were reflected in the opinion of the civil lawyers who were consulted about the ownership of property taken by pirates, following the seizure of Strangeways and his company during 1559. While noting that the captors of the pirates 'had the greater part of their prizes', they acknowledged that goods 'taken by pirates can be lawfully claimed by the owners'.[2] The potential contradiction between competing claims to pirate property, in which the Lord Admiral also had an interest, complicated the recovery and restoration of plundered cargoes, irrespective of the related issue of compensation. This provoked anger and concern among the victims of piracy and disorderly depredation, fuelling suspicions about the connivance of powerful vested interests which undermined respect for legal process. At the same time it threatened to taint the Queen and the court with unseemly allegations about their secret support for pirates and rovers.

The capture of Strangeways was an unexpected success for the new regime, which gave it an opportunity to demonstrate its resolve in dealing with piracy and lawlessness at sea. But the survival of this notorious rover, who was widely known among the Spanish and French as either Enrriex Tranguaz or Estranguitz, exposed a long-standing ambiguity in the handling of the problem. Despite his apparent abandonment of piracy, in April 1559 the Privy Council instructed customs officials in Southampton and Plymouth to prevent Strangeways and an associate, William Wilford, from leaving port, as a result of alarming reports that they intended to raid Madeira with a force of two vessels and 500 soldiers, which apparently included fifty gentlemen. Following a declaration before the council that they intended to go to sea as merchants, Strangeways and Wilford were allowed to proceed on their voyage.[3] Once in the Channel, however, Strangeways seized several Portuguese and Spanish vessels. By July he was reported to have visited Fécamp in Normandy, despite assurances from the French that he would be arrested if he entered their jurisdiction. The English ambassador in Paris, Sir Nicholas Throckmorton, warned the Queen that the French 'will use all the practices they can to make Stranguyse, the pirate, wholly theirs, to be an instrument to impeach her; it would, therefore,' he added, 'be good policy to serve herself by him covertly'.[4]

The regime responded rapidly to Strangeways' return to piracy. In August 1559 the King of Spain was informed that Elizabeth had sent out six ships in search of him, with a warning that 'if it cost her ten thousand pounds she would get hold of him and have him executed, as he had been captured on previous occasions but had been pardoned through the bought favour of her sister's chamber-women'.[5] However, the same report also claimed that the fleet was despatched by the Lord Admiral with the primary purpose of enriching himself from the pirate's booty which was reputedly between 50,000 and 60,000 ducats in value.

Although Strangeways was taken by the fleet off La Rochelle during August, he evaded execution. According to the diary of the London draper Henry Machyn, he was brought to the Tower on 10 August. Several days later he was transferred to the Marshalsea, together with eighty members of his company, in preparation for their trial. They were paraded through the streets of London shackled with fetters, like a band of penitents. The following month Strangeways and seven of his company were arraigned at Southwark and sentenced to be hanged; the rest of the pirates were to be sent to the galleys. Early in October Sir William Cecil, the Queen's secretary, informed Throckmorton of the sentence, although the latter had urged the Queen to delay the execution. While Strangeways and his men awaited punishment, two new pairs of gallows were constructed at Wapping. On the day of execution, however, the pirates were reprieved. Later in the month, the Queen issued a warrant for the release of Strangeways, 'in order to judge of his conduct before his pardon is finally given to him'.[6]

Thereafter Strangeways was given the opportunity to earn redemption through royal service. In January 1560 the French ambassador in England reported that the former pirate, who, he warned, possessed information of the harbours and landing places in Normandy acquired from a French prisoner in the Tower, had been placed in command of one of the Queen's ships. At a time when Elizabeth was prepared to instruct one of her Admirals, in December 1559, to 'pick a quarrel with the French fleet' in Scotland, while publicly maintaining peace with France, there was ample scope for the use of a man of Strangeways' experience and ability.[7] When Elizabeth subsequently intervened in the first war of religion in France during 1562, in an attempt to recover Calais, Strangeways served in command of a royal vessel with a company of seventy men, though during the course of the conflict he was wounded and died at Rouen.

There was nothing new in the employment of pirates in public service, but as an expedient it failed to discourage the growth of disorder at sea. The difficulties in dealing with the problem were underlined by the arrest of Jamey Fobbe and other English and Scottish pirates in Cornwall during December 1559. Although the pirates were imprisoned in Launceston Gaol, an Admiralty officer later reported that Fobbe was released, because no action was brought against him. During the 1560s, therefore, English depredation continued to flourish, becoming more diverse in structure, organization and range. While the selection of targets was often indiscriminate, there was a marked increase in the plunder of Flemish trading and fishing vessels, which was accompanied by the spoil of richer Spanish ships trading between Spain and the Low Countries.[8]

The persistence and diversity of piracy and sea roving were indicated by the growing volume of complaint to the Queen's ministers and council during the early 1560s. In May 1560 Sir Thomas Gresham appealed to Cecil on behalf of a Flemish merchant, who was owed £4,000 by the Queen, whose vessel, the *Abraham* of Enkhuizen, had been taken by William Johnson of Boston. Johnson and his company pretended to be Scots, though the *Abraham* was brought into Boston and sold. In January 1561 the King of Denmark supported a claim for redress to the council from a group of merchants of Hamburg, who had been plundered by English rovers probably under the command of William Holloway of Plymouth. The following month the council was dealing with two rovers who challenged their arrest as pirates, after taking a French vessel, on the grounds that they possessed Scottish letters of marque.[9]

A collection of depositions by Flemish merchants and mariners, drawn up in February 1561, demonstrates the prevalence of small-scale piracy along the Thames and the coast of Kent. Berthelmieu Cornelison, a mariner of Antwerp, complained that he was unable to make a voyage to England peaceably, without being spoiled of clothes and provisions. Even 'before the Queen's palace at Greenwich, they fired at him four or five cannon shot, which tore his sails, which the Queen might have seen from her windows if she had been there'.[10] Other cases of such petty robbery along the shore stretched back over several years. The attacks occurred 'so frequently that no one can sail with safety into England'.

Many of these cases were the result of casual, opportunistic pillage or aggression. Shortly after Christmas 1560 several vessels from Antwerp were attacked by eight or nine English vessels off Margate, after they refused to strike their sails when ordered to do so. In January a Flemish vessel was boarded at Margate by a group of eight or ten armed men who assaulted one of the crew and carried off various commodities. Although their assailants 'wore caps before their faces like masks, and were otherwise disguised', the Flemings knew they were English by their speech.[11]

To some extent this kind of plunder was the product of the spread of river piracy along the Thames. As such it involved small groups of robbers, usually numbering less than twelve men, who were lightly armed with a small range of hand weapons. Operating under cover of night, they stole food and clothing, and anything that could be carried ashore in small rowing boats, including the odd chest of sugar, as well as any money in the possession of the crews of the ships they raided. The men and boys who were involved in this petty criminality relied on surprise and stealth rather than the use of force or violence, although mariners might be intimidated and beaten, like dogs according to one victim. The depositions from Antwerp suggest that small-scale depredation was growing in intensity, with little effective check from law officers or local officials. Albert Jacobsson was able to identify some of the men who boarded his ship at Erith in 1561, and carried off all the clothing and money they could find, 'because one of their number named Guytelier had no nose'. Although they were arrested, local justices 'allowed them to depart with a simple caution'.[12]

Merchants and mariners of the Low Countries were not the only victims of attacks along the Thames, but their grievances were compounded with complaints about pirate raids on the Flemish fishery in the North Sea. This was the work of loosely coordinated groups of pirates operating from various bases along the east coast, which included Boston and Lowestoft. Their leading figures included William Johnson, John Whitehead and John Marychurch. Despite some evidence of local disapproval, they were assisted by shore-based supporters. Two traders from Ostend, who were in Boston during 1561 when Johnson was rigging out his ship, claimed to hear 'the people say that he was going to sea to rob, and said, "Ah, Jonson, Jonson, what mean you to go rob and spoil on the sea, having no need so to do at all"'.[13] According to complaints of the Spanish ambassador, however, the pirates benefited from widespread community support, including the collusion of Admiralty officials. Consequently if they were caught, they were later freed or pardoned 'at the suit of one or other'; sometimes a 'poor knave or two are hanged, but the ringleaders ever escape'.

The pirates operating in the North Sea during the early 1560s sailed in small vessels, of about 40 tons or less, that were adapted for hit-and-run raiding at sea.

Although they carried a limited number of ordnance, the men who served aboard them were armed with a varied range of hand weapons which were usually sufficient for the spoil of small and vulnerable fishing boats. Some of the pirate ships reportedly were painted in distinctive and powerful colours, including black, red and yellow. The vessel that Johnson was preparing in Boston during 1561 was described as a 'black ship with two tops and pointed before, furnished with a quantity of munitions of war, (as pikes, long low bows, arrows, and ordnance)'.[14] These ships acted alone, or in consort with each other, preying on fishing vessels which were spoiled of their catches and provisions. The number of men involved in the boarding of their prey was often small, ranging from four to twelve. Many of the attackers tried to conceal their identities from their victims. Some even operated under the guise of fishing vessels. According to the complaint of the Spanish ambassador, their 'manner … is to go well manned to the sea, and finding a poor fisherman of the Low Countries, to take from him his fish and nets, and make them of the port believe that the fish was of their own catching'.[15]

The depositions of Flemish masters and mariners compiled during 1561, as evidence for the Elizabethan regime, underline the petty character of this form of depredation, though it caused widespread disruption to the North Sea fishery. The company of one fishing vessel was approached by an English pirate ship, 'disguised like a fisherman, armed with bows and darts, with irons … [which] fired twice at them'. A boarding party of five men and one boy entered the fishing vessel, beating the crew with swords and pikes. But the spoil was interrupted by the sighting of two ships in the distance, which persuaded the pirates to depart hurriedly, almost empty handed. Another Flemish vessel was chased by two pirate ships which discharged three or four pieces of ordnance, 'to make them keep underneath, so that they should not see the Englishmen, lest they might be known'. Johnson's company were reported to operate with masks to conceal their identities, but their leader was widely recognised. On several occasions, indeed, it seems that he was concerned to ensure that his robberies were reported in Flanders.[16]

Pirates like Johnson were thus engaged in a specialized form of small-scale depredation. Their prizes were of modest, if not limited, value. Among the Flemish fishing vessels plundered during 1561, the spoil from individual ships included forty barrels of fish and fishing tackle; twelve barrels of fish; 1,000 fish; clothing; fifty pounds of butter; an anchor and an iron pot; twenty barrels of fish; two nets; tackle; butter; and one small gun. Yet the economic cost also included damage to vessels and the wasting of catches. The halyards of one ship were cut in pieces by pirates, who also threw 300 fish and two casks of fish livers into the sea. Another vessel was extensively damaged by pirates, who 'cut in pieces cords of their ship, so that she should not stay there any longer'. But the victims of this attack were left with 500 fish, apparently in response to a remark from one of the pirates, who queried 'shall we take all from one man? We shall meet with enough today or tomorrow'.[17]

Collectively, the damage to the Flemish fishery from English piracy was extensive. In July 1561 the Spanish ambassador claimed that eighty subjects of the King
of Spain, mainly from the Low Countries, had been spoiled by English pirates
during the previous two years. However, the casualties from this wave of piracy
appear to have been limited. While Flemish fishermen were regularly beaten and
abused by pirates, death or serious injury were rare, although the master of one
ship, plundered by Johnson, died from his wounds in Boston.[18] Encounters at sea
indicate that if the companies of fishing or trading vessels surrendered peacefully
to pirates, they avoided serious harm, and were occasionally left with a share of
the plunder.

While the evidence from Flanders reveals that a loosely organized force of
pirate captains raided the North Sea fishery, during the early 1560s pirates and
rovers remained very active in the Channel and the Irish Sea. Scottish men-of-
war continued to range along the east coast. In response to Flemish and Spanish
complaints, indeed, the English tried to shift responsibility for the plunder at sea
onto the Scots. Faced with a thinly veiled warning from Philip II, that he would
be compelled to 'arm some power to the seas' if the spoil persisted, Elizabeth
sent out several royal fleets against the pirates during the summer of 1561. This
failed to impress the Spanish ambassador, who reported that the fleet sent into
the Channel was intended for service in Ireland, allowing the pirates to return to
sea and to continue the daily spoil of foreign shipping. Nonetheless, at the end
of August, Cecil advised the ambassador that Flemish fishermen could proceed
on their voyages, 'without fear of pirates', as a result of the presence of five of the
Queen's ships along the east coast.[19]

As a group, the pirates in the North Sea withdrew to the apparent safety of
remote havens in Scotland. During August 1561 Elizabeth requested the assistance
of Mary, Queen of Scots, in the arrest of Johnson, Whitehead, Marychurch and
other English pirates. At the same time, the English ambassador in Edinburgh,
Thomas Randolph, was instructed to seek redress for the plunder of English
vessels by Scottish rovers, who were allegedly sailing under colour of letters of
marque. Neither request met with success. Johnson and his associates evaded
arrest, joining forces with Thomas Phetiplace. Randolph reported during 1562
that they formed a company of 'three great vessels in good equipage; so that
much mischief must ensue if their devilish purposes be not staid'.[20] With a mixed
force of English, Scottish and Irish recruits, they operated from temporary bases
in the Western Isles and along the west coast of Scotland, ranging into the Irish
Sea in search of plunder. In March 1562 Johnson and Whitehead were reputedly
in the company of Gerald Fitzgerald, 15th Earl of Desmond, who refused to hand
them over to the Lord Justice in Dublin. By June they were at Loch Ryan, in
south-west Scotland, with a rich prize laden with wine and sugar. The Scottish
monarchy issued orders for their arrest, although Randolph reported that 'they
are very strong and come not aland, but have men of the country who repair to
them'.[21] In July, however, he informed Cecil that one of the English pirates, and

some of the Scots, had been apprehended in the isles. Later in the year Alexander Hogg, a Scottish rover who may have consorted with the English pirates, was arrested in Tenby. Several of Hogg's company were executed for piracy. He sought a pardon from the Queen and the restoration of his vessel, offering to 'do service in apprehending the pirates that are now upon the coast'.[22]

This was followed in 1563 by an appeal to the council from Johnson and Phetiplace, from their temporary base at Kintyre, for a pardon in exchange for 'doing some good service in those parts'. John English, who delivered the message in March, informed Cecil that the pirate leaders were prepared to seize James MacDonnell or other noblemen from the isles who were supporting rebel leaders in Ulster, while also offering to take two vessels that had reportedly arrived from Spain laden with munitions. The council was prepared to procure a pardon for the pirates, on condition that they served against the rebels in northern Ireland, including Shane O'Neill, under the supervision of Thomas Radcliffe, 3rd Earl of Sussex, the Lord Deputy in Dublin. Sussex supported Phetiplace's appeal for a pardon, evidently in commendation for his recent capture of Whitehead.[23]

The sequel to these shadowy contacts underlined the inherent dangers in the employment of former pirates by the regime. Although Phetiplace and Johnson were sent out with two ships-of-war by Sussex, at the end of the year they were cruising off the coast of northern Spain, fuelling Spanish complaints against the depredations of English pirates and rovers. Phetiplace, 'an ill man of long time upon the seas', seized a Spanish vessel at Santander, and put to sea in it with seven or eight of his men.[24] His brother, aboard another ship, was forced into Vermeo, where he unsuccessfully tried to conceal several Spanish prisoners from local officials. When the subterfuge failed, the English were arrested and imprisoned. According to a later report Phetiplace's brother died in prison on Christmas Day. In January 1564 a Spanish representative was seeking restitution of the goods taken by the pirates. Several months later Phetiplace presented Cecil with a declaration of his activities and of his submission to authority. Back in British waters, he offered his ship and company of thirty men for service, with a recommendation from the Lord Justice of Ireland for his 'courage and experience'.[25]

The early years of the Elizabethan regime thus experienced the spread of small-scale, organized piracy around the British Isles. In dealing with the problem, the Queen and her council resorted to expediency and past practice, notably in the pardon of pirates for public service. This may have been partly intended to demonstrate the power and authority of monarchy, sometimes in a deliberately dramatic and terrifying way. Machyn, for example, recorded the trial of a large number of mariners for piracy at the Guildhall in London, at least five of whom were to be executed at Wapping, though one was reprieved as the rope was placed around his neck.[26] This dramatic, last-minute action may have been unusual, but it was in accordance with the use of pardons as policy which was encouraged by the active and interventionist policy of the new regime, particularly against Scotland and France. In these circumstances there was both the need and opportunity to employ reformed pirates in the service of the state.

War, privateering and piracy during the 1560s

The widening range of pirates such as Johnson and Phetiplace reveals the way in which small-scale, localized plunder paved the way for longer-range and more ambitious depredation. Although superficially masked by the renewal of Anglo-French hostilities during 1562, the focus for what became a sustained shift into the Atlantic was Spanish trade and shipping. There were times during the 1560s when Spanish ports appeared to be under siege from English pirates and rovers, some of whom began to haunt the Canary Islands in search of richer prey. In the short term the growing clamour in Spain against English plunder disrupted Anglo-Flemish as much as Anglo-Spanish relations. In the longer term it contributed to a lengthening list of grievances, on both sides, that merged with issues concerning access to transatlantic trade. Deteriorating relations with Spain and Portugal paved the way for the emergence of far-reaching, but speculative, oceanic depredation which was linked, at least during its early phase, with aggressive commercial schemes in Guinea.

The war with France led to a revival of organized reprisal venturing, under the guise of which English men-of-war intensified their spoil of Flemish and Iberian shipping, occasionally in partnership with Huguenot adventurers. The outbreak of hostilities was preceded by widespread complaints from merchants against the arrest and seizure of shipping in French ports and at sea. English intervention in the first French war of religion was an opportunistic and unsuccessful attempt to recover Calais. In October 1562 an expedition under the command of Ambrose Dudley, Earl of Warwick, was sent to Newhaven in Normandy, which the Huguenot leadership handed over to the English, in return for their support, until Calais was retaken. But the defeat and defection of the Huguenots isolated the English, and the expedition was forced to withdraw in July 1563. Peace was restored in April 1564. In addition to the military failure, however, the regime struggled to control the unruly activities of men-of-war, which provoked outrage from the Spanish monarchy.

The early months of the conflict were characterized by uncertainty and confusion concerning English aims and activities at sea. In order to maintain the fiction that Elizabeth's intent was 'not to make war or use any hostility against the French King or any of his faithful subjects', the regime made no effort to authorize or encourage the plunder of French trade and shipping.[27] Nonetheless, in January 1563 the council authorized the release of twenty-one pirates from the county gaol of Devon, and eight from Pembroke, on condition that they provided sureties to serve under Warwick at Newhaven. Following complaints from the Spanish ambassador and others, the Queen issued a proclamation in February ordering the arrest of any of her subjects who were aiding French rovers or pirates. According to the ambassador, the governor of Newhaven was issuing commissions to the English for the plunder of Catholics, French and Spanish, as the enemies of God. With reports of eighteen French men-of-war sailing under the command of Francois le Clerc, or Timberleg, alongside English ships, and with more being fitted out in south-coast ports, he warned Philip II that Elizabeth 'was determined to make herself Queen of the Seas'. Several weeks later, in May, he reported alarming rumours that the Queen was involved in a scheme to send out an expedition of five vessels led by the adventurer Thomas Stukely, in association with Jean Ribault, with the purpose of seizing Spanish ships returning from America.[28]

Towards the end of May 1563 the Queen authorized Lord Cobham, Lord Warden of the Cinque Ports, to equip vessels to make reprisals on French shipping, but with potentially confusing instructions not to spoil them, but to compile an inventory of their cargoes. Within the Channel, however, English men-of-war seized the opportunity to use Newhaven as a base for sweeping raids along the coast towards Dieppe. During June, John Bryan, one of Warwick's servants, captured twenty-three Norman and Breton vessels which were brought into Newhaven. More prizes were taken and brought in by other adventurers, including John Appelyard. The Queen tried to limit the disorder at sea, while preventing her subjects from aiding the Huguenots. In July an order by the French monarchy, justifying the capture of English vessels, persuaded her to authorize the seizure of French ships. Within weeks, however, it was qualified by another proclamation against the illegal depredation of the French which was linked with the growth of piracy and robbery along the Thames. Nevertheless, men-of-war remained active in the Channel and the Irish Sea. They included a warship sent out by Sir Thomas Stanley, lieutenant of the Isle of Man, with the support of a group of Chester merchants. In September Stanley's ship seized a French prize, laden with woad, which was brought into Liverpool, to the accompaniment of a 'noble peal of gones, thick, thick, une upon an other', the like of which, it was reported, had never been heard before.[29]

Much of the initial uncertainty over the war at sea reflected the concern of the Queen and members of her council to prevent the piratical spoil of Flemish and Spanish shipping. In response to complaints from the Duchess of Parma, the Spanish regent in the Low Countries, in September 1563 the Queen ordered the captains of naval vessels and private ships-of-war to allow the subjects of the King of Spain to trade and fish freely. Furthermore, if Flemish or Spanish ships were attacked by French men-of-war, they were commanded to aid and defend them, as if they belonged to her natural subjects.[30]

Royal commands did little to stop attacks on Spanish or Flemish vessels, which were justified by claims that they were carrying goods either for or to the enemy. Such claims raised bitterly contested issues regarding neutral rights during wartime which were ill-defined, and subject to strategic and political considerations as much as to a rudimentary code of international law. Efforts to clarify these issues were undermined by the disorderly and piratical behaviour of men-of-war. In February 1563, for example, a Flemish merchant complained of the plunder of a French ship at Bordeaux, laden with wine and feathers, by an English vessel. The Flemish merchant had freighted the French ship, the master of which was able to demonstrate that its cargo belonged to subjects of the King of Spain. Nonetheless, the prize was brought into Tenby, where the wine was sold for £8 per tun. This kind of irregular plunder provoked angry demands for restitution, exposing the limited administrative and regulatory authority of the High Court of Admiralty.[31]

Disorderly privateering in the Channel and off the coast of Spain soon became confused with piratical activity. Both drew on anti-Spanish hostility, damaging the interests of English merchants in Spain, who faced the prospect of retaliation and reprisal. In June 1563 Hugh Tipton, the English agent in Seville, reported a recent attack by two small vessels on a Spanish ship returning from Puerto Rico, off Cape St Vincent. The rovers, who the Spanish claimed were English, 'for that they shot so many arrows that they were not able to look out', plundered the ship of 3,000 coin pieces, ten chests of sugar and 200 hides, as well as its ordnance, cables and anchors. Concerned that English property in Seville would be arrested if the plunder persisted, Tipton informed Spanish officials that the rovers were 'Scots and Frenchmen, and some Englishmen amongst them, a sort of thieves gathered to go a robbing'.[32]

Attacks on Spanish shipping by the English increased during the year. By December 1563 Philip II remonstrated that the spoil of his subjects had reached an intolerable level. According to complaints from Bilbao, within the previous three months English rovers had captured four French prizes laden with Spanish goods, valued at 49,000 ducats, in addition to the seizure of a Spanish vessel in Santander by Phetiplace. A vessel of Bilbao, laden with wool for Flanders, was also spoiled by five English men-of-war off Ushant. Three or four of the crew, including a friar, were killed during the skirmish. The violence at sea spread further south. Tipton reported an incident off Gibraltar in November, when an English vessel attacked a French ship, with loss of life on both sides, which had serious diplomatic repercussions. The English vessel was one of eight trading ships which were ready to depart from Spain laden with wines, raisins, almonds and other commodities. The attack on the French ship was defended as a legitimate act of war. For the Spanish, however, it appeared to be another example of English piracy which was increasingly threatening their trade with America. Consequently, they claimed that all eight vessels were corsairs who had spoiled ships returning from the Indies. Soon after the attack, they were seized by galleys sent out from Cadiz. While the French ship was left unmolested, the Spanish 'took the English banners and hanged them out at the stern of the galleys, dragging them along in the water, as though they had taken their enemies'.[33] At the end of the year several hundred

English mariners were reported to be prisoners of the Spanish, shackled aboard galleys, subsisting on a diet of bread and water.

The incident off Gibraltar seemed to confirm the fears of Sir Thomas Challoner 'that the licentiousness of a few adventurers will be the cause that a number of honest merchants shall be undone'. The arrest of the English ships, and the accusation of piracy, fuelled Anglo-Spanish hostility. The English insisted that the ships were peaceful traders, blaming the French for the clash off Gibraltar. It was not until June 1564 that Philip II ordered the release of the English ships, while thirty mariners remained in captivity at least until August.[34]

Despite Challoner's comments, the spread of English depredation along the coast of Spain could not easily be explained away as the 'licentiousness of a few adventurers'. In particular, an increasing number of English men-of-war, which haunted the Bay of Biscay in search of French prizes, resorted to the plunder of Spanish and other vessels. An English trader in Bilbao reported early in 1564 that there were twenty-five English vessels off the coast of northern Spain, some of which were compelled by contrary winds to bring their French prizes into the Spanish port, where they were arrested on suspicion of piracy. Although English prisoners were reportedly dying daily, the Spanish 'will not let them be buried but abroad in islands'.[35]

Among those involved in the plunder of the Spanish was Thomas Cobham, the brother of Lord Cobham who was a member of the Queen's council. During the latter part of 1563 Cobham was cruising in the Bay of Biscay with three men-of-war, plundering Spanish vessels returning from Flanders. Following his seizure of one vessel, laden with goods valued at 80,000 ducats which were carried off to Waterford, officials in Bilbao and neighbouring ports arrested all English vessels on the coast. The activities of rovers such as Cobham and Stukely, who was involved in a midnight attack on a Portuguese ship in Bayonne during which three of the crew were killed, provoked a furious response from the Spanish. Anger at being attacked 'as if they were mortal enemies' was inflamed by religious hostility. In March 1564 John Cuerton, an English trader resident in Bilbao, reported a growing feeling among Spanish victims 'that what hurt they do to Englishmen they get to Heaven by it'.[36] In these circumstances the difficulties facing English seafarers in Spain seemed to multiply. Oliver Harris and other seamen were arrested and imprisoned in irons at Tolosa, following accusations that they were members of Phetiplace's company. After eight months in prison, during which half of the prisoners died, while the survivors were abused and abhorred as Turks, Harris managed to contact Cecil, begging for assistance. Although they denied the charges of piracy, Harris and four others were sentenced to death.

In February 1564 the Queen tried to curtail the plunder of Spanish and Flemish shipping by proclamation. While claiming that some Spanish ships were carrying French goods, the decree acknowledged that English men-of-war had been too aggressive in searching the vessels of the subjects of the King of Spain for contraband. Accordingly the Queen appointed commissioners to hear and determine complaints of unlawful plunder, while providing rapid redress for the victims. At the same time, the proclamation openly recognized the difficulty in trying to prevent future attacks on the Spanish or Flemings, because of the number of armed vessels at sea and 'specially considering the daily coloring of the French wares by the said King's subjects'. As a result, officials in England and Ireland were ordered to apprehend anybody who was suspected of attacking the subjects of Philip II. If local officers failed to arrest such suspects, they faced punishment 'as abettors to the offenders'. The owners, captains or masters of men-of-war were also instructed to provide sureties for the compensation of the victims of the plunder of Spanish ships or the vessels of friendly rulers. In response to recent complaints, men-of-war were instructed to be particularly careful in their conduct towards Scottish subjects.[37]

The proclamation demonstrated the determination of the regime to curb the piratical activities of men-of-war and other rovers. Its revival of commissioners for depredations, with extensive powers, also showed its concern to respond to overseas complaints about delays in the administration of justice. But the translation of these orders into effective action remained dependent on the cooperation and consent of local officials and communities. The lack of evidence for the proceedings of the commissioners, which may itself be revealing, makes it difficult to determine their effectiveness in implementing royal commands. In practice the attempt of the regime to control seaborne plunder rested on self-regulation among the promoters and companies of ships of war.

The inability of the regime to control or regulate the activities of men-of-war was reflected in the continued plunder of Spanish, Flemish and other shipping during the closing stages of the conflict with France. According to overseas complaints the disorder was accompanied by the use of torture against the masters of neutral vessels, to force them into false confessions. Captain Courteney tortured a Flemish master, John Petersen, with manacles until he confessed that he was a Frenchman. Although Courteney was condemned by the commissioners for depredations, and ordered by the council 'to be punished with some corporall paine for examples sake', he responded with a legal suit of his own against Petersen, for damages of £2,000, though it was halted in January 1565 at the intervention of the Spanish ambassador.[38]

The restoration of peace with France in April 1564 failed to stop the lawlessness at sea. In the aftermath of the war English rovers continued to plunder French vessels in the Channel. The vulnerability of French commerce to attack was underlined by a report in May of the spoil of several traders of France, to the value of more than 5,000 crowns, by an English rowing boat. During an uncertain and ambiguous period, that characterised the slow restoration of more peaceful conditions at sea, the council dealt with widespread complaints of illegal plunder. In August it instructed Sir William Godolphin, John Killigrew and others to restore goods plundered out of a Spanish ship in the south-west, or to compel the offenders to appear before the commissioners for depredations. The following month Sir Thomas Gargrave, vice president of the Council in the North, and other officials were ordered to assist two Frenchmen in the recovery of goods which had been taken and brought into Hull by Percival Wheteley, William Wentworth and their associates. About the same time it dealt with allegations against Sir John Perrot, Deputy Vice Admiral of Pembrokeshire, regarding the arrest of members of the company of Thomas Cobham in Tenby. Several days later the council took the unusual step of appointing searchers for spoils committed on the Spanish along the coasts of Wales, Devon and Cornwall. Sir Peter Carew and Sir John Chichester were subsequently paid £40 for their services in Devon and Cornwall over a period of thirty-four days.[39]

Ineluctably disorderly plunder became confused with piracy, particularly within the Channel. In August the Spanish ambassador reported that the region was still infested with thieves. The 'worst feature of these particular matters', he informed Philip II, 'is that most of the people that are called pirates are simply rogues without means who spend what they steal and after they are condemned at a cost of much trouble and money have not the wherewithal to pay'.[40] In these circumstances the victims of piracy preferred to recover their property, by arrangement with the pirates, rather than pursuing them through the High Court of Admiralty. Although the ambassador was undeniably impressed with the Queen's determination to deal with piracy, the regime struggled to contain the problem during 1564 and 1565.

In an attempt to reassure Spain of its good intentions, in September 1564 the council provided a vessel to convoy a ship of Antwerp, which seems to have taken sanctuary in Plymouth harbour from pirates haunting the south-west, on the last leg of its homeward voyage from Spain. It also sent out two vessels to clear the coasts of Devon and Cornwall of rovers. In another gesture of its resolve to tackle the problem, Sir Peter Carew, one of the Vice Admirals in the south-west, was ordered to arrest Edmond Coke of Plymouth and other men from Falmouth and neighbouring havens, who were accused of victualling pirates. Later in the year Thomas Maynarde of Plymouth was commanded to appear before the commissioners for depredations, after he admitted receiving stolen booty from a pirate, Robert Thirkett. In November, after consulting with the judge of the High Court of Admiralty, the council authorized the mayor and corporation of Bristol to send out ships to apprehend pirates who were haunting the sea between the River Severn and the Scilly Isles. In the following month it issued instructions to the Vice Admirals in the south-west for the arrest and trial of pirates who had been active since the peace with France. The council complained that pirates had been arrested, but none were punished or executed. The Vice Admirals were instructed, therefore, to hold sessions for the speedy trial of suspected malefactors. Those found guilty were 'to be executed upon sum cliffs nere to the sea side, to the example of others'.[41] Officials in the south-west were also ordered to arrest a group of eight men, including John Heidon and John Hope, who were suspected of piracy, and to hold them in custody until they were able to clear themselves of the allegations.

Piratical activity remained concentrated in, but by no means confined to, the south-west. In December 1564 the mayor of Dover was commanded by the council to investigate complaints that a local ship had spoiled a French vessel of a lading of herring. Later in the month it ordered the arrest of three men in Southampton on suspicion of piracy. During January 1565 the Spanish ambassador complained of the robbery of a Flemish ship by Edward Cooke of Southampton. Evidently the plunder was secretly carried ashore by night, to Cooke's house, when some of the robbers were captured, though their leader escaped.[42]

Despite vigorous and vigilant supervision by the council, the spoil of overseas shipping persisted in local waters, while plunder was dispersed across widely scattered coastal regions of England, Wales and Ireland. In April 1565 Carew informed the council of the arrest of one of Stukely's ships at Cork, though a group of other pirates, including Heidon, escaped to the castle at Bearhaven, under the protection of O'Sullivan Beare. In trying to limit depredation at sea, the regime was compelled to rely on short-term expediency, which dealt with the consequences rather than the causes of such disorder, while it struggled to forestall complaints about partiality and slackness in the application of justice. In March 1565 the commissioners in Cornwall were commanded to execute three pirates, unless the assize judges advised otherwise. They were also instructed to send to London a jury of twelve men who had recently acquitted one suspect of piracy, together with the evidence presented during the trial. This concern was to ensure that the trial and punishment of pirates was accompanied by provision for the recovery and restoration of stolen goods, which relied on the cooperation of local officials. In April 1565 Sir Arthur Champernowne, Vice Admiral for Devon, was instructed to assist two Scotsmen in the recovery of their goods which had been spoiled at sea, while Sir Peter Carew was ordered to deliver a vessel, at Dartmouth, to John Petersen of Zeeland, in accordance with a process issued out of the High Court of Admiralty. In May officials in Dorchester were commanded to seize goods, on suspicion that they had been taken by pirates from Frenchmen.[43] But the restoration of pirate booty repeatedly involved the council and the High Court of Admiralty in allegations against the proceedings of local officers, which pointed to wider and deeper weaknesses in the response to piracy.

Yet the regime achieved several striking successes in its campaign against piracy. By May 1565 two of the most notorious adventurers, Thomas Cobham and Thomas Stukely, were under arrest, leading one of Cecil's agents in Bordeaux to claim that there was 'no English pirate left upon the sea', despite French complaints of continued raiding in the Channel.[44] Cobham and Stukely were the leading figures among a group of adventurers whose ambitions for self-promotion and enrichment sustained a wave of speculative and opportunistic plunder along the coasts of Spain and Portugal during the 1560s. Neither Cobham nor

Stukely explicitly identified themselves with the pirates who continued to infest the Channel and the coastal waters of the British Isles, although they drew on localized piracy for support and recruitment. But the search for honour, glory and wealth, which characterized the ambitions of such adventurers, the restless and rootless younger sons of landowners, was overshadowed by their mercenary motives at sea.

Stukely, an extreme example of the type, fashioned a wayward career of divided allegiances and activities, ranging from England and Ireland to Spain and the Mediterranean, which included intermittent piratical venturing from the later 1550s to the mid-1560s. A younger son of Sir Hugh Stukely of Affeton Castle in Devon, though reputedly an illegitimate child of Henry VIII, he acquired extensive experience as a military adventurer before flirting with the attractions of maritime depredation. During the closing months of Mary's reign he was engaged in privateering against the French, which spilled over into the disorderly plunder of Spanish shipping. In June 1563 he was involved in a scheme for a joint Anglo-French expedition with Jean Ribault. Though the expedition was apparently intended for Florida, Stukely's aim was essentially predatory. When the venture failed to proceed as planned, he turned to raiding the coasts of France and Spain from bases in south-west England and Ireland. Stukely's activities provoked angry complaints from the Spanish monarchy. In January 1564 Philip II ordered his ambassador in London to seek redress for his attack on a Portuguese vessel in Bayonne, during which three of the crew were killed. According to Portuguese reports, Stukely sailed with a ship and a smaller vessel, described as a smack, 'under the guise of a merchantman for greater security', preying upon small trading and fishing vessels. During the latter part of 1563 he seized a Portuguese fishing vessel, valued at 1,500 ducats, which had sought shelter in the port of Munguia. On leaving, he captured a Biscayan ship, laden with iron and money, worth 3,800 ducats. He also seized another vessel off Pontevedra, with a cargo of wine, before returning to Ireland.[45]

Although the piratical raids of Stukely and others were especially targeted on local coastal trades, they exposed the vulnerability of the seaborne commercial and communications network that held together the Spanish Empire. Occasionally, moreover, they embarrassed the Spanish with the capture of richer prizes. In February 1564 a Spanish representative in London complained of the seizure of a ship, returning from Flanders with a cargo worth 80,000 ducats and forty convicts, by Cobham, in consort with two vessels from Newcastle. The Spanish claimed that Cobham and his associates 'attacked the ship with artillery as if they were mortal enemies, and killed a brother of the owner'.[46]

The arrest of Stukely and Cobham thus gave the regime an opportunity to respond to diplomatic complaints and grievances from the recently appointed Spanish ambassador in London, Guzman de Silva. Since his appointment in 1564, de Silva had urged the Queen to take stronger action against pirates and rovers.

The Queen's earlier promise that Cobham 'should receive an exemplary punishment if he was [taken] in England', may have aroused Spanish expectations, as expressed in the cautious optimism that crept into de Silva's reports.[47] In August 1564, while informing Philip of the measures taken for the satisfaction of his subjects, he noted that 'the remedy will not be a complete one for all, yet it appears they are doing their best'. Partly in response to de Silva's pleas, the regime tried to regulate more rigorously the activities of men-of-war, while equipping a fleet of royal ships to be sent against pirates. According to the ambassador, Elizabeth was very annoyed at the damage inflicted on peaceful traders, though she continued to claim that many of the pirates were 'Scotsmen who spoke English to avoid being known'.[48]

But the failure of the trials of Cobham and Stukely was another illustration of the regime's inability to combat piracy and maritime disorder. At the same time it appeared to confirm the suspicions of the Spanish that adventurers such as Cobham enjoyed the support of the Queen's courtiers and councillors. In July 1565 de Silva compiled a confusing report that Cobham, a 'bad man and a great heretic', was acquitted by a jury of twelve men; however, the judge of the High Court of Admiralty, 'seeing that they were biased or perhaps bribed, did not submit the whole case to them, but only certain counts, and when they had absolved the prisoner he was taken back to prison again'. The council intervened, charging the jury with bringing in a false verdict. Each juror was condemned with a fine of £20 or imprisonment for six months, and 'put in the pillory with papers stuck on them like a cuirass'.[49] The ambassador was reassured by the Queen's concern to ensure that Cobham was punished. Following a second trial, he reported that Cobham was found guilty and sentenced:

> to be taken back to the Tower, stripped entirely naked, his head shaved, and the soles of his feet beaten, and then, with his arms and legs stretched, his back resting on a sharp stone, a piece of artillery is to be placed on his stomach too heavy for him to bear but not heavy enough to kill him outright. In this torment he is to be fed on three grains weight of barley and the filthiest water in the prison until he die.[50]

Yet the ambassador was soon informed that Cobham's relatives and kin were seeking a pardon for him. Although they did not include Lord Cobham, who reportedly considered 'his brother's crime a disgraceful one', the petitioners included the Earl of Sussex, who privately urged de Silva to intercede with the Queen, 'to suspend the execution of the sentence ... to prevent ... disgrace to their house and kin'. Regardless of the appeal, the ambassador was increasingly doubtful that the sentence would be carried out. Indeed, Cobham seems to have successfully claimed benefit of clergy. In September de Silva was informed by the judge of the High Court of Admiralty that the Queen had been advised after the trial that 'being an ecclesiastic, [he] could not be done to death, by the

A pirate in manacles being pressed. According to a report by the Spanish ambassador, Thomas Cobham was punished in a similar manner during the 1560s, though it is unclear if the punishment was implemented. He seems to have evaded execution for piracy on the grounds of benefit of clergy. (*Buccaneers of the Pacific*)

laws of the realm, and they had sentenced him as they had to deter others from committing like crimes'.[51]

This setback was compounded with the failure of legal proceedings against Stukely due to weaknesses in the evidence presented in court. Stukely's subsequent surprise offer to serve the King of Spain was rebuffed. In 1566 he returned to Ireland with the new Lord Deputy, Sir Henry Sidney, whose instructions included provision for dealing with the problem of piracy across the Irish Sea. But he continued to arouse suspicion and mistrust, particularly with the Queen. In July 1567 Elizabeth ordered Sidney to investigate allegations that he had purchased hides and skins, plundered from the Dutch by Edward Cooke of Southampton. Several years later he fled to Spain, reportedly taking the title of Duke of Ireland, and fuelling fears that he intended to return at the head of an invasion force supported by Philip II.[52]

The failure to punish Stukely and Cobham weakened the Queen's determined drive against piracy. The Spanish ambassador commended Elizabeth's efforts to remedy the situation at sea, while casting aspersions on some of her ministers. But he had a realistic appreciation of the limited impact of royal policy on pirates and rovers. 'As soon as things look a little better', he reported, 'they begin their robberies again, no doubt for the purpose of keeping their hands in'.[53] In these circumstances there was little apparent decline in piratical activity during 1565 or 1566, or any lessening in the support it received ashore.

Although the council coordinated the regime's response to piracy, insofar as its actions amounted to a policy, they were essentially ad hoc in nature. It relied on the cooperation of other agencies for the administration and enforcement of measures that were the result of a reactive, case-by-case approach. Characteristically, in July 1565 the council requested the assistance of the Lord Justice of Ireland in the recovery of a Spanish ship and its cargo which was spoiled by two rovers, James Heidon and Corbett. In the following month it ordered the judge of the High Court of Admiralty to examine Spanish complaints about the plunder of vessels at the mouth of the Thames, and at other places along the coast, with instructions to proceed against pirates, as well as those who aided and abetted them ashore. These demonstrations of concern for 'the conservacion of justice and reformation of … disorders' were followed by a general search for pirates and plunder within Norfolk, Suffolk and Essex, under the supervision of Vice Admirals and local justices.[54] A similar search was ordered for the Cinque Ports under the supervision of the Lord Warden, Lord Cobham.

The council's efforts to encourage or cajole officials into effective action met with mixed results. At the end of August 1565 the Vice Admiral of Essex, George Christemas, was commended for his diligence in searching for pirates 'inhabiting or haunting that coaste'. But he was also admonished for failing to send out vessels to apprehend two rovers at Harwich, on the grounds that he lacked the authority to do so. In future Christemas was instructed to use any means available against pirates who visited the region, as long as it did not burden the

Queen with extraordinary charges. About the same time, in a striking gesture of its determination to combat piratical attacks on Spanish and Flemish shipping, the council authorized the judge of the High Court of Admiralty to proceed against suspected pirates brought to his attention by the Spanish ambassador or any other subject of the King of Spain.[55]

Diplomatic considerations, combined with concern for the security of the seas around the British Isles, compelled the council to maintain close attention to the issue of piracy and disorderly plunder. In September 1565 it ordered the sheriff of Hampshire and the mayor and corporation of Southampton to ensure that the trial of men accused of piracy was dealt with promptly, and that those found guilty were executed. During October it issued orders for the replacement of the *Aid*, one of the Queen's ships sent out to patrol the seas for pirates, by several small vessels which were more suitable for winter service. Shortly thereafter it instructed the Earl of Bedford to assist in the recovery of certain commodities in the north of England, belonging to a merchant of London, which had been taken by pirates. Bedford was also requested to aid Jacob Spinola and others, in the search for their goods, taken by Charles Wilson and his associates at the mouth of the Thames and reputedly stored in the Farne Islands. In addition, the vice president and Council in the Marches of Wales were ordered to send up to London a pirate, Andrew Whyte, for further examination.[56]

Such close supervision and monitoring paid dividends. At the end of October 1565 Wilson and other pirates were captured and brought to London for trial. Two of Wilson's accomplices, John Smythe of Dover and Jeffrey Berrye of New Romney, were also apprehended by Cobham's officers in the Cinque Ports. Both men were ordered to London, so that they could be put on trial with their leaders, in order to assist in the recovery of the plunder. A similar concern to assist the victims of piracy led the council to issue a stay of execution, later in the year, for William and John Hopers who were found guilty of piracy at Southampton, so that they could be examined as to the location of their booty.[57]

Despite his annoyance at the regime's failure to punish Cobham and Stukely, the Spanish ambassador praised its resolute response to piracy during the rest of 1565. Towards the end of October he reported that many pirates had been hanged, while Wilson, one of the more notorious offenders, was in custody. The Queen had also sent out ships to take pirates. Furthermore, de Silva noted that Elizabeth had 'issued very good regulations which were much needed, and if they are carried out, as they appear likely to be, will be of great benefit'.[58]

The regulations which the ambassador referred to represented an unprecedented and wide-ranging attempt to eradicate piracy by linking maritime depredation with criminality and disorderly activity ashore. They included the appointment of commissioners in the coastal counties of England and Wales for the repression of piracy and other disorders. Detailed instructions for the commissioners were drawn up by the council in November 1565. In order to cut off the aid that pirates received from land-based supporters, the commissioners were commanded to appoint deputies within the havens, creeks and other landing places of their jurisdictions. These deputies were to be selected from reputable members of the community. They could be appointed and removed as necessity required. The council anticipated that no haven would 'be lefte unprovided of sufficient persones' to assist the commissioners, who were expected to supervise their deputies by a visit at least once every month.[59] It also required a monthly report from the commissioners of their own proceedings.

Under the terms of the articles drawn up by the council, the piracy commissioners and their deputies were granted extensive policing and supervisory powers. They were instructed to undertake an inquiry of all the ports, creeks and landing places, including a survey of shipping, mariners and fishermen, within their areas of jurisdiction. No vessels were to put to sea without a licence from them. The deputies were to ensure that no prohibited commodities, particularly grain, were exported without the Queen's warrant. They were also given the responsibility for supervising the landing and sale of goods brought in, with authority to arrest and examine any person suspected of illegally acquiring such wares. In addition, the commissioners and their deputies were empowered to arrest suspected law breakers who aided and abetted pirates.[60]

With some qualification, the establishment of the commissioners represented a national strategy for the repression of piracy in England and Wales. Their appointment recognized the wider social dimension to piratical activity which enabled it to flourish in many coastal regions with local support. The maritime counties were placed under the supervision of four or five commissioners who were assisted by a larger number of deputies, though there was no provision for their appointment in Yorkshire, London or Ireland. Elsewhere the new officers included powerful aristocrats, such as the Earls of Derby and Bedford in Lancashire and Northumberland, gentlemen and local officials, including Sir Peter Carew and Sir John Chichester in Devon, or Sir Christopher Heydon and William Paston in Norfolk, as well as the bishops of Durham in the north and of St David's in south-west Wales.[61]

The appointment of the commissioners and deputies may have contributed to the short-term deterrence of piracy, but their impact was uneven and uncertain. While the registers of the council show signs of occasional activity by some officials, there is little evidence of the regular, detailed reporting that was required by their instructions. Their responsibilities, indeed, may have been focused more closely on the enforcement of the ban on the export of grain. Moreover, there was a danger that the activities of such officials would be seen as intrusive by local communities and potentially rival jurisdictions. In December 1565 Richard Arnold of Walberswick in Suffolk was summoned to appear before the council or the Duke of Norfolk, to answer charges that he refused to show 'his cockett to the comyssioners for the sea costes, … and for his evill language used againste them'.[62] In any case local officers lacked effective means for dealing with recalcitrant communities or groups of aggressive pirates or rovers. The commissioners in Radnorshire informed the council during January 1566 of the arrival of Phetiplace at Milford Haven, though they appeared to be powerless to arrest him or his company. The council was also aware of the heavy demands it was placing on the shoulders of unpaid and possibly unpopular agents. Thus, in February 1566, while reminding the commissioners of their responsibilities, it advised them 'not to overcharge themselves or their deputies otherwise then is convenient'.[63]

Despite the novel establishment of the commissioners, the council remained heavily involved in dealing with cases of piracy and disorderly plunder. In November it instructed the Lord Deputy in Dublin to implement a decree, of the High Court of Admiralty, for the recovery of pirate plunder. About the same time it considered allegations made earlier in the year by Reynold Mohun, one of the recently appointed commissioners in Cornwall, against Sir William Godolphin, John Killigrew the elder and younger, and Peter Killigrew, concerning piracy and other disorders in the south-west, which were followed by complaints of the 'evill usage in keeping of a castell'. In November the council renewed an earlier order for the appearance of Smythe and Berrye before the judge of the High Court of Admiralty, to answer accusations that they maintained pirates. At the end of the year, following further Spanish complaints about the plunder of Flemish shipping, it instructed Vice Admirals and others to certify it of such spoils.[64]

While its registers are missing for the remainder of the 1560s, except for the period from October 1566 to May 1567, the council seems to have retained a close interest in the problem of piracy and maritime disorder, particularly as it continued to provoke complaints from Spain. Following an audience with Elizabeth in May 1566 to discuss the plunder of Flemish ships, de Silva informed Philip II that 'the evil is of so long standing that I do not know that any remedy will cure it at once, although the Queen seems anxious to do so'.[65] De Silva was concerned not to see new orders and regulations issued, but with the execution of those already in place.

The concerns of the Spanish appeared to be confirmed by the piratical early career of Martin Frobisher and his brother, John, who came to the attention of the council during these years. Frobisher, who was to become one of the leading maritime adventurers of Elizabethan England, and his associates served as a link between an older generation of pirates, who were still active during the early years of Elizabeth's reign, and a younger group of rovers, who emerged during the later 1560s and 1570s. His disorderly activities at sea underline the confusing interplay between legitimate and illegal depredation which enabled resourceful adventurers to survive while crossing the boundary between piracy and privateering.

Frobisher was a younger son of a minor landed family in the West Riding of Yorkshire. After the death of his father, Martin, as a young and ambitious man, moved to London, finding employment with a relation of his mother, Sir John Yorke, a prominent and well-connected merchant in the city. During 1553 and 1554 he served as Yorke's agent on two trading voyages to Guinea. During the second voyage he was captured and imprisoned for about nine months by the Portuguese. Thereafter, he abandoned any interest in developing a career in commerce, in favour of risky, but potentially rewarding, sea ventures. It is likely that he served on privateering voyages during the Anglo-French war which Elizabeth inherited in 1558. The following year Henry Strangeways claimed that Frobisher was involved in an abortive expedition for raiding along the coast of Guinea. During the war with France from 1562 to 1564, Frobisher, his brother and Peter Killigrew served as captains of three men-of-war sent out by John Appelyard. This small fleet of rovers captured five French prizes, but they were subsequently seized on their return to Plymouth. Frobisher also assisted in the seizure of a Spanish ship which was engaged in a fight with a vessel under the command of Thomas Cobham. The Spanish prize was taken into Baltimore, where Frobisher received part of its lading of wines. Although Frobisher's share of the plunder was confiscated in Devon, he and his associates secured its release, in addition to the French prizes. A dispute with Appelyard over the booty led to the imprisonment of the Frobishers in Launceston Gaol during July 1564, although they were freed later in the year.[66]

The return of peace saw no let up in the Frobishers' attacks on Spanish or Flemish trade. The plunder of a Spanish vessel during 1565 enabled Frobisher to purchase a ship, the *Mary Flower* of 100 tons, which he planned to send out on a trading voyage to west Africa under the command of his brother. In reality this was a voyage of plunder, possibly with a commission issued by the Huguenot leaders in France, which led to the spoil of a Flemish vessel at the entrance to the Thames. The cargo, claimed by merchants of Antwerp, was carried off to southwest Ireland. Frobisher was arrested for his complicity in piracy, but insufficient evidence led to his release in October 1566, on condition that he did not go to sea again without licence.[67]

Frobisher's piratical venturing was part of a wider problem of maritime disorder which was increasingly diverse in character. In August 1566 a merchant of Wexford complained of the spoil of his ship off Land's End by a French vessel under the command of an English captain, and with a crew that included Irish kern (or soldiers). About the same time the council investigated an unusual case of suspected wrecking and spoil within Mount's Bay, involving a Flemish vessel bound for Spain, as well as complaints of piracy along the coast on a Portuguese ship by a group of 'certaine Frenchmen and a negro'.[68] The activities of such mixed groups of rovers reinforced the growing international threat of piracy during the 1560s, as demonstrated in the cooperation between English and French Huguenot men-of-war, privateers and pirates. The French experience of Caribbean plunder served to broaden the horizons of the English, while promoting loose bonds and alliances that could be represented as part of the common cause of international Protestantism against the threat of Catholic Spain.

Despite repeated attempts to tackle maritime disorder and lawlessness, by the later 1560s the Elizabethan regime was faced with widespread overseas complaints against the activities of pirates and rovers. During 1567 the Portuguese complained of numerous piracies committed by the English during the previous decade. The following year they estimated their losses to English piracy at 600,000 ducats. During May 1568 the French King, Charles IX, sought restitution from the Queen on behalf of one of his subjects whose vessel had been seized by English pirates. The Spanish also complained of English rovers who 'openly sail out of port, and having captured ships belonging to the subjects of the King … publicly sell the cargoes and detain the crews'. In addition, the French claimed that their shipping was plundered by groups of English and Huguenot rovers, with the continued support of the inhabitants of the coastal communities of south and south-east England. In one incident a vessel of Marseille, returning to the Mediterranean with a rich cargo from Flanders, was seized by a group of rovers and brought into Southampton. Although the pirates were arrested, they were subsequently released with their prize, allegedly on the orders of the mayor. Against this disturbed background, the regime enjoyed an important success with the arrest and imprisonment of Phetiplace in Chester Castle.[69]

Slave traders, pirates and privateers

The English attack on Iberian trade, which grew in intensity during the 1560s, seriously disrupted Anglo-Spanish relations. Grievances and mutual recriminations concerning commerce and plunder became entangled with political and religious divisions. At a time when the Spanish monarchy was challenged by wide-ranging problems, the spread of English piratical activity not only endangered Iberian coastal waters but also threatened commercial and imperial interests beyond Europe. Under these conditions the growth of English maritime enterprise in west Africa and the Caribbean, partly in competition and cooperation with French adventurers, contributed to a dramatic re-shaping of English depredation during the later 1560s and early 1570s, in which trade and plunder overlapped.

English commercial activity in Guinea originated during the 1540s. From the outset it took the form of an aggressive enterprise which was prone to violence and plunder. It was supported by a diverse group of powerful and well-connected promoters who were initially interested in the profitable trade in gold, ivory and pepper. These adventurers sent out substantial, well-armed vessels that were able to defend themselves against the threat of Portuguese attack, while carrying a sufficient company of men capable of surviving the hazards of long voyages into a deadly tropical environment. The attraction of the Guinea trade, for profit or plunder, appealed to certain types of seafarers, including sea captains such as Thomas Wyndham, who had extensive experience of disorderly and piratical venturing.[70]

The ambiguous relationship between commerce and plunder in the Guinea trade was demonstrated by William Towerson's third and final voyage to west Africa during 1557. Towerson had already clashed with the Portuguese along the coast of Guinea in 1556. The following year, with a fleet of four vessels, he was involved in extensive pillage and plunder, tenuously justified by the war with France, which included setting fire to the African settlement of Shamma. Outward-bound Towerson and his company stopped and searched two vessels of Danzig on suspicion that they were carrying French commodities. Although Towerson and his officers did not want to delay the voyage, in response to demands from the company it was agreed that every man could take out of the vessels provisions and other necessities. In practice, as a subsequent account admitted, Towerson's men ransacked the Danzigers 'and spoiled them so much, that of very pity we gave them a compasse, a running glasse, a lead and a line, certain bread and candles, and what apparel of theirs we could finde'.[71]

A fortnight later Towerson encountered a Spanish naval expedition at the Canary Islands, bound for the Caribbean. Although the meeting between the two fleets was friendly, it threatened to turn violent after Towerson refused to lower his flag to the Spanish Admiral. Shortly after reaching the coast of Guinea the English skirmished with a Portuguese fleet of five vessels. Several days later they clashed with three French ships sailing together, in a determined attempt to stop their trade. The English seized one of the French ships, laden with fifty pounds of gold, but the others escaped. The activities of the French traders, who had acquired 700 pounds of gold by the time of Towerson's arrival, limited the commercial opportunities for their rivals. After struggling to trade with various settlements along the coast, in the face of increasing African hostility Towerson and his men burnt and spoiled the town of Shamma. With disease ravaging the company, and the supply of provisions running out, the expedition returned for England in a desperate condition. One of the ships, the *Tiger*, with a crew that was reduced to six men, was so leaky that it was abandoned at sea. The survivors appear to have been transferred aboard Towerson's vessel, the *Minion*. By the time it reached Cape Finisterre, however, there were only twelve healthy men remaining to complete the voyage.[72]

The predatory characteristics of the early English Guinea trade, which were amplified during the 1560s by a view among some traders of the Africans as prey, invited reprisals and strong diplomatic protests from Portugal and Spain. For the Iberian monarchies, who were concerned to protect their interests beyond Europe, commercial interlopers were corsairs or pirates, whose marauding activities threatened the integrity of vulnerable seaborne empires. As the author of the account of Towerson's voyage of 1557 acknowledged, adventurers engaged in the Guinea trade anticipated retaliation from Portugal or Spain, notwithstanding peace with England.[73]

The condition of the Guinea trade grew worse during the first decade of the Elizabethan regime. Spanish and Portuguese complaints aroused the resentment

of English adventurers who insisted on their freedom to trade in west Africa with
the support of the Queen. The Spanish ambassador repeatedly tried to prevent
English vessels from sailing to Guinea, but Elizabeth's councillors, including Cecil,
aggressively defended such voyaging. Although Elizabeth was more diplomatic in
her response to Iberian complaints, she maintained the right of English adventurers to trade in the region. In November 1564 the Queen informed the Spanish
ambassador that 'she had ordered her subjects not to go to places where the King
held sway, and if they contravened these orders she would have them punished,
but that there was no reason why they should be forbidden to go where the
French went every year'.[74] In fact, leading members of the regime, as well as the
Queen, were increasingly identified with the Guinea trade. While the Queen
loaned ships to Guinea traders, in return for a share in the profits of the voyage,
courtiers and councillors – including Elizabeth's favourite, Robert Dudley, Earl
of Leicester – were members of trading syndicates which included city traders
and naval officials.

The Guinea trade thus became an armed struggle, marked as much by plunder and reprisals as by peaceful commerce and exchange. The expedition led by
George Fenner, in association with his brother, Edward, during 1567 underlines
the unstable relationship between trade and plunder, and its broader implications
for Anglo-Portuguese relations. The Fenners were of a Sussex family, who had
acquired varied interests in trade and shipping, including naval experience. To
some extent they were representative of a growing number of ambitious and
aggressive provincial adventurers who were attracted by the profitable prospects of
Atlantic enterprise. Like the Hawkins dynasty, they would have vigorously repu-
diated accusations of piracy, though their maritime ventures were often predatory
in purpose and piratical in practice.

The expedition to Guinea left Plymouth in December 1566, made up of a fleet
of three vessels, including the *Castle of Comfort*, a powerful and well-armed man-
of-war. During a tense encounter with the Spanish at the Canary Islands they met
Edward Cooke, an adventurer from Southampton, whose activities during these
years aroused repeated suspicions of piracy. When the Fenners reached Guinea
their trade was thwarted by hostility from the Portuguese and their African allies.
Near Cape Blanco a trading party went ashore, but it was attacked by Africans
who were armed with poisoned arrows. Four of Fenner's men later died from
their wounds. Two others were taken prisoner, evidently in retaliation for the
seizure of three Africans by the company of another English vessel cruising along
the coast. Sailing around the Cape Verde Islands, the expedition was welcomed by
Portuguese renegades, but resisted by six Portuguese ships. On the return voyage
to England it was attacked at the Azores by a Portuguese fleet of seven vessels.
After a bloody conflict the Portuguese withdrew, allowing the English to repair
their damaged ships and continue their homeward voyage. As the expedition
entered the Channel, it unexpectedly met a Portuguese ship laden with sugar and
cotton, from which the English acquired forty chests of sugar in exchange for

five Africans. The conclusion to this transaction was threatened by the approach of two armed vessels, suspected of being rovers. In the face of English resistance, the pirates or privateers abandoned their attack, enabling Fenner to acquire ten more chests of sugar in return for protecting his Portuguese trading partner.[75] Although the voyage underlined the inherent risks of the Guinea trade, it also confirmed the naval weaknesses of Portugal in the Atlantic, encouraging the ambitions of English adventurers, despite their limited knowledge of west Africa which left them heavily dependent on the assistance of Portuguese renegades or rival French traders.

In these circumstances English attempts to break into the transatlantic slave trade during the 1560s had far-reaching implications for the expansion of long-distance, organized plunder, as much as for commercial development. The ambivalent character of the voyages promoted by John Hawkins and his part-ners meant that aggressive commercial venturing and depredation reinforced each other. These ventures occurred at a time of growing hostility towards Spain which paved the way for the emergence of militant maritime and colonial ven-turing, while encouraging transatlantic piracy and privateering. The development of more ambitious and diversified forms of depredation was also influenced by French activity across the Atlantic, particularly the attempts of Huguenot adven-turers to establish an outpost in Florida to serve as a base from which to plunder Spanish shipping leaving the Caribbean. The interest that Hawkins and others showed in the French settlement of Florida suggests a speculative approach to slaving, overlaid by the potential for hostile action against Spain, which may partly explain why the English withdrew so rapidly from the trade after the later 1560s.

Hawkins sent out four slave-trading expeditions to Guinea and thence to the Caribbean during the 1560s. The first voyage of 1562 made such a profit that the Queen acquired a stake in succeeding expeditions through the loan of the *Jesus of Lübeck*, a powerful but ageing naval vessel. The second voyage may have earned a profit of 60 per cent, reinforcing the suspicions of de Silva that the English were 'waxing fat on the spoils of the Indies'.[76] However, a third voyage, led by John Lovell, was probably unprofitable. Although the Spanish made a determined effort to stop further voyages to the Caribbean, a fourth and larger expedition was sent out in 1567. Its disastrous conclusion, when Hawkins and his company clashed with a Spanish fleet at San Juan de Ulua, effectively killed off serious interest in the slave trade. Hawkins and a number of survivors, including his younger kins-man, Francis Drake, barely escaped with their lives.

To a considerable degree the commercial success of Hawkins' voyages depended on Iberian cooperation or collusion. During this early phase of ven-turing, Portuguese renegades were a means by which the English were able to establish limited trading contacts in west Africa, though African agency was also an essential characteristic of slave trading. During his last voyage Hawkins estab-lished an opportunistic alliance with an African leader in an attempt to procure

Sir Francis Drake, a pioneer of English piracy in the Caribbean during the early 1570s, when he established an alliance against the Spanish with the cimaroons, runaway slaves who had established their own communities in parts of central America. Drake acquired a remarkable reputation among some of his Spanish victims, who insisted that he was helped by a familiar. (*Sir Francis Drake*)

Qui ʋicit toties ms Fructis classibus hostes
Ille ʋagis HAVKINS ʋitam reliquit in Vndis

Sir John Hawkins, the leading representative of a Plymouth trading and shipowning dynasty, whose members were also engaged in predatory maritime enterprise. During the 1560s Hawkins tried, unsuccessfully, to break into the transatlantic slave trade. In 1577 Hawkins became treasurer of the Queen's Navy. Following the outbreak of war with Spain in 1585, he used his position to promote various schemes for weakening Spain at sea. (*The Fugger News-Letters*) slaves through a joint raid on a rival settlement. On the other side of the Atlantic, moreover, Hawkins was only able to dispose of his human cargo with the connivance of Spanish settlers or colonial officials in scattered markets, ranging from settlements along the northern coast of Hispaniola to the mainland of South America. Thus during his second voyage he relied on Cristobal de Llerena, 'a negro … who had been brought up in Portugal', to act as an interpreter and intermediary in negotiations with Spanish officials at Borburata for a trading licence. Evidently, Llerena was a trader of Jamaica who was probably involved in the slave trade. He was taken, or rescued, by the English in Guinea, where he was a prisoner of a group of Africans. Furthermore, on his final slaving voyage Hawkins received aid at Rio de la Hacha from two runaway slaves who offered to guide the English into the interior, where bullion belonging to the King of Spain was buried, in exchange for their freedom. Following negotiations with local officials, however, the runaways were returned for a ransom of 4,000 ducats. They were subsequently executed by the Spanish.[77]

The failure of the English to establish peaceful commercial relations with the Spanish in the Caribbean helped to turn the region into a theatre for unofficial war, plunder and reprisals which was exposed to inflammatory religious rivalries. Inadvertently, Hawkins' voyages drew attention to the weaknesses of the Spanish Caribbean, where vulnerable colonial settlements could be intimidated or plundered by marauding interlopers. They also enabled the English to gain seafaring experience and expertise of unfamiliar and hazardous waters. De Silva warned Philip II early in 1568 that if the ventures of Hawkins were not stopped, 'they may do much damage by showing the way to the Indies and opening up this business, and also by their religious action in those parts'.[78] The implications of the spread of religious rivalries across the Atlantic were reinforced by reports that the Huguenots in Florida, who were assisted by Hawkins and other English adventurers, provocatively identified the Spanish as hogs, whose unclean status may have been intended to portray them as legitimate targets for Protestant crusading in the New World.

Among the English the growth of transatlantic depredation was encouraged by the withdrawal of Hawkins' London partners following the conflict at San Juan de Ulua. As a result English enterprise in the Caribbean was left in the hands of aggressive provincial adventurers who were prepared to operate in an overtly, if not opportunistic, predatory manner. Among seafaring communities in the south-west, the growth of Caribbean raiding was justified by reports of Hawkins and his company of Spanish treachery and cruelty. This volatile mix of transatlantic reprisals with embryonic Protestantism and patriotism informed the strategic thinking of a generation of Elizabethan sea adventurers. It also favoured the emergence of more ambitious forms of depredation which were linked with schemes for colonial settlement in North America.

In the short term the conflict at San Juan de Ulua contributed to a rapid deterioration in Anglo-Spanish relations, which grew out of the rebellion in the Low

Countries. Spanish complaints about the sanctuary given to rebels in England, with the covert support of the Queen, combined with mounting grievances over plunder, escalated into a damaging diplomatic and commercial breakdown. The consequences of the Dutch revolt were compounded with the wider effects of the renewal of the wars of religion in France. Rebellion and civil war encouraged the spread of disorder and violence at sea, particularly in the Channel. In a notorious incident during November 1568 the Elizabethan regime authorized the seizure of ships carrying silver for Philip II's army in Flanders, after they had sought safety in Plymouth. Although the regime defended the arrest as providing protection for the Spanish against the danger of attack by French men-of-war, the bullion was not restored until 1574.[79]

Against this darkening diplomatic background the Channel was rapidly infested by organized groups of men-of-war of varying legality and number. Although they were dismissed as pirates or corsairs by the Spanish, whose vulnerable trade with Flanders was one of their main targets, many of these adventurers sailed with commissions issued by French or Dutch leaders. Frobisher, for example, was back at sea during 1568 and 1569 with licences from the cardinal of Châtillon, representing Huguenot leaders in France, and from the Prince of Orange, allowing him to seize French Catholic and Spanish vessels. The growth of international privateering or belligerent piracy drew on powerful forces, including religious and political animosities, underpinned by reprisals and revenge, as well as by commercial rivalries and plunder. Although it was linked with the defence of the beleaguered cause of international Protestantism, it also created new opportunities for experienced and hard-bitten rovers like Frobisher, whose seizure of several prizes led to his arrest and imprisonment during 1569.[80]

These conditions promoted the growth and diversification of English depredation. During the later 1560s and early 1570s transatlantic plunder emerged, while localized and opportunistic piracy flourished within the Channel and the western approaches. Both forms of enterprise were focused on the spoil of Iberian commerce. The dangers to Spanish trade and shipping were intensified by the activities of a Huguenot fleet in the Channel, under the authority of the Duke of Condé, which was supported by the English. Although Condé's targets were French Catholics, Huguenot raiding spilled over into attacks on Spanish and Flemish vessels. During 1568 the new Spanish ambassador, Guerau de Spes, whose angry reports from London helped to inflame Anglo-Spanish tension, warned Philip II that ships sailing to Flanders needed to sail in convoy to defend themselves against possible attack. By November the Huguenot privateering force had reportedly seized eleven prizes which were brought into England.[81]

In the following month de Spes informed Philip that the Huguenots had a fleet at sea of about ten men-of-war, manned with 1,200 men. An additional seven or eight ships were expected to reinforce it. In response to Spanish complaints against the use of English ports and havens by the French, the Queen reassured the ambassador that pirates would be punished, though such was the disorder at sea that de Spes was sceptical of the outcome. Indeed, he alleged that Cecil 'wherever he can, favours the pirates, both on account of religious partiality and of the great profit he derives from it'.[82] Spanish concern was fuelled by the activities of adventurers from Plymouth, Southampton and neighbouring ports who were sailing in consort with the French, and by reports that William Winter had led a fleet of six of the Queen's ships to the Huguenot stronghold of La Rochelle.

The spread of Huguenot privateering provided a cover for English adventurers who continued to plunder Spanish shipping. In May 1568 two rovers, including Edward Cooke, seized a Spanish galleon off Guipúzcoa, though it was subsequently recovered by one of the Queen's ships. Among those engaged in what seemed to be an unofficial campaign of reprisals were William Hawkins and Courtenay. Their seizure of several rich Flemish and Spanish ships during 1568 provoked outrage from de Spes, who claimed that they were assisted by friends at the Queen's court. The deep-seated ambiguity of such depredation, which was rooted in the crisis in Anglo-Spanish relations, grew worse following the arrest of English merchants and property in the Low Countries by the Spanish regent, the Duke of Alva. In retaliation, Elizabeth issued a proclamation in January 1569 suspending commercial relations with Spain and Flanders, while authorizing the arrest of Spanish ships and goods within her realm. Diplomatically, the proclamation insisted that Spanish property was not to be spoiled, but to be kept under guard. It also stopped short of allowing reprisals against Spain, leaving adventurers like Courtenay and Hawkins open to charges of piracy.[83]

Nonetheless, the return of the survivors of Hawkins' expedition from the Caribbean early in 1569 provided further justification for the spoil of Spanish shipping. According to de Spes, the seizure of Spanish vessels in English ports was followed by their plunder by Admiralty officials and pirates, despite the Queen's decree to the contrary. In February 1569 he estimated the loss to Spain at about 900,000 ducats. At sea, moreover, Spanish trade continued to be the target for an increasingly international force of privateers and rovers. De Spes complained of the capture of seven merchant vessels off the Isle of Wight by a mixed group of English and Flemish pirates. Several weeks later he expressed concern that the pirates intended to attack Spanish fleets returning from the Caribbean laden with silver and gold.[84]

The Queen tried to contain the disorder at sea through proclamations issued in April and August 1569. Both were in response to the threatening activities of mixed groups of pirates, rovers and privateers, 'of divers nations', who were ranging the North Sea and the Channel, between the coasts of Denmark, Sweden and France, 'robbing and spoiling all manner of honest merchants of every nation without difference'. The first extended existing penalties against piracy by including the supporters of pirates and rovers securely within the jurisdiction of the law. Consequently, those who traded or trafficked with pirates, or who assisted them in other ways, faced the same punishment as the robbers themselves. In suspicious cases, local officials were instructed to take bonds for ships that were not engaged in lawful trade or fishing. If the companies of such ships subsequently resorted to piracy, the officials were to be accountable, suffering imprisonment until the offenders were caught. All pirates and rovers were proclaimed 'to be out of … [the Queen's] protection, and lawfully to be by any person taken, punished, and suppressed with extremity'.[85] These stringent measures were reinforced by the provisions of the succeeding decree against disorder in the Channel. In another attempt to prevent pirates and rovers from being supplied with provisions in England, Vice Admirals and local officers were commanded to apprehend all armed vessels which were not engaged in trade or fishing, or to prevent them from putting to sea. Officials were also instructed not to countenance any ships sailing with overseas licences, but only those which were known as the Queen's, in order that they 'may be sent to the seas for keeping the same free from pirates'.[86]

The regime's attempts to deal with the growing international menace of piracy and privateering in the Channel failed to improve Anglo-Spanish or Anglo-Flemish relations. Early in 1569 de Spes advised Philip II that the English did not deserve an ambassador, 'only an agent, so that when they make captures, reprisals may be at once adopted and their commerce stopped'. This was followed by a steady stream of complaints and allegations about the interests of leading representatives of the regime in the spoil of Spanish subjects. In April the ambassador claimed that Cecil and five or six other members of the council were growing rich from the plunder of the Spanish, and from the bribery that accompanied it. This was 'a road to a host of robberies and rogueries', he complained later in the year, 'and has been devised by some of the council in order to gain great riches for themselves'.[87] Several prominent councillors were alleged to be directly involved in supporting the growth of anti-Spanish venturing. They included the Queen's favourite, Leicester, and the Earl of Pembroke, whose servants reportedly captured a rich Spanish ship returning from Barbary.

Increasingly the reports of de Spes seemed to indicate that the English were engaged in an unofficial war of plunder against the commercial and colonial possessions of the Spanish monarchy. In August 1569 the ambassador reported that the seas remained crowded with pirates. Within the Channel groups of English, French and Dutch rovers plundered Spanish and Flemish shipping from safe havens in south-west England, the Isle of Wight and the neighbouring region. By October de Spes claimed that men-of-war, manned with rovers of Dutch origin, had taken more than thirty vessels, mainly laden with grain, from Spanish subjects. The following month he reported the seizure of four ships by English and French men-of-war under the leadership of the Huguenot commander, Jacques de Sores, who was based in Portsmouth. According to Spanish reports, this Anglo-French force was made up of between thirteen and sixteen strong, well-equipped ships, which were divided into two squadrons. A larger number of scavenging pirate ships also operated in their wake, scouring the Channel in search of prey.[88]

Although these mixed fleets of rovers and privateers continued to plunder the subjects of the King of Spain, they also spoiled vessels of varied origins.

The seizures included two rich Venetian ships, the *Justiniana* and the *Vergi*. The cargo of the former was valued at 130,000 crowns, while the lading of the latter was worth 100,000 crowns. De Spes reported that during the capture of the *Justiniana* the 'pirates hoisted the Queen's standard and pretended to be her officers', though both prizes were subsequently taken to La Rochelle, where their cargoes were declared to be lawful prize. This was followed, during 1570, by the seizure of a hulk of Danzig, of 1,300 or 1,400 tons, which was bound for Portugal.[89]

During the establishment of the Elizabethan regime from 1558 to 1570, therefore, varied forms of depredation survived and flourished. A combination of domestic insecurity and international uncertainty created favourable conditions for the maintenance of small-scale and localized piracy, alongside the development of more purposeful and ambitious piratical venturing within the Channel and along the Atlantic coasts of Spain and Portugal. At the same time, aggressive commercial pioneering beyond Europe opened up new channels for English depredation in Guinea and the Caribbean. While the scale of activity should not be exaggerated, the persistence of piracy and disorderly privateering, and the increasing spoil of Spanish and Flemish trade and shipping, created problems for a vulnerable regime with limited naval experience and resources. Although the official response to these developments betrayed confusion and some degree of tension between potentially competing priorities, the Queen and her council made repeated attempts to curb the excesses of English rovers. While resorting to long-standing expedients, the regime also tried to develop a coherent programme to deal with piracy. However, the limited activities and successes of the commissioners for piracy suggest that it was fighting a losing battle against maritime lawlessness and disorder, particularly given the growth of Anglo-Spanish tension and thinly veiled hostility during these years. In December 1569 the Duke of Alva added to the growing chorus of Spanish complaint against English and French piracies, while warning Philip II that pirates or sea bandits from the Low Countries were operating from bases in England. Alva advised Philip that an open rupture with England would be inappropriate and unwelcome.[90] But the widening range of English piracy, strikingly demonstrated by the return of Drake to the Caribbean, soon brought England and Spain close to a war of mutual reprisals which spanned the Atlantic.

4

Piracy, Plunder and Undeclared War during the 1570s

The international crisis of the late 1560s and early 1570s led to a dramatic and widespread increase in maritime disorder and lawlessness. Conditions in the Low Countries, France and England turned the Channel into a dangerous and violent frontier haunted by privateers, pirates and men-of-war of varied nationality. The attention of these rovers was focused heavily on Spanish, Flemish and French Catholic targets. At times the predators were organized into mixed fleets of Protestant rovers, operating between La Rochelle, Plymouth and the coast of Flanders. The breakdown in Anglo-Spanish relations enabled English adventurers to play a prominent part in an undeclared war on the trade and shipping of the subjects of Philip II, while also offering safe havens to Dutch and French men-of-war. Although the restoration of diplomatic relations during 1573 may have reduced the international tension, and contributed to a lessening in organized plunder in the Channel, it was followed by an upsurge in local and indiscriminate piracy. Within this context, English depredation spread across the Atlantic and into the Caribbean. But the expansion of piratical enterprise also exposed structural weaknesses in deep-sea plunder. The pirate invasion of the Spanish Caribbean was difficult to sustain, particularly at a time of improving Anglo-Spanish relations. By the mid-1570s, indeed, organized piracy and plunder may have been showing signs of decline, in the face of the increasing presence in local waters of foreign men-of-war, many of which were manned with English recruits. This latter practice, which the regime tried unsuccessfully to prohibit, suggests that the decline in activity was more apparent than real. It was certainly short lived, as the subsequent revival of piracy, sea roving and privateering demonstrated.

Crisis in the Channel: piracy and privateering during the early 1570s

The collapse of Anglo-Spanish relations during the late 1560s and early 1570s, and the commercial embargoes in the Iberian Peninsula and in Flanders, were accompanied by an upsurge in piracy and plunder. English depredation contributed to a wider crisis at sea, which was the consequence of rebellion, insurrection and religious conflict in France and the Low Countries. As rulers and rebel leaders resorted to the issue of letters of reprisal or marque against their enemies, the Channel and its approaches became the scene for confusing conflicts involving private men-of-war and trading vessels, in which the legal distinction between legitimate and illegitimate forms of plunder was in danger of collapse.

Despite the instability and chaotic conditions at sea, it is possible to distinguish between several different strands of depredation during these years. Local piratical activity, opportunistic and sometimes amateurish in character, remained a problem as demonstrated by nagging complaints to the council. Although widespread, it was irregular and random in occurrence, and occasionally confused with the illegal arrest of overseas shipping in English ports. Alongside it, more organized and structured venturing continued to develop under the leadership of captains, for whom sea roving was increasingly an occupation. In addition there was a resumption of legally authorized depredation or privateering, but it was limited in scale and volume. Although the Queen was concerned to ensure that English merchants were compensated for the arrest of their goods in the Low Countries, issuing a proclamation in June 1570 that invited claims for losses, there was no general issue of letters of reprisal by the High Court of Admiralty. Commissions seem to have been awarded in a discriminating manner, with some concern for their potential consequences, though this did not prevent their wider circulation, through sale or auction to groups of potential bidders. At the same time, a growing number of captains and adventurers served with French or Dutch privateering fleets, under the guise of commissions issued by Protestant rebel leaders, such as William of Orange or the Queen of Navarre. For the English this provided a veneer of legitimacy for the spoil of Spanish, Flemish and French shipping.[1]

The assembly of a multinational privateering force in the Channel, which had radical implications for English depredation, was the most striking development of these confusing years. It was made up of mixed groups of Huguenot adventurers, Dutch rebels and their English sympathisers. As such it served the interests of a diverse range of seaborne predators, whose motives and methods varied. The Spanish ambassador in London, de Spes, angrily dismissed them as corsairs or pirates. He came close also to portraying England as a rogue nation which openly supported and sponsored robbery at sea.[2] Yet these pan-Protestant groups of privateers could not be lightly discounted, particularly as they were strongly identified with the common cause of Protestantism and liberty in many parts of northern Europe.

GUILIELMUS NASSAVIUS, PRINCEPS
AURIACUS etc.

William of Orange, the leader of the Dutch rebels against Spain until his assassination in 1584. Fleets of privateers serving with his commissions plundered Spanish and other shipping in the Channel during the 1570s, with the assistance of English supporters. Adventurers such as Martin Frobisher served under his authority, skirting a fine boundary between piracy and privateering. (*The Fugger News-Letters*)

This hybrid force of men-of-war, privateers and pirates amounted to an impressive array of shipping. In January 1570 de Spes reported that the corsairs had sixteen strong and well-equipped vessels which were divided into two squadrons or fleets. By June the number had more than doubled, amounting to between forty and forty-five vessels. In October there were fourteen or fifteen ships sailing in the Channel under the Prince of Orange's colours, with a similar number from La Rochelle. The following year, in April 1571, the Spanish ambassador reported that there were twenty pirate ships cruising near Dover, of which seven were described as large, well-armed vessels. In April 1572 Dutch rovers, defiantly assuming the name of sea beggars, had a fleet of twenty-six ships at sea, though most were evidently small vessels. During January 1573 twenty-two vessels from La Rochelle were reported to be sailing along the south coast of England. Although many of the Dutch and French had outworn their welcome in England, in June 1574 de Spes warned that the pirates were preparing to send out a fleet of sixteen small ships from Colchester, while towards the end of the year ten men-of-war from Flushing were at Rye.[3]

The vessels that made up these privateering fleets were well suited for coastal and Channel raiding. Most of them were small and nimble craft, though they were complemented by a number of larger vessels. The ships fitted out in Colchester during June 1574 were less than thirty tons' burden, and described as long and low, with oars as well as sails.[4] Tactically, such vessels depended on surprise, manoeuvrability and weight of numbers rather than on tonnage or weight of ordnance. The guns they carried were intended to disable enemy shipping, allowing large companies of boarders to seize and spoil their prey. Consequently, they were heavily manned with recruits of Dutch, French, English and other backgrounds. According to de Spes the sixteen ships which were at the Isle of Wight in June 1570 were poor vessels, but they were well manned with English and French rogues. Each of the forty or so warships which infested the Channel during these months reportedly included between twelve and fifteen Englishmen among their companies. Although English recruits or volunteers were ordered ashore by the Queen during August, because her own ships were short of men, in the following month de Spes claimed that there were still 200 Englishmen serving with the corsairs. They were, he insisted, 'men of inferior class', who were reinforced by a steady stream of 'mean knaves' from the Low Countries.[5]

Despite the difficulties in maintaining the cohesion of an irregular force of voluntary warships, superficially this group of privateers developed an impressive degree of organization. In December de Spes informed Philip II of discussions to make William of Orange's brother, Ludovic of Nassau, the 'head of the pirates', commanding a fleet of thirty-five vessels which was capable of ranging the Atlantic and the Caribbean.[6] Six months later, in June 1571, the Dutch leader allegedly ordered all the privateers to gather at La Rochelle under Ludovic's command, on pain of death. In reality, however, it was difficult to maintain the organization of such a heterogeneous group of maritime adventurers.

While Spanish perceptions that the rebel leader, William of Orange, was the guiding hand that organized Dutch privateers may be overdrawn, nonetheless he played an important role in commissioning and directing their activities. His agents in English ports issued commissions in his name, as well as supplying shipping and provisions for the rebel cause. In June 1570 one of Orange's servants was at Rye to facilitate the fitting out of two vessels as men-of-war. For the French a similar role was undertaken by Odet de Coligny, Cardinal Châtillon, whose brother, Gaspard, was one of the Huguenot leaders and Admiral of France, and a leading sponsor of French colonial ventures in Brazil during the 1550s and in Florida in the 1560s. Châtillon was a frequent visitor to England during the early 1570s, while some of his servants took up temporary residence, to promote the Huguenot cause. In 1570 his secretary was in the Isle of Wight, collecting a levy on prizes brought in by Huguenot men-of-war.[7]

The activities of the privateers benefited from the support and connivance of local officials, and sympathetic naval and mercantile interests, including John Hawkins and his brother, William. The response to the presence of Dutch and French men-of-war in English waters was heavily influenced by the growth of hostility towards Spain, which was mixed with self-interest regarding their potential strategic value. During February 1570 Châtillon was reported to have presented a proposal to the council 'by which, without cost to themselves but to their profit, they might become masters of the Channel'. The following month the council was also reportedly involved in discussions concerning the despatch of a force of men-of-war to intercept the Spanish fleet returning from the Indies. By June 1570 Antonio de Gueras was convinced that Elizabeth intended to use the corsairs to make war on Spain. At the same time, Philip II was informed that the Queen depended on the privateers to patrol her coasts; with their protection, Elizabeth claimed 'that she had no need of other defence'.[8]

The resort of the privateering fleets to English havens encouraged discussion relating to the seaborne defence of the Protestant cause, which included aggressive schemes for the plunder of the Spanish in the Atlantic and the Caribbean. During the summer of 1570 de Spes kept Philip II regularly informed about Hawkins' plans to lead an expedition to the Indies, with the assistance of a Portuguese pilot, reputedly of great knowledge and experience. The pilot, Bartolome Bayon, was involved in talks with members of the council 'about the project which was discussed here before, to occupy and colonize one or two ports in the kingdom of Magallanes, in order to have in their hands the commerce of the southern sea, and that of Guinea and the coast of Africa, as well as getting as near as they wish to Peru'.[9] Little came of these discussions, but they underlined the potential relationship between seaborne plunder and piracy with aggressive commercial expansion which was to emerge during the 1580s and 1590s.

Spanish reports suggest that Hawkins was planning to join forces with a French fleet which had already departed for Florida. In August 1570 de Spes informed Philip II that Hawkins had twelve vessels prepared for the sea, as retaliation for former losses and injuries. According to the ambassador's Portuguese informant, Hawkins did not intend to 'colonize the Indies, although most of the pirates may stay there'. Instead, he was planning 'to take possession of the island of San Juan de Ulloa, in order to be the master of the fleets which may come and go'.[10] Although the plans were abandoned, Hawkins and his naval associates, including William Winter, were involved in promoting Drake's voyages in the Caribbean during the early 1570s.

The crisis at sea during these years thus generated varied forms of plunder, ranging from the Channel to the Caribbean, within an international context in which political and religious, as well as economic and strategic objectives were closely related. Although de Spes insisted that this bout of spoil and pillage rested on weak foundations, in England it fed the maritime ambitions or visions of leading members of the regime, who were also supporters of the Protestant cause. In January 1571, 'as a sort of boast', Leicester presented Elizabeth with a New Year's gift of a jewel, inlaid with a painting in which Neptune paid obeisance to the Queen, while Spain and France appeared to be covered by waves.[11] In reality, of course, the sea was infested with privateers and pirates, whose activities, while of questionable legality, exposed the fragility and peculiar character of English maritime power and ambitions.

Indeed, the activities of pirates and rovers, as distinct from the raiding of the privateering fleets, remained a persistent problem. During July 1570 John Marten and others were indicted for robbing a vessel of Emden within the jurisdiction of the Cinque Ports. The robbery provoked a strong complaint to the Queen from Anne, the dowager countess of Emden, who alleged also that the robbers were aided by the captain of Dover Castle. Later in the year the council heard complaints against Captain Tyse, a pirate who plundered French traders of goods valued at £300, and against John Wekes, who was accused of the disorderly plunder of Canary wines out of a Spanish vessel. Wekes subsequently tried to justify his seizure and sale of the wine in London. The Duke of Alva, however, scorned the threat to shipping in the Channel from pirates or privateers. In December 1571 he assured the Duke of Medina-Celi that he could sail from Spain for Flanders 'in perfect safety from the pirates, who are all very mean fellows, and dare not attack two armed ships, but have only assailed little packet boats and the like, as they are not the sort of people to run much risk'.[12]

While the privateering fleets were discriminating in their focus on vulnerable targets, their activities led to severe disorder and disruption in the Channel. They seized a large number of prizes, of which a significant proportion was brought into English ports and havens. De Spes' reports from London provide some indication of the heavy toll on trade and shipping. In January 1570 he informed Philip II that the corsairs had captured three Baltic ships bound from Flanders to Spain, in addition to two richly laden Venetian vessels which were taken to La Rochelle. During the following month he complained that the privateers, who were able to land without hindrance in England, had captured a Flemish ship, laden with fruit from Portugal, and a large vessel of Danzig, bound from London to Portugal. In April he reported that the followers of Jacques de Sores had seized a ship laden with salt at Falmouth. The same group allegedly were daily bringing prizes into the Isle of Wight. There was a bustling trade in plundered cargoes on the island which drew on its long-standing importance as a pirate mart. One of the ambassador's agents described the maintenance of a 'great fair of spices, wines, wool, saffron, oil, soap, woad,' and other goods taken from the Spanish, Portuguese and French.[13]

The spoil of shipping continued during the summer and beyond, in the face of widespread complaint. In July three valuable vessels bound from Spain to Flanders were seized and subsequently fitted out, with two other prizes, as men-of-war to reinforce the privateers. Early in September they were 'capturing what they can', including a ship laden with wool from Santander, and disposing of the plunder in the Isle of Wight and other ports along the south coast.[14] Shortly thereafter, the privateers seized several Portuguese vessels laden with Spanish commodities which had run aground, in addition to a Biscayan ship carrying a cargo of wool and iron, captured off Le Conquet, where four other ships had taken refuge. The merchants of the Steelyard in London also complained to the council that their ships and goods were taken at sea and brought into the Isle of Wight as prizes.

In such circumstances de Spes warned that 'if ships continue to come freely in this way trade will simply be to enrich the heretics'.[15] The warning was reinforced by the seizure of six Flemish ships bound for Rouen by the Dutch captain, Schonvall, who had only recently been released from arrest in England because of his disorderly activities in the Channel. Although the council responded to Spanish complaints by issuing orders to prevent the disposal of the plunder in the Isle of Wight, and for the punishment of Schonvall and his associates, it failed to stop the continued pillage of Spanish or Flemish shipping. In December, moreover, French men-of-war were reported to be regularly bringing Spanish commodities into English ports. The plunder included a Flemish vessel laden with fish taken off Dover. At the end of the month the council was investigating further complaints that several vessels belonging to the subjects of the King of Spain had been brought into Colchester. Among the booty was a substantial haul of money which was brought to London, where efforts to recover it by Admiralty officials were frustrated by city officers concerned to defend their jurisdiction against a rival authority. In the face of such activity, de Spes gloomily concluded that 'they are so used to robbing now that it will be very difficult to teach them honesty again'.[16]

Although much of this spoil was concentrated in the Channel, it spread to exposed regions along the coasts of Spain and Portugal. In November 1571 the harbours of Vigo and Bayonne were described as 'the regular refuge and shelter of the pirates as there is nothing there to resist them'.[17] Two men-of-war, the *Printemps* of La Rochelle and the *Castle of Comfort*, an English vessel, had recently sought refuge at Bayonne with a Portuguese prize, taken off the Canary Islands.

The following year, in July 1572, three ships-of-war were fitted out in London for a voyage towards the Spanish coast, particularly Cape St Vincent.

While the evidence is patchy and vague, it is possible that several hundred vessels were seized by the privateers and brought into England during the early 1570s. Undoubtedly many of these prizes were small trading or fishing craft of Flemish or French origin. But a significant number of richer Iberian and Flemish vessels, as well as ships from Italian and Hanseatic ports which were allegedly carrying Spanish or French commodities, were also taken. A steady flow of booty was thus brought into England by the privateers, laying the basis for a flourishing, if clandestine, trade in prize goods in markets along the coast of the south and south-west. De Spes claimed in August 1571 that the plunder from the privateers enriched Dover, the Isle of Wight and other regions along the coast.[18]

Some part of these goods was dispersed as gifts and perquisites to procure the support of courtiers and local officials. Châtillon, for example, marked his departure from the Queen's court in October 1570 with banquets and gifts, paid for out of the proceeds from the privateers. However, a greater part of the booty was disposed of in provincial markets along the coast. These prize marts operated through a combination of exchange and commerce, occasionally at night, and usually to the advantage of buyers who were in a position to acquire plundered commodities at cheap rates. A cargo of cloth brought by French rovers into Tor Bay during September 1571 was worth more than 60,000 crowns, but it was reported that 'they cannot get more than twelve thousand crowns offered for it'.[19]

Although the booming trade in plunder was short lived and localized, it provided some compensation for the disruption to the Spanish and Flemish trades, at least in providing an alternative source for imports. De Spes commented on the demand for Spanish goods among English traders towards the end of 1570, though he noted also that they 'get a sufficient quantity of goods from Andalucia which the pirates steal and bring hither'.[20] While the trade in plunder did not replace commerce with either Spain or the Low Countries, which represented a loss to English customs duties of about 6 per cent, it was on such a scale as to provide a powerful economic incentive to support and shelter the privateers, though it was qualified by retaliatory seizures by the French and Spanish. At the same time, the economic benefits were offset by the damage to England's overseas relations. The activities of the privateers provoked complaints from Spain, France and Flanders, as well as from members of the Hanseatic ports whose trade with the Iberian peninsula was vulnerable to attack. International complaints met with a mixed response in England, although the Queen's sympathy for the privateers was eroded by the gradual improvement in Anglo-Spanish relations

De Spes' reports to Philip II nonetheless presented an unfavourable picture of widespread connivance and collusion with the privateers or pirates, as he insisted on describing them. Their supporters included leading members of the regime. Leicester, for example, was dismissed as a 'light and greedy man who maintains the robbers and lives by their plunder'.[21] The ambassador pursued Spanish and Flemish grievances with the Queen, her council and the High Court of Admiralty, but with varying results. In January 1571 the council ordered the arrest of two Dutch warships which had taken several vessels in the River Meuse, in response to his complaints, with a promise that they would be restored to their owners. In 'the meanwhile', however, he reported that the 'other pirates go on robbing, and very little can be done towards punishing them or recovering their booty'. Although Cecil offered in February to send out two of the Queen's ships against pirates, it was on condition that the merchants of Antwerp contributed to the charge of fitting them out. Several weeks later, the Queen cut short a meeting with one of Alva's representatives from the Low Countries with a 'sort of joke about the pirates; remarking that, as they did not speak English, it was no business of hers to correct them'.

Yet the regime was already adopting a tougher line with the privateers and their supporters in England. In March 1571 Elizabeth took action to prevent the spread of disorder along the coast. This included a warning that 'no pirate of whatsoever nation shall enter any of her ports or the Downs, under penalty of losing the ship which he brings, and imprisonment for himself'.[22] The warning appears to have been particularly intended for the privateers who congregated off the south-east coast, making use of temporary bases and havens in Kent and Essex. Later in the year Frobisher was sent out with four naval vessels, in a more direct attempt to limit the activities of the privateers. Furthermore, during October de Spes reported that the Queen had appointed commissioners to assist in the recovery of plunder which was claimed by merchants and shippers of Hamburg. Indeed, the commissioners arrested some of the privateers and purchasers of their booty in Dover, though de Spes claimed that the former continued to be secretly supplied with provisions. The response of the regime culminated in March 1572 with a proclamation expelling the privateers and sea rovers from English ports. The Queen's subjects were warned that they faced the death penalty if they continued to serve with the privateering fleets.

The actions of the regime had unforeseen consequences for the sea beggars who returned to the Low Countries, seizing Brill in April 1572. Thereafter they acquired bases in Holland and Zeeland, including Flushing, from which they continued their privateering war against Spain. Their sea raiding soon included attacks on neutral and friendly shipping. By June 1573 it was reported that they spared no one they met with, including the English, though three recently captured prizes were released. Their underlying political purpose was underlined by reports that they had taken to wearing the 'device of the crescent' on their clothing, as a sign that 'they would rather turn Turks than abandon' the struggle with Spain.[23] By contrast the maritime activities of the Huguenots, from their base at La Rochelle, were seriously weakened by the massacre of French Protestants on St Bartholomew's day in Paris and the provinces. While the English remained sympathetic to the Protestant cause in France and the

Low Countries, increasingly it was tempered by the diplomatic and defensive concerns of the regime.

Following the restoration of Anglo-Spanish relations and the revival of trade with Spain and Flanders, Dutch and French privateers were in danger of becoming an unwelcome presence in English ports and waters. Even so, the Channel remained infested with Dutch, French and English rovers, many of whom sailed with commissions from William of Orange. Nor was the Queen's Navy able to prevent fleets of privateers from occasionally visiting English harbours either for provision or plunder. When the French ambassador complained to Elizabeth in January 1573 about the continued support for the Huguenots, reportedly she replied 'that as they belonged to the same religion as she did, she could not close her country to them. The sea, she said, was their hunting ground, but if they brought any property of French subjects to her country she would order its restitution'.[24] The seizure of nine French vessels by a group of privateers off the Isle of Wight reinforced the complaints of the ambassador. French concern was inflamed by the arrival in English waters of a fleet of twenty or twenty-two men-of-war from La Rochelle. It soon became the focus for rumours of a relief expedition to the French port under the command of the Duke of Montgomery, one of the Huguenot leaders who escaped to Guernsey after the massacre of St Bartholomew, with the support of maritime adventurers in the south-west, including Hawkins.[25]

The continued threat to shipping was dramatically demonstrated by a piratical attack on a ship carrying the Earl of Worcester across the Channel, to represent the Queen at the christening of the daughter of Charles IX. Worcester was saved by the skill of the master and his company, but an accompanying vessel, with a party of gentlemen aboard, was captured. Four of the company were killed and six or seven wounded, while the gentlemen were robbed of their clothes, jewellery and £500 in cash. According to intelligence sent to Alva from London, the attack was carefully planned, if not 'specially ordered'.[26] It provoked a swift response. While the captain of the Isle of Wight took local action against the privateers and pirates, at sea seven men-of-war were seized by the Queen's vessels under the command of Captain William Holstock.

The support for the Huguenots in England, and the despatch of relief expeditions to La Rochelle, provoked angry complaint from Charles IX. The French claimed that between 1562 and 1573 they were spoiled of goods valued at nearly £30,000 by pirates and rovers based in England. During the summer of 1573, French suspicions were deepened by rumours of various plans for combined action at sea by the Huguenots and their Dutch and English associates. Following his return to the Isle of Wight with a fleet of privateers and several prizes, Montgomery met a representative from William of Orange, reputedly to consider an expedition to relieve the Dutch port of Haarlem. The suspicions of the Catholic party in France, regarding the intentions of the English, appeared to be confirmed in the spring of 1574 when Montgomery invaded Normandy from

Guernsey, in an unsuccessful attempt to raise a rebellion, though Elizabeth denied all knowledge of it.[27]

English depredation was heavily overshadowed by the activities of the Dutch and French privateering fleets within the Channel, but it did not disappear from local waters. While significant numbers of English recruits served with the privateers, pirate ships continued to operate, under conditions, moreover, which deepened the confusion between lawful and unlawful plunder. This was especially the case with those adventurers who acquired foreign commissions, usually against Spain, though the practice was of uncertain legality and met with mixed responses from the regime. Claiming losses against the Spanish in the Low Countries, George Fenner sailed with a commission from William of Orange during the early 1570s. Armed with such authority, he seized a fleet of merchant vessels returning to Flanders from Portugal, laden with salt and bullion, after a running conflict which lasted for two days. The captured vessels were brought into Falmouth during October 1572. At the request of Cecil, however, the legality of the seizures was referred to a group of leading civil lawyers, who reported in November that they should be restored to their owners. Yet this failed to deter the activities of aggressive adventurers, like Fenner, who disposed of plunder overseas. Indeed, Fenner went on to raid the Spanish harbour of Munguia, thereafter sailing to the Azores where he captured several vessels returning from the Indies.[28]

Occasional reports and complaints to the council indicate that piracy and sea roving remained widely scattered and varied, ranging from indiscriminate pillage to the more selective spoil of Spanish and Flemish shipping. During July 1572 the council ordered the return of a Spanish vessel which had been taken and brought into Southampton by a ship of Bristol. It also instructed the Vice Admiral of Essex to arrest the pirate, Captain Blunt, and his company, who were reported to be near Harwich, after committing 'sundrie spoiles and robberies upon the seas against the Queen's ... subjects and others'.[29]

The volume of complaints increased during 1573 and 1574, compelling the council to intervene in various cases of disorderly spoil and plunder. During February 1573 it responded to requests from Sandwich and Dover for a commission for the trial of pirates, partly as a result of local concern at the expense of keeping large numbers of men in prison. The following month the captain of Camber Castle near Rye was ordered to confiscate several prizes brought in by French ships-of-war, although proceeds from the plunder were to be used to offset the charge of imprisoning the companies of the latter. During May and June the Lord Warden of the Cinque Ports was instructed to investigate French and Flemish complaints concerning recent outrages, including the spoil of a merchant of Antwerp at Winchilsea, while taking steps to suppress pirates and their supporters within his jurisdiction.[30]

Much of this was the untidy legacy of the presence of the privateering fleets in English waters, which overlapped with long-standing, localized piratical enterprise. French complaints in February 1573 of the number of English pirates allegedly haunting the coasts, without restraint, were confused with angry concern at the activities of Hawkins and others, who were supporting Huguenot adventurers on the Isle of Wight as well as supplying La Rochelle with provisions and munitions. French and Scottish traders also complained of the 'enormous interest they had to pay to certain brokers at Southampton, to redeem' their ships and cargoes taken by pirates.[31]

In the south-west the following year, the mayor of Dartmouth reported the activities of a group of rovers, 'committing robberies and piracies upon the coast, and having recourse to Torbaye'.[32] They included Captain John Cole who seized a Danzig vessel which was taken to the Isle of Wight. During February or March 1574 John Callice, one of the leading pirate leaders operating during the 1570s and early 1580s, captured a prize, the cargo of which was sold in Cardiff and Bristol. In April 1574 a representative of the King of Portugal complained to the council about the spoil of a ship laden with spices which were brought into Barnstaple. At the same time the bishop of Chichester warned of pirates along the coast of Sussex. Further reports of pirates and sea robbers frequenting the south coast were made by Viscount Howard of Bindon in June. In addition, sixteen ships were reported to be fitting out at Colchester for Zeeland, by a partnership of English, Dutch and French adventurers. Later in the year ten men-of-war of Flushing arrived at Rye, to await a fleet of Huguenot raiders from Calais and other French ports.[33]

Small-scale depredation spread from the Channel into the Irish and North Seas, where it was entangled with Scottish and Irish piracy. Scots pirates were operating in the Irish Sea during 1573. Several were arrested and imprisoned in Ireland, and subsequently dealt with according to a special commission issued by the Lord Deputy in Dublin. During June the Lord Deputy was ordered by the council to arrest two Irish pirates, following complaints of their seizure of several vessels laden with goods claimed by French, Flemish and German merchants.[34]

During the summer pirates and rovers were raiding in the North Sea between England and Scotland. Their targets included vessels from Holland and Zeeland. Cornelis Willemson, the master of one such ship, complained that he was taken and tortured by English pirates near Yarmouth. After being 'hanged until he was almost dead', Willemson was stripped naked and cast into the sea 'eight times tied with a rope and with stones at his legs … until they knew where his money was'.[35] In November the council ordered the arrest of pirates and other suspected persons operating along the coast of Suffolk. By early December one of the pirate leaders, Phipson, was under arrest in the castle at Norwich. Another captain suspected of piracy was taken in the following month. The sheriff of Norfolk was instructed to send both men to London, so that they could be examined by the judge of the High Court of Admiralty. In March 1574 the court issued a writ for the recovery of a French vessel taken by Richard Peacock of Scarborough. Its cargo of Spanish commodities was sold in

Yarmouth, Boston and other places along the coast. Peacock and his company were pursued by a French merchant, Jacques le Duc, who complained later that he 'was not only put in daunger of his lyfe, but also sume of the buyers [of the plunder] commenced an action of slaunder against him, so that he was constrained to relinquishe his … suite'.[36] In June the Scots complained of spoils committed by English pirates, some of whom haunted the Farne Islands, while others cruised off Scarborough and Flamborough Head.

The council responded to the disorder and violence along the east coast by authorizing the Lord Admiral to send out the Vice Admiral of Norfolk against the pirates. But a trading ship was plundered at sea, within sight of the Vice Admiral's fleet. In July 1574 the council issued instructions to the president of the Council in the North, and to officials in Berwick, for the prevention of piracy. They included orders for the arrest of pirates and for an inquiry into the receivers of their goods. The council was keen to ensure that Scottish victims received speedy restitution of any spoil by pirates, though its concern was partly designed to strengthen the claims of English merchants who were the victims of Scottish depredation.[37]

While it remained difficult to combat the threat from pirates who ranged along the east coast and into the North Sea, several rovers were apprehended in Scotland during 1574. In June the English ambassador in Edinburgh, Henry Killigrew, informed Cecil of the capture of Higgins and his company of

The cliffs at Flamborough Head, Yorkshire. This dramatic landmark along the east coast was a favourite haunt for pirates. In 1523 the Admiral or Vice Admiral of the North Sea was sent out to hunt down rovers operating off Flamborough. During the later 1580s a group of locally based pirates haunted the region, disposing of their booty in nearby Hilderthorpe. (Author's collection)

thirty-eight men at Caithness. According to Killigrew's report, Higgins was sailing with a licence from Sir Thomas Smith, though he added that it was 'time to restrain such, for they would make a pique where there is no need'.[38] The capture of Higgins was followed by the arrest of another rover, Robert Isted, a gentleman of Hastings, who was at Montrose with two prizes which were claimed by Flemish traders. Several of the rovers escaped, though at least fifteen remained in custody. They included Peter Fisher, a Scotsman, who admitted to various acts of piracy during the previous eight years. Isted claimed that his prizes were Spanish, and lawfully taken with a commission from William of Orange. In July, however, he and his company, with the exception of two boys who were handed over to Killigrew, were hanged in chains at Leith as an example and warning to others.[39]

Despite these successes, Scottish complaints against English piracy continued. Scottish vessels were spoiled, and their companies ill-treated, along the east coast. In August 1574 Killigrew warned that pirates were 'so openly maintained' by the

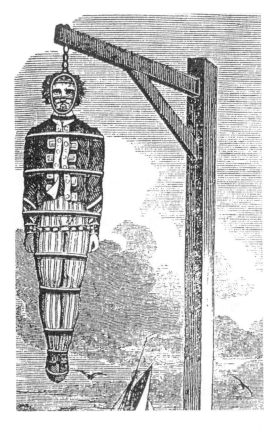

A pirate, William Kidd, hanging in chains at Tilbury in 1701. Pirates were hanged by the sea shore or at Wapping during the sixteenth century, sometimes in chains. The Steward's *Book of Southampton* records the payment of three shillings for making a chain, weighing twelve pounds, to hang the pirate, John Jones, during 1556. (*Pirates: A History*)

inhabitants of Berwick 'that it makes evil blood among them' in Edinburgh.[40] Later in the year the council faced further complaints against groups of rovers, led by Captains Hill and Hudson, who were bringing plundered wheat, rye and other commodities into the border town.

As this record demonstrates, the crisis at sea during the late 1560s and early 1570s was expressed in varied forms of depredation. Within the Channel the distinction between piracy and privateering was profoundly confused. In April 1574, according to report, the sea was so crowded with rovers and men-of-war that 'no ship will escape them, unless a remedy be devised'.[41] But the escalation in maritime violence and plunder, in part the result of wider political and religious divisions, was heavily focused on Spain. In England the lawlessness at sea served as a lightning rod for anti-Spanish enterprise, particularly among adventurers whose interests and ambitions were drawn westward. Within Spain there was mounting concern that the disorder and depredation threatened its Atlantic interests. Against a background of swirling rumours regarding the intentions of the Dutch and French privateering fleets, reports from London suggested that groups of adventurers, including Sir Richard Grenville, reputedly a 'great pirate', were involved in aggressive schemes for transatlantic raiding.[42] What made such reports so alarming was their appearance at a time when English piracy, under the leadership of Drake, had exposed serious weaknesses in an acutely vulnerable region of the Spanish Caribbean.

The pirate invasion of the Caribbean during the 1570s

The spread of piracy into the Caribbean during the 1570s was an ambitious expansion of English depredation. Superficially it was provoked by the clash at San Juan de Ulua in 1568, but its origins lay deeper in the troubled history of Anglo-Spanish relations which can be traced back to the 1540s. It was also related to the vulnerability of Spanish trade and settlements in the Caribbean, which French privateers and pirates were the first to exploit. As Drake's voyages indicate, the success of the English initially depended on cooperation with the French, as well as on the support of the cimaroons, runaway African slaves who had established autonomous communities beyond the jurisdiction of Spanish colonial authority. Their alliance with Drake had profound implications, though essentially it was based on a shared hostility towards the Spanish. In these circumstances English predatory incursions into the Caribbean initiated a small-scale, unofficial war for the riches of Spain's empire in America. Under the resourceful leadership of Drake, who adapted the tactics of pirates and rovers across the Atlantic, initially it met with surprising success in terms of plunder and profit, creating the conditions for a more sustained assault on the region.[43]

The outburst of marauding in the Caribbean by the English, between 1570 and 1574, involved at least ten separate ventures, about half of which were organized by Hawkins and his associates. Thereafter the number declined. From 1574 until the outbreak of the Anglo-Spanish war in 1585 evidence survives for four ventures.[44] The inability of English adventurers to capitalize on the success of Drake during the early 1570s reveals the difficulties in sustaining a transatlantic campaign of plunder under unfavourable political conditions. Yet this was an experimental phase of trial and error when English rovers opportunistically probed for areas of weakness, while acquiring the confidence and experience to survive in a new and hazardous environment.

Drake was in the forefront of English raiding in the Caribbean, though it was his later reputation which lent the expeditions of the early 1570s their allure. His self-image also demanded that these voyages were presented as legitimate revenge and reprisal. There is little doubt that he would have strenuously denied any accusation of piracy, despite his lack of a covering commission. His three voyages into the Caribbean during these years have the appearance of small, speculative ventures which at first may have combined trading with raiding. They occurred at a time when the number of French and Dutch pirates or privateers was increasing. Among the Dutch, rovers from Flushing claimed to be the subjects of the Prince of Orange, operating under his command. Spanish reports suggest that English activity was initially overshadowed by other Europeans. Although the English soon came to play a prominent role in Caribbean plunder, it was probably based on close coordination with Huguenot raiders.[45]

In the aftermath of Hawkins' last slaving voyage, Drake was involved in two poorly recorded voyages to the Caribbean, in 1569 and 1571. In the first he sailed with two small ships owned by William Hawkins, possibly with the intention of combining trade and plunder. During 1571 he appears to have sailed as part of a small fleet of three vessels sent out by John Hawkins in partnership with William Winter and his brother, George. Drake was in command of the *Swan* of 25 tons, the company of which included Richard Dennys, a merchant of Exeter who was also one of the promoters of the venture. In consortship with a group of French rovers, and with the aid of an African guide, Drake raided the region around Rio Chagres near the Panama isthmus, an exposed and defenceless part of the Spanish Caribbean that was already a favourite haunt for pirates. He returned with a substantial haul of booty, raising ambitious expectations among his supporters for the success of another voyage.[46]

Drake's third and last expedition in this sequence amply fulfilled these expectations, but the outcome of the voyage lay in the balance until he gained the assistance of the cimaroons, and was reinforced by French adventurers led by Guillaume le Testu. Drake set out from Plymouth in May 1572 with two vessels, the *Pascha* of 70 tons and the *Swan* of 25 tons, and a company of seventy-three men and boys, including his brothers, John and Joseph. The *Pascha* also carried three pinnaces, ready to be assembled across the Atlantic, for use along coasts and rivers. Returning to familiar territory, Drake and his men constructed a fort at Port Pheasant, a secure harbour with good resources of fish and game. Though

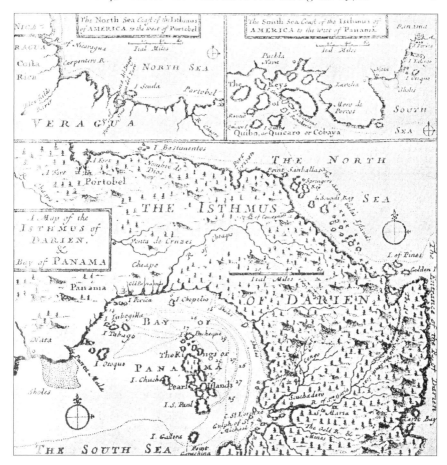

The isthmus region of Central America, from a map of 1705. Long a focal point for pirates and rovers, it was here that Drake raided the mule train in 1572, with the support of the cimaroons and a group of French rovers. (*Buccaneers of the Pacific*)

intended as a temporary base for raiding, it was the first English habitation in America; it included thatched buildings and a small shipyard.[47]

The arrival of James Ranse with a company of thirty men, in a vessel owned by Sir Edward Horsey, captain of the Isle of Wight, strengthened the English presence in the region. Led by Drake, a combined force attacked Nombre de Dios in a pre-dawn raid, but it was misjudged and based on poor intelligence. Although Drake tried to rally his discontented men, claiming to have 'brought them to the mouth of the treasure of the world', the attack was abandoned with one fatality and many wounded.[48] A Portuguese account by Lopez Vaz, subsequently published by Richard Hakluyt, presented an unflattering portrait of fearful English pirates who fled in the face of limited Spanish resistance, abandoning their equipment and stripping off their hose to escape aboard their pinnaces.

Central America, from a map of 1705. During the second half of the sixteenth century the Spanish Caribbean became a theatre for piracy, irregular warfare and commerce. English privateers visited the region in large numbers during the war with Spain from 1585 to 1603. During its closing stages a growing number of raiders combined plunder with trade, and occasionally logwood cutting. (*Buccaneers of the Pacific*)

Following Ranse's departure after the failed raid on Nombre de Dios, Drake reconnoitred the coast of the Spanish Main as far as Cartagena, taking several small vessels. Ashore he kept his company busy with a schedule of work and recreation, which included the construction of a building for meetings, a visible projection of the cooperation, consent and community that deep-sea pirate leaders tried to promote. The English traded with the local Indians for provisions, from whom they received gifts of fruit and bows and arrows, as well as information regarding Spanish activity. Contact was established with the cimaroons, who indicated their willingness to aid Drake. According to the account of Vaz, it was the cimaroons who informed Drake of the mule trains which crossed from Panama to Nombre de Dios laden with silver and gold.

But time appeared to be running out for the pirates. Later in the year they heard alarming reports that Spanish frigates, manned with Indians armed with poisoned arrows, had been sent to hunt them down. During November, moreover, the company was ravaged by sickness. Many died of fever within two or three days. The death toll was devastating. By the end of the year Drake's company was reduced to about thirty men. Among the fatalities were his brothers: one was killed in a skirmish with the Spanish, the other died from sickness.

In these difficult circumstances, the support of the cimaroons became crucial. While providing Drake and his men with vital provisions and intelligence about the Spanish, they reinforced the depleted and demoralized company with experienced warriors and guides, who taught the English to live off the land. Without their assistance it is difficult to see how the raid across the isthmus could have gone ahead. During a visit to a cimaroon settlement Drake heard a detailed account of their conflict with the Spanish, who 'they kil like beasts, as often as they take them in the woods'.[49] News of one cimaroon leader, who was reportedly capable of sending out 1,700 fighting men, reinforced Drake's determination to establish closer relations with these rebels against Spanish colonial authority. According to a later account of the expedition by Philip Nichols, a clergyman, published in 1628, which 'was reviewed by ... Drake ... before his death', this included attempts to convert the cimaroons to Protestantism. Although they lacked priests, evidently 'they held the crosse in great reputation'. At Drake's persuasion, 'they were contented to leave their crosses, and to learne the Lords prayer, and to be instructed in some measure concerning Gods true worship'.[50]

Even with the support of the cimaroons, the first attempt to seize the mule train failed. At this stage the English were reinforced by the arrival of le Testu with news of events in Europe, including the massacre of the Huguenots in France. The French agreed to join Drake and the cimaroons in another attack. It was spectacularly successful. The raiders seized as much gold as they could carry, though they were forced to bury the silver, most of which the Spanish later recovered. Spanish officials estimated their losses at more than 80,000 pesos in gold. Once the plunder had been divided Drake returned for England. Before leaving he exchanged gifts with the cimaroons, who appear to have expected him to return in the future. The expedition arrived back in Plymouth on Sunday 9 August 1573. After it entered the harbour, during 'sermon-time', the church emptied as the congregation flocked to 'see the evidence of ... our captains labour and successe'.[51]

Drake's raid on the isthmus was more than piracy or outlawry. The alliance with the French, acknowledged with an exchange of gifts, appeared to represent an extension of the predatory reach of international Protestantism which envisioned a godly war across the globe against the forces of Catholicism. At the same time the alliance with the cimaroons cast pirate leaders, and some former slavers, in the role of freedom fighters who were prepared to support rebellious slave communities in guerrilla warfare against Spain.

For Spanish colonial officials the league between the English and the cimaroons was a shocking and dangerous development which provoked widespread alarm. According to one stark warning of May 1573, if Nombre de Dios was taken by the English, Panama would be 'theirs as easily as the words are said', because of the rumoured support of 2,000 cimaroons.[52] If this happened, furthermore, 'they have the means to settle along the Pacific and build ships outside Panama'. Among the Spanish, piracy was confused with the threat of English expansion. Officials urged Philip II to take action to prevent future raids and to forestall the possibility of pirate settlement, by stationing galleys along the coast. Against a background of prolonged French raiding, Drake's incursion appeared to be part of a concerted campaign that threatened to drain Spanish America of its wealth. In November 1573 representatives from Nombre de Dios complained of the loss of gold and silver during the previous seven years, reputedly worth two million pesos, and of the deaths of more than three hundred people on land and at sea.[53]

Despite these alarming reports, English pirates and rovers were unable to build on Drake's success in 1573. Revealingly, Drake did not return to the Caribbean until 1586. Pirates continued to sail thence during the 1570s, but the successors of Drake met with mixed success. In 1574 a pirate group, led by John Noble, pillaged various vessels along the coast of Nombre de Dios. However, the pirates were captured and executed, except for two boys who were sentenced to servitude in the galleys for the rest of their lives. Early in January 1575 another group of rovers, led by Gilbert Horsley, joined forces with French corsairs in an expedition up the San Juan River, in Nicaragua, daringly seeking to sack weakly defended settlements in the interior. Though the Spanish were taken by surprise, the pirates retreated after encountering and spoiling several vessels sailing downstream to Veragua. Horsley and his company of twenty-five men, who included a Portuguese pilot, plundered the vulnerable coasting traffic, reportedly torturing various passengers either for money or information, though they withdrew to avoid clashing with stronger vessels.[54]

There may have been a brief upsurge in pirate activity, both English and French, during 1576 and 1577. In March 1577 five pirate ships were cruising off Veragua, the smallest of which was manned with eighty men. By April the number had increased to sixteen sail, 'all out with the intention to sack these cities of the Main, and cross to the Pacific'.[55] But the English expeditions expose the underlying limitations of this early wave of Caribbean depredation, while indicating its appeal for leading members of the regime. During the summer of 1576 Andrew Barker, a merchant of Bristol who claimed to be seeking compensation for losses sustained in the Canary Islands, set forth with a small expedition, made up of the *Ragged Staff* and the *Bear*, the promoters of which included Leicester. It was a quarrelsome, mutinous and unsuccessful voyage. Barker captured a number of vessels off Trinidad and along the coast of the Main, allegedly throwing the crew of one ship overboard. The prizes included a ship laden with gold, silver and emeralds, valued at £500. Among the passengers was a friar who had an emerald, set in gold, hidden around his thigh. Growing discontent among Barker's men exploded in mutiny off the island of La Guanaja. Barker and several others were forced ashore, where they were surprised and killed by the Spanish. Their heads and one hand were subsequently displayed as war trophies before the municipal authorities of Trujillo. The survivors went on to raid the neighbouring island of Ruatan, seizing several small vessels in which they set sail for England. The shipwreck of one of the vessels off Cuba persuaded the company to return to the Honduran coast, where several were captured and later executed by the Spanish. A number returned to Plymouth during 1578, and were arrested to stand trial as accessories to the death of Barker. According to Hakluyt's account of the voyage, the ring leaders received lengthy prison sentences, while some of the others 'shortly after came to miserable ends'.[56]

The expedition led by John Oxenham, who was with Drake in 1572, was more ambitious in scope, though much less successful in outcome. Oxenham left England during April 1576 in command of a vessel of 100 tons and a company of fifty-seven men, with the intention of trading with the cimaroons for gold and silver. In reality this was a pirate voyage which drew on Drake's earlier experience. Shortly after arriving in the Caribbean, Oxenham established contact with the cimaroons, who were keen to know 'if captain Francis was among them'.[57] Oxenham's company spent the winter at the cimaroon settlement of Vallano, during which time they constructed a pinnace for raiding in the Pacific. The following year, in February 1577, with a company of about fifty men, which was reinforced by nine or ten cimaroon leaders, the English raided the Pearl Islands off Panama. The attack caught the Spanish completely by surprise, confirming the fears of colonial officials about the security of the coastal trade between Panama and Peru.

Oxenham's success at the Pearl Islands was striking, but short lived. Spanish reports indicate that the raiders carried off a substantial haul of plunder, including gold, silver and pearls, as well as seventy slaves who were handed over to the cimaroons. It was accompanied by a furious outbreak of iconoclastic violence, with the destruction of images and crucifixes, and the public assault and humiliation of a friar, who was forced to wear a chamber pot on his head. In another powerful example of symbolic violence, a Spanish colonist had an iron collar placed around his neck by one of the cimaroons. The raid on the Pearl Islands was followed by the seizure of a rich vessel laden with gold and other commodities off Guayaquil.[58]

The Spanish responded by sending out expeditions to hunt down the pirates, while launching raids against cimaroon settlements. During the six months following the raid much of the booty was recovered. Oxenham's company dispersed, suffering heavy casualties at the hands of the Spanish. The ferocity of this campaign appears to have weakened support for the English among the cimaroons. Oxenham later claimed that they blamed the English for their ruin, and consequently treated them badly. Spanish hostility was intensified by rumours of increasing pirate violence across the Main. This 'new development', according to one Spanish report, included the castration of two Franciscan friars.[59] By October 1577 Oxenham and seven members of his company had been captured. More were rounded up later in the year, though a small group managed to escape, possibly returning to England. Oxenham and his principal officers were subsequently taken to Lima and executed in November 1580.

For the Spanish, the spread of English raiding into the Pacific starkly demonstrated the dangers to colonial commerce and settlement from small-scale provincial adventurers, who seemed to be capable of promoting piratical ventures with little check from the regime. Oxenham informed the Spanish that 'no licence or permission of anybody was necessary, for these and more can depart out of England without there being required more licence than their will to go'.[60]

However, Oxenham's voyage came at a time when English depredation in the Caribbean was losing momentum. In part this was the result of the inherent dangers and difficulties of transatlantic plunder. These grew progressively worse as Spain improved its defence of the isthmus region, helped by the failure of the English alliance with the cimaroons to develop. At the same time an unfavourable political and diplomatic environment in England weakened support for a direct assault on Spain's colonial possessions in America, though the Queen's interest in more indirect and discrete activity was demonstrated by her support for Drake's voyage of 1577. Furthermore, the seafaring infrastructure appeared to be ill-suited for sustained predatory venturing across the Atlantic, particularly as piracy and sea roving were flourishing in the seas around the British Isles. Most of the piratical ventures into the Caribbean during the 1570s were undertaken by small-scale, marginal operators from provincial bases in the south-west, who were unable or unwilling to bear the hazards of a dangerous and mercenary business.

Nonetheless, this introductory phase of Caribbean piracy was a formative experience for the English, during which traditional tactics, practices and forms of organization were tested under new and challenging conditions. Secrecy, subterfuge and surprise remained essential characteristics of piratical enterprise, though when opportunity arose they could be accompanied by displays of bold theatricality. As 'becomes their calling', noted one Spanish official about Drake's attack on the mule train, 'they did not arrive by the public entrance'.[61] If surprise failed, the raiders would often withdraw, for fear of sustaining heavy casualties. On occasion pirates might herald their arrival with a trumpet call or appear with their faces daubed with charcoal and red dye. Much of their raiding was concentrated in the south-west corner of the Caribbean, around a key strategic and commercial region, though some pirate groups ranged further along the coast of the Main or cruised off the more accessible islands. In small, fast-sailing vessels, and armed with a variety of hand weapons, they raided along coasts, lying in wait around capes and headlands, while reconnoitring river systems with the assistance of local guides. In this way they played a part in the unintended and unrecorded exploration of the Caribbean, the results of which may have been widely shared, becoming part of an oral culture and inheritance that circulated among pirate bands as part of a rudimentary survival kit.

Caribbean depredation rapidly developed its own rhythm and mode of operation that newcomers were able to imitate or adapt. By 1569 French rovers had developed the practice of following fleets from Spain, awaiting an opportunity to pick off stray vessels. Geographical conditions enabled pirate groups to use small offshore islands or secure coastal areas as temporary bases, providing the English with their first real experiences of life in the New World. These habitations developed varying degrees of contact with the cimaroons and to a lesser extent with Indian groups, enabling pirates to develop tactics for raiding on land and at sea during extended stays in the Caribbean.[62]

In varying ways the pirate invasion of the isthmus region during the early 1570s depended on these cross-cultural relationships. For the cimaroons, whose war against the Spanish included night-time raids on settlements, such as Nombre de Dios, the arrival of the pirates created a potentially powerful force of allies who shared a common purpose in the acquisition of booty. In May 1573 Spanish officials in Panama reported that the cimaroons 'advertise that they have allied and confederated themselves with the English and French to destroy this realm, a thing not until this year ever seen or imagined'.[63] Yet Spanish reports also present a complex picture of relations between the English and the cimaroons which may reflect the uncertainty of short-term relations that were both local and trans-atlantic in character.

During the early 1570s the Spanish were alarmed that the cimaroons would teach English pirates the 'methods and means to accomplish any evil design they may wish to carry out and execute'.[64] Several years later, as colonial authorities sent out expeditions to attack their settlements, they were equally concerned that the cimaroons were trained by the English in military tactics. Under the leadership of men such as Juan Vaquero or Anton Mandinga, the cimaroons supported pirate groups in exchange for a share of their plunder, including supplies of wine and linen. In some circumstances, as the experience of Drake suggests, groups of cimaroons may have undergone a form of conversion. According to Spanish reports, the group who assisted Oxenham in the attack on the Pearl Islands were instructed in the doctrine of Lutheranism. When one of Oxenham's men danced about wearing an alb, so delighted were the cima-roons that they uttered 'I, English; pure Lutheran'.[65] But the depth and extent of these conversions were problematic. In addition, the loyalty of the cimaroons to the English was stretched by the successes of Spanish military expeditions during the later 1570s. Many were reported to be unhappy with Mandinga for helping the survivors of Oxenham's company. By 1579 several cimaroon com-munities were ready to make peace with the Spanish in exchange for written guarantees of their freedom. As a result Mandinga moved to the north coast to await the English, who he expected to return in greater numbers within two or three years. According to a statement by a cimaroon known as Pedro, 'a black flag was the signal agreed upon between them, to be made from the sea, that they might be recognized'.[66]

The use of the black flag, which subsequently became a powerful sign and symbol for pirates, raises intriguing questions about the social organization of English piracy in the Caribbean during these years. Although English pirates and rovers were not part of a deviant sub-culture, of the kind which was to emerge within transatlantic piracy during the second half of the seventeenth century, they did form a loose fraternity, based on similar backgrounds and shared experiences, which was the focus of growing recognition, if not admi-ration, in England. Within the Caribbean, piracy found expression in adaptable forms and patterns of behaviour which ranged from the pathologically cruel and violent to the humorous and teasing. Such conditions created fertile ground for the emergence of that radical egalitarianism which flourished

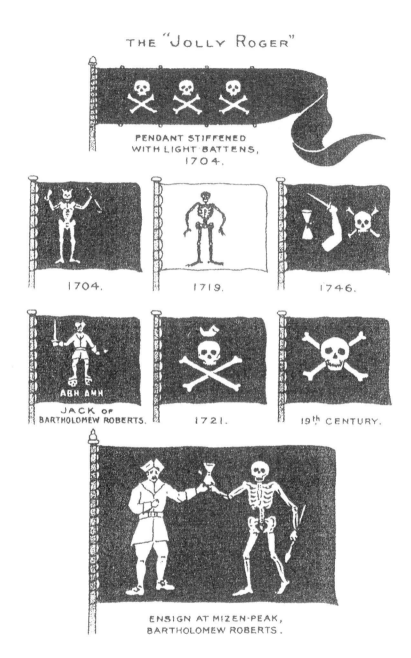

THE "JOLLY ROGER"

PENDANT STIFFENED
WITH LIGHT BATTENS,
1704.

1704.

1719.

1746.

JACK OF
BARTHOLOMEW ROBERTS.

1721.

19th CENTURY.

ENSIGN AT MIZEN-PEAK,
BARTHOLOMEW ROBERTS.

A selection of pirate flags from the early eighteenth century. Such menacing symbols were not used during the Tudor period, though the 'bloody flag' was used by men-of-war. In the Caribbean the black flag was used by some adventurers, including Drake. (*Pirates: A History*) among later pirate groups and communities, though its development during the 1570s was constrained by the modest scale and extent of piratical activity. While estimates for the number of English pirates operating in the Caribbean must be treated cautiously, particularly as they were part of a broader pattern of depredation which included temporary alliances with other European rovers, at its height it may have involved seven or eight vessels, manned with crews that ranged in number from about thirty to eighty men and boys, giving an overall total of between 210 and 560 recruits.[67] In some years the total may have been considerably less.

Many pirates, including leaders such as Drake, were young men from seafaring backgrounds. A significant proportion probably came from the maritime communities of south-west England, including Plymouth and Bristol and their wider hinterlands, though pirate companies undoubtedly were complemented by migratory recruits whose residence was either casual or temporary in nature. During his examination by Spanish officials, Oxenham admitted that his company of fifty Englishmen included 'many youths and seamen, and second class seamen not fit for war'.[68] Of the company of seventy-three men and boys who left Plymouth with Drake in May 1572, the eldest was aged fifty, the rest were under thirty.

Although the crews of pirate ships seem to have been predominantly English in origin, they included a handful of recruits from more diverse backgrounds. Among Andrew Barker's company there were at least three Frenchmen, in addition to a Dutchman and Philip, a Welshman. One of Oxenham's leading officers was an Irishman, John Butler, known as Chalona to the Spanish, who had lengthy experience of living in the Indies which enabled him to serve as an interpreter for the expedition. Among Oxenham's company Chalona was described by a Spanish official as the 'principal corsair of all, and the one, it is understood, who induced them to come to these parts, and led them into the bush'.[69] Spanish reports indicate that Chalona spoke with a Portuguese accent, possibly to conceal his real identity.

Little is known of recruitment to pirate ships, or the terms and conditions under which recruits served. Oxenham stated that he bought a vessel, 'and with his men he came to an understanding and signed them on for the voyage', though he failed to elaborate on its nature. Drake's company of 1572 were described as 'all voluntarily assembled … [and] richly furnished, with victualles and apparel for a whole yeare'.[70] As was customary among pirates or privateers sailing in European waters, these men served for a share in the plunder taken during the course of the voyage rather than for a wage. It was this prospect, of sharing in a rich prize laden with gold, silver, pearls and other valuable commodities, which lured young men into the Caribbean, despite the dangers of disease or death at the hands of the Spanish.

Evidence for the operation of this system is provided by the papers of Captain Barker, which were seized by the Spanish. They included several sheets described as a true note of all the gold, silver and jewels that were shared among the company.[71] Individual rewards were based on an allocation of shares. Accordingly, the captain and master were allotted eight and seven shares, the officers and surgeons were allocated four, the ordinary sailors were granted two or three, while the two boys were to receive a half-share each. A company of soldiers were awarded individual shares ranging from one to four.

The division of the plunder was undertaken by five representatives of the company, made up of the quartermasters and one of the boatswains, who were nominated or elected for that purpose. This system managed to present an image of cooperation and community, among a group of men who shared the dangers and rewards of the voyage, while reaffirming the traditional hierarchy of shipboard life. But the division of booty could be the source of festering suspicion and discontent. It may have been a serious issue among Barker's crew, contributing to the mutiny off La Guanaja in 1577. After the captain's death, a gold chain was found in his chest which was divided among the surviving members of the crew. In one of the earliest recorded notices of a practice that was to become commonplace among pirate crews operating in the Caribbean, Barker's company also made provision for the allocation of shares for members of the company who died during the voyage.[72]

Although the practice of dividing plunder along an agreed or recognized system of shares was partly intended to promote harmony among unruly, potentially uncontrollable, groups of aggressive young men, it was possibly underpinned by popular and radical, though ultimately self-serving attitudes towards property and wealth. According to Spanish evidence, during the course of Oxenham's raid on the Pearl Islands some of the company found a child's school book which was read out by Chalona, enabling him to reinterpret one of the Ten Commandments in a revealing manner. Thus when 'he came to the commandment: Thou shalt not steal, he laughed loudly at it, and said that all goods were common property; and all of them laughed and jeered at the commandments and remarked that one was missing, for there should be eleven commandments'.[73]

But the vision of good fellowship and commonalty, which the social organization of piracy was partly intended to promote, was difficult to realize in the Caribbean. Later accounts might portray the pirates, especially Drake and his men, as a community of gallants, but their conduct and lack of self-regulation points more towards a fraternity of angry and aggressive youths and young men, whose hatred of Catholicism and hostility towards Spain served to justify intimidation, terror and gratuitous violence. This was an ill-disciplined, irregular force that was difficult to control. During 1572 Drake faced mutterings of discontent against his leadership, though he was prepared to consult with his men, even to the extent of constructing a building for that purpose.[74] Other pirate leaders faced more overt challenges to their authority and leadership. Even during this early stage of English transatlantic piracy, therefore, it appeared to contain the seeds of its own fragmentation and dissolution.

By the later 1570s it seemed to some observers that the Spanish were winning the war against piracy in the Caribbean. According to Lopez Vaz the provision of two galleys along the coast of the Main had an almost immediate effect on improving the defence of the region, with the seizure of six or seven French ships during their first year of service. Once 'this was knowen', indeed, 'there were no more Englishmen or Frenchmen of warre that durst adventure to approach the coast', until Drake returned under very different conditions in 1586.[75]

The challenge of overseas privateering and piracy

The faltering development of English depredation in the Caribbean contrasted with the underlying strength of piracy and other forms of plunder across the Atlantic, though a subtle shift in focus appears to have been in progress during the mid-1570s. In the face of repeated provocation, the spoil of English shipping by foreign privateers or pirates became a serious problem, arousing widespread anger which did little to weaken support for localized piracy or sea roving, particularly by adventurers who portrayed their activities as unofficial retaliation or reprisals against overseas attack. At the same time the growing practice of English adventurers serving with foreign commissions or men-of-war presented the regime with a potentially dangerous and divisive problem.

Despite the restoration of trading relations with Spain and Portugal, and a treaty with France designed to improve Anglo-French trade, the revival of English overseas commerce, especially with the Low Countries, was severely disrupted by the activities of men-of-war operating from Flushing, Dunkirk, La Rochelle and the Channel ports of France. In January 1575 warships from Flushing seized an English ship bound for Ostend, laden with a cargo of cloth, which was justified as a necessity of war, 'without any intention of injuring the English'.[76] Following further attacks on shipping, in June the Queen sent a mission, led by Daniel Rogers, to the rebel leader, William of Orange, remonstrating against the activities of Flushing privateers in English waters. Rogers' purpose was not only to complain of the disruption to trade, but also about the damage to the Queen's honour. In September he provided a report on his attempts to secure the restitution of English plunder in the Low Countries, which included the spoil of vessels sailing along the coast between Rye and Dover as well as from London to Weymouth.

Furthermore, English shipping was exposed to attack by French men-of-war. Negotiations for an Anglo-French commercial treaty during 1575 were threatened by the grievances of English merchants who were the victims of French depredation, for which it was claimed that they were unable to obtain redress. The French countered with their own complaints, and a request that Elizabeth send out ships to suppress rebel pirates or rovers, serving under commissions issued by Huguenot leaders, who were operating in English waters. Although draft articles for the treaty contained provision for the abolition of the use of letters of reprisal, in June 1575 the Queen was reported to have granted commissions against France, in response to the continued plunder of English merchants. The companies of French men-of-war also faced arrest and legal action in England. During August members of the company of the *Crescent* of La Rochelle were indicted before a court held in Padstow, for unlawfully attacking a ship of the Isle of Man. More Frenchmen were detained for piracy during September. Others, who were condemned for piracy in October, were executed.[77]

While the Queen and her councillors resorted to diplomacy to try and recover English vessels and cargoes taken by foreign privateers and rovers, the activities of the French in particular provoked unofficial retaliation which was easily confused with piracy. During 1575 William Michelot of St Malo was arrested, apparently as a reprisal action by Captain Courtenay of Dover. Although Michelot was released, he was subsequently apprehended at the suit of merchants of Chester, in retaliation for the spoil of two local ships by men-of-war from the French port. A ship of St Malo also was seized off Ireland by the *Castle of Comfort*, whose owners now included Hawkins. Such actions revived long-standing, cross-Channel rivalries, creating a breeding ground in which a younger generation of pirates and rovers, like John Callice, could flourish.[78]

The problem of overseas depredation was complicated by the practice of English recruits serving aboard Dutch, French and Flemish men-of-war. The regime was acutely concerned about the number of seamen and soldiers serving overseas in 'troublesome times of civil wars, some on the one side and some on the other', because of the divisive domestic and damaging international consequences.[79] Volunteers for Spanish service provoked particular concern. The adventurers who served at sea included William Cotton and Henry Carey, who were granted letters of marque or reprisal, in April 1575, by officials in Castile and Flanders. Both men were authorized to capture Dutch shipping; in addition, they were promised a bounty of six crowns for every rebel they seized. English prisoners in Spain were offered pardons on condition that they served aboard the vessels of Cotton and Carey. The Queen complained to the Spanish of the practice, claiming that the 'worst sort of her people … [were] secretly enticed on both parts to serve on the seas, under colour of which … most become common pirates'.[80] The dangers were underlined by the plunder of several ships off the coast of Essex by a man-of-war operating from Dunkirk in the service of the Spanish monarchy, and manned by Englishmen.

In an effort to suppress the practice, during October 1575 the Queen issued a proclamation prohibiting her subjects from serving overseas. The prohibition was justified by the increase in spoil and robbery in English ports, as a result of which 'a great number of … mariners and fishermen be turned from good subjects to appear rather to be pirates and sea rovers'.[81] English recruits employed by foreign princes, without licence from the Queen, were commanded to return home to their customary occupations or trades. Those who refused would be considered as rebels. Admiralty officers and local officials were instructed to apprehend and imprison anyone who ignored the proclamation. Office holders who failed to implement the instructions faced dismissal and severe punishment. These measures appeared draconian on paper. In practice they were probably unworkable, if only because they rested on a degree of local cooperation and administrative efficiency that was, at best, sporadic. In any case the regime lacked either the persuasive power or compulsive force to prevent volunteers from serving overseas, whether for mercenary or ideological motives.

The activities of a group of English adventurers who were engaged in privateering from Dunkirk provoked particular concern. One of the leading members of this group, William Cotton, was involved in sending out several English captains on voyages of reprisal. Cotton's associates included Richard Flodde and George Phipson, who was freed from arrest during 1576 after successfully clearing himself of charges of piracy. Complaints against Cotton's unnatural behaviour, in spoiling English vessels, were voiced during March 1576. But the rebellion in the Low Countries presented opportunities for predatory enterprise, in a godly cause, which Cotton and others eagerly exploited. William of Orange complained bitterly of English adventurers trading with Flanders, who subsequently acquired letters of reprisal, under false pretences, against the rebels. The activities of alienated and committed Catholics in the Low Countries had more dangerous implications. Thus, in January 1577, Cotton, a 'lewd and most horrible varlet', was portrayed as a supporter for setting up Mary, Queen of Scots, as a challenger to Elizabeth.[82]

Yet it was Dutch men-of-war or privateers which continued to inflict heavy damage on English commerce during 1576. In an early indication of subsequent inflammatory disputes over flag honour in the Channel, an English vessel was spoiled off Dover by four warships of Flushing, for refusing to strike its topsails. In April it was claimed that during the course of one month privateers from Flushing had taken thirty English ships. Burghley complained of the 'universal barbarism' of Dutchmen, who he dismissed as a 'rabble of common pirates, or worse, who make no difference whom they outrage'.[83] The plunder of English shipping provoked repeated complaints and demands for restitution, which included allegations of the use of gratuitous violence and torture by privateering companies serving under the authority of William of Orange.

In July 1576 Sir William Winter led a diplomatic mission to the Low Countries to complain of the activities of the privateers of Flushing, though it met with little success. William of Orange responded with Dutch grievances against the English. Later in the year, however, he acknowledged the damaging effects of the disorderly spoil by captains sailing with his commissions. The continued seizure of English ships by the Dutch, which were claimed as good prize allegedly on the grounds that they refused to strike their sails to William of Orange's vessels, thus aroused widespread complaint. In order to deal with such losses, in November the regime suggested that the Estates of Holland and Zeeland should provide insurance for English merchants against the spoil of their goods at sea.[84] Evidently the plunder of English shipping was on such a scale that the Estates were reluctant to accept an open-ended and potentially costly commitment.

The regime struggled unsuccessfully to combat the menace of overseas piracy and privateering, particularly when it involved the Dutch. Naval patrols were sent out in an effort to improve the security of the seas, but they met with mixed success, partly as a result of widespread sympathy for the rebel cause and a concern not to alienate William of Orange. In November 1575 the Queen instructed the Lord Admiral to send out two vessels to repress pirates and freebooters in the Channel. The following year, in March 1576, the Lord Admiral was directed to arrest ships of Flushing, in retaliation for the plunder of English vessels. The instructions for Captain Henry Palmer, who was sent out in May 1576 with a fleet of six vessels, indicate that an exception was made for privateers sailing with commissions issued by the Dutch leader. Later in the year William Holstock was sent out in command of three vessels, with instructions to scour the Channel and arrest all ships of Flushing, in response to their continued attacks on English shipping. The limitations of these and other measures adopted by the council during the summer were demonstrated by complaints that thirteen men-of-war from Flushing were in Tor Bay. Yet the reaction of the council to such reports was deeply ambivalent. To some extent, moreover, this reflected a wider ambivalence towards the Dutch and their rebellion against Spain, which might be detected in the complaints of London merchants against cowardly English mariners who surrendered with little or no resistance to privateers from Flushing. While the council insisted that the allegations were an 'infamous slander', it also warned that those accused of cowardice would be proceeded against as traitors.[85]

In the last resort, and with reluctance on the part of the Queen and Burghley, the regime authorized the issue of commissions of reprisal in retaliation for the plunder of English vessels by French or Dutch men-of-war. The number of such commissions was small and carefully controlled by the council. The recipients included Henry Jolliffe of the Isle of Wight, who was granted permission in September 1576 to send out shipping against a French pirate, Captain Gilliam, on condition that he provided bonds for good conduct at sea. Later in the month Richard Gooche received a commission for use against the ships of Flushing. In November Captain Burbaige was granted a licence to arrest vessels of Brest or Le Conquet.[86]

While the Queen complained of the activities of French raiders, however, she acknowledged that they were not pirates, but lawfully commissioned men-of-war. These circumstances may have reinforced a preference for diplomacy over the use of reprisals, although the Queen warned that if English property was not restored, she would be forced to issue letters of marque.[87] A similar concern to limit or avoid the issue of commissions for the plunder of overseas shipping was revealed during the negotiations with Portugal, in October 1576, for the restoration of diplomatic and commercial relations. By the terms of the ensuing treaty, both parties agreed to implement more effective measures for the suppression of piracy, while suspending the use of letters of marque or reprisal for three years.

Despite diplomacy and the threat of reprisals, English trade and shipping remained vulnerable to attack by Dutch, Flemish and French men-of-war. In April 1576 sea rovers from Newhaven reportedly were robbing all the English ships they met at sea. During the course of discussions in August 1577, concerning the French spoil of English shipping, Sir Amias Paulet, the recently appointed ambassador in Paris, claimed that 'for one pirate in England they had ten in France, and that … all their havens were full of rovers and thieves'.[88] Earlier in the month, the Queen sent out three vessels against pirates; nonetheless, several weeks later one of her representatives, Robert Beale, who was travelling to Germany on diplomatic business, was 'miserably spoiled by Flushingers and others, pretending to serve under the Prince of Condé'.[89] To the annoyance of the regime, French captains sailing with commissions issued by the Huguenot leader, Condé, continued to use the Isle of Wight as a temporary base for their privateering ventures.

The persistence of disorderly depredation became a source of mutual suspicion and discontent between England and France during the later 1570s. In January 1578 Walsingham expressed concern at the plunder of English ships, noting that it was an 'opening to a plain cause of hostility'.[90] One Exeter man, Richard Adern, whose case may have come to Walsingham's attention, was twice plundered by the French, while Henry Jolliffe claimed to have been spoiled six times by French rovers. The French responded with their own complaints, though they only served to provoke righteous indignation among the English. On being informed by the governor of Calais that a group of English adventurers had been captured and brought into the harbour, one of Paulet's servants replied, 'if they were pirates he would do well to have them hanged, and that he might be sure they would not be received in any port in England'.[91]

For Paulet the unregulated issue of letters of marque, which he described as 'next neighbours to open hostility', only served to encourage the plunder of English shipping by French rovers. But English complaints provoked a vicious circle of claim and counter-claim. The governor of Normandy insisted that 'for every crown which those under his government had taken from the English, the … [latter] had spoiled them of 500'.[92] Against this, Paulet estimated English losses at the hands of Norman rovers, during the two years from April 1576 to March 1578, at 33,000 crowns. The scale of the problem led to a suggestion for an Anglo-French fleet to be sent out to clear the seas of pirates, though it met with little enthusiasm on either side of the Channel. As a result, indiscriminate attacks on English shipping by French rovers continued. By July 1579 English losses at the hands of French pirates or privateers, since July 1562, were estimated at more than £70,000 in value.[93]

The threat from overseas predators during the mid-1570s diverted attention away from the persistence of domestic piracy within the waters around the British Isles. At the same time it provided favourable conditions for the maintenance of varied forms of localized depredation. While the plunder of English ship-ping provoked retaliation against the Spanish, French or Dutch, the disruption to commerce may have helped to swell the number of available recruits among unemployed seafarers. The prolonged lawlessness at sea in north-west Europe thus created an environment in which piracy, privateering and sea roving flour-ished under conditions of undeclared war. The inability of the Elizabethan regime to regulate or repress the disorder, and the opportunities available to aggressive adventurers, were reflected in the activities of men such as Captain Sawyer of Rye, who was sent out by the council on an intelligence-gathering mission to the coast of Spain in 1576, during which he spoiled a French vessel.[94] In these cir-cumstances the spread of English depredation into the Caribbean had profound implications for the future development of piracy and privateering, though in the short term it was the resurgence of local piratical enterprise, particularly in south-west England and Wales, which appeared more threatening.

The Profession of Piracy from the mid-1570s to 1585

The growing ambition of English pirates and sea rovers was strikingly demonstrated by the contrasting experiences of the period from the mid-1570s to the outbreak of the war with Spain in 1585. Localized piracy remained an endemic problem. Its prevalence and persistence encouraged a greater degree of organization among pirate groups under the leadership of professionalized rovers, such as John Callice or his associate Robert Hicks. Operating under uncertain, but favourable, international conditions, these pirates plundered a varied range of overseas shipping, usually in an opportunistic and haphazard manner. By contrast, deep-sea plunder was increasingly and insistently anti-Spanish in focus. The threat to Spain was alarmingly revealed by Drake's 'Famous Voyage' from 1577 to 1580, when he became the first Englishman to circumnavigate the globe. This remarkable expedition, which went ahead with covert support from the monarchy, indicated the immense riches to be had from oceanic plunder. Foreshadowing a new phase in the development of English depredation, it was accompanied and followed by a rash of anti-Spanish projects that linked predatory ambitions with visions of settlement in North America. Among a small, but vocal group of Protestant warriors and colonial promoters, the plunder of Spain was projected as a patriotic duty, as a means of defending the Protestant cause while weakening the 'great whore of Babylon'.[1] In these circumstances deep-sea depredation merged with wider political and religious goals.

Callice and company: local piracy and plunder during the later 1570s

Although local spoil and pillage remained widespread during the 1570s, increasingly it was concentrated within a region encompassing south-west England, south Wales and south-west Ireland. Under a group of prominent pirate captains, it was organized as a small-scale, commercialized and profitable enterprise, which flourished with community encouragement and support. The regime struggled to combat the problem, appointing piracy commissioners for the maritime counties during the later 1570s. But the renewed campaign against piracy was inconsistent and ambiguous. Of necessity, moreover, it was focused more on the consequences rather than the causes of maritime plunder.

Conditions during these years favoured the formation of a loose brotherhood of pirates, which anticipated the development of pirate communities in bases within the Mediterranean and the Caribbean. The social organization of piracy was based on varying degrees of contact and cooperation between pirate captains and companies. It was expressed in a disorderly code of conduct which flouted convention, occasionally in behaviour that appeared to combine mockery and mimicry with robbery at sea. The pirate Captain Clarke reportedly haled vessels with a glass of wine which was thrown into the sea when empty. Pirate life may have been informed by a rich oral tradition of outlawry, as suggested by the circulation of stories about Robin Hood. For some, the sea may have served as the greenwood, with its prospect of riches, good fellowship and freedom. The vision of creating a band of good fellows was realized in the sociability and hospitality which were shared between pirate companies, often in association with friends and families ashore. The close relationship between some captains was demonstrated in a letter of June 1575 from Hicks to his 'brother Callys', from Milford Haven, where he had brought in a prize laden with corn, affirming that 'all he has is at his service'.[2] At sea, pirate captains were capable of combined action, operating in hunting packs of two or three ships. The *James* of London was attacked by the pirates Hodges, Clarke and Worald, probably during 1575, when four of the company were killed. The scale and prevalence of piracy thus suggests that these years were a formative period in the development of pirate culture, creating a lifestyle which was to be elaborated and enriched by subsequent experience.

From a range of scattered evidence it is possible to identify at least thirty pirate captains who were active during the years from 1575 to 1580. Assuming that pirate companies could range in number from twenty to seventy, this suggests that between 600 and 2,400 men were involved in piratical activity. If the total was towards the higher end of this scale, it would provide a striking comparison with subsequent outbreaks of piracy, including the later seventeenth and early eighteenth centuries, when about 2,000 pirates were active along the eastern seaboard of North America and in the Caribbean.[3] Piracy on such a scale represented a serious danger to the security of the seas, and an alarming threat to trade and shipping.

The victims of the pirates were selected indiscriminately, though there was a tendency, despite the violent attack on the *James*, to plunder foreign, rather than English, ships. Much of this venturing took the form of short voyages to frequently haunted regions that cut across busy shipping lanes around the British Isles, including the western approaches and the Irish Sea. In January 1579 the west coast of Ireland was reportedly infested with English pirates. Later in the year Burghley was informed that around Guernsey the 'sea was never so full of pirates'.[4] This kind of small-scale depredation flourished with the assistance and cooperation of shore-based supporters, who provided markets for pirates and other rovers, exchanging provisions for a varied range of plundered commodities, including wine, salt, corn, assorted cloth, carpets and jewellery. In some areas visiting pirates supported local service industries, while encouraging the spread of disorderly drinking houses and prostitution.

As a business, however, piracy was characterised by inherent ambiguities. While maritime robbery on this scale acquired the appearance of an illicit and irregular trade which involved a significant redistribution of wealth, few of those directly engaged in it appear to have gained great profit. In part this was because 'golden prizes come not every day'.[5] But it also reflected the economics of an enterprise where the advantage usually lay with the land-based suppliers of pirates. In many cases it seems likely that the latter were able to acquire goods at cheap rates of exchange, or even as gifts, which were later sold for profit at market prices. Either through choice or necessity, pirates could be remarkably generous in giving gifts to friends or associates ashore. Such behaviour may have been one of the defining features of pirate culture. It grew out of the life cycle of poor men, often from struggling seafaring backgrounds, for whom piracy was part of a wider economy of illicit enterprise, and in which the rewards of plunder were easily dissipated in nights of 'jubilee'.

The character of this kind of depredation is illuminated by the career of one of its leading practitioners, Callice, whose activities at sea spanned the period from about 1574 to 1585. Callice came to the attention of the council during April 1574 as a result of his capture of the *Grace of God*, apparently while in the service of Sir John Berkeley. The prize was brought into Cardiff where part of its cargo was sold. The remainder was disposed of in Bristol. As he came from Tintern, Callice was very familiar with the Severn region and its wider hinterland, where the maritime communities of south Wales served as safe bases and accessible entry points to widespread markets for the disposal of plundered cargoes.

According to evidence which Callice subsequently presented to Sir Francis Walsingham, as part of a plea for a pardon, during these early voyages he sailed in association with Captain Sturgis of La Rochelle, under the authority of a Huguenot commission. This veneer of legality did not last for long. In January 1576 the council ordered his arrest for various piracies, including the spoil of a Spanish vessel off the Scilly Isles in consortship with Captain William Battes. Callice went into hiding in Denbigh, north Wales. By February he was reported to be in Ireland with Battes and Heidon. In May the council turned its attention to the pirate's supporters in Cardiff and Glamorganshire.[6]

These early voyages established a pattern of highly localized enterprise, based on petty plunder and raiding within the Channel, which rested on informal networks of shore-based supporters, especially in south Wales. Later in 1576 Callice spoiled four French ships, including a Newfoundland fishing vessel which was attacked off Belle Isle, allegedly worth 20,000 livres in total. Faced with complaints from the French, the council made a renewed attempt to apprehend Callice, who was haunting the coast of Wales during October. Although one of his associates, Robert Thresher, was taken in Poole, Callice successfully evaded capture. In December he was at Newport. The following month the council complained that he was allowed to escape after being 'lodged and horsed' in Haverfordwest.[7] Six of his company were seized during February 1577 by Sir John Perrot, but Callice remained at liberty, plundering French, Danish and Scottish vessels.

This promising career of piracy was interrupted by Callice's capture on the Isle of Wight. The council was informed of the news on 7 May. Three weeks later Callice was a prisoner in the Tower of London. In expectation that the pirate would be pardoned, one of his Scottish victims, Thomas Browne, petitioned for its award, presumably in the hope of recouping his losses. In June, however, at the council's command he was handed over for trial to the judge of the High Court of Admiralty. The case against him was reinforced by complaints from the King of Denmark concerning the seizure of several Danish vessels in association with Hicks earlier in the year.[8]

Although the Queen was prepared to hand Callice over to the Scottish ambassador if a request was made for the restitution of the plunder of Scottish shipping, on her instructions in July he was brought from Bristol to the court at Havering. The visit led to his pardon, but on condition that he served with Sir Humphrey Gilbert, an ambitious and well-connected adventurer from the south-west, who was assembling a large expedition for a transatlantic enterprise with a commission from the Queen. Among Gilbert's supporters was Henry Knollys, whose father, Sir Francis, was a member of the council and a cousin of the Queen. Knollys commanded three of his own vessels during Gilbert's badly organized and abortive expedition, including the *Elephant* in which Callice and several other recruits had previously committed acts of piracy. With Walsingham acting as Gilbert's patron, the growing strength of the anti-Spanish party within the regime was creating a more favourable environment for aggressive schemes of plunder, and opportunities for the redemption of resourceful pirates such as Callice.[9]

Although Walsingham may have played a part in the pardon of Callice, it may also have been the result of the pirate's own initiative. While in custody, either on his own or with assistance, he produced an impressive case which amounted to a powerful plea for clemency. It included a contrite confession in which he offered to reveal the names of his accomplices and supporters; details of the capture of six ships, with information about the purchasers of their cargoes; as well as an account of money that was either owed to him or which remained in the hands of Hicks; and intelligence of French scheming in Ireland. It amounted to a compelling appeal, revealing the ability and ingenuity of one of the most notorious pirates of the 1570s, who might well have expected to be shown little mercy.

Callice's carefully crafted petition to Walsingham mixed spiritual with secular concerns. Lamenting his former woeful and wicked life, he hoped for redemption through the forgiveness of God, while craving mercy from the Queen.[10] If Elizabeth spared his life, he offered to clear the coasts of other pirates. With his possibly unrivalled knowledge of the regions frequented by pirates, and of their supporters ashore, Callice claimed that he would 'do more therein then if hir Majestie shold send Shipps abroade to that end', thus saving the Queen at least £20,000. As a sign of his good faith he identified the purchasers of the cargoes of three vessels he had taken in association with Sturgis and Battes, though he was unable to remember the names of several buyers from Gloucester who bought part of the lading of a Portuguese ship, at Penarth near Cardiff. However, he claimed to have gained little money from these transactions, receiving in exchange victuals and other supplies. In the case of a Scottish ship, claimed by Thomas Browne, he admitted to being present at its capture, but denied having any part of the cargo. The prize was taken to Cardiff and Newport, where its lading was sold by some of the servants of Sir William Morgan, who was one of Callice's leading supporters in south Wales. Callice insisted that Morgan's men should provide compensation for Browne. Furthermore, he offered to restore a Danish vessel which was in the hands of Hicks.

This confession was accompanied by intelligence, albeit anecdotal and uncorroborated, of French designs against the English in Ireland. In deploying this material Callice sought to portray himself as a patriotic pirate whose loyalty to the Queen was unquestionable. Thus he claimed to have been in conversation with O'Sullivan Beare, at his castle at Bearhaven, about the rebel James Fitzmaurice during which he refused to support a planned expedition to Ireland by the latter with French support. Despite the offer of gifts, to serve as a pilot for Fitzmaurice, Callice proclaimed that he 'wold not consent or joyne with any rebel against the Quenes Majestie, but hoaped of hir mercy in tyme to come'.[11] Several months before his capture, he received a similar offer from a French captain, of long-standing acquaintance, who he encountered in Tor Bay. In exchange for entering the service of the King of France, Callice was promised a pardon for his spoil of French shipping, as well as 3,000 crowns and an annual pension. But he rejected the offer, replying 'that whatsoever shold become of me I wold never be sworne to any foren prince', despite a warning from the French captain that he would never receive the same preferment in England.

The petition presented to Walsingham included details of Callice's financial dealings, effectively a summary of his personal estate. The pirate claimed that he had £530 in cash, though it was with Hicks aboard one of the Danish ships they had taken. In addition he was owed about £350, much of which was accounted for by grants of money to Nicholas Herbert and Sir William Morgan, on the promise that they would secure a pardon for him. These debts included small loans to local traders, such as £5 to John Williams of Margam or £2 10 shillings to William Francklin of Swansea, and several outstanding payments from the purchasers of the pirate's plunder. They included George Herbert, who acquired a cable and an anchor out of a French ship for £7, though Callice claimed they were worth £20 in total. Furthermore, William Herbert of Cardiff evidently held £130 in safe keeping for him. On paper this was an impressive sum of money, amounting to more than £1,000, but very little of it was in Callice's own hands. When he was captured on the Isle of Wight, he was in possession of £20 7 shillings. While the recovery of pirate debts was difficult, by November 1579 the owners of the Danish vessel had received £505 by way of compensation, much of which may have come from Callice and Hicks.[12]

Callice's case was skilfully and successfully presented. But the issue of a pardon during the summer of 1578, evidently at the suit of the regent of Scotland, failed to curtail his piratical activities. Indeed, his later career indicates how small-scale, localized piracy merged with, and reinforced, more ambitious schemes for oceanic depredation in the Atlantic and the Caribbean. During the latter part of 1578 he was involved in Gilbert's expedition which sailed with a large number of pirates and rovers, including James Ranse, who was with Drake in 1572, and Simon Fernandes, a Portuguese renegade. Gilbert's intentions were shrouded in secrecy, though his commission from the Queen suggested that he was planning to establish a settlement along the eastern seaboard of North America, partly modelled on the earlier example of the French in Florida.[13] It was a speculative and hazardous enterprise that drew on the aggressive resources of pirate groups. A small, temporary habitation, organized by a company of private adventurers, could expect to face fierce opposition from Spain, though in the short term it might serve as a profitable base for raids on Spanish shipping, while enabling the English to acquire first-hand knowledge and experience of an unknown and potentially valuable region that would pave the way for future colonization.

Gilbert's backers were made up of gentlemen, especially from the south-west, including members of his own family, and London merchants, such as Thomas Smith who had wide-ranging interests in overseas commerce. Although Gilbert enjoyed the patronage of Walsingham, there were few high-ranking courtiers or officials among his supporters, with the exception of the Earl of Sussex. With such support Gilbert assembled a large expedition of ten vessels and 500 men. Among the captains were Gilbert's younger half-brother, Walter Ralegh, and Henry Knollys, who contributed three of his own ships to the expedition.

Gilbert's venture was based on an uneasy association of potentially competitive interests. Soon after reaching the coast of Ireland, Knollys' ships effectively abandoned the expedition in favour of piracy and plunder. Gilbert made some attempt to proceed across the Atlantic, but he was forced back by bad weather. It was an embarrassing, though revealing failure, particularly for the small and rather isolated group of promoters for American colonization. Spanish suspicions of Gilbert's schemes appeared to be confirmed when several ships from the expedition plundered the coast of Galicia, raiding cattle and pillaging a shrine, which was followed by the spoil of French vessels.[14]

There can be little doubt that Callice and his associates were heavily implicated in this opportunistic resort to piracy. An inquiry of 1579 failed to investigate the matter effectively, however, leaving him free to continue his irregular roving at sea. According to a report of June 1580 he was ambushed and taken prisoner on one of the Orkney Islands, after landing to take on fresh water. Several years later, during 1583 and 1584, he provoked renewed complaints about the spoil of French shipping. By this time he was associated with Court Hellebourg, who was based on the Isle of Wight, and sailing with a commission issued by Don Antonio, the pretender to the throne of Portugal. Under such dubious authority, on the eve of the war with Spain, in March 1585, he was involved in attacks on Iberian shipping with William and Edward Fenner.[15]

The activities of Callice and others during the later 1570s demonstrated that small-scale, organized piracy had become a deep-seated problem. As in the past, it easily spread across the Irish Sea, threatening to become entangled with native resistance towards the Elizabethan regime in remote regions of Ireland. At the same time it was complicated by an upsurge in Scottish depredation, which also ranged across the Irish Sea. Although such activity depended on local support, in some areas it provoked confusing allegations and counter-allegations concerning the conduct of officials or the connivance of members of communities. Such claims raised difficult questions about the enforcement of law and order. At times they suggested also that the regime was in danger of losing control over those parts of the coast where pirates were able to operate with immunity from the threat of arrest.

A wide range of reports and complaints reveals the extent and nature of piratical activity, as well as the demands it placed on the regime. The south-west remained a fertile breeding ground and reception area for pirates and rovers. It attracted some of the most notorious pirates operating during these years, including Robert Hicks, who came from Saltash, John Piers of Padstow, and Callice. Pirates of varied backgrounds were able to congregate in favoured locations such as Tor Bay, Purbeck, Portland or the Isle of Wight, where loose bonds of community were renewed at informal social gatherings, on land and at sea, providing an opportunity for the exchange of news and gossip, the disposal of plunder and the tending of the sick or wounded. In secure locations ashore pirates indulged in prolonged drinking sessions, though entertainment and recreation could be

ANTHONIUS de Coninck van Portugael en Algarben.

Don Antonio, the pretender to the throne of Portugal, who served as a figurehead for a group of anti–Spanish adventurers during the 1580s, including Drake. English adventurers sailed with his commissions, plundering Spanish and other shipping. However, Don Antonio failed to get much support from the Queen, and his penurious circumstances contributed to the disorderly activities of his captains at sea. (*The Fugger News-Letters*) diverse. Simon Fernandes, an associate of Callice, later boasted of his skill in horse riding, 'a thing that few mariners can wel doe', which he acquired 'on a great horse at Sir William Morgayns, … when he … bremyd hym [the horse] with a cudgel abowt the beak head afore and the quarters abaft'.[16] As Callice's narrative indicated, moreover, such gatherings enabled pirate leaders to maintain contact with French rovers. Despite the disapproval of the regime, French men-of-war continued to visit the coastal waters of England and Ireland. During October 1577 Sir Arthur Champernowne, the Vice Admiral of Devon, arrested fifteen French warships off Plymouth.[17]

But small-scale, localized depredation was not confined to south-west England. In south Wales there were several pirate captains operating in the shadow of Callice. They included Edward Herbert who, like Callice and Hicks, was able to dispose of plundered commodities in Cardiff and Milford Haven. In May the Cinque Ports were so troubled with pirates that the Lord Warden, Cobham, appealed to the council to send out ships against them. At the same time pirate groups ranged along the east coast. In July 1577 the *Fortune* of Aberdeen was taken off Lowestoft by Captain Phipson; one member of the pirate's company was apprehended in Yarmouth while trying to hire new recruits. Acting in consort with Captain White, Phipson spoiled fourteen Dutch vessels of linen, cheese and other goods. Both pirates resorted to a safe haven along the coast of Yorkshire, near the mouth of the River Humber, where they were able to land and receive assistance from local people. Across the river, in

Padstow Bay, Cornwall. This small Cornish port was the home of John Piers, a notorious pirate who sailed in local waters, haunting Lundy Island, to prey on trade and shipping. He was aided by other members of his family, including his mother, who was reputed to be a witch. (Author's collection)

Lincolnshire, pirates frequented small creeks and havens to dispose of plunder. During August 1577 Lancelott Grenewell, captain of the *Elizabeth* of Chichester, brought a ship laden with rye into Englemans haven which was also known as 'Theefes creeke'.[18] Subsequently, Grenewell was captured by several armed vessels sent out by the mayor and corporation of Hull. Further south, complaints that pirates were haunting the mouth of the Thames compelled the Queen to send out two of her ships to apprehend them.

The activities of Callice indicated the continued importance of Ireland for much of this piracy and spoil. The presence of English and Welsh pirates in Irish waters may have been with the encouragement of Gaelic leaders, such as O'Sullivan Beare, who identified them as potential rebels against the regime. In these ambiguous circumstances Callice and others were welcomed in remote regions of south-west Munster, including Bearhaven and Dingle, though an alliance between the pirates and Irish rebels failed to materialize. Most pirates seem to have retained an underlying, if self-interested, loyalty to the Queen. Hicks was captured in Ireland, and thereafter employed in service against a Scottish pirate until he was despatched to London by Sir William Drury, the president of Munster. In any case Irish reactions to English and Welsh piracy were tempered by the spoil of local shipping. During 1579 Drury complained to the council of a piratical attack on two Breton ships, and the spoil of a merchant of Drogheda, by Alexander Vailes of Aldeburgh. To some extent, moreover, piracy in Irish waters was influenced by the activities of the rebel, James Fitzmaurice, who possessed a French or Spanish commission for the plunder of English and Huguenot vessels. Reports that Fitzmaurice seized an English ship, the company of which were 'sent to the Inquisition and executed', may have provoked hostility from patriotic pirate captains, encouraging them to provide officials with intelligence regarding his preparations for a landing in Munster.[19]

Most of these pirates continued to operate in an opportunistic and indiscriminate manner, at least in their plunder of foreign shipping. The result was a mixed haul of booty from vulnerable trading and fishing vessels, much of which was readily disposed ashore, for modest returns, often in the form of provisions, hospitality and occasionally credit. It may have been possible for some pirate captains to accumulate wealth, but this depended on resourcefulness as well as luck, and a willingness to venture to the coasts of Spain and Portugal in search of richer prizes. Hicks, for example, returned from a voyage to the coast of Galicia, during 1577, with a Spanish ship laden with iron and other goods.[20]

In the waters around the British Isles, where too many rovers may have been in search of potential prey, pirate groups operated in highly contingent circumstances, appearing at times almost as seaborne vagrants. Phipson's activities along the east coast suggest that piracy might have been part of a wider creative, sometimes criminal – though not always successful – response among the labouring poor to hard times. According to the report of the local deputies to the recently appointed commissioners for piracy in Yorkshire, he was cruising off the coast as early as 1574, when he arrived in Scarborough in a small boat of 5 or 6 tons, with a company of about twenty men, to await the arrival of a larger vessel from Ireland. The boat was carrying several rolls of linen cloth which aroused the suspicions of the town bailiffs. Consequently, Phipson was arrested and sent to appear before the lord president of the Council in the North at York. Within a week he was back in Scarborough, although sickness apparently prevented him from putting to sea with the rest of his company for a brief foray along the coast. Shortly thereafter the pirates returned, bruised and beaten, after sailing to Flamborough Head, 'where they enterprised upon a Frenche ship & were repulsed'.[21] Nonetheless, they acquired an anchor and a piece of cable which were brought ashore and stored in a cellar in Scarborough. Although Phipson's men were arrested and sent to York, they were not detained.

During 1576 the pirates returned to the region, arriving at Filey in a small vessel armed for war. On this occasion the local deputies reported that Reynold Farley and his wife went aboard the ship and purchased barrels of soap, pewter ware and other goods. A few days later, two other rovers came into Filey, including one of Phipson's associates, Captain White, who 'dranke & made merry in dyvers houses in the towne'.[22] Phipson came back after several weeks, in search of victuals, purchasing beer and bread from two local men. The following year Phipson and his company were further north along the Yorkshire coast, seeking supplies of fresh water in the small haven of Skinningrove. Faced with local obduracy the pirates threatened to use force, but an attempt to land was repulsed. In response they seized a boat belonging to Robert Patteson, described as a very poor man; it was returned after he supplied Phipson and his company with water. By 1577 Phipson's activities along the east coast had come to the attention of the council. In February 1578 it was dealing with the complaint of a Scottish trader, who stated that the pirate had plundered sheep skins and other goods which were sold to a beer brewer in Ipswich.[23]

An analysis of the plunder taken during these years, though inevitably based on incomplete data, provides some indication of the commercial consequences of persistent, but local, depredation. Collectively, the pirates seized a significant number of trading and fishing vessels. Many of these prizes were small and laden with various commodities which were of limited or modest value. Small French coasting vessels were particularly vulnerable to attack, but most pirates made little distinction in the spoil of foreign ships. During 1577 John Granger of Plymouth seized a French fishing vessel returning from Newfoundland; Hicks plundered several vessels belonging to merchants of the Steelyard in London, as well as a Danish ship which he took in consort with Callice; while Captain Clarke took a French vessel in Dartmouth harbour. In addition, Edward Denny returned to the Isle of Wight with two prizes – one of which was French, the other Spanish – and Gilbert Horseley brought two French hoys laden with coal into Shoreham. Some prizes were of such little value that they appear to have

Filey Brigg and Bay, Yorkshire. This exposed bay was regularly visited by pirates during the 1560s and 1570s. In December 1577 the piracy commissioners for Yorkshire reported the recent arrival of Captain Phipson, who sold barrels of soap and pewter ware to the local inhabitants. (Author's collection)

Dartmouth harbour, Devon. Dartmouth had a long-standing interest in seaborne plunder, including piracy and privateering, which persisted throughout the sixteenth century. In 1577 Captain Clarke captured a French ship in the harbour. Nearby, Tor Bay was an important meeting place for large numbers of pirates, especially during the 1570s. (Author's collection)

been abandoned by their captors. Two small vessels taken by Phipson were left in the Humber or nearby, where one was salvaged by local watermen, while the other was driven ashore at Kilnsea.[24]

Most pirates tacitly refrained from plundering English vessels, though this was a practice that was not always adhered to. During August 1577, for example, the council issued orders for the arrest of a ship in Portsmouth harbour, owned by Christopher Andrews and others, on the grounds that its company had spoiled subjects and allies of the Queen, especially the Scots. At a time of uncertain and uneasy Anglo-Scottish relations, the regime was acutely concerned about the spoil of Scottish vessels, particularly as it provoked retaliation, including Scottish attacks on Cornish fishermen in the Irish Sea. While the diplomatic damage might be contained, Scottish victims continued to complain of long and expensive legal suits for the recovery of their property.[25]

The scale and vigour of local piracy during the later 1570s had far-reaching consequences, apart from the disruption and damage to commerce. While piratical venturing served as a safety valve for organized violence and aggression, especially among young men from seafaring backgrounds, it also strengthened the recruiting ground for deep-sea depredation. The companies of captains like Callice and Hicks provided the human resources for the oceanic expansion of English piracy and spoil. But the underlying links between these different forms of plunder served to complicate the official response to seaborne robbery and commercial warfare. The survival of Callice, as well as the re-emergence of Drake, demonstrated an ambivalent attitude towards piracy and sea roving, which deepened as it became more focused on Spain.

The commissions for piracy during the later 1570s

The regime responded vigorously to the growing threat of local piracy during the later 1570s, but with mixed success. A patchwork of agencies were involved in dealing with the problem, creating a multi-layered structure, though it was weakened by conflicts of interest between rival jurisdictions and the unreliability of local officials. The Lord Admiral and the judge of the High Court of Admiralty were closely involved in handling complaints of piracy. But the Queen and her council remained deeply concerned about the spread of piracy and spoil within English waters, not least because of the shadow it cast over royal jurisdiction and honour.

The council was the key agency in responding to complaints and reports of pirate activity. Its surviving registers indicate that these occurred on a weekly, sometimes daily, basis during these years. The result was a rapidly expanding volume of business. At times the council struggled to cope with complaints of piracy, delegating some matters to regional bodies, such as the Council in the Marches of Wales and the Council in the North, or to local corporations and officials. To a considerable degree the effectiveness of the regime's response to the disorder at sea depended on the cooperation of the latter, which included Vice Admirals and their deputies, acting increasingly in association with officers representing the High Court of Admiralty in London.

Much of the official response continued to be characterized by short-term expediency as the regime sought to deal with two separate, but interrelated, issues concerning the incidence of piracy at sea and the support it received on land. The range of business relating to these matters was reflected in an unrelenting flow of commands, directions and instructions issued by the council during the later 1570s. Directions for sending out one of the Queen's ships, the *Foresight*, in October 1577 and April 1579, for the suppression of pirates were interspersed with commissions of July 1578 authorizing private adventurers to set forth ships for their apprehension. Commands were issued periodically for the arrest of pirates, and for their speedy trial under commissions of oyer and terminer in Hull, Newcastle and other ports, as well as for the discovery of pirate plunder. Suspected pirates and their supporters, particularly of gentry status, were ordered to appear before the council. On one occasion during May 1578, however, it was so busy with other matters that Roger Puttocke of Fareham, who appeared to answer allegations of buying pirate goods, was dismissed on bond. Letters of assistance of various kinds were circulated for the recovery of captured vessels and cargoes or to support and reinforce the legal process in the High Court of Admiralty.[26]

The council was especially concerned with complaints from Scotland, issuing a general warrant in August 1577 for the recovery of all Scottish goods brought in by pirates, though it was generally determined to show its regard for overseas grievances. During November it ordered that fines levied on the supporters of pirates were to be used to compensate their victims. On several occasions thereafter the council ordered the payment, out of such fines, of £80 to a Danish merchant; of £260, subsequently increased to £300, to Adam Fullerton, a Scot; and £20 to another Scot whose case was recommended by James VI.[27]

By various means the council also encouraged or cajoled local officials to discharge their duties. In September 1578 the captain of the Isle of Wight was commended for his efforts in trying to capture Captain Clarke. Although Clarke escaped, at least two men and one boy from his company were taken. Later in the month, however, officials on Guernsey were reprimanded for their evident unwillingness to take action against a group of French pirates. The council was determined that the pirates be 'proceeded against as public enemies pronounced by civil laws &c', though such cases of local obduracy often grew out of long-standing and jealously guarded rights and privileges.[28] Shortly thereafter, indeed, officials in Queenborough refused to deliver Captain King, arrested on suspicion of piracy, claiming exemption from the jurisdiction of the High Court of Admiralty.

The determination of the regime to repress piracy was underlined by its search for a comprehensive and long-term solution, based on the re-establishment of commissioners for piracy with expanded powers and responsibilities. By comparison with the earlier ineffective commissions of the 1560s, there was greater pressure on officials to take action against pirates, while providing an effective means for the recompense of their victims. Under the supervision of the council these commissions laid down a procedure for community policing and enforcement which, despite evident weaknesses, had wider implications for the consolidation of the authority of the Tudor state, especially in remote and disorderly regions.

During September 1577 the council appointed commissioners in England and Wales with detailed instructions for the suppression of piracy. As during the 1560s these appointments were drawn from the ranks of leading representatives in the maritime counties, including landowners and office holders. As commissioners they were instructed to survey all the havens, creeks and landing places in their regions, and to nominate deputies for each area. The procedure is indicated by practice in Cornwall, where the commissioners, who included Sir John Killigrew, John Arundell and Francis Godolphin, met for the first time on 11 January 1578 when they nominated their deputies, with instructions to appear before them six days later 'to receave ther charge by othe according to the instructions'.[29] They certified the council of the names of thirty-three deputies who were to take charge of various locations along the coast. The deputies were responsible for making presentments to the commissioners, copies of which were to be sent to the council, with details of cases of piracy and other suspicious activity. The commissioners were expected to investigate these matters by examining suspected pirates and their supporters, with the assistance of juries of local men. Officials in Kent informed the council that they had empanelled a jury of 'the most honeste, sufficient and least suspected persons from all parts of this shyre'.[30]

The council instructed the commissioners to compile an account of their proceedings. This was to include information regarding the value of the lands and goods of offenders, particularly those who purchased pirate plunder, in order that they could be fined accordingly. The magistrates of Norfolk, for example, were requested to provide a true valuation of the property for 'every person named to be offenders for causes of pyracye' who resided in the county.[31] In collecting this material the magistrates were forced to rely on constables and other local officers.

At the same time as re-establishing the piracy commissioners, the regime took action to regulate and control the movement of shipping, partly in response to overseas complaints against the plunder and spoil of trade. This included attempts to prevent ships from putting to sea, unless engaged in trade and fishing, without a commission from the Queen or council, signifying that they were sent out either for royal service or for the discovery of new trades. Vice Admirals and piracy commissioners were given extensive powers to supervise shipping, especially vessels suspected of evil intent. They included the authority to prevent the departure of suspicious vessels frequenting 'any arme of the sea, navigable river, landing places or darke corners of this realme'.[32] Collectively, the regime's actions represented an ambitious and demanding programme for the eradication of piracy. It was a striking affirmation of its determination to tackle a deep-seated problem which had damaging consequences for overseas relations.

The revived campaign against piracy was driven by a combination of domestic and international concerns. In particular, it reflected the concern of the Queen and her council to remain on good terms with France during an unsettled and difficult period in cross-Channel diplomacy. Paulet's mission to France during 1577 drew attention to the anger and recriminations engendered by piracy and disorderly privateering. In an audience with the French King, Henry III, he complained that the English were 'robbyd, spoyled and killed on the seas daylie; that they had made sondry and often complaints [but] that no justice was ministered unto them'.[33] While the King was sympathetic, attributing the increase in maritime depredation to the 'malice of this tyme', he responded with comparable complaints of French merchants and mariners at the 'wrongs done to them, and … the shorte justice they founde in England'. Paulet piously replied that the

English 'would be ashamed that any pirate or murtherer notoriously knowne should escape unpunished'. Later in the year, during discussions with one of Henry's ministers, Paulet insisted that the best way of promoting Anglo-French amity was to 'ponishe with severitie all pirates and robbers on the seas, pestilent enemyes to all comone welthes'. By then the English were deeply angered at the seizure of more than fifty trading vessels on the grounds that they were men-of-war which were trafficking with Huguenot rebels at La Rochelle. Paulet continued to exchange complaints with French ministers, claiming that English losses greatly exceeded those of the French, while asserting that more than 100 'restitucions had been made to the Frenche within theise few years, and verie few or none at all made unto us'.[34]

If there were pressing diplomatic reasons for the firm reaction to piracy by the regime during the later 1570s, the scale and nature of the response suggests that it was also part of a broader campaign against disorder and organized criminality, which was intended to discipline and reform a growing number of men who were in danger of being identified as beggarly outcasts or dangerous outlaws. Although it is difficult to gauge opinion and attitudes, a new tone appeared to be creeping into the social labelling of pirates, as suggested by Paulet's description of them as pestilent enemies of the commonwealth. While the wider social response to piracy and sea roving remained deeply ambivalent, this changing emphasis appeared to foreshadow the deliberate marginalization of pirates during the later seventeenth century.

Although the regime achieved some success in its attack on piracy, it was uneven and impossible to sustain. Piracy commissioners assembled in many parts of England and Wales in an impressive attempt to fulfil the orders of the council. On paper this seemed to be a model example of the mobilization of unpaid, local officials whose reports and certificates provided the council with a mass of information on piracy, which was unprecedented in its scope and level of detail. In practice, however, the work of the commissioners was heavily qualified and variable in effect.

Delays in the proceedings of commissioners were probably unavoidable, though at times they may have been the result of local indifference or hostility. Officials in Somerset excused their slowness in returning certificates to the council by drawing attention to the sickness and unavailability of several commissioners. In Cornwall officials blamed their apparent lack of diligence on the uncooperative attitude of Sir John Killigrew. Commissioners in Carmarthenshire informed the council during February 1578 that they were too few in number to proceed: one lived forty miles from Carmarthen and was too busy with other matters to attend, while another had gone to London on business. In Hampshire officials also admitted that their delayed proceedings were due to the lack of sufficient commissioners. In Gloucestershire, too, the commissioners warned that they were too few in number to proceed, and consequently there was a marked delay in responding to the council.[35]

Nonetheless, across the maritime counties, during 1578 and 1579 commissioners met to discharge their duties. They provided the council with variable information, inadvertently revealing weaknesses in the regime's effort to suppress piracy. While officials in some areas put together extensive reports of piratical activity, with detailed lists of local supporters, others provided brief and unrevealing summaries. Given the nature of the problem they were dealing with, commissioners and their deputies were occasionally in danger of being identified as the unwelcome agents of an intrusive regime, whose legal authority was questionable. Thus in December 1577 Lord Thomas Howard reported that the mayor and other officials in Poole refused to cooperate with the commissioners in Dorset. The latter requested greater power to deal with such intransigence, but they faced more difficulties in other parts of the county as a result of local collusion and connivance with pirates. In January 1578 one member of the commission warned Walsingham that:

> as longe as some be comyssioners wee shall doe but smale good about Lullworthe side where all pirates doe resorte, specially bycause wee have no aucthoritie to swere anye other but suche as be our deputies, and such as shalbe of the jurye, and manye there be that are to be examined, and oughte to be examined by force of an othe or else they will saye nothinge…. [Furthermore] there is suche cunynge & fyne devises used that suche persons as wee send for and woulde have them to be our deputies about Lullworthe ether they must be sycke, ether from home at London or Exeter, or taken some falle that they cannot, maye not or dare not come before us to do there duties.[36]

The situation in south Wales, especially in and around Cardiff, underlined the problems facing the regime in orchestrating its campaign against piracy. Concerned at the way in which Callice almost flaunted his presence in the town and the surrounding region, the council made several unsuccessful efforts to arrest him. During November and December 1576 an Admiralty officer, James Crofts, pursued the pirate and his company across south-west England and Wales. In Cardiff he heard of two prizes off Penarth, one of which had been taken by Callice. But the local inhabitants refused to assist Crofts in the capture of the pirates, 'althoughe', he reported, 'in speche every sorte of people colde saie, it were well donne to take them'.[37] Crofts also complained that the townsmen of Cardiff and local gentlemen bought plundered goods off Callice and his accomplices.

While he was at Cardiff, Callice's prize was taken to Newport by servants of Sir William Morgan, the Vice Admiral of Monmouthshire. Crofts' attempt to arrest it was rebuffed by Morgan's deputy, William Morgan, with the statement that 'he did not care for the commission, nor me'.[38] Unable to get assistance from the local justices, who were unwilling to interfere in the affairs of the Vice Admiral, Crofts was forced to leave Cardiff after four days, during which time goods from the prize were 'verey disorderlie conveyed away … by daie and night in lighters and botes, to places unknowen', while the captive crew 'lamentablie cried for aide & relief'. The most significant result of Crofts' visit may have been the compilation of a lengthy list identifying the purchasers of Callice's plunder, with the names of the brewers and victuallers who supplied him with provisions.

In the aftermath of Crofts' failed attempt to arrest Callice, Sir John Perrot, one of the leading landowners and officials in south-west Wales, was forced to defend himself against allegations that he was a maintainer of pirates. During February 1577 he advised the council to take strong action against the inhabitants of Cardiff and the county of Glamorganshire on the grounds that they harboured the receivers of pirate booty. According to Perrot, support for piracy was part of a wider problem concerning the growth of violence and disorder among local inhabitants who 'are become a warr lyke people for thear ys not almost one that goeth to the plowe amongst them, but he ys armed and weaponed'. It was, he added, an 'ill example by their doings bothe by sea and lande'.[39]

In a further attempt to deal with such disorder, on the orders of the council in London, the Council in the Marches appointed Fabyan Phillips, Thomas Lewis and Perrot to investigate suspected pirates and their support-ers in Cardiff. Phillips and Lewis were forced to proceed without Perrot, 'by reason of infirmities as it seemeth by his letteres of excuse'.[40] They examined at least sixty people, acquiring the names of a large number of pirates who were lodged in the town, and from whom the inhabitants had received much of their plunder. Local people were acutely aware of the discredit that the pirates brought to the town. Indeed, traders and others travelling overseas 'dare not well be knowen or to avowe the place of theyr dwelling at Cardiff'. Even so, the inhabitants refused to cooperate with the investigation, in some cases because of fear or intimidation. Thus Phillips and Lewis complained that 'they have taken a generall rule, that they wooll neyther accuse one another, nor yet answer to any matter that toucheth them selfes upon othes'.[41] Faced with similar intransigence from one of the captured pirates, William Chick, the two officials handed him over to the council, in the hope that a spell of confine-ment in manacles would make him talk.

Although some of the chief suspects accused of receiving pirate goods, including one of the customs officials, David Roberts, had left town following their arrival, Phillips and Lewis continued to gather evidence during 1577. They bound five men, including William Herbert and John ap John, to appear before the council at the end of April, but there is no indication that they appeared on the required day. In January 1578 six men of Cardiff were examined at Hampton Court, before the judge of the High Court of Admiralty and two other officials, when they confessed to receiving goods and gifts from pirates or to supplying them with provisions. John ap John admitted 'that he kept company with pirates in the town of Cardiff, as generally all men there did'.[42] Five others, including Roberts, who failed to appear, were sent for. They included John Thomas, who was accused of providing bail for Court Hellebourg, though he denied the charge, claiming that somebody else had used his name without his knowledge. Most of those who appeared before the judge were fined £10, though two men were punished with fines of £200.

Community support for piracy was widespread in many other parts of England and Wales. In character it ranged from chance contact and barter to regular relations and commercialized exchange. Organized criminal activity on this scale and extent was impossible to prevent without local assistance and knowledge. Even with such support, there were serious difficulties in gathering and interpreting evidence against pirates, as demonstrated by the situation in Cardiff. Without a confession from pirates or their supporters, investigators were forced to rely on information from informers or on anecdotal allegations which were self-interested, partial and often coloured by local rivalries or personal animosities. One way of dealing with these difficulties, which the council appeared to resort to occasionally, was the threat or use of torture, which included the racking of pirates.

In these circumstances perhaps the best the regime could hope for was to deter the supporters of piracy ashore, while seeking to contain its spread at sea. But this called for a level of surveillance and policing which placed heavy, if not insupportable, demands on local officials. It was also dependent on maintaining a regular system of naval patrolling that may have been beyond the resources or capability of the regime. While the collection of fines may have helped to deter the supporters of pirates, and to provide compensation for their victims, this rested on their punitive impact which in some cases may have been insufficient. The evidence against John ap John of Cardiff suggested that he made £40 from dealing with Callice, though he appears to have been fined £10 by the council.[43]

Yet the regime met with some success, even if its campaign to suppress piracy was short lived and unsuccessful. Greater vigilance on the part of local officials, under the supervision of the council, led to more arrests. In February 1577 Perrot informed the council that he had arrested six pirates belonging to the companies of Callice, Hicks and Herbert. Several months later Callice was captured on the Isle of Wight. The following year Hicks was apprehended in Ireland and executed. Along the east coast Thomas Hitchcock was taken in or near Yarmouth, while Richard Scarborough was arrested in Lincolnshire. About the same time Philip Boyt, notorious for his plunder of a Spanish ship in the Straits of Malaga, was under arrest, though reports of his execution were premature. In obscure circumstances Boyt was reprieved, but in July 1580 the council was 'informed there is great misliking conceaved' against a stay of execution.[44] As a result it ordered Boyt's trial and execution, with several other pirates.

Under such conditions there was little reduction in the scale of pirate activity during the later 1570s. Nor was there any let up in the burden of business on the council, which included a variety of matters concerning piracy and depredation. In January 1579 it dealt with complaints concerning the plunder of vessels from the Low Countries off the coast of Kent by English pirates. Thereafter it handled cases concerning the spoil of French, Spanish and Scottish shipping, while trying to restore plundered goods which were brought into such scattered ports as Winchilsea and Waterford, as well as the Isle of Wight and in south-west England and south Wales. In addition it investigated allegations from the merchants of the Steelyard against pirates, issuing orders for the restitution of goods taken by Richard Scarborough which were brought into Grimsby, while dealing with a warning that another pirate, Captain Wilson, was lying in wait for their ships off Margate. It also faced repeated complaints against Henry Seckford, whose vessels were engaged in wide-ranging spoil during these years. A court official, trader and shipowner, Seckford survived several allegations of piracy; after 1585 his vessels were engaged in disorderly privateering.[45]

An increasing volume of business that came to the attention of the council concerned the business of receiving and dealing in the plunder of pirates. Early in 1579 it ordered the arrest of suspected supporters of pirates in Boston. Several weeks later it charged Thomas More of Gorleston, near Yarmouth, with handling goods from pirates. Faced with the refusal of some offenders to pay fines, it was forced to introduce more effective procedures for dealing with the recalcitrant. Bonds for the payment of fines were taken in Devon and Cornwall. But in March the collector of fines in Cornwall was admonished for the delay in paying in fines into the Exchequer. The difficulties in imposing financial penalties were revealed by the case of a group of men, accused of involvement in piracy, who were pardoned but unable to pay their fines because of poverty. Instead they were ordered to serve on a voyage to Iceland. Thereafter the council faced a steady stream of business dealing with the plunder and disposal of goods by pirates, which could only have raised doubts about the effectiveness of the piracy commissioners in some parts of the country.[46]

By 1580 the Elizabethan regime was struggling to contain the spread of piracy around the coasts of England, Wales and Ireland. Repeated attempts to eradicate it only revealed how deep seated and extensive the problem had become. While a growing band of pirate captains flourished in the local waters of the British Isles, a smaller number of resourceful and ambitious leaders, such as Callice, were also ranging into the Atlantic and beginning to enter the Mediterranean in search of richer prey. All too often the regime was left in the position of reacting to reports and complaints of piratical activity, while remaining dependent on inefficient or corrupt officials whose failings were strikingly exposed by the ease with which pirates either evaded capture or escaped from custody. Even when pirates were apprehended and executed, they were readily replaced by new recruits. Indeed, piracy was given renewed vigour by the cultivation of a new generation of leaders. Clinton Atkinson, a member of Boyt's company who entered the Mediterranean in 1578, soon earned notoriety as a pirate captain. Although he was apprehended and imprisoned in Exeter gaol, during the summer of 1580 he managed to escape.

An illustration of the execution of a pirate at Wapping, a well-established site for the punishment of piracy. Public executions were an opportunity for the display of repentance, but some pirates, such as Purser and Clinton, refused to play the part expected of them. (*Buccaneers of the Pacific*)

Underlying much of this piratical enterprise there was a widespread degree of complicity, which was reinforced by a vague patriotic impulse that pirates were attacking real or potential enemies of the realm. In May 1580 Philip Boyt defended his seizure of a Spanish ship by claiming to be under the apprehension that war was declared between England and Spain.[47] Although Boyt's defence was unsuccessful, the prospect of a war of plunder against Spain moved a step closer following the dramatic return of Drake, later in the year, with a rich haul of Spanish booty, after an absence of nearly three years during which he had circumnavigated the globe.

Oceanic plunder and schemes for overseas expansion

Drake's voyage was a landmark in the development of English depredation. Though it grew out of a dense background of organized, but highly localized petty marauding, it dramatically illuminated the oceanic capability of predatory enterprise. Characteristically it proceeded in highly ambiguous circumstances. Despite the regime's resolute response to piracy during the later 1570s, the Queen and some of her ministers covertly supported Drake's venture, though more as a speculative adventure than a strategic design. At the same time, the emergence of oceanic depredation was driven by anti-Spanish hostility which appeared to be capable of initiating a private or surrogate war of plunder against Spain's far-flung empire. Political and religious rivalries with Spain, inflamed by fear and aggression, were intensified by Philip II's acquisition of Portugal and its seaborne empire during 1580. The pretender to the Portuguese throne, Don Antonio, who travelled between England and France in search of support for his cause, served as a figurehead for a varied group of adventurers, including Drake, who were determined to promote aggressive action against Spain in the Atlantic. These hostile ambitions helped to focus attention on the strategic potential of North American settlement. Under these conditions during the early 1580s, the interweaving between piracy, privateering and transatlantic expansion appeared to be laying the basis for a national assault on Spain and its empire.

Concern at the Spanish reaction to Drake's voyage meant that its purpose was shrouded in secrecy. When the expedition left Plymouth during November 1577 it was publicly given out that Drake was bound for Alexandria in the Mediterranean. The survival of a damaged draft plan for the voyage indicates that it was an ambitious venture for trade and discovery along the east and west coasts of South America not yet occupied by, or under the obedience of, any other Christian ruler. Evidently it was motivated by the 'great hope of gold, silver, spices, drugs, cochineal, and divers other special commodities, such as may enrich her Highness' dominions, and also put shipping a-work greatly'. The plan anticipated a voyage lasting thirteen months, with Drake returning 'by the same way ... as he went out'.[48]

In reality, trade and discovery concealed a deeper intention, aimed at the plunder of Spanish commerce and shipping in one of the most vulnerable regions of the Hispanic Empire. According to Drake's version of the expedition, as subsequently reported by one of his company, this was a voyage of reprisal or revenge which grew out of discussions with Walsingham and the Queen. During the course of a speech to the company, which was intended to reinforce his authority at a difficult stage in the voyage, Drake indicated that the Queen had sought his advice on how she might 'be revenged on the King of Spain … and said further that he was the only man that might do this exploit'.[49] In addition, he claimed to have a commission from Elizabeth for the voyage, as well as a bill of adventure demonstrating her investment in it. Although the Queen was probably an investor in the venture, it seems unlikely that she provided Drake with a written commission for the voyage. Indeed, Drake was undoubtedly aware that if the expedition failed, it would be publicly disavowed by Elizabeth.

Drake's advice regarding the Queen's desire for revenge against Philip II, that 'the only way was to annoy him in his Indies', was a strategic challenge and a beguiling prospect.[50] But it emerged within a wider context of growing English interest in long-distance commercial expansion and vague, as yet unrealized, schemes for colonization in America. In these circumstances, the essentially predatory purpose of the voyage was linked with equally speculative ambitions which played some part in influencing its outcome. The flexibility of the venture thus created the opportunity for exploration along the eastern coast of North America, and for commercial reconnoitring in the East Indies, while not distracting from its primary goal. At the same time, however, it drew on Drake's experience in the Caribbean. Among the company was a cimaroon, who aided Drake in 1572 and had since been in his service. It is possible that Drake was intending to return to the region around Panama, with the hope of renewing his alliance with the cimaroons and of establishing contact with Oxenham, who had departed on a plundering expedition to the isthmus eighteen months earlier. As such, the voyage has been seen from one perspective as a sequel to English raiding in the Caribbean during the mid-1570s.

The supporters of the venture demonstrated the willingness of leading members of the regime to promote anti-Spanish enterprise across the Atlantic and beyond. In addition to the Queen, the investors included the Lord Admiral, Leicester, Walsingham and Sir Christopher Hatton, as well as Sir William and George Winter and Hawkins. While Drake's subscription amounted to £1,000, the Winters and Hawkins invested £1,750 in the voyage.[51] This range of support indicated a close community of interest between prominent courtiers and officials, including the navy, with one of the leading representatives of the predatory tendency in English maritime enterprise. Although the employment of redeemed pirates by the regime was neither unusual nor unprecedented, at least in European waters, the Queen's support for Drake's voyage was of a different order to her willingness to use men such as Strangeways or Callice. In political, diplomatic and financial terms this was a gamble with high stakes.

With this backing Drake assembled a fleet of five vessels of modest size, the largest of which, the *Pelican*, subsequently renamed the *Golden Hind*, was of about 100 to 150 tons. The expedition was well armed and equipped for its purpose. Drake's ship, the *Pelican*, itself carried medium-sized ordnance and a variety of hand weapons such as muskets, pikes and bows and arrows, as well as fire bombs, which were intended for use in the seizure of prizes rather than for sustained battle at sea. About 160 men sailed with the expedition, including Francis Fletcher – a minister and the author of an account of the voyage – and a group of about ten gentlemen. As a demonstration of sea power this was modest in scale; in reality it was more a projection of a well-established tradition of irregular, private depredation than of royal naval enterprise.

The voyage was marked by widespread plunder and punctuated by high drama and adventure. After leaving Plymouth the expedition cruised southward along the coast of Africa, seizing several Iberian prizes of limited value.

The *Pelican*, a vessel of about 100 tons, and armed with eighteen ordnance. Drake sailed in this ship during his circumnavigation from 1577 to 1580. It was renamed the *Golden Hind* in honour of the courtier Sir Christopher Hatton, a prominent investor in the voyage, after the execution of his servant, Thomas Doughty. Drake was knighted aboard the vessel in 1581. (*Buccaneers of the Pacific*)

Off the Cape Verde Islands a Portuguese vessel was taken. Its pilot, Nuño da Silva, was retained for service in navigating along the coast of Brazil, which the English reached in April 1578. In poor weather Drake scouted south before deciding to winter in Port St Julian, a safe harbour which Magellan had previously used. It was here that Drake faced down the mutinous discontent of the gentlemen, with the trial and execution of Thomas Doughty. Social rivalry and indiscipline were always a potential problem among unruly groups of mariners serving on long voyages, but they were intensified by the presence of gentlemen volunteers whose expectations of an easy life at sea were a provocation to most seamen. Drake complained to his company after the execution of Doughty that there was 'such controversy betwixt the sailors and the gentlemen, and such stomaching between the gentlemen and the sailors, that it doth even make me mad to hear it'.[52] In an impassioned exhortation, which was both popular and radical in implication, Drake demanded that 'the gentleman … haul and draw with the mariner, and the mariner with the gentleman', for the sake of the unity of the company and the success of the venture. But it was an awkward and short-term solution to a problem that was to become more overt after the outbreak of the war with Spain in 1585, as growing numbers of gentlemen were attracted into service at sea by the appeal of privateering.

The expedition, now reduced to three vessels, passed through Magellan's Strait during August 1578. In bad weather the fleet separated: one ship was lost at sea, another returned for England. Drake continued the voyage in the *Golden Hind*, sailing north along the coast of Peru. By December he had reached and ransacked the small coastal settlement of Valparaiso. A ship laden with wine and gold was seized in the harbour. Sailing further north, he captured another valuable prize and raided the harbour at Callao, where he heard about the recent departure of a richly laden vessel, the *Nuestra Señora de la Concepcion*, also known as the *Cacafuego*, for Panama. Drake gave chase and seized the vessel, laden with a cargo of gold and silver worth 360,000 pesos, close to Cape San Francisco. Though he continued sailing north, taking several smaller prizes and raiding the small harbour of Guatulco along the coast of Mexico, Drake's main aim was to return to England with this rich haul of plunder. Fortunately, he had acquired two Spanish pilots from one of the prizes, who were experienced in sailing to the Philippines.[53]

During an extended cruise along the west coast of North America, which may possibly have been linked with the search for the Northwest Passage, Drake landed in the vicinity of San Francisco, where he was ceremoniously welcomed by the native people who treated the English as gods. In naming the region Nova Albion, he also claimed it for the Queen. At the end of July the expedition began the Pacific crossing, reaching the island of Ternate, the ruler of which was apparently keen to establish commercial relations with Europeans other than the Portuguese. After a brief stay, and the acquisition of six tons of cloves, Drake departed, hoping to reach the Moluccas. But the *Golden Hind* was nearly shipwrecked along the coast of Celebes. In perilous circumstances Fletcher, the minister, 'made them a

An illustration of the fight between the *Golden Hind* and the *Cacafuego* near Cape San Francisco. When commanded to surrender, the master of the Spanish ship apparently responded: 'What old tub is that which orders me to strike sail? Come on board and strike sail yourselves'. But the Spanish put up little resistance, and the vessel, richly laden with gold and silver, was easily taken. The 'old tub' became one of the most famous vessels in Elizabethan England. After returning to London, it was laid up at Deptford and became an attraction for visitors. (*Buccaneers of the Pacific*)

sermon and they received communion all together and then every thief reconciled himself to his fellow thief'.[54] The ship was saved by a change in the wind, and the jettisoning of some of the cargo of spices and several pieces of ordnance. However, bad weather drove the vessel past the Moluccas to Java, from whence the *Golden Hind* returned to England by way of the Cape of Good Hope. After a voyage of nearly three years, Drake sailed into Plymouth harbour towards the end of September 1580.

Drake's success provoked a clamour of complaint from the Spanish. The Queen failed to respond to repeated demands for the restoration of the booty. Indeed, the survivors of the voyage were allowed to keep £20,000, half of which was

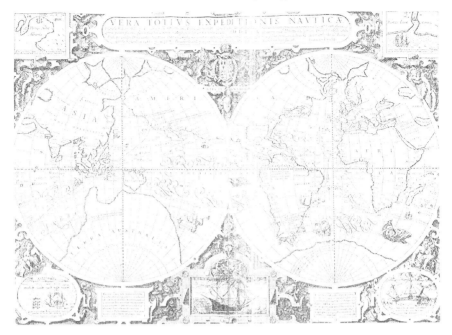

A Dutch map of 1595, indicating the voyages around the world by Drake and Cavendish. Drake's voyage was primarily a voyage of plunder, though it may have included provision for exploration and commercial reconnoitring. The success of the voyage helped to transform Drake into a popular hero. (*Sir Francis Drake*)

for Drake's personal use. The following year, in April 1581, he was knighted by Elizabeth aboard the *Golden Hind*. Though the acclaim was far from universal, the response to the voyage began the transformation of Drake into a folk hero, exploiting and embellishing the image of the pirate as a righteous outlaw. The growth of Anglo-Spanish suspicion and tension was also a vital element in the wider reaction to Drake's success, particularly as it provided an opportunity to portray the piratical assault on Spanish shipping as a lawful means of reprisal. Reports of May 1582 that the King of Spain had offered 20,000 ducats for Drake's head only served to confirm his status as a patriotic leader, who inspired emulation among a small host of Protestant champions eager to win renown and honour at sea while sharing in the spoil of the Spanish empire.[55]

If Drake's voyage caught the popular imagination, contributing to a new-found sense of confidence in Elizabethan England, it also encouraged a variety of schemes for commercial and colonial expansion which were linked with plunder. Across the Atlantic these ranged from the Straits of Magellan, where a naval station was proposed for the purpose of intercepting Spanish trade, to Newfoundland, the focus for several proposals in favour of the seizure of Iberian fishing vessels. They also included plans for the settlement of North America, which a small group of adventurers was beginning to promote, though there was an unresolved tension between an overtly aggressive and more pacific approach. In addition, projects were put forward for the capture of Spanish fleets returning from the Caribbean or for raiding along the coast of Spain.[56]

In practice many of these schemes were unrealistic. Additionally, the Queen's determination to avoid open war with Spain left them in the hands of private adventurers, who were unable to provide clear direction to largely uncoordinated ambitions for Atlantic depredation. Nonetheless, these circumstances provided an opportunity for the proponents of westward expansion, such as Richard Hakluyt the younger, to present imaginative proposals for the employment of pirates to advance English interests in America.[57]

The arrival of Don Antonio in England had the potential to lend greater shape to these schemes. He soon became a focal point for the ambitions of a mixed group of anti-Spanish adventurers which included courtiers, naval officials and maritime entrepreneurs, as well as pirates. The Queen was concerned that the presence of Don Antonio would provoke Philip II, though the Portuguese pretender was reportedly so poor in 1581 that he lacked clothing. However, Elizabeth did not prevent him from issuing commissions against the Spanish to his English supporters, nor did she stand in the way of an ambitious plan for an expedition to the Azores during 1581, which was supported by leading members of the regime and involved Drake. Although the expedition failed to proceed as intended, a small fleet of four vessels, under the command of Captain Henry Roberts of Bristol, was despatched to Angra, and may have played a vital role in conserving the island for Don Antonio. Failing to get more effective assistance from the Queen, he moved to France, where he gained sufficient support for an expedition to the Azores in 1582, though it was heavily defeated by the Spanish.[58]

Under the camouflage of commissions from Don Antonio, a motley and disorderly force of privateers was involved in the plunder of Spanish and other shipping during the early 1580s, anticipating to some extent the rapid expansion of English privateering after 1585. While these commissions were justified as legitimate reprisals against Spain, they were also an implicit claim to sovereignty by the pretender to the throne of Portugal, even if in practice many of the recipients behaved in a piratical manner. Their activities provoked grievances not only from the Spanish, but also from the Dutch. Spanish complaints against Henry Knollys, who was cruising with the ships of Don Antonio off the Isle of Wight during 1581, forced the latter to apologise to Walsingham, though he insisted that the Englishman was disregarding his orders. In November 1581 the Dutch complained that ships fitted out in England, under the pretext of aiding Don Antonio, were spoiling vessels sailing to the Low Countries.[59]

While the Dutch demanded that those involved in these attacks should be dealt with as pirates, there seemed to be genuine uncertainty in England regarding the status and legality of vessels operating under Don Antonio's commission.

The seizure of a Spanish ship returning from Santo Domingo, which was brought into an English port, provoked discussion about its adjudication as lawful prize. In September 1582 the Spanish ambassador complained of Roberts' seizure of two Portuguese caravels returning from Brazil with cargoes of sugar, though he expected that the matter would not be favourably resolved. Indeed, it was reported in April that the Queen 'intends not to meddle in Roberts' sugars', though one of the prizes was subsequently restored.[60]

At least eleven English captains were sailing with commissions from Don Antonio during 1581 and 1582. Such was the apparent appeal of serving under the Portuguese pretender that in July 1582 it was reported that forty ships were expected to be sent out by English adventurers in his support. Earlier in the year, a German adventurer offered to aid him, leading an expedition against Spain to the Indies, if he was supported by the Queen. The prospect of Don Antonio becoming a figurehead for pan-Protestant adventurers, including French Huguenots sailing with commissions from the King of Navarre, who were intent on pursuing a war of plunder against the Spanish and Portuguese, receded following the failure of the expedition to the Azores in which several English captains served. In July he left Tours and went to sea, though he was forced to sail without any of his captains, who were in prison for debt. According to one report, 'no man can tell whether he needs not be afraid to be robbed, for he has not a penny more than the poor grey friar'.[61]

About the same time, the cause of the Portuguese pretender among Protestants was discredited by reports that he had issued a declaration promising protection to merchants trading with Spain under his licence. Early in 1584 he was allowed to return to England, but on condition that he would not reside near the coast. He was reported to be in such difficult circumstances that he wanted to move to Guernsey. By September he was in the Netherlands, issuing letters of marque or reprisal to Dutch adventurers. Evidently he hoped to mobilize a force of twelve ships. Through agents in England he continued to issue similar commissions to his English supporters, who included the Fenners and their new associate Callice.[62]

Although the legality of English depredation under the auspices of Don Antonio remained uncertain, it provided the regime with an opportunity to maintain the pressure on Spain at sea, while denying any hostile intent. Under these conditions privateering served as an instrument of policy, albeit one that was inherently hazardous. At the same time it provided an outlet for the activities of pirates and the aggressive propagandists of overseas expansion. While it was recognized in February 1583 that the Queen could not assist Don Antonio with 2,000 men without risking conflict with Spain, the case for continuing to support him with men-of-war seemed to go unchallenged. For some this was an irresistible opportunity to penetrate the Portuguese and Spanish seaborne empires through a combination of trade and plunder.[63]

While there was a danger that such irregular privateering would degenerate into piracy, it strengthened English venturing into the Atlantic during the early 1580s. English captains were involved in expeditions to the Azores during 1581 and 1582, either with others or on their own. They included Captain Kenne of Bristol, who seized several prizes off Terceira which were brought into Southampton. In 1582 William Hawkins and his brother, John, received a commission for a voyage of discovery to Africa and America, authorizing them to assist the Portuguese pretender against his enemies. With the benefit of this authority Hawkins led an expedition, which included two ships owned by Drake, to west Africa with the intention of trading thence to Brazil. Faced with hostility at the Cape Verde Islands, and learning of an increased Spanish presence along the coast of Brazil, the fleet sailed for the Caribbean, where a profitable cargo of commodities was acquired. Further north, adventurers turned their attention to the vulnerable fishing fleets off Newfoundland. In November 1582 the Spanish complained of the spoil of more than twenty ships at the fishery by Henry Oughtred of Southampton.[64]

But the growth of deep-sea plunder endangered peaceful plans for commercial expansion within neglected regions of the Iberian empires. The ambitious, but unsuccessful voyage of Captain Edward Fenton during 1582 and 1583 underlined the dangers, particularly with expeditions which suffered from weak or divided leadership. Ostensibly the purpose of the voyage was to establish a trading outpost in the East Indies as a means of exploiting Drake's contact with the Moluccas. To some extent, however, it was a legacy of the abortive expedition to the Azores of 1581. It attracted a similar range of investors, as well as arousing the interest of a group of merchants who were prominent figures in the Muscovy Company. Leicester was the leading promoter of the venture, purchasing the *Galleon Oughtred* from Henry Oughtred at a cost of £2,800 for the voyage. Of this amount, £800 represented Oughtred's share in the voyage. According to the terms of the sale, Leicester was to procure a commission from Don Antonio authorizing the plunder of Spanish and Portuguese shipping. Drake was among the other investors, who included Walsingham and his son-in-law, Christopher Carleill.[65]

Fenton, the leader of the expedition, was an experienced soldier who served with Frobisher on the ill-fated Northwest Passage ventures during the later 1570s. He harboured grandiose visions of wealth that turned the voyage into a disorderly and unsuccessful quest for Iberian prizes. He commanded a fleet of four vessels and a company of more than 230 men. Oughtred's ship, renamed the *Galleon Leicester*, a large vessel of about 400 or 500 tons, armed with forty-two pieces of ordnance, served as the Admiral for the voyage. The officers included William Hawkins the younger, a nephew of John Hawkins, though Carleill pulled out of the voyage after clashing with the former. John Drake, one of Drake's cousins, was in charge of a pinnace, the *Bark Francis*. In addition Simon Fernandes, who was accused of bragging about his piracies during the course of the voyage, served as chief pilot. The expedition sailed with two clergymen, John Walker and Richard Madox. Neither survived the voyage, but both of them kept diaries that reveal their mounting concern at the piratical inclinations of members of the company.[66]

Fenton's instructions, which were approved by the council, indicate the commercial purpose of the voyage and a concern to avoid antagonizing the Spanish. Thus the expedition was to avoid the Straits of Magellan, unless in an emergency, sailing to the East Indies and returning thence by way of the Cape of Good Hope. Furthermore, Fenton and his company were instructed not to spoil the Queen's 'friends or allies, or any Christians, without paying justly for the same', while dealing as 'good and honest merchants, traffiquing and exchanging ware for ware' with the people they encountered, 'as well ethniks as others'.[67]

Yet commercial aggrandisement of this nature was marked by deep-seated ambiguities. Revealingly they were exposed partly by Madox during his sermon to the company on the eve of the departure of the fleet from Southampton. Taking his cue from the first verse of Psalm 24, the clergyman raised several issues regarding the lawfulness of travel and trade in general, including traffic with non-Christians, reaffirming that England had the best claim to the Indies. For some the sermon reinforced the essentially predatory purpose of the venture. In May 1582, as Oughtred informed Leicester that the fleet was ready to sail, he was unable to conceal his wish for its safe return with 'all the Kinge of Spayne his gold in theyr bellyes, to temper the pryde of such a tyrawnte'.[68]

According to the narrative of William Hawkins, drawn up shortly after the return of the expedition, Fenton denied any intention of seeking to emulate Drake in playing 'the pirate and theefe', claiming instead to have 'thre strings to his bowe' which would make for a profitable voyage.[69] Nonetheless, the shadow of Drake's voyage hung over this expedition, arousing high expectations for its success. Consequently plunder was always a likely option. Among the company, moreover, the mariners served on their own adventure, in expectation that a share of the proceeds of the voyage would replace a wage. The expedition had barely left the coast of England before leading members of the crew were expressing their hope of meeting with a rich carvel laden with sugar and wines. Fenton resisted calls to attack a vessel, with the support of the clergymen, whose sermons reminded the company of the purpose of the voyage. However, Madox noted that some of the men declared that they 'wer bound in duty to spoyl all papists, as enemyes to god & our sovereign, of what cuntrey so ever they were'.[70] Fenton's failure to give chase to a possible prize thus provoked an undertow of disaffection and disunity that persisted for much of the voyage.

Despite careful preparation and clear guidance, the expedition was an embarrassing failure. From the outset it was endangered by the ambitions of Fenton to undertake some notable action which would win him honour and profit. Unfortunately, he was a weak, vainglorious commander, mockingly described by Madox in his private diary as 'our little king'.[71] On several occasions Fenton spoke openly of turning to plunder or piracy, arousing the expectations of many members of the expedition, but he lacked either the courage or boldness to suc-ceed as a successor of Drake.

In accordance with their instructions, after leaving England the fleet sailed southwards. At the direction of Fernandes the vessels maintained a course for the Canary Islands, apparently intending to acquire goats, though Madox noted that most of the company were 'set on purchase'.[72] Although bound for the Cape Verde Islands, it was agreed by a council of officers to sail for Rio de la Plata, across the Atlantic, on the advice of the pilots concerning the navigation of the Cape of Good Hope. The Atlantic crossing was delayed by a decision to sail for Sierra Leone in search of fresh water. Unaccountably the fleet spent two months off the coast of west Africa, during which sickness broke out among the company, killing at least ten men aboard the *Galleon Leicester*. The English had a small trade with a group of Portuguese merchants, acquiring rice and ivory in exchange for one of their smaller ships. While they were on the coast Madox viewed a party of slaves acquired by the Portuguese, one of whom, a woman, he sketched. Several male slaves were purchased by the English to replace members of the company who had died.

It was during this period that Fenton conferred with Madox about a startling proposal for the settlement of the island of St Helena, as a base from which to plunder Portuguese vessels returning from the East Indies. Since its discovery by the Portuguese in 1502, the island had been used by returning vessels from the east as a resting place to take on fresh water, but its use was irregular because of the difficulty in locating it. Fenton's proposal was opportunistic and ill-consid-ered, though it appears to have been shared by some of his officers. It may have been made to test the reaction of Madox who, along with Walker, was known to be against the predatory direction of the voyage. At the same time, it dem-onstrated the shifting priorities of the leaders of the expedition. Shortly after Fenton discussed the scheme with Madox, the clergyman discovered that he 'had promised many among us that he would never return to our native land before he rewarded them with wealth'.[73] Failing to win support from the clergymen, Fenton considered returning to the Cape Verde Islands, but he was eventually persuaded to proceed across the Atlantic.

Before leaving the coast of Africa, the plan for sailing around the Cape was given up in preference for passing through the Straits of Magellan. It was also agreed that when the expedition entered the Pacific it was 'to deale as occa-sion should be given'.[74] In effect the original purpose of the voyage was tacitly abandoned. Further change was suggested during the Atlantic crossing, when Fernandes advised a council of officers to sail directly for the Caribbean in search of plunder. Although the two clergymen dissuaded Fenton from pursuing this course, soon after reaching the coast of Brazil, in December 1582, the fleet seized a small prize carrying a group of passengers, which included seven friars. The capture of the vessel provoked angry disagreement among Fenton's com-pany concerning competing claims to pillage and plunder. Madox recorded that it was 'sent away in peace but still slightly plucked so as to satisfy our rapacious and greedy sailers in some measure'. The spoil, including a net, axes, iron hoops, bills, small amounts of sugar, ginger root and some sweet meats, amounted to £10.[75]

It became evident along the coast of Brazil that Fenton was unwilling to undertake the revised plan. Following information from the passengers aboard the prize that a Spanish expedition had been sent to guard the straits, he assembled the company to request their advice on the best way of proceeding. Opinion was divided, and Fenton's subsequent decision to change direction, and sail northwards, aroused widespread concern, reinforcing rumours that the 'voyage was bought & sold' before their departure from London.[76] At this stage the *Bark Francis*, with John Drake in command, left the fleet in an unsuccessful attempt to make for the straits. Drake's departure appears to have unnerved Fenton, who now tried to persuade his officers of the profit to be made from trading with the Portuguese in Brazil. Within twelve months, he claimed, they would be able to return home with an honest, if modest, profit. But the revised plan had no appeal for men such as Fernandes or Hawkins. For the former the decision to engage in trade, rather than robbery, was greeted with incredulity. After the Christmas celebrations, he spoke out against Fenton's new scheme, claiming that it would reduce the company to beggary and worse, particularly as he was already impoverished and in debt. Though motivated by raw self-interest, undoubtedly Fernandes was speaking for many other members of the company who had little to lose and much to gain from illegitimate depredation. But his attempt to represent these piratical interests in a favourable light, by trying to convince Fenton and the clergymen that he possessed a licence from members of the council to wage war against the Spaniards, met with no success.[77]

Fenton's scheme for peaceful commerce failed. The Portuguese refused to trade with the English, though they were prepared to supply them with provisions. As the two remaining ships sailed along the coast of Brazil, they encountered three Spanish vessels off the port of São Vicente. During the ensuing conflict one of the Spanish vessels was sunk. Thereafter the English ships became separated. Both were short of water and provisions. Consequently both ships returned to England, though Fenton considered making course for Newfoundland. When he reached Ireland in June 1583 many of his company were discontented and rebellious. By the time the *Galleon Leicester* reached the Thames one of the officers, Hawkins, was in irons as a result of a violent brawl with Fenton.

What began as an ambitious and peaceful trading venture turned into a disorderly and dangerous voyage. Yet the expedition was symptomatic of the increasingly predatory and opportunistic nature of English maritime expansion. The evidence of Madox's diary, moreover, suggests that this was in the hands of men who were habituated to piracy. But the development of deep-sea plunder raised challenging questions about its operation. Fenton's scheme for the settlement of St Helena may have been impractical; nonetheless, it points to the emergence of new and possibly radical ideas for the establishment of overseas pirate bases which may have been circulating among seafarers, though the experience of the voyage indicated that conditions during the early 1580s did not favour their implementation. Madox's summary of the reasons by which Fenton was 'induced at last to honest trading' provided a revealing insight into the confused discussion of such ideas, and the response to them. Evidently Fenton appealed to his company:

> if we once give ourselves over to piracy, any place suitable for habitation must be contemned and to return home enriched with plunder is neither safe nor honest. And after plundering to return home in poverty is an offense punishable by death. Even if all are charged with the same guilt and all are authors with me in robbing others, yet the harshest blame would fall on me should I return. But to remain is a harsher lot, for I find no one who would willingly wish to die an exile from his country, and I cannot remain alone.[78]

Fenton's 'troublesome voyage', and the confusion which overtook it, thus illuminated the speculative and uncertain response to the opportunities for oceanic plunder that Drake so spectacularly pioneered.

Piracy and disorderly privateering during the early 1580s

If deep-sea depredation emerged in hazardous and hesitant circumstances, local piracy around the British Isles continued to flourish in various guises despite the commissions of the later 1570s. Experienced pirate captains, such as Callice, survived into the early 1580s, but they were joined by a group of younger leaders who reinvigorated the pirate brotherhood, particularly in favoured haunts in south-west England and Wales. The activities of men such as Clinton and Purser, whose exploits were embellished in ballads and song, pointed towards the consolidation and elaboration of a pirate culture which was acquiring sharper and more defiant definition.

A steady stream of complaints and reports to the council revealed the extent of the problem. In May 1580 an Italian ship was seized along the Thames by a Dutch rover sailing with an English captain. Several weeks later a group of English soldiers and sailors spoiled a ship in the harbour at Youghal. In addition pirate ships were active along the east coast, ranging northwards from Orford Ness. The *Elizabeth* of London was plundered by John Coates and his company off Flamborough Head, a regular haunt for pirates who preyed on vulnerable coasting vessels. Although much of this activity was opportunistic, and justified as retaliation against overseas attack, organized piracy flourished along the coasts of south and south-west England. In April 1581 Henry Howard, son of Viscount Howard of Bindon, was accused of associating with pirates at Lulworth.[79]

Further along the coast, the increase in the number of pirates and rovers off the Isle of Wight was blamed on the negligence of Sir Edward Horsey's lieutenant. Later in the year the council ordered Lord Cobham to send out ships for the apprehension of pirates who had plundered merchants of Rye while crossing to Dieppe. Two London merchants, Samuel Knollys and Philip Fish, were also commanded to appear before the council to answer charges that their vessel, the *Bark Roe*, had spoiled two Turkish ships in the Mediterranean.[80]

Despite greater vigilance and supervision, pirates and rovers continued to frequent well-established havens with little fear of arrest or punishment. One of Burghley's agents, John Johnson, provided a detailed report concerning the situation on the Isle of Wight, which was regularly visited by English, Dutch and French rovers during the early 1580s. Under the protection of local officials a flourishing trade in booty, including the redemption of captured vessels, was maintained in the form of unregulated seaside markets. In small ports, such as Cowes or Newport, the disposal of pirate plunder attracted gentlemen, farmers, fishermen, craftsmen and the servants of Sir Edward Horsey. In April 1581, with at least four men-of-war anchored around the island, Johnson reported that about thirty boats thronged around the rovers, carrying passengers from ship to ship for a fee of twelve pence to do business with the pirates. It was like a fair, with 'bynge and selling and barteringe'.[81] Aboard the men-of-war every sailor had his share of the booty laid out on display, while bargains were made with visiting buyers. Johnson, who was trying to recover the property of English and Flemish traders, aroused the suspicions of the rovers because he purchased nothing. His report to Burghley suggests that he narrowly escaped with his life after being identified as a spy. The captain of one of the rovers threatened to put him on trial before a jury selected from the company, but he was dissuaded by appeals from the master and others, including one of Horsey's men. Instead, he was forced to swear never to reveal the identities of the rovers or the purchasers of their plunder. Thereupon the captain 'made [him] good cheare' in his cabin, promising him two shirts.[82] Meanwhile, the company disposed of their wares. A cargo of cloth and linen, reputedly worth £1,400 or £1,500, was sold in less than two days; much of the proceeds appear to have been dispersed by the pirates in daily visits ashore.

Under these conditions the regime struggled to maintain its firm response to piracy. The punishment of pirates continued to be influenced by considerations of policy or undermined by the negligence and corruption of local officials. In June 1581 the commissioners for piracy in Dorset bound Adam Sampson, a Scottish rover, to appear before the council, though they were one of the few commissions still active. The following month Samuel Bigges, sentenced to death for piracy, was reprieved. In August the council was informed that William Daniel and another pirate had been allowed to escape. Although two pirate captains were in custody by October 1581, their contrasting experiences indicated similar weaknesses. One of them was John Piers, who was widely suspected of operating in league with his mother, Ann, reputedly a witch of Padstow. According to various

Lulworth Cove, Dorset. Under the protection of local landowners such as Sir Richard Rogers, pirates and rovers visited the harbour during the 1570s and early 1580s, consorting with the local inhabitants. Among those associating of consorting with pirates was Henry Howard, the son of Viscount Howard of Bindon. (Author's collection)

reports Piers was freed without facing trial by the mayor of Rye. Although he was arrested a second time, he escaped from Dorchester Gaol with the connivance of the keeper. He was recaptured and hanged in chains along the shore of Studland Bay at the command of the council. The other prisoner, Fludd, avoided execution during 1581. On the eve of the Anglo-Spanish war, with the reputation of a 'valiant and skilful pirate', he offered to survey the coast of Spain for the Queen.[83]

The limited success of the council in regulating local officials was demonstrated by the activities of the servants of Sir John Killigrew, one of the commissioners for piracy in Cornwall. In January 1582 other members of the commission accused Killigrew's servants of spoiling a Spanish ship in the harbour at Falmouth, and of attempting to rescue a pirate captain. Faced with repeated allegations of conniving with pirates, Killigrew fled Cornwall. According to one report he was 'secretly lurking in London', although another informant suggested that he was in Ireland.[84] In April he voluntarily appeared before the council. After a short spell of confinement, he was allowed to return to the south-west.

From the perspective of the council, the problem of dealing with such cases was complicated by malicious complaints, which often grew out of local rivalries that were difficult and time consuming to disentangle. In July 1582 Gilbert Peppitt, an Admiralty official in Exeter, was accused of allowing Clinton Atkinson to escape two years earlier. But the accusation appears to have been

Carrick Roads, Cornwall. A long-standing haunt for pirates and rovers, and the power base for the Killigrew family, whose members were repeatedly in trouble for their maritime activities and dealings with visiting rovers. (Author's collection)

part of a campaign to discredit Peppitt, who was subsequently exonerated of any wrongdoing. To some extent, the growing use of officials from the High Court of Admiralty in London to search for pirates and their supporters was intended to override these difficulties, though officers from London remained dependent on local cooperation and compliance. James Swift, the marshal of the Admiralty, compiled a detailed report on piracy during 1581 which contained a mine of information, sometimes of a very personal nature. The pirate, George Burde, for example, was described as suffering from a 'stump foot'.[85] Yet without the support of local officials, much of this information was of little value, as Swift inadvertently acknowledged. His comments on the procedure for the arrest of pirates drew explicit attention to the long-standing problem posed by negligent constables.

As a result piracy remained a flourishing business, especially within the Channel and western approaches. In February 1582 a ship of Don Antonio's was taken and brought into Kinsale by a group of pirates. A fishing boat was attacked within sight of Rye during June. About the same time, the French complained of the seizure of five ships by Court Hellebourg, and the capture and sale of another vessel in Poole by Atkinson. Later in the year Francis Hawley, the keeper of Corfe Castle in Dorset, presented an alarming report of his inability to repel visiting pirate ships. The 'place of their repaire is here', he informed Walsingham, 'where in trueth they ar my masters'.[86] Hawley sought to defend himself against rumours concerning his relations with the pirates, claiming that 'their comforte in landing here is not the cause of their accesse unto us, for their captaines (who seldom or never come ashoare) ar verie unwilling therunto'. In any case, when pirates came ashore they were 'so stronge and well appointed as they cannot be on soddine repulsed'. While Hawley admitted that he had been recently involved in discussions with Purser, about the recovery of a French ship, he advised Walsingham that a group of Southampton men had offered £600 for the recovery of the vessel, which they intended to sell back to the original owners.

The activities of pirates and rovers within and beyond the waters of the British Isles encouraged retaliation, including the arrest of English shipping in overseas ports, which provoked appeals for letters of reprisal among merchants and shipowners. During 1581 the *Minion* of Plymouth was arrested in Spain on suspicion of piracy. The owners of an English vessel which was arrested in the port of Civitavecchia were awarded a commission of reprisal. It was accompanied by the issue of a similar licence against Lübeck. In addition the raids of French and Scottish rovers led to angry complaints from ports such as Chester, Liverpool and Yarmouth. Merchants of Chester repeatedly demanded letters of reprisal against France and Spain to recoup their losses at sea. Among those claiming losses against Spain was Henry Oughtred of Southampton, although the Spanish countered with their own complaints about the raid on the Newfoundland fishery by his vessels in 1582.[87]

Corfe Castle, Dorset. The estate of the castle was acquired by Sir Christopher Hatton in 1572. During the early 1580s the keeper of the castle, Francis Hawley, warned one of the Queen's ministers that he was unable to prevent pirates from visiting the region. The castle was occasionally used to stage trials for pirates. (Author's collection)

The damaging impact of disorderly plunder and piracy aroused widespread concern. One report partly blamed the decline of Southampton on piracy. During the past ten years it was claimed that pirates had haunted the coast. They seized many ships bound for the port, disposing of their plunder locally and in other parts of the county. The pirates 'robbed & spoyled many of our merchants even at their owne dores, & sold away their goods as it were before their own faces, to the undoing of many which shall never be able to recover themselves againe'.[88] In addition, the upsurge of Scottish piracy was particularly damaging for trade and fishing along the east coast. By June 1584 Scots pirates had taken more than fourteen vessels belonging to the fishing ports of Suffolk. Later in the year, North and South Shields claimed to have suffered damages amounting to £1,100 at their hands. Concern at the activities of the Scots was accompanied by complaints from the coastal communities of the south-east against Dutch men-of-war, including the 'hell-hounds' of Flushing.[89]

Although the economic cost is impossible to quantify, the damage inflicted on English trade and shipping by overseas pirates and privateers may have been considerable. During Anglo-French negotiations concerning the plunder of shipping in the 1590s, the English claimed losses against the French of £104,000, of which 'there was never one penie restitution made'.[90] More than one quarter of the total value of this spoil was taken during the first half of the 1580s, with losses of more than £17,000 during 1580 and 1581, followed by a sharp drop, before the amount began to increase during 1584.

The scale of cross-Channel plunder and reprisals rendered redundant a renewed Anglo-French attempt to agree on articles for the abolition of piracy during 1583. French complaints concerning the activities of Hellebourg and Callice appear to have persuaded the regime to send out Captain Richard Bingham in September with a commission to take pirates in the Channel, though in reality it may have been a cover for the seizure of Dutch vessels as recompense for outstanding debts. This did little to ease French hostility at sea. The violence and disorder were inflamed by reports of cases such as the seizure of a Breton vessel by Henry Knollys, which rotted away at Southampton, while its owner went mad and died pursuing the case in the High Court of Admiralty, leaving behind a widow and children in starving circumstances.[91]

The seas around the British Isles consequently remained profitable hunting grounds for pirates and privateers of varying background and legality. Some regions were infested with rovers. Within a few days of leaving the Thames, Fenton's expedition encountered more than six suspicious ships, two of which were taken and brought into Southampton as prizes. Off Dover it met four small vessels which were suspected to be men-of-war. One was a pirate ship, manned with at least nine men who were originally recruited for the expedition, but who abandoned it in favour of piracy, when Frobisher was replaced by Fenton. Under Captain Watson – and with Willobye, 'a tawl [bold] feloe of Dover', among the company – the pirates seized a vessel which they later exchanged for a Flemish ship.[92] As Fenton's fleet sailed from Dover to Southampton, it met and chased two vessels under the command of Captain Heyns, a notorious pirate. It also stopped and boarded a man-of-war, sailing under a commission from Don Antonio, with a French prize. As the expedition approached Southampton it was boldly greeted by Captain Clarke with his customary salute of a glass of wine.

The pirate groups operating during these years were led by a mix of experienced and well-established captains, some of whom, like Callice or Clarke, had been active for more than a decade, while there existed a group of younger leaders, including Clinton Atkinson and Thomas Walton of Cheshire, alias Clinton and Purser. In March 1583 Clinton was spoiling vessels at the mouth of the River Shannon, in a ship of 100 tons and with a company of eighty men. A few months later, he was reported to have seized one of the Queen's vessels, defiantly threatening to enter the service of the King of Spain or to support the rebellion of Gerald Fitzgerald, 15th Earl of Desmond, in Ireland. Towards the end of the year, in consortship with Atkinson, he plundered several Irish ships in Mount's Bay. One of the victims, Maurice Fowler of Cork, was subsequently awarded a licence to beg, as a means of alleviating his losses.[93]

Despite the plunder of Irish shipping by Clinton and Purser, English pirates and rovers received varied support in the remote regions of south-west Ireland, renewing contacts which were to flourish during the early seventeenth century.

As in parts of England and Wales piracy encouraged the growth of widespread, if sporadic, networks of trade, exchange and gift giving. Along the isolated and rough hewn coast of Munster pirates were provisioned and provided with recruits, many of whom came from transient groups of seafarers and fishermen. The presence of an increasing number of soldiers in Ireland created a wider pool of potential recruits. It was a mixed group of soldiers and sailors, for example, who plundered a vessel in the harbour at Youghal during 1580. The discharge of soldiers in Ireland, many of whom lacked the resources to return to England, dramatically increased the number of poor and vagrant in some communities. According to a report of February 1582, unemployed soldiers were begging on the streets of Dublin.[94] Such conditions favoured the growth of organized, though petty, criminality both on land and at sea.

On the eve of the outbreak of the war with Spain, therefore, conditions at sea were profoundly confused. Localized piracy, indiscriminate and opportunistic in character, remained a serious problem, with the connivance or cooperation of shore-based supporters. During March 1584 officials in Poole, including the mayor, faced allegations of dealing with pirates. In 1585 the inhabitants of Lydd were accused of relieving rovers, including Atkinson. The regime appointed another commission to investigate piracy in the south-west during 1584, while Drake and Carew Raleigh were authorized to apprehend pirates at sea. In October Sir Julius Caesar drew up proposals for combating piracy, partly in response to complaints from merchants of Aberdeen, in favour of leaving the problem to be dealt with by the Lord Admiral and the judge of the High Court of Admiralty, whose powers were to be enhanced. Although the proposals were not adopted immediately, Caesar's own admiralty circuit in the south-west during the early 1590s demonstrated what might be achieved with closer supervision.[95]

Yet one of the underlying problems was the peculiar criminal characteristics of piracy. While it often began in violent and random circumstances, for many it was casual, part-time employment. It attracted recruits of varied backgrounds, especially mariners and men from related occupations, including soldiers and other landsmen. Robert Titley, a soldier from Blandford in Dorset, served with Callice and Hellebourg during the early 1580s. Aged about thirty-four or thirty-five, he was to sail on many other voyages thereafter. By 1592 he had acquired ten or twelve years' experience of the sea, including service on reprisal ventures into the Caribbean.[96] At times piracy could be portrayed as a contested crime, with extensive social roots, which was driven or justified by economic necessity. The testimony of a group of men who were arrested and accused of piracy during 1584 illustrates the difficulty in trying to police an organized form of petty but popular criminality, which combined robbery and force with good fellowship. The oldest member of the group, Richard Thomas, a fisherman of Penryn, aged about fifty, insisted that he was taken by the pirate, Charles Jones, while fishing in Falmouth haven with two men and a boy. John Harris, a boy aged about fourteen, claimed that he was detained by the pirates in Studland Bay, and employed as their cook. At least two other men joined the company at Studland, including John Deamon of London, a sailor aged about thirty, and John Adams of Christchurch, a labourer of similar age, who went aboard Jones' ship 'hoping to fynd some frind-shipp there'.[97] In addition, William Glover of Bideford, a husbandman aged about twenty-four, was recruited while serving in a fishing boat in the west. Robert Hawley of Ipswich, a sailor aged about twenty-one, joined Jones' company at Kinsale.

This pattern of recruitment and venturing was one of the defining features of local piracy during these years. Jones and his company were involved in a voyage that lasted for about one month, during which they seized a vessel laden with alum, wax and other commodities, near Newhaven along the coast of France. Thereafter the pirates sailed for Ireland where the booty was exchanged for provisions. Following a conflict with another French ship, when one of the pirates was killed and thirteen others were wounded, Jones returned to England. According to Thomas, while the pirate ship was anchored in Stokes Bay it was supplied with provisions of beef, mutton, wine and bread by boats from Portsmouth and Hamble. The pirates were chased by Captain Gilbert Yorke in one of the Queen's ships, and at least six of the company were captured, though Jones and twelve others escaped ashore.[98]

The persistence of such forms of piracy and sea roving encouraged the development of varied practices and patterns of behaviour among pirate groups. While the bravado of some pirate captains reflected the ethos of young, masculine and potentially violent groups, it may also have represented a rejection of respectable society, or at least that part of it which was concerned to promote moral reform. The behaviour of captains like Clarke flaunted the good fellowship and comradeship aboard pirate ships. At the same time it may have been intended to mimic and mock social convention. One of the associates of John Piers, for example, who was described as a 'very eavell disposed mane', claimed that the Queen was his godmother.[99] Pirate agency may have been an appealing and subversive force, as well as a means of acquiring wealth. It was manifested in various ways; moreover its creative energy was probably inspired by the rich oral culture which bound seafaring communities together. During Fenton's voyage, for example, Madox recounted the 'good sport' he and others had, from listening to the surgeon recite 'Robynhood rymes'.[100] Tales and rhymes provided entertainment at sea, encouraging friendship and community, but they were also a way of circulating ideas, sometimes to promote or justify piracy and spoil.

Although there was a tendency to idealize piracy during these years, it remained a dangerous criminal activity in which intimidation, violence or murder were never far removed. Captain Clarke and his company seized a Dutch ship which was carried off to a remote part of the coast of Northumberland, where the master was persuaded into buying back his vessel and its cargo. If he refused to sign a bill of sale, Clarke threatened to hang him from the yard arm of his own ship.[101] Some pirates developed a pattern of pathological behaviour which passed

Studland Bay, Dorset. This wide arcing bay served as a safe haven for a large number of pirates during the 1570s and early 1580s. At least forty prizes taken by pirates were brought in during the early 1580s, attracting dealers from a wide hinterland. (Author's collection)

The Foreland, Studland Bay, Dorset. Possibly the site for the execution of John Piers in 1582, who was hanged in chains on the order of the Privy Council. Piers was a particularly violent character. He had already been captured twice before, but on the first occasion he was freed by the mayor of Rye, while on the second he escaped from the gaol in Dorchester. (Author's collection)

from sea to shore. John Piers reputedly killed four French mariners with his dagger. Described as a 'crewell mortherer and a bloody varlet … [who] dowthe seeke nothinge mor but to embrace his hands in the bloud of strangers', he had allegedly been twice pardoned for similar offences.[102] During the course of a visit to the Isle of Wight in 1581, he attacked and raped the daughter of a local man.

At times the behaviour of pirate leaders indirectly challenged the authority and jurisdiction of the regime. Purser was captured and executed before he was able to carry out his threat of supporting Desmond's rebellion. Nonetheless, it was a defiant statement and an alternative to the supposed patriotism of Callice and others. The executions of Purser and Clinton, who were hanged at Wapping with seven other pirates during 1583, furnished an opportunity for both men to indulge in a theatrical display that seemed to mock the pretensions of the wealthy in a way that reaffirmed community with their followers. According to John Stow's subsequent description, the pirates were richly dressed for the occasion. Clinton wore velvet and gold lace. Purser's attire included 'venetian breeches of crimosin taffata' which he cut up and distributed 'to such [of] his old acquaintance as stood about him'.[103] Purser's conduct contained real and symbolic messages for the audience. His unwillingness to play the part expected of him, to the apparent disapproval of Stow, suggested a defiance that reflected a deeper ambivalence about piracy as a crime. These ambiguities were appropriated and exploited by ballad writers and dramatists. Thus the execution of Purser and Clinton was followed by the publication of at least three ballads, though the text of just one has survived. While serving as a means to portray the penitence and alleged patriotism of the pirates, unintentionally such material laid bare conflicted loyalties, in the process of trying to explain their aberrant behaviour.[104]

The ambiguities of local piracy were carried over into more ambitious venturing into the Atlantic, under the uncertain legality of commissions issued by Don Antonio. The cause of the Portuguese pretender enabled enterprising English adventurers, including Drake and Hawkins, to promote predatory ventures against Iberian trade and shipping. The deterioration in Anglo-Spanish relations pointed in a similar direction. On Christmas Day 1584 Ralph Lane, a military adventurer who was closely associated with Walter Ralegh, requested a commission from the Queen to lead an expedition of seven ships to the coast of Spain. Although Elizabeth remained reluctant to sanction open hostility towards Spain, the availability of licences from Don Antonio authorized voyages of plunder which drew on the experience and resources of the pirate fraternity. During the latter part of 1584 William Fenner of Chichester and his uncle, Edward, set out with their ship, the *Galleon Fenner*, to serve against Spain under his authority. The Fenners sailed with a company of about seventy men, with Callice as their lieutenant. William Fenner's account of the voyage, though intended to clear him of charges of piracy, indicated that this was a disorderly venture during which French and other shipping were plundered on the grounds that they were trading with Spain and Portugal or carrying Iberian goods.[105]

Sailing along the coast of Spain, the *Galleon Fenner* encountered five French ships, all but one of which were plundered of provisions, ordnance, canvas and cloth. The English also seized a vessel of about 400 or 500 tons of Lübeck, carrying timber, copper, wax and other commodities for Spain. Its plunder was justified by Fenner on the dubious grounds of providing compensation for damages 'susteyned in fight'.[106] Thereafter the English were chased by two French men-of-war. During the ensuing skirmish one of the vessels was taken. It was laden with plunder from the Portuguese and English, including 100 chests of sugar. As was customary Fenner placed some of his company, under the command of Callice, aboard the French prize. This was followed by the seizure of a Portuguese ship laden with sugar and spices.

As the weather grew increasingly stormy Fenner decided to return for England. During the homeward voyage the *Galleon Fenner* and its prizes were separated. Evidently Callice, whose vessel was forced into Ireland, was arrested on the orders of the Lord Deputy, while the Portuguese prize was captured by the pirate William Wise, and taken to Wales. Much of the remaining plunder was used to purchase provisions in Ireland, distributed among the company or given away as gifts to Fenner's family and friends. When the ship was arrested in March 1585, on orders from London, only twenty-two chests of sugar remained. In seeking to justify his conduct at sea, Fenner insisted that he had only seized Spanish or

Portuguese goods, except necessary provisions and victuals. He hoped, therefore, 'that he hath not broken the lymitts of his commission or incurred the daunger of her Majesty's lawes'.[107]

By the early 1580s the Elizabethan regime appeared to have lost its campaign against piracy. Essentially this was due to the varied and intractable nature of the problem. In the waters around the British Isles pirates exposed serious limitations in the naval resources of the regime, while on land they challenged its policing and regulatory powers. The prevalence of sympathetic attitudes towards piracy, and a growing awareness that it was often related to the uncertain and irregular work cycles of the seafaring population, undermined the response of the regime which, in any case, was divided in its willingness to sponsor ambitious schemes for oceanic depredation. For the early propagandists of empire, indeed, the remedy lay in the employment of seamen in the cause of overseas expansion. In 1584 Hakluyt tried to advance English colonization in North America by claiming that longer, transatlantic voyages would prevent poor and idle mariners from falling into piracy. It was an appealing suggestion. Before it could be put to the test effectively, however, conflict between England and Spain had broken out. The war at sea which followed soon provided alternative employment for large numbers of seafarers, including pirates and other rovers.

6

War, Reprisals and Piracy
from 1585 to 1603

The Anglo-Spanish conflict from 1585 to 1603 had profound consequences for English piracy, privateering and sea roving. The state of undeclared war, which was justified by the English as a legitimate response to the arrest of shipping in Spanish ports during 1585, led to widespread and general reprisals against Spain and Portugal. By these means the Elizabethan regime sanctioned a private war of plunder against its enemies that drew on earlier precedents and practices. At the same time the regime became a partner in an uneasy coalition of interests which assumed responsibility for promoting larger-scale, semi-official expeditions against the Spanish monarchy. While this was a highly effective means of mobilizing private resources to maintain the war at sea, under the control of seasoned veterans of maritime raiding and spoil, it suffered from limited direction and a lack of coherence. Moreover, its rapid development unavoidably exposed an underlying tension between strategic or tactical goals and financial imperatives. Under these conditions a state-sponsored war of reprisals, conducted by men-of-war sailing alone or in small hunting packs, was overlaid by a naval conflict, involving larger and more ambitious expeditions which included the Queen's ships. Collectively, these sea raiders captured a substantial haul of booty which in terms of value, at least, more than compensated for the loss of trade with Spain. But this was a war which grew increasingly piratical, particularly in European waters, provoking complaints and retaliation from neutral and friendly states. By the early seventeenth century the damage to England's diplomatic position within Europe appeared to suggest that the war at sea had outlived its strategic usefulness.

Sea war and transatlantic venturing: the opportunities and challenges of the 1580s

The outbreak of the Spanish war was a defining moment for the Elizabethan regime, when the Queen demonstrated her reluctant willingness to assume the mantle of the defender of international Protestantism, while acting as the protector of the Dutch rebels against Philip II. Although the assassination of the Dutch leader, William of Orange, in 1584 provided a catalyst for these events, the war was also the product of Anglo-Spanish tension which was inflamed by the predatory activities of sea warriors, such as Drake, who looked to Don Antonio, the pretender to the Portuguese throne, as a figurehead for their cause. Elizabeth's strategic goal in the Netherlands may have been essentially defensive, but her support for the Dutch revolt represented a substantial commitment to a prolonged and internationally divisive cause.[1]

Consequently, the conflict with Spain presented the regime with a serious challenge. By necessity and choice it relied heavily on private enterprise to organize the campaign at sea, hoping to weaken a powerful enemy through the unremitting spoil of trade and shipping. In doing so, it was able to draw on a varied and versatile tradition of depredation which increasingly encompassed ambitious schemes for transatlantic colonization. At the same time it exploited economic and social resources, including shipping and seamen, which might otherwise have lain dormant during the war. The challenge for the regime was to provide direction and discipline to an irregular or auxiliary force of voluntary vessels which operated beyond its effective control.

During 1585 the council drew up regulations for the recipients of letters of reprisal, which were intended to serve as a code of conduct for the maritime conflict, while maintaining the convenient fiction that England and Spain were not at open war. These were shaped by previous practice, though subsequently subject to modification in response to international complaint. Thus merchants and others who required commissions of reprisal were to demonstrate proof of their losses in Spain either before the Lord Admiral or the judge of the High Court of Admiralty. Those who were awarded such commissions were to provide bonds for good behaviour, which included provision for the return of all captured ships and cargoes to England, where they were to be inventoried and appraised; after their appraisement such commodities could be sold in open market as lawful prize. Adventurers sailing on voyages of reprisal were instructed not to 'break bulk' by disposing of their plunder elsewhere, or to attack any of the Queen's subjects and allies.[2] The council's regulations codified the division of prizes into three equal parts, distinguishing between merchants and shipowners, victuallers and the companies who served aboard reprisal vessels. Although the regulations omitted any mention of the adjudication of prizes by the High Court of Admiralty, this was remedied later in 1585.

In theory the publication of this code of conduct drew a clear line between lawful reprisals and piracy. However, in practice it became increasingly difficult to maintain a distinction between legitimate plunder, disorderly venturing and outright piracy. The structure of regulation almost invited such confusion. Although the conduct of the war of reprisals was the responsibility of the Lord Admiral, Charles Howard, 2nd Lord Howard of Effingham, and his deputies in the maritime counties and officials in the High Court of Admiralty, their ability either to control or supervise the activities of men-of-war was undermined by corrupt or vested interests and the lack of an effective policing force. In effect the sea war soon came to depend on self-regulation, particularly as the need to prove losses or provide bonds was rapidly dispensed with. Shortly after the outbreak of the conflict the regime promoted general reprisals against Spain, creating the conditions for a flourishing trade in commissions, with little restraint or regulation. In addition the financial stake of the Lord Admiral in lawful prizes, demonstrated in the collection of a levy of 10 per cent, known as tenths, encouraged persistent intervention in the judicial process.[3]

From the outset, the war with Spain met with an enthusiastic response. For self-appointed anti-Spanish crusaders, who had been engaged in surreptitious hostilities for more than a decade, it was long overdue. Among the pirate fraternity, an unruly but potentially valuable resource of experienced and aggressive seafarers, it provided an appealing opportunity for redemption and service in a public cause. In June 1585 Sir George Carey, the governor of the Isle of Wight, informed Walsingham:

> that one Flood, a valiant and skilful pirate, weary as he protesteth of his former trade, vowing to lead a new and better life, seeketh to come in upon my word, and maketh offer of his service to be employed upon all the coast of Spain to discover what is in action or intended against us, only craving to be victualled, and if therefore he shall be found to deserve his pardon, then to have it.[4]

The appeal of a better life, linked with popular patriotism and animated by deep-seated hostility towards Spain, may have spread widely among the seafaring community, especially in ports and regions where the loss of the Iberian trades was a serious threat to employment. The Spanish war thus benefited from a broad constituency of support within English society which was mobilized by the interplay between plunder and overseas expansion, Protestantism and national identity, combined with service for the Queen. The result was the creation of an impressive host of voluntary vessels, sent forth by promoters and adventurers of varied backgrounds, who were prepared to bear the risks of war either independently or in partnership with the Crown.

The first real test of this approach to the maritime war was Drake's raid on the Caribbean during 1585 and 1586. This was an impressive demonstration of English sea power, driven by predatory motives and informed by previous piratical enterprise in the region. It was also a state-sponsored expedition, the largest of its kind so far to challenge Spain across the Atlantic. Although no written instructions appear to survive, Drake's purpose was to plunder the Spanish silver fleet while raiding settlements in the Caribbean, including Panama, possibly with the intention of establishing an advance base for continued depredation. Given the timing of the expedition, Drake probably planned to support or reinforce Ralegh's recent settlement at Roanoke. In outline at least, this looks like an ambitious strategy for developing the Atlantic war, linking plunder with American colonization in a manner that played on religious and political rivalries. It may have included plans for the destruction of the Iberian fishery off Newfoundland, which was raided by Captain Bernard Drake during 1585. As envisaged by Richard Hakluyt, the leading propagandist of westward enterprise during the 1580s, Spanish and Catholic tyranny would be overthrown by a combined force of English Protestant imperialists with the assistance of discontented natives and slaves. Although this flattering and self-serving image was never shared by the Queen, whose interest in the sea war was primarily pragmatic, to some extent it was influenced by Drake's own experience in the Caribbean, including his relations with the cimaroons, which may have exaggerated the expectations of a group of adventurers who identified themselves as God's warriors.[5]

The promoters of the expedition represented a powerful alliance of naval and maritime interests who had long been in favour of aggressive action against Spain. Drake and Hawkins probably contributed eleven vessels to the venture, while most of the other shipping was provided by their associates or supporters at court, including Leicester and the Lord Admiral, and merchants in London and Plymouth. The Queen furnished two vessels, the *Elizabeth Bonaventure* of 600 tons, in which Drake sailed, and the *Aid* of 200 or 250 tons. In all, the promoters mobilized a force of twenty-five ships and eight pinnaces, manned with a complement of more than 2,000 sailors and soldiers. Under the leadership of Drake, the captains included Martin Frobisher, Thomas Fenner and Francis Knollys, who possessed extensive sea experience, and a group of kinsmen and loyal associates, including Thomas Drake, William Hawkins and Richard Hawkins. Christopher Carleill, the son-in-law of Walsingham, served as captain of the *Tiger* and was in command of the land forces. Also included among the company was Pedro, an Indian originally from the island of La Margarita, who had been with Drake for about twelve years and was to serve as an interpreter.

Maintaining command of this large, amphibious expedition, while fulfilling the expectations of its promoters, presented Drake with unprecedented responsibility. Although he held councils with captains and officers, and maintained discipline through improvised courts to deal with offenders, as during the circumnavigation, he appears to have sailed in dread of the danger of sedition and faction among the company. At Cape Verde he became embroiled with Knollys in a dispute over the administration of an oath which threatened to turn into a re-run of the Doughty affair. The quarrel rumbled on, with Knollys facing a court martial, but it never reached a crisis point, possibly because of his connection to the Queen.[6]

The expedition left Plymouth on 14 September 1585. Shortly thereafter the *Tiger* captured a French vessel returning from Newfoundland with a cargo of fish. Claiming the vessel as lawful prize, on the grounds that it was bound for Spain, the English shared out their catch of fish and used timber from the ship as a supply for firewood. A few days later the expedition reached Bayonne, where it was supplied with fresh water and provisions. During these uneasy but generally peaceful contacts Drake provided local officers with official justification for the voyage, offering them a choice between peace and war, in retaliation for Philip II's embargo of English shipping earlier in the year. Drake made it clear that he was acting in the service of his sovereign; subsequently, he was to be enraged at being described by Spanish officials as a corsair. While the fleet lay at Bayonne, however, Drake's company sacked a religious house. The iconoclasm grew more furious during the course of the voyage, reflecting the spread of popular Protestant radicalism among mariners, which encouraged the misuse, vandalism and destruction of churches. Off the coast of Portugal the fleet encountered about twenty sail of English men-of-war, from London, Bristol and Southampton, which had raided and burnt the port of Viana. From the Iberian coast the expedition sailed on to the Canary Islands and thence to the Cape Verde Islands, where the abandoned settlements of Santiago and Porto Praya were set on fire. As the fleet crossed the Atlantic, the company were afflicted by the outbreak of a deadly disease which accounted for several hundred casualties. The extent of the losses may have had a crucial bearing on the subsequent course of the expedition, and in dissuading Drake from leaving a small occupying force in the Caribbean.[7]

Following a brief stay on the unsettled island of Dominica, at the end of December the expedition arrived off Santo Domingo, once one of the most important settlements in the Spanish Caribbean, now in decline. The English encountered little resistance. During an occupation that lasted one month, they systematically looted and burnt the city. As churches were vandalised and destroyed, some of Drake's men argued with the Spanish over matters of theology. The destruction only came to a halt when the defenders agreed to pay a ransom of 25,000 ducats, although the amount was a disappointment to Drake and his captains who had expected much more. In addition to the ransom, the English departed with an assortment of plunder, including church bells, ordnance, hides and three ships, which were exchanged for two old vessels out of the fleet, as well as eighty slaves, Turks, Frenchmen, Greeks and Africans.[8]

This devastating assault on Santo Domingo was followed by an equally damaging raid on Cartagena, which Drake may have considered holding as an outpost for future use. According to one report, the English fleet arrived 'flying black banners and streamers and menacing war to the death'.[9] Although the Spanish were forewarned, after a confused clash along the sea shore, during which the English sustained casualties, the defenders reportedly fled like sheep. The capture of Cartagena strengthened a view among some of the English that God fought for them, overwhelming their enemy with blindness and fear. Most of the inhabitants escaped to a safe retreat in the interior; the fort was abandoned and two galleys were set on fire. The English stayed at Cartagena for more than five weeks, burning the town as negotiations proceeded for its ransom. Though amounting to 107,000 ducats, again the amount was less than Drake anticipated. As at Santo Domingo the attackers ransacked the town of ordnance, church bells and anything else made of metal, while slaves of varied backgrounds were freed. By the time the expedition departed, at the end of March 1586, the English had accumulated as many as 200 Turks and a large number of Africans, who may have been intended as unwitting reinforcements for Ralegh's settlement at Roanoke.[10]

Although the Spanish put up little resistance to the raiders, the English suffered heavy losses to sickness and disease during their occupation of Cartagena. According to one report the losses amounted to 100 men. Cumulatively the rate of attrition discouraged Drake from proceeding to attack Panama. In February 1586 a decision was made to return home. During the return voyage to England the expedition destroyed the Spanish outpost of San Agustín, along the coast of Florida, partly to protect Roanoke from possible attack. When Drake made contact with Ralegh's settlers in June, however, it was apparent that they had experienced a difficult and discouraging year of hunger and increasing native

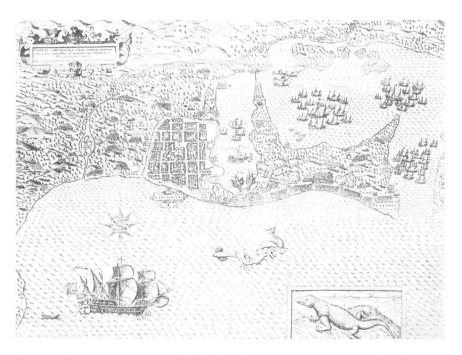

The port of Cartagena, on the Spanish Main. This is one of several illustrations of Drake's raid during 1585 and 1586. English forces can be seen marching on the town from the right. Drake reportedly attacked with black banners and streamers flying, threatening war to the death. (*Sir Francis Drake*)

Santo Domingo, on the island of Hispaniola, formerly one of the most important settlements in the Spanish Caribbean. It was raided and plundered by Drake in 1586. Although the booty was disappointing, the raid exposed the vulnerability of key regions of Spain's empire to attack by privateers and others. (*Sir Francis Drake*)

hostility. Drake offered the settlers a small vessel to re-settle in a more favourable location in Chesapeake Bay, but it was lost during stormy weather. Although the colonists were offered a replacement, they abandoned Roanoke and returned with Drake to England. While the early Roanoke voyages suggested that plunder and plantation could be combined profitably, encouraging the re-establishment of a small settlement in 1587, Ralegh rapidly lost interest in colonization in favour of privateering.[11]

Drake's expedition was a striking, but mixed, success. It dramatically revealed the range and capability of English maritime power, exposing the weakness of the Spanish monarchy within a vulnerable region of its American empire. The trail of plunder, destruction and iconoclastic violence was a damaging blow to Spanish reputation. The surprising ease with which Santo Domingo and Cartagena were taken suggested that Spain's colonial settlements were deeply disorganized and demoralized, although the prospect of more damaging activity was foreclosed by the spread of disease among the English. The seizure and sack of Cartagena provoked rumours among the Spanish that Drake was going to inform Philip II about the unpreparedness and weak defences of the region. With both settlements stripped of their ordnance, local officials warned Philip of their exposure to further attack. Thus Santo Domingo was reported to be unarmed and 'defenceless against any corsair who may undertake to finish us off'.[12] Spanish reports from the Caribbean indicate that the damage may have been as much psychological as physical. As such the expedition exposed the fragile integrity of an expanding Iberian monarchy, by exploiting or revealing rivalries between the Spanish and the Portuguese, and reviving concern about the possibility of an alliance between English raiders and discontented natives and slaves. Drake's challenge to Spain, moreover, was accompanied by reports that he would be followed by Don Antonio in command of a large fleet.

For Drake and his associates the expedition amounted to a resounding declaration of war against Spain which provided a model for future development. In effect this anticipated the merging of the pirate tradition with royal service, creating the conditions for private adventurers to organize an Atlantic campaign against the Spanish monarchy, in cooperation with the regime. Yet there were signs that this alliance was problematic and unstable, not least in the ambitious expectation that strategic goals could be accomplished while the war not only paid for itself, but also earned a profit for its supporters. Indeed the financial return from Drake's expedition was a disappointment: the plunder, estimated to be worth £60,000, failed to provide its promoters with a profit. According to Spanish report, although Drake:

> had promised the Queen of England to fetch her a million as her share … he was disturbed to see how little profit he had so far obtained [at Cartagena]; and even all his captains and soldiers were aggrieved because he had promised them so much and they saw that their part would be small, and so all the gentlemen said that he would not again find any to go out with him from England.[13]

When set against the heavy human losses, amounting to more than one-third of the expedition's company, this cast a shadow over the ability of the English to sustain such a conflict against Spain over a prolonged period. In addition, the failure of North American colonization, partly as a result of the counter-attraction of maritime depredation, left the development of a transatlantic strategy in disarray. The confusion was compounded with the Queen's reluctance to exploit the advantage against Spain. In the immediate aftermath of the expedition she claimed that Drake had 'exceeded his instructions'.[14] In these circumstances it appeared likely that the latter would continue hostilities in the service of Don Antonio, possibly with the assistance of the Dutch.

Nonetheless, the expedition had far-reaching diplomatic and international implications, placing England at the head of the forces of international Protestantism which were arrayed against Spain. Its value as anti-Spanish propaganda was underlined by the publication of an edited account of the voyage by Walter Bigges, with Latin and French editions in 1588, followed by English and German versions during 1589. Dedicated to Robert Devereux, 2nd Earl of Essex,

A raid on a Spanish settlement in America by French rovers during the sixteenth century. The French led the way in attacking Spanish trade and towns in the Caribbean, establishing a form of enterprise which others adapted and developed. English pirates, including Drake, often acted in partnership with French Huguenot men-of-war. (*Scourge of the Indies*)

Bigges' *Summarie and True Discourse* was intended to maintain morale at a critical time while promoting the cause of the war party, by demonstrating 'what great victories a fewe English men have made upon great numbers of the Spaniardes, even at home in their owne countreyes'.[15]

Drake's celebrated raid on Cadiz during 1587 appeared to provide strong support for a forward campaign at sea, despite the Queen's caution and misgivings. The raid, an amphibious expedition of royal and privately owned vessels, was meant as a pre-emptive strike against the Armada which was assembling in Spanish and Portuguese ports for the invasion of England. As a reprisal venture, partly promoted by private adventurers, it was also intended to provide its backers with a profit. While there was no apparent incompatibility between these strategic and financial goals, the underlying uncertainty over their priority was a source of tension which may have been reflected in divided leadership and rivalry between Drake and the Queen's leading officer, Vice Admiral William Borough, which flared into open hostility during the voyage.

An illustration of a conflict between French and Spanish forces during the sixteenth century. As English pirates and privateers ranged into and across the Atlantic, so they faced the growing danger of Spanish hostility. Yet the greatest threat on such long-distance voyages often came from the outbreak of disease. (*Scourge of the Indies*)

Drake left Plymouth in April 1587 at the head of a fleet of twenty-three vessels. Of these, six were owned by the Queen and eight belonged to London merchants, including four from the Levant Company. Drake contributed three of his own vessels, while the Lord Admiral furnished another. Despite the Queen's late and abortive attempt to stop it sailing, the fleet departed on a wave of high expectation. The company, Drake informed Walsingham, was united as 'one body to stand for our gracious Queen and country against Antichrist and its members'.[16]

An account by Robert Long, a volunteer with the expedition, provides a fascinating narrative of the voyage, which employs classical and biblical allusions to portray Drake as the champion of England against the enemies of the gospel. Such propaganda seems to represent Drake's increasingly strident fundamental Protestantism, though it also concealed the innate flexibility and potentially hazardous nature of the enterprise. On leaving England the expedition sailed for the coasts of Spain and Portugal, where Drake acquired valuable information from two Dutch ships about the shipping and provisions which were being assembled in

HIC TVVS ILLE COMES GENEROSA ESSEXIA NOSTRIS
QVEM QVAM GAVDEMVS REBVS ADESSE DVCEM

Robert Devereux, 2nd Earl of Essex, in a pose as the Queen's military champion. A supporter of the last voyage of Drake and Hawkins, Essex tried, unsuccessfully, to re-shape the war at sea during the mid-1590s. (*The Life and Death of Robert Devereux, Earl of Essex*)

Cadiz. Three days later the English sailed into Cadiz harbour, sinking and burning about thirty vessels. Although the expedition encountered resistance, unexpectedly Spanish naval forces inflicted little damage on the fleet. Despite the dangerous and unfavourable location, the galleys of Spain were ineffective against a force of sailing vessels. Thereafter Drake sailed to Cape St Vincent, where he put ashore a company of 800 men who captured and set fire to local fortifications. Faced with little opposition at sea, the fleet cruised along the coast, anchoring unchallenged in sight of Lisbon, while taking prizes and laying waste to the coastal fisheries.[17]

The raid on Cadiz was a tactical success, but it failed to provide Drake with sufficient plunder to make the voyage profitable. Consequently, after sending sick members of the expedition home, he sailed for the Azores in search of richer prey. Within twenty or thirty leagues of the islands he captured a Portuguese carrack, the *San Felipe*, using tactics widely employed by pirates and corsairs. It was a profitable catch. The ship was laden with cloth, silks and spices, subsequently valued at £100,000; a casket of rich jewels was retained by Drake for the Queen. He also freed 400 Africans aboard the carrack, who were apparently intended as slaves in Portugal and Spain, providing them with a vessel 'to goe whether they lyst'.[18] The capture of the *San Felipe* deeply alarmed the Portuguese and Spanish. The latter were reportedly in despair at the threat to the Indies fleet. For Drake, however, the expedition had fulfilled its aims, and by the end of June 1587 he was back in Plymouth.

The expedition was a provocative challenge to Philip II. It exposed serious weaknesses in Spanish sea defences in home waters, and revealed the vulnerability of Portuguese shipping returning from the East Indies. Among the Spanish, the shock and disbelief fed suspicions that Drake worked with a familiar, while English reports claimed that the action at Cadiz hastened the death of the Spanish High Admiral, the marques of Santa Cruz, the intended leader of the armada. At the same time the venture served to affirm the striking effectiveness of the English sea war, demonstrating the profitable and tactical benefits of rapid mobilization and action. For Drake in particular, it underlined the case for aggressive action against Spain, and in a way that defined the defence of the realm with the godly cause. During April he wrote several letters to supporters and friends in England about the raid on Cadiz and other recent events. One, addressed to Walsingham, contained news of the fleet that the King of Spain was assembling, ending with an urgent appeal to 'prepare in England strongly, and most by sea. Stop him now, and stop him ever'.[19] Another was addressed to John Foxe, the preacher and martyrologist, and appealed to the clergyman for his remembrance and spiritual support, so 'that we may have continual peace in Israel'.

While the raid on Cadiz delayed and disrupted preparations for the Armada, possibly with critical consequences for its leadership, it did not prevent its departure in 1588. After the raid, moreover, Drake was less concerned with inflicting further damage on Spain than with ensuring that the voyage made a profit. His angry dispute with Borough, culminating in dangerous accusations of mutiny and desertion, may have grown out of the latter's cautious approach to the attack on Cadiz, but it seems to have originated in the jarring tension between commanders of different maritime traditions and service, with differing perceptions of the sea war and naval command. In the short term the implications of this tension were papered over by the need to prepare for the Armada, but they became increasingly difficult to reconcile as the war proceeded.[20]

In these circumstances the departure of the Armada was testimony to the resources and resilience of the Spanish monarchy, as well as to the religious mission of Philip II, for whom the enterprise of England represented a crusade as much as a means of protecting the integrity of Iberian territory and trade. In place of the original commander, Santa Cruz's unwilling successor, the Duke of Medina Sidonia, was saddled with a difficult, possibly unworkable, plan for the Armada to convey an invading force of veteran Spanish troops from the Netherlands across the Channel. Regardless of English maritime defences, the success of the expedition depended on precision, timing, logistical support and a knowledge of north-western European waters that tested to the limit Philip's grand strategy against a resourceful opponent.[21]

While the English had yet to develop a clear strategic shape or direction for the war at sea, as a counter to the threatened Armada leading members of the war party urged the regime to adopt offensive action against Spain. Concerned at the apparent hesitation of the Queen, and aware of the mounting charge of the navy, in February 1588 Hawkins presented Walsingham with a choice between 'a dishonourable and uncertain peace … or … a settled war as may bring forth and command a quiet peace'.[22] To achieve the latter he argued in favour of maintaining a naval presence on the coast of Spain to seize local shipping and to lie in wait for the returning Indies fleet. A force of six of the Queen's ships was continuously to patrol the coast, based on a regular period of service lasting four months. It was to be supported by a fleet of six smaller vessels which would cruise between Spain and the Azores. Although Hawkins estimated the monthly cost, in wages and victuals, at £2,700, he claimed that it would be more than covered by the capture of enemy prizes. It was an imaginative and appealing argument for a naval blockade of the enemy, to create the conditions for a peace 'with honour, safety and profit', though it was not without risk and had little chance of being implemented, at least in the short term.

Hawkins' radical plan for re-shaping the conflict at sea was accompanied by a call for a declaration of open war, which was an implicit condemnation of the Queen's diplomatic determination to maintain the confusing fiction that England was engaged in a campaign of legitimate reprisals against Spain. To some extent it was supported by Drake, who claimed that 'the continual going to the seas of the smaller sort of … shipping daily upon letters of reprisal … can do little good'.[23] Not only was there a lack of suitable prizes along the coasts of Spain, as most shipping sailed in convoy with provisions for the Armada, but also English raiders faced the risk of capture by fleets of Flemish men-of-war from Dunkirk.

As the threat of the Armada loomed, Drake appealed to the council, at the end of March, to be allowed to sail for Spain with a fleet of fifty vessels. He repeated the appeal to the Queen several times during the following month, hoping to seize the 'advantage of time and place' by fighting the enemy in his own waters.[24]

At this very time, however, the regime was struggling to assemble shipping to assist in the defence of the realm. Appeals from the council to local officials in the ports for a levy of vessels, particularly belonging to merchants and shipowners who had benefited from reprisals against Spain, met with a mixed response. During April the council received reports, ranging from Hull to Exeter, about an inability to provide ships for service. The mayor and aldermen of Poole begged to be discharged from the responsibility of providing one ship and a pinnace for service. In their defence, they claimed that as local merchants were not involved in reprisal venturing, they had gained nothing from the war at sea. Moreover the town was suffering from a lack of trade, losses at sea and robberies by pirates who haunted Studland Bay. Although officials in the neighbouring port of Lyme Regis sent a pinnace of 40 tons to Plymouth, they insisted that no one of the town had received 'any benefit by reprisals, except one stranger very lately come in amongst us'.[25] The mayor and aldermen of Southampton likewise drew attention to their poverty, exacerbated by losses from reprisals of at least £4,000, and warned of murmuring and unrest among local inhabitants at the anticipated charge of providing two ships and a pinnace. In Ipswich, indeed, there was open resistance from one local gentleman to the attempts of the bailiffs to collect a rate for the levy of three vessels. Local recalcitrance tended to collapse in the face of angry reprimands from the council; inadvertently, however, it may have reinforced the Queen's determination to prevent the costs of the campaign from spiralling out of control.

Against a Spanish fleet of 130 vessels, which was manned with 22,000 sailors and soldiers, the English mobilized a force of about 180 ships. The English fleet was a hybrid complement of naval and maritime resources: thirty-four of the Queen's vessels were reinforced by a large body of private shipping, including thirty that were roughly equal, in terms of tonnage and armament, to the former. The English fleet was commanded by Howard, with Drake serving as his Vice Admiral, supported by a host of sea captains of varied experience. This seaborne militia collectively represented a tradition of maritime and naval enterprise that favoured flexibility and initiative against an inflexible and less adaptable fleet and strategy. Although there may have been a degree of crude parity between the rival forces, the campaign of 1588 exposed differences in the organization, armament and employment of seaborne forces that aided the English, despite early warning signs of logistical and financial problems affecting the supply of recruits and gunpowder.[26]

As the Armada sailed up the Channel it was shadowed, and occasionally harried by the English, who had the weather gauge. Remarkably it reached the coast of northern France almost intact. One of the few Spanish losses was the *Nuestra*

Lyme Bay, Dorset. During the 1560s and 1570s pirate groups were able to operate along exposed and vulnerable coastlines with little fear of arrest. The region was an important recruiting ground for pirate ships, particularly during the 1560s and 1570s when growing numbers of mariners were seeking employment. Small ports, such as Lyme Regis, continued to be involved in organized plunder during the 1580s. The *Julian* of Lyme Regis, for example, seized two prizes during 1589 which were valued at £30,000. (Author's collection)

Señora del Rosario, which was disabled and subsequently taken by Drake in an operation that has been endlessly discussed. Although Drake's decision to abandon his post, in order to seize the Spanish vessel, endangered the formation of the English fleet, leaving the Lord Admiral in an exposed position, it was an opportunistic, almost reflex action, by a commander whose experience was rooted in plunder. Nor was Drake condemned for his behaviour. Although Frobisher angrily insisted on receiving a share of the prize from Drake, threatening to 'make him spend the best blood in his belly', his comments were the product of petty rivalry between two men of similar background over a division of booty.[27]

The arrival of the Armada off Calais exposed fatal flaws in the Spanish plan. While Parma's troops were being assembled, the activities of Dutch men-of-war along the coast presented an unforeseen and potentially crippling hazard to their embarkation. Under Justin of Nassau, the Dutch force effectively locked in the Spanish army, preventing it from leaving Dunkirk or Nieuport. Seizing the advantage, the English used fire ships to disperse the Spanish fleet. During the only sustained conflict of the campaign, off Gravelines, the superior gunnery of the larger English vessels inflicted significant damage on the Spanish. According to William Winter, about 500 shots of various kinds were fired from his ship during the course of the day. This was a rate of fire power that the Spanish were unable to match, though it left many English vessels dangerously short of powder and shot. Howard reported afterwards that the English sank three enemy vessels, while another four were so leaky and damaged that they were forced ashore. In disarray the Armada was inexorably driven north by the weather. Howard 'set on a brag countenance and gave them chase', at least until the Spanish vessels cleared the east coast of England.[28]

The Armada campaign battered both sides to near exhaustion. At times improvised, English provisioning appeared to be close to breaking down. As Howard followed the Spanish fleet in the North Sea with his supply of powder and shot nearly spent, some members of his company were reportedly forced to eat beans and drink their own urine.[29] Inadequate supplies of victuals and fresh water encouraged the outbreak of sickness and mortality which spread rapidly among men who had been at sea for a prolonged period, with little pay or fresh clothing. The casualties among the company of one vessel, the *Elizabeth Jonas*, amounted to more than 200, contributing to a groundswell of discontent over pay and conditions. On 26 August Hawkins reprimanded Burghley for seeking to save

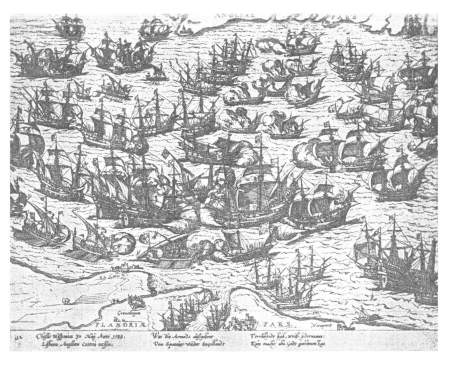

An illustration of the conflict off Gravelines between the Spanish Armada and the English fleet. Badly damaged, the Spanish were forced to return home around Scotland and the west of Ireland. The organization and character of the English force, in which Drake and Frobisher served, demonstrated the value of the piratical tradition to English naval enterprise at this time. (*The Fugger News-Letters*)

money by the death or discharge of sick men. Shortly after Howard complained of the shortages in provisions, and warned that future recruitment to the navy would be affected if there was no improvement. Many of the Spanish suffered worse. Severely weakened and scattered by autumn gales, the Armada was forced to return to Spain around the dangerous coasts of Scotland and Ireland, where as many as twenty vessels were wrecked with the loss of thousands of men. In Ireland widespread reports indicate that some of the survivors were robbed and killed, often along the sea shore.[30]

The failure of the Armada, despite the survival of nearly two-thirds of the shipping sent against England, was profoundly damaging to Spanish morale. As the scale of the failure became more apparent in England, relief and thanksgiving gave way to optimism and commemoration which were subsequently translated into myth and memory. The publication of Hakluyt's *Principal Navigations* in 1589, with its epic celebration of English maritime enterprise, appeared to capture the changing mood, although its attempt to revive interest in North American colonization was short lived. In any case the sea war continued to present more pressing, and potentially profitable opportunities.

In a bold attempt to exploit the defeat of the Armada, the Queen authorized a large-scale expedition against Spain under the command of Drake and Sir John Norris. Although one of its key aims was to complete the destruction of the Armada, the survivors of which were huddled in Santander and other harbours in the Bay of Biscay, following discussions between the leaders and Don Antonio a more radical and comprehensive scheme emerged. This included a plan to restore the Portuguese pretender with possible assistance from the King of Morocco, followed by an attempt to intercept the Indies fleet. In order to promote the expedition, in October 1588 Don Antonio offered Burghley the tempting prospect of establishing the East Indies trade in England. It was left to a group of London clergymen to affirm the legitimacy of Protestant support for the restoration of a Catholic ruler, following a disputation during November, but only as a means of weakening the 'capital enemy' of Spain.[31]

Against this shifting background the instructions for Norris and Drake, drawn up in February 1589, emphasized two purposes, which involved the destruction of Spanish ships in Santander and neighbouring ports and the seizure of the Indies fleet at the Azores. The restoration of Don Antonio was to proceed only after the leaders were satisfied that he would be supported by the Portuguese people. A council of experienced soldiers from the Netherlands, including Sir Roger Williams and Sir Edward Norris, and maritime adventurers, such as Thomas and William Fenner, was appointed to assist the leaders.[32]

The expedition represented a substantial investment in the business of war. Despite Burghley's concern at its mounting costs, a force of about 100 ships, manned with more than 20,000 seamen and soldiers, some of whom were withdrawn from the Netherlands against Dutch protests, was assembled during 1589. The Queen contributed seven of the largest vessels. The rest of the shipping was owned by a diverse range of private adventurers, including Drake, his associates and supporters at court, and a growing number of merchants and shipowners who were acquiring a prominent role in the war of reprisals against Spain, such as Thomas Cordell and John Watts. The mobilization of such an impressive strike force seemed to demonstrate widespread support for offensive and potentially profitable action at sea, but it was based on confusing goals and high expectations of success. Such was the appeal of honour, profit and service that the Earl of Essex, a penurious, but leading representative of a younger generation of courtiers and Protestant champions, risked the Queen's anger by volunteering to accompany Drake and Norris with his friends, followers and kinsmen.[33]

The expedition failed to accomplish any of its goals, raising questions about command and leadership, and demonstrating the difficulties of organizing the sea war when strategic objectives were confused with financial ambitions. Before departing from Plymouth, during April 1589, Drake and Norris informed the council of their intention to sail for the coast of northern Spain, following the receipt of information that 200 vessels of varied nationality had lately arrived with supplies for the enemy, effectively setting aside one of their key goals. By 24 April the expedition had reached Corunna. The English captured the lower town and wasted the surrounding countryside. The inhabitants set fire to a Portuguese galleon which had served in the Armada, while Drake seized several ships in the harbour. Unable to take the upper town, the English withdrew and sailed for the coast of Portugal, neglecting the opportunity of destroying about half of the survivors of the Armada which were harboured in Santander. On hearing news of the action at Corunna, the Queen caustically commented on the negligence of Norris and Drake in failing to perform what they had promised, preferring instead to raid 'places more for profit than for service'.[34]

As the expedition sailed south for Lisbon the extreme heat took a heavy toll among the soldiers. Although the raiders met with little initial resistance, they were not welcomed as liberators by the Portuguese. Indeed, Sir Roger Williams complained that they did more harm than good. Soldiers and sailors were demoralized by the outbreak of disease, indecision among the leaders and a lack of supplies from England. Drake admitted that a 'little comfortable dew from heaven, some crowns or some reasonable booty', were needed to revitalize the company.[35] While the expedition seized more than sixty vessels in the harbour, laden with corn and other provisions, it was unable to take Lisbon, which had been forewarned and reinforced as a result of the raid on Corunna. After a week of indecisive skirmishing ashore, Norris and Drake withdrew, intending to sail for the Azores, but the spread of sickness and contrary winds forced them back to England.

It was a costly and damaging failure, particularly for the Queen who had invested £49,000 in the expedition. It provoked bitter recriminations and fuelled debate over the character and direction of the sea war. Among the explanations offered for the failure of the venture, there was a tendency to use the opportunistic attack on Corunna as an excuse, though at least one report also drew attention to a lack of counsel and consultation. Anthony Wingfield's discourse on the voyage indicates that the expedition went ahead despite misgivings and opposition in some quarters. Nonetheless, Wingfield was convinced that seaborne expeditions remained the best way to bring Spain to its knees, while forcing the enemy on the defensive, in order 'to free ourselves from the war at our own walls'.[36] Neither Drake nor Norris escaped censure for their conduct during the voyage. In October 1589 both men were charged by the council with failing to carry out their instructions. The expedition damaged the reputation of Drake, whose career in royal service seemed to be over. Above all, however, its failure exposed the underlying tension within the coalition of interests between the state and private enterprise, and the danger, as Elizabeth recognized, of strategic objectives being subverted in favour of spoil and profit.

The early years of the Anglo-Spanish War thus provided a real challenge for the English organization of the conflict at sea. Maritime and naval resources were rapidly mobilized and energetically deployed, but with mixed results. In particular there was little evidence that a conflict on this scale would be cheap or, as yet, capable of paying for itself. While the war generated strategic ideas and initiatives, they were overshadowed by the failure of the expedition of 1589. The poor success of squadrons despatched to the coast of Spain and the Azores during 1590 and 1591, in search of the Spanish silver fleet, also raised doubts about the value of offensive action at sea. By the early 1590s, moreover, the regime was faced with the alarming prospect of the land war spreading into northern France.[37] In these circumstances the Queen's enthusiasm for further large-scale seaborne expeditions cooled, leaving the maritime conflict in the hands of private adventurers who were ostensibly engaged in legitimate reprisals against the Spanish monarchy.

Reprisals and piracy during the 1580s and early 1590s

The war of reprisals which flourished during the later 1580s and 1590s was a powerful example of the Elizabethan regime's ability to exploit private resources to weaken the enemy. A campaign of sustained plunder inflicted severe damage on Iberian trade and shipping, compensating for the disruption to English commerce, while providing employment for unemployed mariners and occasionally producing spectacular profits for promoters. But this was an improvised and indiscriminate way of waging a maritime war. English vessels sailing on reprisal voyages were subject to uncertain and self-interested supervision by the Lord Admiral and his officials; once at sea the conduct of English men-of-war essentially depended on self-regulation. From the outset, therefore, the maritime war was at risk from disorderly and illegal depredation. The vessels

of friendly and neutral states were exposed to repeated spoil by English predators, on the grounds that they were supplying Spain with provisions identified
as contraband. At the same time the sea war masked, but could not conceal,
piratical enterprise of varying forms. Indeed, it created the conditions for an
undercurrent of piracy to persist with increasing vigour into the early seventeenth century.[38]

To a considerable extent this private war at sea was promoted and planned by
the merchants of London. Although the length of the war allowed for a considerable turnover of promoters and adventurers, overseas traders and shipowners
played a leading role in maintaining the business of reprisals. A significant group
of these adventurers had been heavily involved in the Iberian trades before the
outbreak of hostilities. Among the London trading interest many seemed to represent a younger generation of merchants whose ambitions, aggressive drive and
increasing interest in the potential profit of long-distance enterprise encouraged commercial expansion, while paving the way for a revival of interest in
colonization after 1603. The more successful promoters, who included members
of the Levant and Barbary Companies, combined commerce with plunder in
a specialized but flexible form of enterprise, which was particularly suited to
ventures that required larger, heavily armed vessels, such as in the Mediterranean
and African trades.[39]

In London, John Watts was one of the most active merchant supporters of
the sea war. By 1585 he was a well-established trader with extensive commercial interests in Spain, as well as with the Canary Islands and the Azores.
Claiming losses of £15,000, as a result of the confiscation of five vessels in
Spanish ports, Watts was soon involved in sending out ships on reprisal voyages. His partners included merchants and shipowners with similar interests,
such as John Bird and John Stokes, with whom he sent out at least five ships
against Spain during 1585 and 1586, though he was more regularly associated with members of his own family and household. As in the case of
other leading adventurers, Watts' interest in reprisals merged imperceptibly
with the public, more official war at sea. He was a leading supporter of the
expedition to Cadiz in 1587, during which three, possibly four, of his vessels served. Two of these ships stayed on the coast of Spain, following Drake's
return to England, seizing a number of rich prizes. During the Armada campaign, Watts served aboard one of his own ships, leading the scramble to
share in the capture of a Spanish vessel which had run aground near Calais.
Thereafter he became one of the leading promoters of ventures to the Spanish
Caribbean. During 1595 four of his vessels sailed on Drake's last voyage.
The failure of that expedition was offset by the profit from James Lancaster's
daring raid on Pernambuco in Brazil, in which he was heavily involved.
Furthermore, in 1598, he was a prominent supporter of an expedition led by
George Clifford, 3rd Earl of Cumberland, which raided Puerto Rico. Among
Cumberland's fleet, six vessels were owned by Watts.[40]

Although Watts was one of the most important promoters of reprisal ventures, there were a number of powerful and wealthy merchants in London who developed similar interests in the sea war, including Paul Bayning and Thomas Cordell, and who tended to reap most profit from it. In addition there was a much larger group of more modest merchants from London and some of the leading ports in the south-west, especially Bristol and Plymouth, who sustained a serious interest in promoting reprisal ventures, turning the Spanish war into a profitable business enterprise, while providing the regime with the maritime equivalent of a voluntary militia, made up of strong, well-armed vessels which were capable of inflicting serious damage on the enemy.

Merchant promoters were not the only adventurers to try their hand at the business of reprisals. The appeal of profit, honour and glory, in a godly and patriotic cause, mobilized a varied range of adventurers. They included men with a professional interest in the sea or seafaring, such as naval officials and other royal office holders, as well as sea captains who owned or partly owned their vessels. Among the former were well-connected promoters, including the Lord Admiral and his brother-in-law – Sir George Carey, governor of the Isle of Wight – Sir John Hawkins and other captains in the Queen's Navy, including Sir Walter Ralegh and Sir Robert Cecil. The latter group included experienced captains such as William Parker of Plymouth, who led several expeditions to the Caribbean, culminating in a bold attack on Porto Belo in 1601, and Christopher Newport, who was involved in a series of voyages to the West Indies in the service of merchants such as Watts.[41]

At the other extreme to such experienced and professional promoters was a small but significant group of landowners, or men of landed background, whose interest in the sea war, while rooted in the promise of financial gain, was encoded with chivalric ideals of knightly service. Their leading representative was Cumberland, who in 1600 claimed to have spent £100,000 in sending out his own fleets against Spain. Partly seeking to salvage his debts through the plunder of the enemy, Cumberland had two ships at sea during the first year of the war. They were followed by a second voyage in 1588, though neither met with much success. In these early ventures Cumberland regularly employed vessels owned by the Queen alongside his own, occasionally commanding in person, combining private ambition with public duty. During the later 1590s, however, he became associated with leading London merchants, such as Watts, Cordell and Bayning, who were among his chief supporters for an ambitious expedition of 1598 which led to a successful, though unprofitable, raid on Puerto Rico. Unusually, as a result of the association, Cumberland became a prominent proponent of the Londoners' shifting view of the war, as an opportunity to deploy English sea power for commercial aggrandisement within the seaborne empires of Spain and Portugal. Despite some striking successes, he failed to restore his fortune, lamenting at the end of the war that he 'threw his land into the sea'.[42]

Although leading promoters of such backgrounds helped to shape the private war at sea, they were supported by a much larger number of smaller investors who were of particular importance in the lesser provincial ports such as Rye, Poole, Dartmouth and Barnstaple. The economic structure of reprisal ventures, which came to maturity during the 1580s and 1590s, facilitated the development of a substantial passive investment in the business which mobilized or exploited the resources of adventurers of modest means. As a joint stock venture based on a customary distinction between shipowners, victuallers and the ship's captain and company, there was ample opportunity for shipwrights, carpenters and other craftsmen, shop keepers, butchers and bakers, ale-house keepers and others to contribute to fitting out a vessel for a reprisal voyage, in exchange for a share in captured prizes. This structure spread the risks of reprisal ventures across local communities. At the same time it widened support for the war, generating a self-interested patriotism that was dependent on plunder and increasingly liable to provoke disorderly or piratical enterprise.

The scale of reprisal ventures amounted to a form of national sea power. Expeditions sent out by well-funded partnerships rivalled royal fleets in size, strength and capability. Moreover, the practice of consortship at sea brought together significant numbers of men-of-war of considerable force. But the private war of reprisals was not a national conflict. Geographically it was restricted to certain regions of England, while its social base was sectional in character. Evidence for the three years following the Armada campaign, from 1589 to 1591, indicates that English adventurers were involved in promoting about 100 reprisal voyages a year, involving about as many vessels. Though subject to short-term fluctuation, this capability was sustained throughout the war. In 1598 more than eighty recorded voyages occurred. These are minimum estimates, based on limited and patchy evidence. Nor do they include the potentially significant number of unlicensed vessels operating along a porous borderline between legitimate reprisals and disorderly, piratical enterprise, which grew in volume during the closing stages of the conflict.[43] In sum, the actual number of vessels annually engaged in lawful and disorderly depredation, as well as in piracy, fluctuated between 100 and 200, and in some years it may have been even greater.

This private sea war was heavily dominated by London, with the support of Bristol, Plymouth and other ports in south-west England. Approximately one-half of the recorded total of 236 ships sailing on reprisal from 1589 to 1591 came from London, Plymouth and Bristol; the proportion was more than 70 per cent when other ports along the south-west coast, from Poole westwards, are included. The importance of London grew during the course of the war. By 1598 it accounted for half of the eighty-six vessels known to have been operating with letters of reprisal. This trend was accompanied by an apparent decline in activity within the south-west, especially at Bristol. London's leading role was underscored by the tonnage of shipping employed in the war. While small ships of less than 100 tons accounted for more than half of all vessels sent out on reprisal during the early

Æmulus æquorei, admiratorque Draconis
Commodiore via, et spacijs brevioribus Orbem
Circumagens, patriam multa cum laude revisi;
Pleraque Neptuno et dignißima Marte peregi.
Si Mare Cretensis nescit, tum nesciet Anglus
Oceanum, et viuet positis inglorius armis.

Thomas Cavendish, one of several gentlemen adventurers, who sought to emulate Drake during the 1580s and 1590s. He circumnavigated the globe from 1586 to 1588, seizing a rich Spanish galleon along the coast of California. He embarked on another voyage in 1591 to repeat this success, but died during the course of the voyage, possibly by committing suicide. (*The Fugger News-Letters*)

phase of the conflict, London contributed about two-thirds of the small number of larger and stronger ships, of 200 tons and above. By the closing years of the war, as the number of smaller vessels declined, London's share of the latter had increased significantly, accounting for more than 80 per cent of such ships operating during 1598.[44]

As might be expected, given its potential targets, the sea war attracted little or no interest in ports and harbours along the east coast or the north-west. In addition, neither Welsh nor Irish adventurers appear to have been heavily involved in sending out ships on reprisal. Indeed, Irish vessels were vulnerable to English attack on the grounds that they were trading with the enemy.

Although an impressive volume of shipping was employed during the sea war, it represented a mixed force made up of miscellaneous vessels of varied tonnage, armament and manning. Many were small or modest trading ships adapted or converted to carry more men and ordnance. Such ships increased in size during the 1580s and 1590s, especially those which were engaged on long-distance trading voyages into the Mediterranean, creating a body of strong, well-armed vessels readily adaptable to the functions of private men-of-war. A small number of larger vessels were constructed to serve in the latter capacity; appropriately named, they were comparable in most respects to the Queen's ships. One of Cumberland's vessels, the *Red Dragon*, built to serve as a warship in 1595 and subsequently re-named the *Malice Scourge*, was of 600 tons burden. But successful plunder often depended as much on speed and manoeuvrability as on strength and armament. As a result small vessels such as the *Catherine* of Weymouth, of 35 tons and armed with four small ordnance, continued to operate very successfully, much as many pirate ships had done during the 1560s and 1570s.[45]

These vessels were engaged in the plunder of Iberian trade and shipping, within and beyond Europe. Many of the hunting grounds visited by English men-of-war were regular haunts for pirates, whose knowledge and experience of sailing in familiar and unfamiliar regions helped to pave the way for the more extensive and organized campaign of reprisals after 1585. The Channel, western approaches and the Bay of Biscay were regularly infested with large numbers of lesser predators, involved in short raids on vulnerable trading and fishing vessels that were increasingly indiscriminate in the selection of targets. Larger vessels haunted the coasts of Spain and Portugal, particularly at headlands and capes, preying on coastal traffic, and occasionally consorting together in anticipation of meeting richer prizes returning from the Caribbean, Brazil or the East Indies. In December 1587 forty English vessels were reportedly sailing about Cape St Vincent, effectively laying siege to the coast and taking booty worth 250,000 crowns. Two years later there were reports of 100 English ships off the Cape, taking 'every ship, French or Spanish, that seeks to pass'.[46] Voyages to the Canary Islands and the Azores were an outgrowth of this raiding which also encouraged transatlantic venturing. During the 1590s English ships in the Mediterranean began to combine trade with plunder, though it rapidly became disorderly and piratical in nature.

Although hunting grounds within European waters attracted most of these raiders, the Caribbean also became a frequented haunt for ships sailing on reprisal. The incursions of English men-of-war during the 1580s and 1590s turned the region into a dangerous and defensive frontier zone for the Spanish monarchy. In effect the conflict at sea was a means by which transatlantic piracy was transmuted into lawful plunder, in a way that represented an unofficial extension of sea power in the service of commercial as well as predatory ambitions. Within a widely scattered and exposed region, which Spain struggled to defend, English predators rapidly developed the experiences of pirate groups from the 1570s. As during the early wave of illegal depredation, moreover, they benefited from the occasional assistance of renegades or native groups. During the war at least 235 men-of-war, accounting for seventy-six expeditions, sailed to the Caribbean, while the actual total may have been well in excess of 100 expeditions and 300 vessels. After a slow start, reprisal ships of varying size and armament swarmed in the West Indies, raiding local shipping along the coasts of Cuba, Hispaniola and Jamaica, the Tierra Firme coastline – especially east of Cartagena – and within the Gulf of Honduras. The palpable threat to commerce and shipping, as demonstrated by the presence of thirteen English vessels off Havana in 1592, revived widespread alarm and anxiety among Spanish officials and settlers. Despite attempts to improve local defences, settlements even in sensitive strategic areas remained dangerously vulnerable to English assault.[47]

The character of activity in the West Indies acutely revealed the underlying strengths and weaknesses of English depredation. Although the Spanish repeatedly identified the English as corsairs, questioning the legitimacy of operations within the Caribbean, in practice many of those involved in such raiding were among the leading supporters of the war against Spain. But they were not the spearhead of an offensive maritime campaign which was organized and controlled by the state; instead they operated in a private and strategically uncoordinated capacity. Though sanctioned by the regime, the monarchy was directly involved in only two major ventures of 1585 and 1595, both of which had mixed results. In these circumstances plunder and profit overshadowed tactical or strategic purposes. Furthermore, there were occasions when English men-of-war were as much competitors in the search for Spanish prizes as they were collaborators in a war against the enemy. The mixed groups of raiders who haunted the Caribbean during these years may have been among the more dynamic element of the war effort, but they were also opportunistic, fragmented and ill-disciplined in character.[48]

The evidence for several ventures sent out from 1588 to 1591 demonstrates the dangers and difficulties of prize hunting in the West Indies and beyond. The 1588 voyage of the *Examiner*, set forth by John Watts with his brother, Thomas, as captain, was marked by an undercurrent of discontent between the master and the latter. It culminated in a violent attack on Thomas, who was left with a crippled arm as a result. In the following year an expedition led by John Chidley, a gentleman from Devon, originally intended for the South Sea, ended disastrously due to the outbreak and spread of disease, demoralization and mutiny. Although the expedition broke up after the death of Chidley, one vessel, the *Delight*, sailed on for the Straits of Magellan, only to turn back in the face of the continued loss of life. It returned to England with only six of the original company of ninety-one men and boys alive. Such dangers were compounded by the ever-present threat of Spanish hostility. Thus in June 1591 the *Content*, a man-of-war sent out by Sir George Carey, was caught off the western coast of Cuba by a fleet of enemy warships. The ensuing conflict raged from seven o'clock in the morning until eleven at night. The ship was badly damaged, while one member of the company was killed and two others were wounded. The number of casualties might have been greater, but for the fact that at least ten of the crew had taken refuge in the hold. A change in the weather, described by one of the survivors as a gale from God, enabled the *Content* to evade further action.[49]

Despite such dangers, English reprisal ships seized an impressive haul of enemy prizes. Within the first three months of the conflict twenty-seven Spanish ships were seized, while more than 1,000 vessels may have been taken during the war years.[50] A significant number of neutral vessels were also taken, allegedly because they were trading with the enemy in contraband goods. In addition, an unknown number of ships were piratically spoiled or seized. According to the regulations governing the conduct of the sea war, all captured vessels were to be returned to England to be adjudged as lawful prize by the High Court of Admiralty, but there were powerful motives and opportunities for the companies of men-of-war to dispose of their captures illegally in overseas markets, especially in the ports of south-west Ireland and north Africa. During the first two years of the war, plunder from at least fifteen vessels, most of French origin, was brought into Irish ports and sold, often with the approval of local officials. The booty included a ship taken by Captain Courtenay, which was laden with sugar, wool, oil and an abundance of silver.[51]

Even so, reprisal ships operating within the confines of the regulations returned with varied and sometimes rich returns. There were wide fluctuations in the seizure of enemy prizes, ranging in annual value from £100,000 to £200,000. The most common type of prize, accounting for about one-half of the total number of captured cargoes, was made up of European commodities, particularly wine, timber, corn and fish. The more valuable prizes were of American goods, including sugar, hides, logwood, ginger, gold, silver and pearls, though ships laden with treasure were rarely taken. In total they accounted for more than three-quarters of the total value of prize cargoes. Because of their size and armament, few vessels returning from the East Indies were captured. However, one of the richest prizes taken during the war was a Portuguese carrack, the *Madre de Dios*. This huge prize was captured in 1592 off the Azores, on the return voyage from the east, but only after a prolonged conflict involving five of Cumberland's ships acting in consortship with a fleet of men-of-war, in which the Queen had an interest, and other reprisal ships. The value of the cargo, of spices, jewels, perfumes and gold, was close to £500,000, but the prize was so extensively pillaged that Cumberland and the other promoters were left to share out £140,000. For the principal adventurers, this may have barely covered the cost of the venture.[52]

Characteristically the war of reprisals served competing and complementary interests. By promoting the sea war, the regime created an outlet for the employment of private resources and investment, as well as for the expression of anti-Spanish hostility. While the nature of the conflict reduced the Crown's control over strategy, weakening its ability to direct operations at sea, it may have been well suited to the maintenance of a defensive war against one of the greatest powers in western Europe. At a time when the Queen was forced into an increasingly burdensome commitment in the Netherlands and northern France, the maritime conflict provided her with the opportunity to harass and weaken the enemy in a potentially profitable way, while limiting the dangers of employing the navy in risky and costly offensive actions. But the length of the war, which was still in progress at the time of the Queen's death, had unforeseen and contradictory consequences. On the one hand it encouraged the development of better organized, business-like enterprises, as the more amateurish and unsuccessful adventurers were forced out of business; on the other hand it led to growing disorder at sea, within a context of mounting international competition involving English, Dutch, French and Flemish men-of-war. There was an inherent danger that the so-called 'wild men' of the war of reprisals would subvert public and private ambitions, while weakening the coalition of interests which sustained the conflict at sea, by their disorderly behaviour.[53]

The scale and length of the war thus had unexpected consequences for maritime depredation. The later 1580s and early 1590s were marked by overseas complaints against English pirates, which became more widespread and intense as the war progressed. In some parts of Europe it appeared that the English were engaged in an unprecedented attack on neutral trade and shipping as well as on Iberian commerce. Much of this overseas complaint was about the seizure of contraband, or the capture of neutral vessels carrying enemy cargoes, rather than piracy as such. But the disorderly activities of reprisal ships undermined the ability of the regime to maintain the distinction between legitimate privateering and piracy. As a result the sea war provoked a cycle of irregular spoil, piracy and violence at sea, encouraging overseas reprisals and retaliation.

Maritime depredation confused profound issues of strategy, property rights and international law. Although the regime justified the seizure of munitions and provisions aboard neutral ships as a lawful means of weakening the enemy, in practice there was no widely accepted definition of contraband of war. In June 1586, for example, the French insisted on their right to trade freely with Spain, England or the Low Countries, citing in their defence English practice during the last

Franco-Spanish war, when English merchants traded with both countries. To some extent the difficulty was an unavoidable consequence of the limited development of international law, especially as it applied to neutral rights and practices. But it was also the result of self-interested political and economic considerations. In the Netherlands the issue was a source of discord among the rebels against Philip II, with the merchants of Amsterdam and other ports in Holland insisting on the right to trade with Spain, against the demands of those who tried to restrict or halt it. At a time when the regime in England was seeking to promote the 'common cause' of international Protestantism, while preventing the spread of hostilities in France, the seizure of neutral shipping was an acutely sensitive issue, which threatened to embroil it in protracted and damaging disputes with friends and allies.[54]

Against this background the opening years of the war witnessed an onslaught on shipping in the Channel which endangered the distinction between lawful reprisals and piracy. Vulnerable French trading and fishing vessels were especially exposed to disorderly spoil by the English. In May 1586 the *Jonas* of Rouen, laden with a cargo of sugar from the Canary Islands, was taken by two English men-of-war off Cape Finisterre and brought into Bridgewater. It was followed by the seizure of five or six ships, laden with corn, during June and July, several of which were carried off to Flushing, then in the hands of an English governor and garrison, where they were adjudged as lawful prize. The spoil of French shipping aroused widespread anger and resentment. In July Burghley was informed that the recent plunder of sixteen vessels provoked such hostility towards the English in St Malo that they were afraid to be seen in public. It also led to concern among merchants in the West Country that they would be debarred from trading across the Channel. During September, complaints of the seizure of ten or twelve French vessels were accompanied by reports that their companies had been cast overboard and drowned. Shortly after, it was reported that ten headless corpses, bound together, were washed ashore along the coast of Treguyer. The following month Henry III complained to the Queen about the seizure of wheat and rye laden aboard two English ships at Hamburg for the governor of Calais. The grain was taken into Zeeland by Captain Henry Griffin and declared to be legal prize, in spite of objections from the English Lord Admiral.[55]

The regime appeared to be powerless to prevent this determined assault on French shipping. In January 1587 William Waad, visiting Paris on other diplomatic business, was informed that 150 traders or shippers had been spoiled by English men-of-war. These complaints were aggravated by allegations concerning the difficulty and delay in securing justice in England, which led to a suspension of Anglo-French trade in January. Although it was lifted in May, by then the issue of disorderly depredation was complicated by the plunder of naturalized Spaniards resident in France.[56]

The seizure or spoil of at least sixteen French vessels during the period from March to June 1587 led to violent retaliation. In June two English ships bound for

La Rochelle were plundered by men-of-war from Dieppe. The French report-edly 'used great cruelty towards the men, slaying divers of them a sang froid, and leaving some of them most barbarously upon certain rocks, to the end they might perish … for want of succour'.[57] Despite intervention from Sir Edward Stafford, the English ambassador in Paris, in support of French complaints, by November 1587 commissioners acting for Henry III were considering the issue of letters of reprisal against England. Early in 1588 Stafford warned Burghley of the diplo-matic damage from the unruly spoil of French ships: 'these continued sores upon sores will mar all in the end', he cautioned, compelling the French into 'thinking that we desire to have quarrels with them'. As England prepared to meet the threat of the Spanish Armada, its relations with France seemed to be endangered by the corrosive issue of maritime depredation. French representatives continued to complain of piracy and illegal spoil by adventurers such as Captain Leye, 'who makes war without any warrant', as well as by disorderly captains in the Queen's service. In addition the plunder of vessels from the Huguenot stronghold of La Rochelle threatened to damage relations with Henry, King of Navarre, the leader of the Protestant interest in France and heir to the throne.

Although French shipping bore the brunt of English disorderly depredation during the early years of the war, the assault on neutral trade provoked wider overseas complaint. The concern of the regime to prevent the traffic in war mate-rial and provisions to Spain from northern Europe turned the Channel into a battleground for contraband trade and neutral rights. While ships from Norway arrived in Spain during August 1586 having 'met no man of war all the way', the regime saw the supply of the enemy with certain commodities, especially ordnance, as a 'very bad and unconscionable trade'.[58] Even among friendly states, however, there was disagreement over the extent of the English definition of contraband. While the King of Denmark agreed to accept gunpowder, ordnance, saltpetre, pitch, tar and other naval supplies in a list of such prohibited goods, he objected to the inclusion of wheat and rye. Under these conditions neutral traders either sought guarantees from the Queen that their ships would not be attacked, or they diverted their vessels around Scotland to avoid the dangers of the Channel.

But the issue of contraband was soon clouded by disorderly and indiscrimi-nate attacks on trading vessels, regardless of their intended destinations. During 1586 Dutch merchants complained of rovers and freebooters, with or without commissions, who disposed of plundered goods in London, Dover and the Isle of Wight, the proceeds of which were used to wage war against Spain. The cap-tures included the *Hope* of Flushing, which was taken under colour of reprisals by a vessel sent out by Watts and his London partners. The following year the King of Denmark threatened to arrest English shipping if his subjects were unable to obtain redress for such spoil. The Queen apologized for the unruly activities of English reprisal ships, providing compensation for their victims. But she also urged the Danish monarch 'to consider how hard it is to restrain men-of-war from outrages by sea and land, in times of hostility between princes'.[59] As a result, Danish complaints continued. In January 1588 the King angrily complained to Elizabeth of the damage to his honour and reputation, following the seizure of a fishing vessel returning from Iceland by two English captains, Wickes and Wood, who evidently tore up a royal passport and letter of safe conduct. The company of the vessel were spoiled of their victuals and clothing and set ashore in Ireland, while the cargo was sold at Chester. Faced with daily complaints against the activities of English pirates, the King threatened to 'use his own means for revenge of these outrages'.[60]

The early years of the war at sea thus witnessed the establishment of a pattern of maritime enterprise which dangerously confused the distinction between lawful depredation and piracy. Despite the regime's prohibition of reprisals against targets other than Spain and Portugal, English adventurers launched an indiscriminate campaign of plunder against neutral trade and shipping. Although it defended such attacks as a legitimate means of denying Spain supplies of contraband of war, its position was undermined by the activities of captains such as Diggory Piper. During 1585 and 1586 Piper was one of several captains who deliberately targeted French and Danish shipping. His seizure of a Danish vessel under colour of reprisals was described by the civilian lawyer, Dr Hammond, as 'plain piracy'.[61] In order to reduce the level of piratical activity, the author of an undated paper, of c.1587, called for rapid legal action against pirates, including summary executions without any prospect of pardon, as well as more effective regulation of the sea war by Admiralty officials. But the suggestion that the plunder of neutral vessels should be regarded as piracy, which would have overwhelmed the High Court of Admiralty with offenders, underlined the difficulty in trying to maintain a clear distinction between illegal and legal enterprise.[62]

The response to English depredation was overseas complaint and condemnation, accompanied by retaliation which generated a violent cycle of reprisals and piracy. Thus the raids of Dutch and Flemish men-of-war aroused anger among the south-east ports, while the French response provoked widespread concern in the south-west. The disruption and damage to peaceful trade, particularly in provincial ports, swelled the ranks of unemployed mariners, increasing the pool of potential recruits for irregular maritime venturing, including localized piracy. Under such conditions the violence and disorder at sea were sustained, and justified, by mutual grievances and hostility. In August 1588 the Lord Admiral warned that the ill-treatment of English subjects by the French forced men into piracy.[63]

If the sea war bred disorderly reprisals, it also served as a cover for the persistence of small-scale piracy. The legal distinction between both forms of activity was deeply compromised by the actions of captains like Piper. As during the 1540s, however, there was a tendency for the former to concentrate on overseas targets, while pirates spoiled domestic as much as foreign shipping. Localized piracy was heavily overshadowed by the scale and vigour of the reprisal war; nevertheless, it remained a problem in the coastal waters of the British Isles, reinforcing and occasionally merging with more ambitious forms of depredation.

During the years preceding the Armada campaign, much of this activity was an attenuated survival of the organized piracy which had flourished so widely during the 1570s. With local support, it persisted particularly within the Irish Sea and along the coast of East Anglia. In June 1586 the council complained to magistrates and the commissioners for piracy in Wales about the presence of pirates in Cardiff and the neighbouring region; local constables who had allowed them to escape were to face exemplary punishment. The pirates included several groups who operated off the coast of north Wales, spoiling ships sailing to and from Ireland. Later in the year the council was informed that pirates openly resorted to Gorleston, where 'disordered persons keep the town in awe'.[64] Various reports of 1586 and 1587 identified the leading offenders as Captains Wise, Beare, Cooke, Smith, Kanter, Cole and Strangewich, but there were undoubtedly others who were engaged in the business. Cooke seems to have been engaged in the spoil of local shipping within the Irish Sea, disposing of plunder in Milford Haven and Carmarthen, possibly with the continued connivance of local officials. The apprehension and punishment of such rovers remained dependent on the cooperation of local officers, with varying results. In August 1587 a servant of the Lord Admiral, who was sent to Margate to apprehend certain pirates, encountered the master of 'their fellowship and confederacie', but he escaped when an official in the town refused to assist in his arrest.[65]

Piracy was confused with the spoil and pillage of foreign shipping. Along the east coast groups of pirates attacked Scottish and other overseas vessels, provoking repeated complaints. According to the Deputy Vice Admiral for Yorkshire, most of the members of one group, who 'have reigned too long upon that poor coast', were fugitives.[66] Under Francis Concette, captain of the *Doe* of London of 50 tons, in October 1586 they plundered a vessel off Flamborough Head, of furs, stockings, silk lace, pearls, as well as 500 or 600 dollars and fourteen pieces of gold. Most of the booty ended up in the hands of William Concette, a yeoman of Hilderthorpe further south along the coast, who was the only member of the group 'of ability to make satisfaction' to the victims.

At the same time the council heard a growing number of cases and complaints against the activities of other pirates and rovers. During 1587 it was informed that Melchior Strangewich and Fox piratically seized a Danish ship which was brought into Helford, where the cargo was sold. Another Danish vessel was taken by John Mers, a rover who was sent out by Sir Walter Leveson, the Deputy Vice Admiral of north Wales. Mers, who boldly took the prize in a Danish harbour, was also involved in the spoil of Dutch fishermen in the North Sea. The Dutch subsequently complained that he and his associates spoiled three fishing boats off the Scottish coast, plundering them of goods valued at £2,850; furthermore, some of the fishermen were 'murdered and buried in the sands near the Isle of Wight, "not as Christians, but as dogs"'.[67] About the same time Lawrence and Thomas

Dutton, set forth by their father, John Dutton of Dutton Hall in Cheshire, pirati-cally spoiled a French vessel.

The council acted promptly to deal with these and other complaints, partly out of concern at the prospect of overseas retaliation. A servant of Edward Seymour, who purchased Danish goods in Helford, was summoned to London, while his master was ordered to compensate the Danes for their losses. Dutton and Leveson were also instructed to appear before the council. The registers of council meet-ings demonstrate its concern to deal with the disorder at sea, and its determination to support the legitimate complaints of neutral traders against unruly English men-of-war and pirates. Yet there were limits to what the council could achieve. Josias Calmady, a gentleman who sent out Diggory Piper, claimed that he was too poor to answer a bond for good behaviour. Piper was also acquitted of piracy by two juries. Although Strangewich was captured during 1587, two years later the council was investigating his escape from custody in Dorset. In some cases attempts to deal with these and other problems were threatened by long-standing claims to Admiralty jurisdiction in ports such as Southampton and Newcastle. In November 1589 the judge of the High Court of Admiralty, Sir Julius Caesar, put forward a novel plan for a yearly circuit to try matters of piracy, which might have resolved these issues, but little came of it.[68]

The Armada campaign appears to have brought a brief respite to the disorder at sea, though it did not disappear. In April 1588 Margaret Johnson petitioned for the recovery of a vessel which was taken by a group of pirates, who killed her husband. The following month William Pitts robbed a vessel off Hilbre Island bound for Dublin. During August the Lord Admiral informed Burghley of his capture of a pirate in the west. When 'charged … with his piracies, he cursed, and said he had dealt against none but Frenchmen; and he said he was forced to it, for he had complained two years together of his losses by Frenchmen'.[69] Several French vessels had recently been taken by other pirates, including a group led by Robert Smyth, and their cargoes of wine sold in Galway and Kinsale. In response, during September the council authorized two merchants of Bristol to send out ships to apprehend pirates and recover French goods. Later in the year another French ship was taken and brought into Helford by Captain Harwell, and its cargo of corn sold. In December the council appointed commissioners to assist in the search for pirate plunder, partly in response to reviving French and Danish complaints.[70]

The failure of the Armada was followed by a resurgence of English depre-dation, as adventurers sought to take advantage of Spanish weakness. The war of reprisals reached a new level of intensity, throwing into relief the confusion between lawful plunder, disorderly spoil and piracy. Men-of-war of varying legal-ity crowded the coasts of Spain and Portugal. In January 1589 Venetian vessels were reportedly afraid to leave Lisbon, for fear of capture by English pirates. Later in the year rovers were swarming off the islands of the Azores, preying particularly upon vulnerable Portuguese ships returning from Brazil. In addition the Channel

Hilbre Island, Cheshire. Though the island can be reached by foot at low tide today, it was occasionally frequented by pirates and rovers during the sixteenth century, who preyed on the trade of Chester and Liverpool. (Author's collection)

The Dee estuary, Cheshire. Pirates and rovers were attracted to the region by the trade of Chester across the Irish Sea. They ranged across the coast of north Wales, to Holyhead and beyond. (Author's collection)

and western approaches continued to attract a large number of seaborne raiders of varied backgrounds, who attacked local and coastal traffic while lying in wait for the return of fishing vessels from Newfoundland.[71]

Attempts by the regime to justify the seizure of foreign ships failed to convince or appease most neutral traders. Responding to the Armada as an act of open war, later in 1588 Elizabeth warned the merchants of Hamburg that she would not allow them or other members of the Hanseatic ports to carry gunpowder, provisions or ordnance and other weapons to her enemies. At the same time the regime's efforts to clarify and regulate the sea war, by prohibiting attacks on French, Scottish and other friendly vessels, and through the issue of a revised list of prohibited goods in 1592, met with little success. Indeed, as the council continued to be inundated with overseas complaints, during the 1590s there was a real danger that the rising tide of disorder and piratical activity would overshadow, if not discredit the legitimacy of the war at sea.[72]

French shipping remained the most common target for unruly English men-of-war and pirates, though the seizure of Danish vessels continued to provoke controversy and complaint. French prizes were regularly taken during 1589 and beyond. In June and July the council heard complaints concerning the seizure of a vessel bound for Spain with grain and munitions by Captain Thomas Maye, who was sailing with a commission from the King of Navarre, and of the plunder of a cargo of wines claimed by a merchant of La Rochelle. In August Sir Walter Ralegh and one of his captains, John Chidley, were ordered to restore two vessels of Cherbourg. The issue of letters of reprisal against the Catholic League in France provided a coating of legality for some of this spoil. For many French merchants and shipowners, however, English activity was essentially piratical in nature, which was aggravated by lengthy legal suits for the recovery of ships and cargoes. In an attempt to limit the damage, during 1591 the French ambassador requested that English men-of-war should be prohibited from attacking French vessels without a new commission from the Lord Admiral and himself, 'on pain of being treated as pirates and having their ships confiscated'.[73] Under prevailing conditions, it had little chance of being accepted.

The vulnerability of French vessels remained an irresistible temptation for disorderly reprisal ships and pirates. In October 1591 the Princess of Navarre complained to the Queen and Burghley about the seizure of a vessel, carrying her passport, which was returning from North America with a cargo of fish, oil and a large quantity of rich furs. In June 1592 the port of Bayonne claimed to have suffered losses to English pirates of at least 50,000 crowns. Despite the French King's threat to issue letters of reprisal to the victims, a few months later at least twenty warships were reported to be cruising between the Scilly Isles and Ushant, waiting to intercept fishing vessels returning from Newfoundland to Bayonne and other ports.[74]

Attacks on Danish and Dutch vessels also led to angry and persistent complaints. In both cases, the response of the regime was influenced by wider political and strategic interests affecting the common cause against the enemy. Thus in August 1589 the council ordered that Danish complaints in the High Court of Admiralty were to be handled with extraordinary favour. It also ordered the restoration of a ship recently seized by Strangewich, and a search for concealed Danish plunder in London. In response to protests from Christian IV against the plunder of Danish ships in Norwegian havens, dating back to 1587, the Queen promised prompt action. By the end of 1589 commissioners in England were dealing with at least fourteen cases of disorderly spoil, in some cases stretching back over twelve years. On the defensive, the regime insisted that some of the malefactors had been executed for piracy. Further complaints to the council during the early 1590s indicated that Danish vessels remained targets for English men-of-war or pirates. While a representative for Elizabeth reassured the Danish King in 1590 that 'his subjects should be treated with the highest favour in her realms', he warned that pirates of different backgrounds 'infested English waters and some Englishmen, especially in war time, attacked Englishmen and others indifferently'.[75]

The seizure and spoil of Dutch shipping strained Anglo-Dutch relations, despite their shared hostility towards Spain. Although the Dutch defended their commerce with Spain on the grounds of economic necessity, doing business with the enemy was a contentious and divisive issue. Reports of 1589 indicated that Dutch traders were shipping various commodities to Spain around Scotland, contrary to Admiralty warnings, because of the profit from the trade. The scale of the English attack on Dutch trade thus aroused widespread anger in Holland and Zeeland. By 1589 the High Court of Admiralty and other agencies were hearing at least forty Dutch claims concerning disorderly or illegal depredation. According to the States-General, Dutch losses amounted to 1.6 million florins. One solution to the problem, put forward during 1589, was to allow the Dutch and other traders from northern Europe to trade with Spain in what was described as non-harmful goods, while paying for licences to sail unmolested through the Channel. It was anticipated that more than £200,000 would be raised by these means for the benefit of the Queen and the Dutch. The States-General showed some interest in the scheme, but it attracted little or no support from the Dutch merchant community.[76]

Despite the Queen's frustration and annoyance, the Dutch insisted on their right to maintain commercial relations with Spain. The English maintained that it was 'a strange kind of war, both to traffic and make war with your enemy', but their own position was undermined by evidence of the supply of contraband to Spain by English merchants.[77] This tangled issue thus provoked mutual complaints, though on the Dutch side it was inflamed by reports that English captains, including Cumberland, tortured their victims into confessing that they were carrying goods belonging to the enemy. In 1592 Dutch traders claimed losses of more than £60,000 in three vessels taken by the English. Such 'continual spoils and cruelties at sea threatened … ports', such as Middelburg, 'with ruin'.[78] The Dutch demonstrated their determination to deal swiftly and severely with unruly and unlawful predators by executing about forty members of the company of the *Diamond* of Bristol for piracy, despite a plea for clemency from the council.

Although the regime tried to limit the damage to neutral and friendly states, the disorderly activities of English men-of-war spread to include shipping from northern and southern Europe. The publication of a remonstrance in July 1589 against the ports of the Hanseatic League supplying Spain with provisions for war, which coincided with the return of Drake from Lisbon with more than thirty Hanseatic vessels, aroused widespread anger and resentment. The diplomatic damage, and strident demands for retaliation in Hamburg and Lübeck, subsequently led to the release of the ships and their cargoes. But the seizure of vessels from Lübeck, Emden, Danzig, Stettin, Hamburg and ports in the Baltic continued. The English used international law and custom to defend the prohibition of war supplies to Spain, but as in the case of the Dutch and the Danes, there was serious disagreement over the definition of contraband. Complaints from Lübeck in 1590 about the spoil of shipping carrying lawful goods were followed by the seizure of four vessels from Hamburg by Cumberland's fleet of men-of-war. About the same time the *Red Lion* of Bremen was taken by John Perryman and other notorious pirates and brought into Chester, where its cargo was illegally sold.[79]

During the early 1590s, Italian shipping also became a target for English rovers either sailing along the coasts of Spain and Portugal or cruising into the Mediterranean. Although the number of captures was small, they raised complicated legal issues that could take years to settle. During the latter part of 1590, for example, a Venetian argosy was brought into Plymouth by two men-of-war. Drake was instructed by the council to investigate the matter, while apprehending one of the captains and confiscating a rich cargo of pepper and jewels. The incident led the Queen to issue a proclamation warning that future attacks on the ships of friends and allies would be dealt with as cases of piracy. Nonetheless, the dispute over the ownership of the cargo turned into a fiercely contested legal case, with the captors claiming that the prize was taken 'by way of reprisal, and that the merchants' marks on the cargo' had been fraudulently changed.[80] As the case was referred to arbitration during 1592 it was overtaken by the plunder of another Venetian vessel by Captain Edward Glenham.

Although unruly English depredation increased in range, the seas around the British Isles remained the scene for varied forms of opportunistic piratical enterprise which, for a time, became focused on Irish and Scottish shipping. In January 1589 a group of Dublin merchants complained of the capture of a ship by Captain Fulford, who carried his prize off to Tor Bay. In August the council issued a letter of assistance to a merchant of Waterford for the recovery of Spanish wines taken by the pirate Noe Randall and his company. By the end of the year Scottish traders were complaining of the spoil of their ships. They included a complaint of George Paddy against Sir John Wogan, dating back three years, for losses amounting to £400. The Scots merchant claimed that one of the vessels was plundered twice by pirates, who were assisted by Wogan and his three sons.

Although the council provided compensation for some Scottish victims, Paddy's long-running complaint case against Wogan lay unresolved in 1593.[81]

Localized piracy and disorder continued to be a persistent problem. In April 1589 there were complaints that the inhabitants of Poole were dealing with pirates. The following year the council was informed of the spoil of a vessel at Yarmouth by a group of masked raiders, who seem to have originated from nearby Gorleston, 'a receptacle for all disordered and masterles persones, daily committing fowle abuses'.[82] In August 1590 the commissioners for piracy in Pembroke and Carmarthen were ordered to arrest the pirate, Nashe, and his confederates. Later in the year, in the face of renewed Scottish grievances, Burghley was compelled to disavow English piracies, insisting 'I hate all pirates mortally'.[83] During June and July 1591 there were complaints of English pirates haunting the coasts of the Orkney and Shetland Islands, and of two pirate ships cruising around the Scilly Isles. The merchants of Caernarvon complained in October 1592 that they were robbed by pirates as they sailed to Bristol fair. Pirates were operating in the Severn estuary during 1593, among whom Hillary Brocke of Jersey was one of the chief suspects, while later in the year a case of piracy and murder in Hull was investigated by the Council in the North.[84]

Though subject to control and regulation, the early years of the sea war established a confusing pattern of legitimate reprisals, overlapping with widespread disorder and violent spoil, which was in danger of merging with overtly piratical activity. At the same time, small-scale and opportunistic piracy continued to flourish. In some regions it may have been linked with a wider problem of disorder and unrest ashore. Under these conditions, therefore, by the early 1590s the regime was in danger of losing control of the maritime conflict, to the detriment of its relations with friendly and neutral states.[85]

The strain of war: plunder and piracy to 1603

Although the coalition of interests which maintained the war at sea continued to function, the maritime conflict acquired its own momentum during the 1590s, responding and adapting to changing conditions. The failure of Drake's last voyage of 1595, followed by the gradual withdrawal of the regime from offensive operations at sea, upset the balance of forces within what was always a temporary alliance, while further weakening its ability to control reprisal enterprise. Despite the short-lived ambitions of a younger generation of patriotic sea warriors, to reinvigorate and re-shape the maritime conflict, it continued to be characterized by small-scale actions. Consequently it remained disorderly in application and purpose, particularly as the raids of enemy men-of-war increased the competition for prizes in dangerously crowded hunting grounds. From the perspective of neutral or friendly states, English depredation appeared deliberately to confuse the distinction between lawful reprisals and piracy. By the later 1590s, the strain of organizing a private and semi-official sea war was beginning to expose deep-seated problems which lay unresolved by the time of the Queen's death.[86]

Yet the strategic and economic benefits of fighting Spain in partnership with private enterprise still seemed to outweigh the potential disadvantages. At little financial charge, it enhanced the Queen's Navy and its maritime capability, providing her, in the words of one observer, with a 'force by sea far exceeding any other nation's'.[87] This force undertook damaging raids along the coasts of Spain and Portugal; it disrupted and delayed the sailing of the Indies fleet; and it supported an offensive, if necessarily ill-organized, assault on the Spanish Caribbean. The seizure of one vessel returning from the West Indies, with a cargo reputedly worth 800,000 crowns, fed hopes early in 1591 that the entire fleet could be taken, precipitating the collapse of Spain in revolt, as a result of war weariness and poverty. In spite of the presence of two galleys off Havana, in 1592 it was reported that English men-of-war 'daily braved them at their own doors'.[88] The intercepted letters of enemy merchants underline the vulnerability, or brittleness, of Spain to this kind of maritime assault. With the coast infested with pirates and rovers, merchants appear to have withdrawn from trade in the face of severe disruption and mounting losses.

The impact of the maritime conflict was strikingly demonstrated by the activities of private adventurers during 1595. In April an expedition of reprisal ships sent out by a group of London traders, including Watts, under the command of James Lancaster, raided the Brazilian port of Pernambuco. With the support of Captain Edward Fenner, and aided by a fleet of French raiders, Lancaster occupied the port for one month, during which a rich haul of booty to the value of £50,000 was acquired. Lancaster returned with profitable Brazilian commodities, including sugar and dye wood, as well as the even more valuable cargo of an East Indian carrack, which had been forced into Pernambuco, and a number of prize ships. The raid illustrated the peculiar strengths and weaknesses of the offensive reach of English sea power, especially in seeking out areas of weakness within the widely scattered and vulnerable Portuguese seaborne empire, which was ruled by Philip II. At the same time Cumberland's fleet of predators was reported to 'go about their ordinary purchasing' under commissions from the Queen.[89] Within a few years Cumberland was trying to follow up Lancaster's raid on Pernambuco, in association with a group of London merchants.

There was renewed interest in a transatlantic offensive against Spain during the mid-1590s, which brought together experienced leaders, such as Drake and Hawkins, with a younger generation of ambitious courtiers and strategists, represented by Essex and Ralegh. Though these schemes remained uncoordinated, they were marked by a mix of expansionist and predatory motives which were manifest in heady visions of looting Spanish America. Ralegh's expedition to Guiana during 1595 appeared to encapsulate this ideological projection of empire, gold and anti-Spanish aggrandizement. These ambitions were shared by Essex, a younger and more powerful rival of Ralegh at court. In the wake of the return of the latter, Essex's entertainment for the Queen, which made use of an Indian youth, portrayed a glorified image of the expulsion of Spain from America in accordance with ancient prophecy. Although these ambitions were of limited appeal to the Queen, Essex played a key role in persuading her to send out Drake and Hawkins in command of an expedition to the Caribbean, in a bold attempt to seize the initiative in the war against Spain.[90]

Although intended for Drake's old hunting ground, which may have included provision not only to raid, but also to retain Panama, the aim of the expedition was subject to late modification, effectively turning it into a treasure hunt. It included a plan for an opportunistic raid on Puerto Rico, where a richly laden vessel reportedly lay exposed to capture. At the same time, the Queen's concern for honour and profit was qualified by the security of the realm. Accordingly she expected that Drake and Hawkins 'shall not need … to tary out longer then six monthes at the furthest'.[91] Unfortunately, preparations for the voyage were disrupted by unforeseen delays which bred discontent among some of the company, enabling Spain to acquire details of its purpose. Even before the departure of the fleet from England towards the end of August, a Spanish force was preparing to sail to safeguard the treasure at Puerto Rico.

Drake and Hawkins left at the head of a large expedition made up of twenty-seven vessels, manned with a company of about 2,500 sailors and soldiers. With 'such a fleet and such numbers of gallant men', Sir Thomas Baskerville, the commander of the army, protested to Essex that he would 'rather be buried alive then any such disgrace shuld happen'.[92] The fleet was made up of six large royal vessels, including the recently constructed *Garland* of 660 tons, and a varied force of private ships, at least four of which were owned by Watts. As in the organization of reprisal ventures, the company served for a share of one-third in any prizes and plunder. Some of the officers were investors in the voyage, including Baskerville, who received a bill of adventure for £500 instead of pay.

Though launched with high expectation of placing Spain on the defensive, from the outset the expedition was weakened by tension between Drake and Hawkins, and by confusion between public and private interests. Both were evident in the emergence of rival forces and factions within the fleet, which cruelly exposed the limitations of ageing sea commanders. The awkward hesitancy of Hawkins and the brash overconfidence of Drake were exacerbated by their old and out-of-date intelligence of the Spanish Caribbean. But the conduct of the expedition also pointed to deeper weaknesses in the organization of the war at sea which, in the short term, strengthened a view that Caribbean enterprise was best left to 'filtchinge men of warre' rather than large, albeit hybrid, fleets.[93]

Against the advice of Hawkins, outward bound the expedition visited the Canary Islands in search of fresh water and provisions. It was a brief, but ominous, diversion. Drake's company sustained several casualties, while Spanish officials sent a vessel to the Caribbean warning of the arrival of the fleet. When the English reached the West Indies, the Spanish fleet despatched earlier in the year seized a straggling vessel, the *Francis*. Its company provided valuable information of Drake's presence and of his intended destination.

The attack on Puerto Rico did not go according to plan. While the English fleet approached in some confusion, the defenders sank several vessels in the mouth of the harbour to hinder their approach. The attackers inflicted some damage on the fort with their ordnance. However, a night-time attempt to destroy the Spanish ships went disastrously wrong when the raiders were illuminated by the light from their fireworks. After three days, during which the English sustained significant casualties, Drake withdrew. Among the dead was Hawkins. The Spanish claimed that he was killed in conflict, 'shewinge divers signes & markes of him', but the cause of death was a lingering sickness.[94] Drake also had a lucky escape off Puerto Rico, when a stool on which he was seated, while drinking a pot of beer, was struck by a stray shot from the shore.

Departing from Puerto Rico, Drake boasted that he would take the company to twenty places more profitable and easier to take. In December the expedition seized the town of Rio de la Hacha along the coast of the Main. Although abandoned, and lacking much in the way of booty, the English took many prisoners, including African slaves who voluntarily surrendered. While the town was ransomed for 24,000 pesos, Drake raided the neighbouring pearl fishery, capturing a vessel laden with wine and some money. As the fleet cruised along the coast, finding other settlements forewarned of its arrival, Drake avoided an attack on Cartagena in favour of sailing directly for the isthmus.[95]

Landing at Nombre de Dios, the commanders decided on a rapid march to Panama in the hope of finding hidden treasure. But the march was abandoned in the face of unexpected resistance from the Spanish, mounting casualties and concern at spoiled and short supplies. According to Thomas Maynarde, a close associate of Drake, among the survivors the ordeal sapped morale and support for the expedition. Early in January 1596 Drake called a council of officers, at which it became painfully apparent to Maynarde and others that he was 'at the furthest limit of his knowledge'.[96] The council agreed to sail for Nicaragua. Before the fleet departed, the English set fire to Nombre de Dios, sinking fourteen small frigates and acquiring a modest amount of gold and silver.

With Drake troubled in mind, the fleet anchored off an uninhabited island in search of fresh provisions. Only a few tortoises were taken. The toll of casualties mounted, as a result of the spread of disease and short rations. Sailing for Porto Belo, Drake could barely conceal his grief from Maynarde:

> protestinge … hee was as ignorant of the Indies as my sealfe and that hee never thought any place could be so changed … yet in the greatnes of his minde hee would in the end conclude with these words. It matters not man God hath many things in store for us, and I knowe many meanes to doe her majestie good service & to make us ritch, for wee must have gould before wee see Englande.[97]

But the arrival of the fleet at Porto Belo was marked by the death of Drake. He was buried at sea in a lead coffin.

Baskerville attempted to salvage the expedition by sailing for Santa Marta along the Main. In stormy weather, and with the fleet in danger of being dispersed, he changed course for Jamaica. With fourteen vessels under his command, Baskerville reached the southern coast of Cuba where, off the Isle of Pines, he met a Spanish fleet under the command of Bernadino Delgadillo de Avellaneda. Boldly challenging Avellaneda to a duel, Baskerville led the expedition into battle against the Spanish force of twenty ships. It was a hot contest, involving close action between rival fleets of warships. Although both sides claimed victory, the English sustained few casualties, inflicting greater damage on Avellaneda's fleet. The English claimed that the latter was 'sore beaten and racked thorough'.[98] The Spanish shadowed the English ships, but they showed little desire to renew the conflict, enabling Baskerville and his company of survivors to leave the Caribbean for England.

Soon after reaching the Scilly Isles in May 1596, Baskerville informed Burghley of the unexpected failure of the expedition. He returned with some silver and pearl, as well as ten Africans, who the council ordered to be transported out of the realm. As Baskerville anticipated, the plunder failed to cover the cost of the venture. Furthermore, he faced allegations of cheating the Queen out of £30,000, though he resolutely defended himself, complaining to his wife that he was at least £1,000 poorer as a result of the voyage.

Baskerville explained the disastrous outcome of the expedition by drawing attention to the intelligence which the Spanish had of English plans. This appeared to raise deeper issues regarding the delayed preparations for the voyage, which touched on the Queen's role, though understandably he refrained from making any comment on these matters. Additionally, he drew a veil over the problem of divided leadership, declining to offer any judgement on the command of either Drake or Hawkins. By contrast Maynarde drew subtle lessons from the failure of the voyage, which reflected on the wider conduct of the maritime campaign in the Caribbean. Without a base in the region, he argued that large fleets would accomplish little. Consequently, unless the Queen was prepared to 'dispossesse … [Spain] of the Landes of Porterico, Hispaniola & Cuba,' it was reprisal ships, the 'filtchinge men of warre', who were capable of achieving greater success and profit.[99]

The last voyage of Drake and Hawkins was also the last expedition into the Caribbean in which the monarchy was involved as a major partner with private adventurers. By default the conflict in the region fell into the hands of the privateering interest. For the English, therefore, the Caribbean remained a crowded arena for private war and reprisals, creating the conditions for the subsequent growth of piracy and buccaneering. During the later 1590s the sea war also paved the way for the emergence of ventures which combined plunder with trade or logwood cutting. The *Anne Francis* of London set out in September 1598, carrying

letters of reprisal, with the intention of acquiring a lading of wood. On the uninhabited island of Nevis the company, who served for wages, cut about 120 tons of
logwood, pioneering a form of enterprise which was to be adopted and adapted
by groups of rovers in other parts of the Caribbean.[100]

Across the Atlantic the maritime conflict was reinvigorated by the emergence
of Essex as the champion of the war party, in favour of offensive action against
Spain. Drawing on the ideas of Hawkins, Drake and others, he promoted a
coherent and compelling strategy designed to weaken the enemy while defending and enriching England. He relegated the significance of the reprisal war,
eschewing the 'ways of sharking seamen', identifying the struggle with Spain as
a contest over religion and liberty, rather than a disorderly pursuit for plunder.[101]
But profit was not neglected. Within a short time, 'a great part of the golden
Indian stream might be turned from Spain to England', creating the foundations
for an imperial monarchy which would enable Elizabeth to 'give law to all the
world by sea'. Apart from this powerful strategic vision, Essex's plans appeared
to contain an inherent social dimension which anticipated the assertion of
aristocratic control over the sea war, against the disorderly and embarrassingly
piratical behaviour of private men-of-war. In that sense they drew on lingering
ideas of chivalry which helped to sustain the ambitious enterprises of adventurers such as his kinsman, Robert Dudley, the illegitimate son of Leicester, whose
search for the gold of El Dorado was also intended to burnish the mirror of
knighthood.[102]

As the survivors of the West Indies expedition returned during 1596, a major
fleet was prepared for action on the coast of Spain. This was a royal venture, led
by the Lord Admiral in association with Essex. Its primary purpose was to destroy
shipping of the Spanish navy, to forestall aggressive action in Ireland, though it
was also intended to plunder the Indies fleet. It was made up of more than 100
vessels, of which seventeen were from the Queen's Navy, and carried a force
of nearly 10,000 men. With Spanish coastal defences unprepared, the fleet sailed
into Cadiz harbour, burning and sinking ships, including several galleons. But it
missed the chance of capturing a fleet bound for the Indies, laden with goods
reputedly worth twelve million ducats, which was sunk in the harbour to avoid
its seizure and spoil. Nonetheless, the English took and held Cadiz for two weeks,
during which it was extensively looted. A proposal by Essex to retain it, as a base
to be used as a stranglehold on Spanish commerce, met with little support, and
the expedition returned for England. Three vessels owned by Watts stayed behind,
to lie off Cape St Vincent, hoping to acquire prizes. Although the Cadiz expedition was an impressive military and political success, which seriously embarrassed
the Spanish monarchy, it was a financial loss for the Queen, whose share of the
plunder amounted to little more than £12,000.[103]

The following year a serious attempt was made to take and hold a base on the
coast of Spain, though it ended in confusion and failure. With a force of seventeen
royal vessels and 5,000 men, Essex was also instructed to destroy a Spanish fleet at

Ferrol. The plan was changed after the original expedition was forced to return due to bad weather. Although Essex departed later in the year with a reduced force, the attack on Ferrol was abandoned in preference for a blockade of the Portuguese coast. But this scheme was soon surrendered. Instead, Essex sailed for the Azores in the hope of meeting the Indies fleet. Under Essex's weak command, however, the expedition scattered at the islands, missing the fleet which reached Spain without loss. As the expedition returned to England, a Spanish force was within striking distance of the coast of Cornwall. Although it was battered by autumn gales, the threat to English security, combined with the incalculable risk of offensive operations, affected the subsequent conduct of the war at sea.[104]

The expedition effectively ended Essex's career as a sea warrior and strategist. Faced with the spread of rebellion in Ireland, against a background of increasingly hazardous international relations that included peace between France and Spain, the regime's interest in offensive maritime action weakened, in favour of concentrating on essential defensive measures within the Channel. By 1598, the peace party at court appeared to be gaining the upper hand, though the war drifted on for another five years.

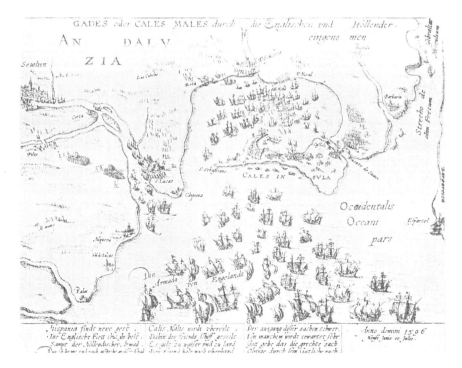

A Dutch illustration of the English attack on Cadiz in 1596. Under the leadership of Essex and Howard, the Lord Admiral, the raid strikingly revealed the capability of English sea power. However, Essex's ambitious plan to retain Cadiz as a base was abandoned. (*The Fugger News-Letters*)

Despite these changing conditions, the private war at sea flourished. A voluntary force of predators continued to expose alarming weaknesses within Iberian commercial and colonial networks. While a large and disorderly group of men-of-war haunted the Channel or congregated along the coasts of Spain and Portugal, others ranged into the Caribbean or the Mediterranean. There was also an attempt to build on Drake's success in the South Sea, with an expedition of 1593 led by Richard Hawkins. Although he was captured by the Spanish, and held in captivity until 1603, the expedition underlined the persistent vulnerability of the region to opportunistic incursions. According to a report of October 1600, another adventurer, Captain Benjamin Wood, who had been at sea for four years, acquired a rich haul of booty in the South Sea, only to lose it all disastrously. During the return voyage the company 'was driven to … [such] want that they were faine to eate one another, and forced at last to put into Porto Rico, where all that were left are taken and theyre wealth lost'.[105] Even so, the relentless assault on enemy trade continued to pay rich dividends, especially for experienced mercantile promoters.

At the same time the reprisal war continued to provide an opportunity for large-scale expeditions to be sent out by Cumberland, sometimes in association with the Queen but increasingly in partnership with London traders and ship-owners. In effect these were auxiliary fleets which were intended to undertake offensive action against Spain and Portugal. Cumberland's sea venturing culminated in 1598 with a major expedition to the West Indies, made up of twenty vessels. Outward bound the fleet cruised along the coast of Portugal, hoping to intercept rich carracks returning from the East Indies. The Portuguese insisted on describing Cumberland as an arch-pirate. Nevertheless, in May it was reported from the Iberian coast that 'the small forces of an English Earl … shut in both the East and West India fleets'.[106] Within the Caribbean, the expedition raided San Juan de Puerto Rico, gaining control of the island, which Cumberland intended to retain. The plan was given up, however, following the loss of about 400 men to disease. The expedition returned with several prizes, laden with sugar and ginger, valued at between £15,000 and £16,000. For Cumberland this was a financial disaster. The booty, one letter writer noted, failed to cover half of the charge of setting out the fleet. In addition the scale of the human casualties underlined the dangers of Caribbean venturing. Sustaining heavy losses, Cumberland withdrew from sea service. He retained an interest in several ventures on a much-reduced scale, which included associations with Sir Robert Cecil, Burghley's son and political heir. In 1601 he promoted an ambitious, but abortive plan for a venture to use the island of St Helena as a base for the plunder of Iberian shipping.[107]

Cumberland's ventures dramatized the deep-seated ambiguities of the sea war, especially the tension between short-term profit and longer-term strategic goals. The balance between these distinct, occasionally complementary, but competing goals was destabilized during the latter part of the conflict, as the competition for plunder intensified between English, Dutch, French and Flemish men-of-war. During the 1590s private enterprise grew progressively parasitic, diverting resources, including recruits, away from royal service. While the navy resorted to pressing men, not always successfully, there was no shortage of volunteers prepared to serve aboard private ships. Under these conditions the character of the war at sea also began to change. On the one hand, as the conflict progressed, London's share of reprisal venturing became more dominant. In part this was the result of widespread difficulties in the provincial ports, which were struggling to cope with the disruption and decline of trade. At the same time it reflected the greater concentration of professionalized and experienced adventurers among the merchants and shipowners of the city. On the other hand, the growing dominance of London was accompanied by increasing disorderliness at sea. To some extent this was an inherent characteristic of large-scale, organized depredation, particularly over a prolonged period. It was rooted in the organization of reprisal ventures, whereby recruits served for a share of the spoil, and fuelled by the greater freedom that prevailed aboard men-of-war. At times legitimate plunder provided a cover for piracy, though it became increasingly threadbare during the later 1590s and the early years of the seventeenth century.[108]

Conditions at sea during this period became widely confused and disorderly. An unruly group of captains and their companies, who repeatedly came to the

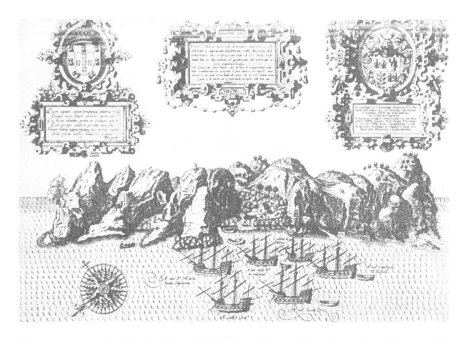

The remote, rugged and isolated island of St Helena, from an illustration of 1599. Occasionally used by Portuguese ships returning from the East Indies, there were various suggestions during the sixteenth century that it might be employed as a base by English pirates or privateers. (*Buccaneers of the Pacific*)

attention of the High Court of Admiralty or the council, ignored the regulations governing the reprisal war, provoking outrage and retaliatory action. Unlawful spoil was associated with violence, occasionally torture and murder, and was often concealed by the illegal disposal of prizes in overseas markets ranging from southern Ireland to north Africa. Those who engaged in it came close to mimicking the behaviour of pirates, following a path pioneered by Callice and others. In turn they established a pattern of roving which was to be copied or adapted by pirate groups operating after the 1604 peace with Spain.[109]

Among the victims, French traders and shippers continued to bear the brunt of this tide of disorderly depredation. But Dutch shipping was also subject to repeated spoil, as were vessels from the Hanseatic League, as well as from Denmark, Poland and Scotland. In addition, English and Irish merchants who continued trading with the enemy were exposed to attack, though Irish trade to the Iberian peninsula was unofficially tolerated because it provided the regime with valuable intelligence from Spain. In March 1597 a leading Dublin merchant, Nicholas Weston, who had two servants employed as spies in Spain, complained that one of his ships had been pillaged while returning from Bilbao. It was the fourth occasion during the year that one of his vessels was spoiled. As he informed Cecil, it was 'very dangerous now to venture abroad, by reason of so many English men-of-war, which spare nobody that comes'.[110]

The activities of unruly or unlicensed reprisal ships aroused a clamour of overseas protest. During the second half of the 1590s the council was faced with a stream of complaints from foreign merchants and shipowners against unlawful depredation or piracy. The nature of the problem is indicated by a sample of cases heard by the council from January to June 1596. During these months, among a wide range of other business, it dealt with grievances concerning the seizure or spoil of at least nine foreign vessels. Four of these ships were of French origin, while the rest were of Dutch or north European background. In most cases their capture was apparently justified by letters of reprisal, though the owners of goods aboard a ship of St Malo, taken during a return voyage from Lisbon, denied that it was lawful prize. Indeed, the spoil of two other French vessels led the council to issue warrants for the arrest of those involved, who it accused of piracy. In at least two cases an attack on neutral ships was accompanied by outrageous behaviour and conduct. Thus the *Jonas* of Rotterdam, returning from Malaga with a lading of sugar, wine and raisins, was violently boarded by Captain Morrice and his company, in a man-of-war set forth by Sir Thomas Norris. At some stage during this encounter, in obscure circumstances, the master and crew of the Dutch vessel were all slain, while the cargo was taken to Limerick to be sold. In a separate incident Captain Webb, in command of the *Minion* of Bristol, seized a ship of Danzig returning from Lisbon, the master and company of which were tortured and then cast overboard.[111]

The complaints heard by the council included an example of sharp practice by an experienced captain, which may have been commonplace. It concerned the seizure of a Dutch vessel off Santo Domingo in the Caribbean, by Captain Thomas West. The prize was laden with a rich cargo of ginger and other commodities, valued at £15,000, which was returned to England. But the High Court of Admiralty was unable to proceed with the case, because the bills of lading and other documents from the vessel had been dispersed by West to others, who he refused to identify, 'albeit his examinacion was taken upon oathe'.[112]

The range of grievances which came to the attention of the council reveals the opportunism and tactical versatility of the captains of many men-of-war. Nor was unlawful plunder or sharp practice restricted to the wilder element among the promoters of reprisal ventures. The council heard repeated complaints from Dutch, German and French traders against captains serving under Cumberland. In December 1597 it ordered the restoration of the cargoes of two Hamburg vessels, only to discover that some of the goods had been sold secretly. With little sign of any lessening in the disorder, special commissioners were appointed to deal with the spoil of friends and allies, though they had little success in limiting the damage at sea, particularly when it was the result of ventures involving high-ranking or well-connected officials. During the closing years of the war persistent allegations of unlawful plunder were heard by the council against Sir John Gilbert, captain of the fort at Plymouth, the son of Sir Humphrey Gilbert and the nephew of Ralegh, with whom he sailed to Guiana in 1595. Gilbert was involved in reprisal venturing with Ralegh and Cecil, and occasionally as an associate with Richard Drake, an esquire of the Queen's stable. At various times between 1600 and 1603 he was embroiled in suits before the High Court of Admiralty involving the plunder of Scottish, Dutch, German and Italian goods. In September 1601 he sought the assistance of Cecil in a case which had dragged on for three years, involving a contested claim to booty 'for more than I am worth'.[113] Cecil, unlike his father, was also engaged in several irregular ventures to the coast of Spain and into the Mediterranean as a partner with the Lord Admiral.

These ventures demonstrated the way in which powerful officials effectively subverted or ignored the regulations governing the sea war, exploiting their own and the Queen's resources in voyages for public and private purposes. During 1597 Captain Martin Bredgate was sent out in the *Truelove* on a trading voyage to Barbary, with instructions from Cecil to seek 'intelligence and purchase' along the Spanish coast.[114] The vessel had been recently constructed for Cecil and the Lord Admiral, who authorized Bredgate to dispose of prizes in north Africa if they were not worth returning to England. Bredgate's associates included Richard Gyfford, who was involved in several subsequent ventures in the Mediterranean promoted by Cecil and others, which aroused angry complaints of piracy.

It was within the Mediterranean that the slippage between disorderly privateering and piracy became an acute problem, provoking anger from neutral traders. English predators of varying shades of legality made a distinct contribution to a long-standing pattern of war, slave raiding, commerce and corsair enterprise, in

which the hostility between Christendom and Islam was qualified by other rivalries. The opportunistic incursions of raiders cruising along the coasts of Spain and
Portugal, initially restricted to the western Mediterranean, were overtaken during
the later 1590s by more purposeful and aggressive raiding by men-of-war who
ranged further east, attracted by the prospect of rich, vulnerable prizes of dubious
legality, trading with Turkey and the Levant. The activities of these adventurers
were facilitated by access to the ports of north Africa, where rulers welcomed
potential allies against Spain. In exchange for a levy or tax, the regents of the
Barbary ports provided English rovers with overseas bases and markets, creating
the means for a flourishing trade in plunder and prisoners.

These borderland encounters represented a new departure for the development
of English depredation. While access to overseas havens had far-reaching implications, encouraging the growth of Mediterranean piracy after 1604, the association
with Turkish rulers and their agents provoked moral opprobrium, engendered by
fears of English rovers and pirates 'turning Turk'.[115] Closer contact with Barbary
failed to break down such suspicion and hostility, which were reinforced by the
growing use of sermons and collections in London and elsewhere in support
of the redemption of captives in Turkish imprisonment. The Turkish connection
thus helped to weaken support and sympathy for piracy within England in the
aftermath of the war with Spain.

Among the earliest English adventurers to venture into the Mediterranean
during the war was Edward Glenham. An ambitious but inexperienced captain,
Glenham sold his estate in Suffolk to support a venture to the Canary Islands,
which led to a raid on the Azores. Thereafter the voyage became increasingly
disorderly and piratical. The capture of a rich Venetian vessel laden with sugar
within the Mediterranean may have laid the basis for Glenham's subsequent
indictment for piracy. A second voyage of 1594 was another failure. Short of supplies, Glenham put into Algiers where he 'unnaturally' left eight of his men 'in
pawne for victualles'.[116] But he died too poor to redeem them. Consequently, the
council authorized a collection for their redemption, though they remained in
captivity at least until 1600, by which time several had been released after con-
verting to Islam.

The activities of rogue adventurers like Glenham provoked alarm in Venice,
whose rulers were concerned at the wider threat to their commercial interests. Alarm turned to outrage during the later 1590s as an increasing number
of men-of-war invaded the Mediterranean. In December 1597, the Venetian
ambassador in France complained to the English agent of piracies and violence
committed by English vessels within the jurisdiction of the republic. By 1598
the Venetian ambassador in Spain warned that 'the English, not content with
piracy on the high seas, are thinking of the Mediterranean too, where they
have begun to make themselves felt'.[117] The danger seemed to increase with a
report from Vienna, the following year, that the sultan in Constantinople had
granted the English a port on the coast of Barbary for use against Spain. Though

inaccurate, the use of the Barbary ports encouraged and sustained a growing number of disorderly predators who attacked friends and enemies.

By 1600 it was claimed that there were as many as thirty English men-of-war operating in the Mediterranean. In fact the number was inflated, possibly deliberately so. It seems to have been based on the confusion between trading vessels and rovers or pirates, particularly among the Venetians, whose complaints against the 'villanous English' were in part provoked by the threat to their trading interests in the Levant from London traders.[118] Nonetheless, such uncertainty reflected a real problem which was beginning to reach the eastern Mediterranean. Within a busy trading region, crossed by well-armed English trading vessels capable of combining trade with plunder, unlawful depredation was a tempting, at times overwhelming, opportunity.

The voyage of the *David* of London during 1597 demonstrated the powerful appeal of such opportunities, encouraging opportunistic plunder, which appeared to confirm Italian suspicions that all English vessels sailing within the Mediterranean were corsairs or pirates. The ship was freighted by two London merchants, Thomas Offley and Edward Parris, for a trading voyage in the Levant. Sailing from Scanderoon to Zante in August, the English sighted and gave chase to a vessel close to the island of Crete. The latter was subsequently identified as the *St John Baptist* of Chios, which was bound from Ancona to Alexandria with several Italian merchants aboard. As the *David* gained on its quarry, a group of the company appeared to abandon the vessel, seeking to escape in a boat with a substantial amount of money. This was revealed when the English caught up with the boat, through the interpretation of one of the quartermasters who spoke some Italian. A mad scramble for booty ensued. Richard Willett, a servant of the merchants, later described how the members of the company of the *David* rushed to board the boat in such an unruly fashion that the master lost control, while some of the money was lost in the sea.[119]

The master, William Greene, struggled to reassert his authority and recover the money, by searching his company as they returned aboard the *David*. Philip Wistbrowe, the boatswain's mate, who was one of the first to enter the boat, admitted to acquiring a bag of money and a cap nearly full of money, while having more hidden up his sleeve, though it was recovered by Greene. Although Wistbrowe managed to retain some of the booty, which he hid in a jar of water in the gunner's room, it was later discovered by the master. The *St John Baptist* was rifled of any remaining money and allowed to depart with water, wine and some biscuit.

According to the quartermaster, who acted as an interpreter for his English companions, the master of the *St John Baptist* voluntarily confessed that most of the money was owned by Spaniards, except for 3,712 dollars which belonged to merchants of Florence. This was contradicted by one of the merchants aboard the plundered vessel, who insisted that only 1,500 ducats were Spanish owned; Florentine traders owned the rest. Faced with threats from the English that they would sink the vessel, however, the merchant admitted that he advised the master to say that the money was Spanish for fear of being cast overboard.[120]

One of the most striking features of this encounter, which was related in detail before the High Court of Admiralty, was the apparent disunity among the company of the *David* over the spoil of the *St John Baptist* and its boat. A servant acting for the owners of the English ship instructed the quartermaster to inform their victims 'that they were merchants & used continuall trade in Italy & therefore would not offer wronge to eany Italians or take eany thinge from them'. While it was agreed to break off from the voyage, in order to return to England with at least two of the Italian merchants, the master, Greene, remained profoundly uneasy at the behaviour of some of his men. Several members of the crew described him as growing frantic or being troubled in mind after the spoil of the *St John Baptist*. Greene later claimed that ten days thereafter he 'fell sicke and was disquieted with a feare in such sorte that he could not abide the money in his chist'; indeed, 'he was in such a hatred therewith' that he handed it over to the servants of the merchants.[121]

Even so, when the *David* put into Tunis during the return voyage for London, the master was among other members of the company who were 'continually ashore & brought many things & spente much of the money in providing victuals for the ship & themselves'. At the same time the ruler of Tunis, the captain of the fort and the French consul all received gifts from the English mariners. During the stay at Tunis a warning from one of the Italian merchants, that the booty would have to be restored, provoked a dispute among the English, a group of whom were in favour of throwing their prisoners into the sea.[122]

Following the return of the *David* to London, the council was faced with angry complaints from Florence against the unjust and illegal spoil of the *St John Baptist*, amounting to losses of 32,000 crowns. Although the matter was handed over to the High Court of Admiralty, the council retained a close interest in the case to ensure that the Italians received compensation. Partly in response to such actions, in February 1599 the Queen issued a proclamation instructing English men-of-war sailing into the Mediterranean not to harm friendly shipping. In addition the declaration warned that anyone caught breaking bulk or disposing of plunder before legal proceedings would be executed as pirates.[123]

Yet the piratical conduct of English rovers within the Mediterranean persisted. As the lawlessness and disorder increased, the regime was faced with mounting Venetian grievances. The coastal waters of Provence and the Aegean Sea, between Zante and Crete, were favoured haunts for the English where they plundered Venetian and French shipping laden with cargoes of sugar, spices and silk. Venetian agents at Constantinople, moreover, continued to claim that they were unable to distinguish between English trading vessels and men-of-war. According to one report, 'all of them were hampered with artillery, and provisioned for a year, even to the water, and in order that they might be handy in fighting they were kept clear, leaving not only the quarter deck but also the main deck, where goods are usually placed, free for the artillery'.[124]

The activities of disorderly men-of-war and pirates threatened English commercial and diplomatic interests in the Mediterranean. Early in 1601 the Duke of Florence was reported to have arrested English goods in Leghorn and Pisa in retaliation for the seizure of a vessel claimed by his subjects. Reports of attacks on Turkish vessels weakened the position of English merchants at Constantinople. Later in the year, further complaints concerning the spoil of a Turkish vessel led to the arrest of English merchants at Tripoli. Prominent London merchants, such as William Garway, expressed concern at the disruption and damage to their trade with the Levant.[125]

In order to deal with the problem, during 1600 the regime tried to regulate English men-of-war, sailing on voyages of reprisal, which entered the Mediterranean. At the same time consuls and merchant representatives in the Levant, such as Matthew Stocker who was based at Patras, were ordered to arrest English vessels sailing without a special licence from the Queen or the Lord Admiral. In March 1602, following further complaints against disorderly spoil and piracy, the Queen sent one of her vessels into the Mediterranean to hunt for pirates. Such measures were ineffective. Indeed, they only served to emphasize the piratical conduct of men-of-war who operated independently from bases that included Patras, Coron and Modon, as well as Algiers and Tunis. Thus Stocker informed the English ambassador at Constantinople that he was unable to do anything against the captains who frequented the port, because the local ruler was their confederate and received a share of the plunder.[126]

English depredation thus remained a problem within the Mediterranean until the end of the reign. It included a diverse mix of disorderly men-of-war and hard-bitten pirates or rovers who were in danger of being perceived as renegades. English merchants at Zante insisted that the sea robbers were outlaws, for whom they could not be held responsible. According to the report of March 1603 by the captain of an English ship at Zante, there were twelve men-of-war based at Tunis whose companies 'were all exiles from England, in disgrace with the Queen, and being driven to desperation they are resolved to plunder all and sundry whom they may fall in with, even those of their own nation'.[127] This peculiar and ill-fitting collection of rovers included Captain William Piers and Sir Thomas Sherley and his brother, who acquired notorious reputations in parts of the Mediterranean during the early seventeenth century. Piers came from Plymouth, reputedly of a wealthy background. He sailed in a well-armed vessel, carrying twenty ordnance, with a company of between seventy and eighty men, who included William Lancaster, 'a man of evil fame and little or no substance'. Piers operated independently at sea from various bases. In 1603 he plundered the *Veniera*, near Zante, laden with a rich cargo belonging to Venetian merchants. According to the report he married a Turkish wife, who benefited from gifts of silk dresses and sequins. When taxed by one English captain, 'that he had ruined the Levant trade and earned a halter', allegedly he retorted 'I may as well lose my life for a lot as for a little; and I would have done more if I could'.[128]

If the career of Piers foreshadowed the emergence of a new breed of pirate who would flourish after 1604, the activities of the Sherley brothers appeared to represent the dying species of the gentleman adventurer. The poorly organized, erratic and often wild enterprises of such promoters brought little profit or honour to their leaders. Sir Thomas Sherley came from a financially troubled, landed background. During the later 1590s he turned to sea venturing in an attempt to restore his fortune, raiding the coast of Spain with a fleet of six vessels. In 1602 he ventured into the Mediterranean with his brother and several ships. Following the disintegration of the fleet, he led a desperate and abortive attack in early 1603 against the island of Kea. He was captured and imprisoned by the Turks. On his release in December 1605 he returned to England, where his financial troubles continued. Thereafter he sold his family lands, 'married a whore' and secured a small sinecure as a royal park keeper on the Isle of Wight.[129]

The growing lawlessness at sea during the later years of the war was partly the result of too many predators in search of too few prizes. In 1603 one of Cecil's captains, Joseph May, reported a striking lack of lawful prey along the coast of Spain. As there 'was little trade by Spaniards … for the most part our English men-of-war do make their voyages upon the French. All sailors of late', he added, 'are fallen into such vile order that they shame not to say that they go to sea to rob all nations, and unless the captain consent thereto, he is not fit for this time'.[130] During one later voyage, May's company grew discontented and mutinous, threatening to stow him under the hatches following the seizure of a French vessel reportedly carrying a cargo worth £10,000, which he released 'without diminishing one penny'.

Conditions during the later 1590s reinforced an underlying trend towards the emergence of organized deep-sea piracy which depended on overseas bases and markets. This development, which was especially evident in the Mediterranean, overshadowed the lingering persistence of traditional forms of depredation around the British Isles. While local piracy, as such, was not eradicated, it was much reduced in volume and intensity, bearing the characteristics of a marginalized activity undertaken by fugitives whose activities were both elusive and fragmentary.

Nevertheless, small groups of pirates operated intermittently during the later years of the war. They were involved in small-scale, opportunistic piracy and sea roving. As an enterprise that was distinct from the disorderly actions of ships sailing on voyages of reprisal, it continued to attract the attention of the regime. In February 1596 the council heard a complaint concerning the arrest in Scotland of the *Hopewell* of Dunwich by Patrick Stewart, the lord of the Orkney Islands, 'upon pretence of some wrongs done him … by Gwin, an English pirate and fugitive'.[131] One year later it dealt with the complaints of two merchants against Matthew Drew and other pirates, who boarded a vessel in the night at Christmas time, and spoiled it of iron. In May 1597 it was informed of an act of piracy by Captain Thomas Venables and company on the *John* of Waterford. The plunder, including goods owned by Thomas Butler, 10th Earl of Ormond, was later sold in the Isle of Man and at Chester. Several months later it pardoned George Green, who was accused of piracy for stealing two anchors and two cables valued at forty shillings. In August it ordered the arrest of a group of pirates, as well as the buyers and receivers of their goods, in south Devon. Another warrant for the apprehension of pirates, who spoiled the *Judith* of Guernsey of a cargo of Newfoundland fish, followed in January 1598.[132]

Several years later there were signs of a revival in Ireland of coastal raiding by Gaelic rovers, who had previously been identified as rebels as well as pirates. In October 1600 a Scottish trader was spoiled by Tibbot ne Long, the son of Grainne O'Malley, along the coast of Mayo. Yet the activities of such raiders were circumscribed by the presence of one of the Queen's ships, the *Tremontana*, under the command of Captain Charles Plessington, which was patrolling the coast of Connacht and Ulster to prevent the supply of rebel forces by Spain. During a cruise of two months in 1601, the only vessel sighted by Plessington was a galley 'with thirty oars, and … 100 good shot', sent out by the O'Malleys on a raiding voyage against the McSweeneys around Lough Swilly and Sheep Haven.[133] It was forced ashore after a brief skirmish with the English. The decline of this form of sea raiding did not indicate an end to Irish piracy or roving. In November 1601 a Scottish ship was taken, near the harbour of Cork, by Captain Myagh, Walter Bethell and others. For Myagh this was the start of a piratical career which was to flourish after 1603, sometimes in association with English pirates who returned to haunt the coast of south-west Ireland following the war with Spain.[134]

During these same years, however, English men-of-war and pirates faced increasing competition from a growing number of overseas rovers, especially of Dutch and Flemish origin. Dutch privateering vessels provided strong competition for the English, particularly in the Atlantic and the Caribbean. In January 1599 the Dutch were reported 'to laugh to see the English … keep this river [at Lisbon], while they may take the Indies'.[135] More alarmingly, men-of-war from Dunkirk, sailing under Spanish authority, made sweeping raids along the east coast, occasionally straying into the Irish Sea, disrupting local and coasting trades. Sailing in packs of three or four vessels, and occasionally operating in larger fleets of between nine and twelve, the Dunkirkers dramatically exposed the vulnerability of English waters to external attack. Their growing presence along the east coast aroused fears that they intended a landing at Scarborough in 1599 and an assault on Harwich the following year.[136]

The war with Spain was still raging when Elizabeth died in March 1603. Her successor, James VI of Scotland, brought the conflict to an end with the peace of 1604. The sea war had been a formative experience for English maritime enterprise, with profound consequences for its predatory aspects. It encouraged a rapid and sustained growth of privateering, under the guise of reprisal venturing, which seemed to be accompanied by a decline in piracy. Yet this surprising development was more apparent than real. The organization and operation of the sea war, based on a dynamic but unstable coalition between public and private interests, led to widespread disorderly spoil and plunder. The way in which the conflict was conducted also confused the distinction between piracy and lawful depredation. Even in its dying days, adventurers of varied backgrounds, such as Pierce Griffith in north Wales, embarked on unlicensed voyages during which neutral shipping was subject to spoil or capture. Griffith's attack on a vessel of Hamburg was followed by his seizure at Cork, and his subsequent trial and imprisonment. John Ward of Plymouth, who earned renown and infamy during the reign of James I as a pirate who 'turned Turk', was also involved in piracy on the 'Spanishe seas', which included the plunder of French and Danish ships.[137] Over the course of the long war with Spain, therefore, reprisal enterprise served to re-direct and re-shape piratical activity. But the scale of the ensuing assault on overseas shipping earned the English an unenviable reputation as a nation of pirates among maritime communities across Europe.

Epilogue

In 1598 Paul Hentzner, a German visitor to England, noted that the English were 'good sailors and better pirates, cunning, treacherous, and thievish'.[1] He claimed that more than 300 pirates were hanged annually in London. This was an impressive number of executions to stage during the course of one year. Undoubtedly it exaggerated the actual number of men executed for piracy; however, it registered a response to a serious problem that appeared to be out of control. By the closing years of the reign of Elizabeth, English piracy and disorderly privateering were arousing alarm and anger in many parts of Europe. Nor was there any sign that the end of the Spanish war and the recall of men-of-war by the new monarch, James VI of Scotland, would lessen the disorder at sea. During the summer of 1603 officials in Plymouth, Dartmouth and Bristol warned the council of the persistence of robbery and spoil, while overseas complaints cast a shadow over the King's efforts to restore peaceful relations with Spain.[2]

After nearly twenty years of authorized maritime depredation, involving large numbers of ships and seamen, for many the restoration of peace was an unwelcome development, which encouraged an increasing number of recruits to continue a private war against Spain by sailing under Dutch commissions. Although the new regime tried to prohibit the practice, it provided employment for groups of demobilized men who had served aboard reprisal vessels. Even so, the peace with Spain created a serious problem of unemployment which encouraged the transfer of disorder and lawlessness from sea to land. In June 1603 the mayor of Plymouth presented the council with an alarming report on the influx of a 'great number of sailors, mariners and other masterless men, that heretofore have been at sea in men-of-war, and being now restrained from that course do still remain here and pester our town which is already overcharged with many poor people'.[3] Faced with an uncertain future, many of these men resorted to stealing from boats at night-time, robbing English as well as French owners.

Among those employed in such petty piracy and theft was John Ward, who was shortly to acquire widespread notoriety as a pirate and renegade in the Mediterranean. Ward, whose unusual and challenging career after 1604 earned him celebrity and condemnation, was at the forefront of a new breed of pirates who were to re-shape, in a radical and unsettling manner, the character of English piracy. By using overseas bases, which also served as places of habitation, some of these pirates adopted a way of life that seemed to be a deliberate rejection of their origins and background. The self-avowed alienation and hostility of Ward and others, including a concern to re-create their lives in a different setting, represented a profound change in the attitudes of pirates and rovers, which became more common with the oceanic expansion of sea robbery as it spread along the maritime frontier of a wider commercial and colonial network.[4]

While the period covered by this book might be seen as a necessary prelude to the so-called 'golden age of piracy' which flourished between 1650 and 1720, it had its own distinctive character which was expressed particularly in the prevailing confusion between piracy, privateering and sea roving. From the 1520s to the 1590s the overlap between these varied forms of maritime depredation became ever more confused. Piracy flourished during these years, but as an ambiguous enterprise. It was maintained with widespread community support and with varying degrees of connivance on the part of successive regimes. While the monarchy was concerned to protect its jurisdiction and to defend its honour at sea, there was no sustained campaign against pirates or their supporters during the period of Tudor rule. At sea, naval patrolling was expensive, irregular and often ineffective. On land the establishment of piracy commissioners during the 1560s and 1570s represented important initiatives in local government and policing, but they were short lived and unsuccessful. Despite the apparent rigour of the law, an increasing number of recruits were prepared to participate in sea robbery, either in the hope that they would not be caught or in the expectation of a pardon.

Under these conditions the growth of piracy and other forms of maritime depredation was marked by an underlying shift in its range and vigour, which was accompanied by short-term upsurges in the incidence of local spoil and plunder. The revival of small-scale piracy around the British Isles during the 1520s and 1530s was powerfully reinforced by the spread of disorderly privateering during the 1540s. This created an opportunity for the growth of more organized, long-distance plunder, the success of which was strikingly demonstrated by Reneger's raid off Cape St Vincent. A traditional form of indiscriminate, petty piracy and spoil thus became linked with more ambitious and increasingly anti-Iberian enterprise. During the 1550s and 1560s aggressive commercial venturing

The Jolly Roger flying over Studland beach. It testifies to the modern fascination with pirates and piracy, though the subject is often perceived in a very romantic or nostalgic fashion. Flags such as this were not used until the later seventeenth century. Most pirates active during the earlier period rarely revealed their identities in such a public or threatening manner, though the use of the 'bloody flag' may have been proliferating. (Author's collection)

to Guinea, which blurred the boundary between trade and plunder, served as an outlet for this predatory force, attracting the interest of men such as Frobisher and Strangeways. In combination with an upsurge in piracy and sea roving within the Channel and along the coasts of Spain and Portugal, which were justified as legitimate, if irregular reprisals, these developments led to the pirate invasion of the Caribbean during the 1570s. Led by Drake, the spread of English piracy was encouraged and favoured by external forces. Exploiting the weaknesses of Spain and Portugal, it followed in the wake of French raiders, while it was most successful when undertaken in alliance with the cimaroons.

The tension between potentially contradictory and complementary forms of plunder, linked to its widening range, was acutely exposed during the 1570s and early 1580s. Under the leadership of captains such as Callice, Hicks and Piers, a large number of pirates and rovers made a living from organized, but essentially localized, piracy, while activity within the Caribbean appeared to falter. Nonetheless, Drake's voyage from 1577 to 1580 revealed the rich rewards to be gained from preying upon vulnerable regions of the Spanish Empire. Oceanic plunder encouraged far-reaching predatory commercial schemes, while it also strengthened the appeal of anti-Spanish colonial and military projects. In these circumstances the outbreak of the war with Spain during 1585 was followed by the transformation of privateering into a large-scale business, especially in the hands of merchants and shipowners. Under the dubious legitimacy of reprisal venturing, the war provided an opportunity for the consolidation of previous practices and structures, while charting a new direction in the development of long-distance plunder. But the loose regulation of privateering on this scale produced widespread disorder and illegal depredation.

Against a crowded and confused background, therefore, the period from the 1520s to the 1590s was a crucial stage in the development of English piracy and privateering. While local, short-distance piracy flourished almost unchecked, it was during these years that organized, long-distance depredation emerged. As this study demonstrates, both were woven into the fabric of English seafaring enterprise. For thousands of seafarers and others, robbery and plunder at sea were a form of employment. For some, it was a way of life, the basis for an embryonic culture which was to develop during the second half of the seventeenth century. At a time when the early modern English state was compelled to compromise with unruly predatory forces, piracy, privateering and sea roving acquired an unusual significance. Maritime depredation served varied commercial and military purposes, occasionally providing the shock troops for an embattled and beleaguered regime, although it was impossible to control and regulate effectively. Consequently, the export of organized violence and criminality, which was under way at the close of the sixteenth century, inaugurated a new phase in the history of English piracy, culminating in the creation of a community of outcasts whose survival challenged the commercial and colonial interests of an expanding seaborne empire.[5]

Endnotes

Abbreviations

APC: J.R. Dasent (ed.), *Acts of the Privy Council 1542–1604*, 31 vols. (London, 1890–1907)

BL: British Library

Calendar: J.C. Appleby (ed.), *A Calendar of Material relating to Ireland from the High Court of Admiralty Examinations 1536–1641* (Dublin, 1992)

CSPD: R. Lemon et al. (eds.), *Calendar of State Papers Domestic 1547–1603 and Addenda*, 7 vols. (London, 1856–71)

CSPD Edward: C.S. Knighton (ed.), *Calendar of State Papers Domestic Series of the Reign of Edward VI 1547–1553* (London, 1992)

CSPD Mary: C.S. Knighton (ed.), *Calendar of State Papers Domestic Series of the Reign of Mary I 1553–1558* (London, 1998)

CSPF: W.B. Turnbull et al. (eds.), *Calendar of State Papers, Foreign Series, 1547–89*, 23 vols. (London, 1861–1950)

CSPI: H.C. Hamilton et al. (eds.), *Calendar of State Papers relating to Ireland 1509–1603*, 11 vols. (London, 1860–1912)

CPR: *Calendar of Patent Rolls preserved in the Public Record Office 1461–1582*, 24 vols. (London, 1897–1986)

CSPS: M. Hume et al. (eds.), *Calendar of Letters and State Papers relating to English Affairs, preserved principally in the Archives of Simancas 1558–89*, 4 vols. (London, 1892–99)

CSPV: R. Brown et al. (eds.), *Calendar of State Papers and Manuscripts, relating to English Affairs, existing in the Archives and Collections of Venice 1558–1603*, 9 vols. (London, 1890–97)

EHR: *English Historical Review*

EPV: K.R. Andrews (ed.), *English Privateering Voyages to the West Indies 1588–1595* (Hakluyt Society, Second Series, 111, 1959)

HCA: High Court of Admiralty, The National Archives

HMC Salisbury: *Calendar of the Manuscripts of the Most Hon. the Marquis of Salisbury*, 23 vols. (Historical Manuscripts Commission, London, 1883–1973)

Law and Custom: R.G. Marsden (ed.), *Documents relating to the Law and Custom of the Sea*, 2 vols. (Navy Records Society, 49 & 50, 1915–16)

List and Analysis: R.B. Wernham (ed.), *List and Analysis of State Papers Foreign Series Elizabeth I 1589–1596*, 7 vols. (London, 1964–2000)

LP: J.S. Brewer et al. (eds.), *Letters and Papers, Foreign and Domestic, of the Reign of Henry VIII and Addenda*, 22 vols. (2nd edition, London, 1920–32)

MM: *Mariner's Mirror*

Monson's Tracts: M. Oppenheim (ed.), *The Naval Tracts of Sir William Monson*, 5 vols. (Navy Records Society, 22, 23, 43, 45, 47, 1902–14)

NAW: D.B. Quinn (ed.), *New American World: A Documentary History of North America to 1612*, 5 vols. (London, 1979)

ODNB: C. Matthew and B. Harrison (eds.), *The Oxford Dictionary of National Biography*, 60 vols. (Oxford, 2004)

Pays–Bas: K. de Lettenhove (ed.), *Relations Politiques des Pays–Bas et de l'Angleterre sous Le Règne de Philippe II*, 11 vols. (Brussels, 1888–1900)

PN: Richard Hakluyt, *The Principal Navigations Voyages Traffiques & Discoveries of the English Nation*, 12 vols. (3rd edition, Glasgow, 1903–5, repr. New York, 1969)

Select Pleas: R.G. Marsden (ed.), *Select Pleas in the Court of Admiralty*, 2 vols. (Selden Society, 6 & 11, 1894–97)

SP: State Papers, The National Archives

Tudor Proclamations: P.L. Hughes and J.F. Larkin (eds.), *Tudor Royal Proclamations*, 3 vols. (New Haven, 1964–69)

Introduction

1. A. Corbin, *The Lure of the Sea: The Discovery of the Seaside in the Western World 1750–1840* (London, 1994), pp. 1–15; N.A.M. Rodger, *The Safeguard of the Sea: A Naval History of Britain 660–1649* (London, 1997), pp. 79, 97.

2. S. Rose, *The Medieval Sea* (London, 2007), pp. 123–6; N.A.M. Rodger, 'The New Atlantic: Naval Warfare in the Sixteenth Century' in J.B. Hattendorf and R.W. Unger (eds.), *War at Sea in the Middle Ages and the Renaissance* (Woodbridge, 2003), pp. 237–47; K.R. Andrews, 'The Elizabethan Seaman', *MM*, 68 (1982), pp. 249–51; F. Braudel, *The Mediterranean and the Mediterranean World in the Age of Philip II*, 2 vols. (2nd edition, London, 1972), II, pp. 865–9.

3. Rodger, 'The New Atlantic', p. 240; Rodger, *Safeguard of the Sea*, pp. 115–28, 143–56. Elizabethan privateering, it has been argued, was a form of 'government by licence', see M.J. Braddick, *State Formation in Early Modern England c.1550–1700* (Cambridge, 2000), pp. 202–3.

4. J.E. Thomson, *Mercenaries, Pirates, and Sovereigns: State–Building and Extraterritorial Violence in Early Modern Europe* (Princeton, 1994), pp. 23, 67–8 argues that the activities of the so–called 'sea dogs' of the Elizabethan period amounted to 'state–sponsored terrorism'. The navy's war against piracy did not, of course, end the problem, see P. Earle, *The Pirate Wars* (London, 2003), pp. 209ff.

5. J.S. Brewer et al. (eds.), *Calendar of the Carew Manuscripts 1515–1603*, 4 vols. (London, 1867–70), I, p. 20.

6. K.R. Andrews, 'The Expansion of English Privateering and Piracy in the Atlantic *c.*1540–1625' in M. Mollat (ed.), *Course et Piraterie*, 2 vols. (Paris, 1975), I, pp. 196–230.

7. For a typology distinguishing between officially sanctioned piracy, commercial piracy and

deep-sea marauding (either organized or anarchic), see R.C. Ritchie, *Captain Kidd and the War against the Pirates* (Cambridge, Mass., 1986), pp. 11–26.

8. For a case of poachers wearing visors and with painted faces see *CPR 1558–60*, p. 44.

9. *Monson's Tracts*, I, p. 130; J.K. Laughton (ed.), *State Papers relating to the Defeat of the Spanish Armada*, 2 vols. (Navy Records Society, 1 & 2, 1894), II, p. 249. The *Elizabeth Bonaventure* formed part of Drake's expedition to the Caribbean in 1585 and to Cadiz in 1587. During the sixteenth century many pirates used a variety of flags to disguise their activities. By 1700 the black flag was synonymous with 'pyratical Colours', D. Defoe, *A General History of the Pyrates*, ed. M. Schonhorn (London, 1972), pp. 68, 139, 143, 216, 299, 343 (though Defoe's authorship of this work is now contested). Men-of-war and some pirates also used the red or 'bloody flag' as intimidation, Ibid., p. 101; W.S. Stallybrass (ed.), *Esquemeling: The Buccaneers of America* (London, n.d.), p. 400. On flags see M. Rediker, *Villains of All Nations: Atlantic Pirates in the Golden Age* (London, 2004), pp. 4, 77, 121–2, 164–7, 202, and www.bonaventure.org.uk/ed/flags2.htm.

10. HCA 1/40, ff. 151–1v. For shares and pillage see *Monson's Tracts*, IV, pp. 19–21.

11. For an exploration of law and legal attitudes see C. Harding, '"*Hostis Humani Generis*"– The Pirate as Outlaw in the Early Modern Law of the Sea' in C. Jowitt (ed.), *Pirates? The Politics of Plunder, 1550–1650* (Basingstoke, 2007), pp. 20–38.

Chapter 1: *War and Maritime Plunder from the 1480s to the 1540s*

1. Sir G. Warner (ed.), *The Libelle of Englyshe Polycye: A Poem on the Use of Sea-Power 1436* (Oxford, 1926), pp. 32, 41–2; M. Opp. enheim, *A History of the Administration of the Royal Navy and of Merchant Shipp. ing in Relation to the Navy from 1509 to 1660* (London, 1896, repr. Aldershot, 1988), pp. 15–18; D. Loades, *The Tudor Navy: An Administrative, Political and Military History* (Aldershot, 1992), pp. 25–8; Rodger, *Safeguard of the Sea*, pp. 145–7.

2. I.F. Grant, *Highland Folk Ways* (London, 1961), pp. 253–5; Rev. J. MacInnes, 'West Highland Sea Power in the Middle Ages', *Transactions of the Gaelic Society of Inverness*, 48 (1972–74), pp. 529–45; Rodger, *Safeguard of the Sea*, pp. 166–8; *Orkneyinga Saga: The History of the Earls of Orkney*, trans. H. Palsson and P. Edwards (London, 1978), pp. 215–6 for an account of a 'good Viking trip' which indicates the early significance of feasting, plunder and gifts. For raiding and the persistence of piracy into the early seventeenth century see A. I. Macinnes, *Clanship, Commerce and the House of Stuart, 1603–1788* (East Linton, 1996), pp. 33–5, 64–5, 68.

3. A.L. Rowse, *Tudor Cornwall: Portrait of a Society* (London, 1941), pp. 108–9; F.E. Halliday (ed.), *Richard Carew of Antony: The Survey of Cornwall* (London, 1953), pp. 210, 226–7.

4. C.L. Kingsford, *Prejudice and Promise in Fifteenth Century England* (Oxford, 1925, repr. London, 1962), pp. 87–102. For earlier examples see *Calendar of Inquisitions Miscellaneous (Chancery): Volume VII 1422–1485* (Woodbridge, 2003), pp. 27–8, 38, 89–91, 93–6, 124–5, 131–4; C.F. Richmond, 'The Earl of Warwick's Domination of the Channel and the Naval Dimension to the Wars of the Roses, 1456–1460', *Southern History*, 20–21 (1998–99), pp. 6–14.

5. *CPR 1476–85*, pp. 146, 355–6, 517–8, 545.

6. *CPR 1476–85*, p. 79.

7. *CPR 1476–85*, pp. 78–9, 356, 370–1.

8. *CPR 1476–85*, pp. 493–4; Kingsford, *Prejudice*, pp. 105–6.

9. *CPR 1476–85*, p. 520.

10. Kingsford, *Prejudice*, pp. 105–6; S. Cunningham, *Henry VII* (London, 2006), pp. 261–2.

11. *CPR 1485–94*, pp. 105, 108; *Tudor Proclamations*, I, pp. 25–6.

12. G. Connell–Smith, *Forerunners of Drake: A Study of English Trade with Spain in the early Tudor Period* (London, 1954, repr. Westport, CT, 1975), pp. 38, 58.

13. *CPR 1494–1509*, pp. 44, 61; *Tudor Proclamations*, I, pp. 44–5. The Magnus Intercursus of 1496 also included provision for dealing with piracy and reprisals in a diplomatic way. C.H. Williams (ed.), *England under the Tudors 1485–1529* (London, 1925), pp. 254–5; Loades, *Tudor Navy*, pp. 46–7.

14. *CPR 1494–1509*, p. 290.

15. *LP 1509–14*, I, pp. 289, 593, 599, 605; I.F. Grant, *The Social and Economic Development of Scotland before 1603* (Edinburgh, 1930), pp. 342–3.

16. *LP 1509–14*, I, pp. 593, 605; II, p. 1425.

17. *LP 1515–18*, I, pp. 221–2; II, pp. 1118, 1124, 1182–4, 1232, 1374–5; J.A. Williamson, *Maritime Enterprise 1458–1558* (Oxford, 1913), p. 365.

18. *LP 1515–18*, II, pp. 1374–5; *LP 1519–23*, I, p. 91; *Tudor Proclamations*, I, p. 131.

19. *LP 1509–14*, I, p. 718 (the petition was dated 1513).

20. *LP 1509–14*, I, p. 718.

21. *NAW*, I, pp. 160–71; D.B. Quinn, *England and the Discovery of America, 1481–1620* (London, 1973), pp. 163–8.

22. *LP 1515–18*, I, p. 72; *LP 1519–23*, I, pp. 75, 131; II, p. 1392. As the King's lieutenant in Ireland, Surrey also responded vigorously to the threat from pirates, Brewer et al. (eds.), *Carew Manuscripts*, I, pp. 11, 20.

23. *LP 1524–26*, p. 791; *LP 1526–28*, pp. 1627, 1852, 1886; *LP 1529–30*, pp. 2172, 2257, 2264; M. St Clair Byrne (ed.), *The Lisle Letters*, 6 vols. (London, 1981), I, pp. 183–4, 396–7.

24. *LP 1529–30*, pp. 2650–1, 3193; *LP 1534*, p. 447.

25. *LP 1531–32*, pp. 14, 190, 198, 424–5, 707.

26. *LP 1531–32*, pp. 424–5; Byrne (ed.), *Lisle Letters*, I, pp. 258, 545, 663.

27. *LP 1533*, pp. 54, 66–7, 75, 110, 129, 175.

28. *LP 1533*, p. 512; *LP 1534*, pp. 85, 135, 535, 587; *LP 1535*, I, pp. 75, 87, 89, 175; Byrne (ed.), *Lisle Letters*, II, pp. 72–4, 101–2, 111, 189. The report of Broode's execution indicated that it was for treason rather than piracy.

29. *LP 1535*, II, pp. 291, 354, 365, 377; HCA 1/33, f. 9.

30. *LP 1535*, II, p. 354; *LP 1537*, I, p. 274; *LP 1540–41*, pp. 446, 448; H.A. Lloyd, *The Gentry of South–West Wales, 1540–1640* (Cardiff, 1968), pp. 161–2.

31. *LP Addenda*, I, part 1, p. 339; Byrne (ed.), *Lisle Letters*, II, pp. 112–3.

32. *LP Addenda*, I, part 1, pp. 339–40.

33. G.R. Elton (ed.), *The Tudor Constitution* (2nd edition, Cambridge, 1982), pp. 158–9; P. Williams, *The Tudor Regime* (Oxford, 1979), pp. 244–5.

34. *LP 1537*, I, pp. 339, 421, 525; II, pp. 81–2, 90, 167; HCA 1/37, ff. 1, 9, 16v–9v; HCA 1/33, ff. 16–9v; Byrne (ed.), *Lisle Letters*, IV, p. 293.

35. *LP 1536*, II, pp. 115, 122, 442–3; *LP 1537*, II, pp. 225–6.

36. *LP 1537*, II, pp. 159, 220–1, 224, 305; Byrne (ed.), *Lisle Letters*, IV, pp. 273–6, 367, 415. Pirates were also active off the coast of Kent and the Isle of Wight, D. Childs, *The Warship Mary Rose: The Life and Times of King Henry VIII's Flagship* (London, 2007), p. 151.

37. Byrne (ed.), *Lisle Letters*, V, pp. 38, 55; *LP 1538*, II, p. 158.

38. *LP 1538*, p. 61; HCA 1/33, ff. 60–70v and for the rest of this paragraph.

39. *Select Pleas*, I, pp. 73–4. Pirates and rovers used stones, fireworks and a variety of small weapons, G.V. Scammell, 'European Seamanship in the Great Age of Discovery', *MM*,

68 (1982), p. 368 reprinted in *Ships, Oceans and Empire: Studies in European Maritime and Colonial History, 1400–1750* (Aldershot, 1995).

40. *LP 1538*, p. 431; *LP 1539*, I, pp. 365, 436; II, p. 43. About the same time, a Breton ship was attacked by pirates off the Scilly Isles, and members of the company were bound and cast overboard, HCA 1/33, ff. 47–8.

41. HCA 1/33, ff. 41–5.

42. Byrne (ed.), *Lisle Letters*, V, p. 387; *LP 1539*, I, p. 97.

43. HCA 1/33, ff. 16–8v.

44. *LP 1539*, I, pp. 27, 105, 111, 127.

45. *LP 1539*, I, pp. 436, 455, 477; HCA 1/33, ff. 47–8.

46. Connell–Smith, *Forerunners*, p. 140; HCA 1/33, ff. 10–11.

47. R.G. Marsden (ed.), 'Voyage of the Barbara to Brazil, A.D. 1540' in *Naval Miscellany II* (Navy Records Society, 40, 1912), pp. 3–66.

48. *LP 1540*, pp. 365, 502; *LP 1540–41*, pp. 21, 70–1, 160, 165; R.K. Hannay (ed.), *The Letters of James V* (Edinburgh, 1954), pp. 401–2, 407, 413.

49. *LP 1540–41*, p. 493; Hannay (ed.), *Letters*, pp. 401, 430–1, 407, 413.

50. *LP 1542*, pp. 343, 369–70, 456, 531. (Hereafter referred to as council).

51. *LP 1544*, II, p. 337.

52. *LP 1543*, I, pp. 186, 189, 231, 239; Connell–Smith, *Forerunners*, pp. 130–2; Rodger, *Safeguard of the Sea*, pp. 182–4.

53. *LP 1543*, I, pp. 199, 231, 282, 287; *APC 1542–47*, pp. 108–10, 112, 115. In 1522 Fletcher was described as one of the 'wisest masters within the town of Rye', C.S. Knighton and D. Loades (eds.), *Letters from the Mary Rose* (Stroud, 2002).

54. *LP 1543*, I, p. 245; II, p. 3; Connell–Smith, *Forerunners*, pp. 134–6; *ODNB*, 'Sir John Russell'.

55. *LP 1545*, I, p. 622.

56. *Select Pleas*, I, pp. 139–41.

57. *LP 1544*, II, p. 177; J.A. Williamson, *Sir John Hawkins: The Life and the Man* (Oxford, 1927), pp. 9–19.

58. *LP 1544*, II, p. 337; Oppenheim, *Administration*, p. 88; Knighton and Loades (eds.), *Letters*, p. 108.

59. *LP 1544*, I, pp. 122, 128.

60. *LP 1544*, II, pp. 337, 359, 361–2, 370–1, 379.

61. *APC 1542–47*, p. 123; *LP 1544*, II, p. 456; *Tudor Proclamations*, I, pp. 345–6. On the damage to fishing see W.G. Hoskins, *The Age of Plunder: The England of Henry VIII 1509–1547* (London, 1976), pp. 185–7.

62. *APC 1542–47*, pp. 158, 176–7, 187–8; Williamson, *Maritime Enterprise*, pp. 265–8, 270–5; Williamson, *Hawkins*, pp. 26–30; Connell–Smith, *Forerunners*, pp. 137–8.

63. *LP 1545*, I, pp. 454–5, 533–5; Williamson, *Maritime Enterprise*, pp. 272–3; Connell–Smith, *Forerunners*, pp. 141–52.

64. *LP 1545*, I, pp. 460, 612; *APC 1542–47*, pp. 220–1.

65. *LP 1545*, I, pp. 105, 130, 145; G.V. Scammell, 'War at Sea under the Early Tudors: Some Newcastle upon Tyne Evidence', *Archaeologia Aeliana*, 38 (1960), pp. 95–6.

66. *LP 1545*, I, pp. 234, 245, 331; *Select Pleas*, I, pp. 136–7.

67. *Tudor Proclamations*, I, p. 348; Loades, *Tudor Navy*, p. 130.

68. *LP 1545*, I, p. 636; *CSPI 1509–73*, pp. 72, 74; HCA 1/34, ff. 22–2v, 26v, 30–1v.

69. *LP 1545*, I, pp. 631, 653; II, pp. 3, 66, 153; Williamson, *Maritime Enterprise*, pp. 392–3. It

has been argued that cheaper iron ordnance aided the spread of piracy after 1544, P. E.J. Hammer, *Elizabeth's Wars: War, Government and Society in Tudor England, 1544–1604* (Basingstoke, 2003), p. 80.

70. *APC 1542–47*, pp. 206, 208, 210–11.

71. *APC 1542–47*, pp. 275, 282. The arrest of Irish shipping in Spain also led to demands for reprisals against Spanish and Flemish ships, *CSPI 1509–73*, p. 72.

72. *LP 1546*, I, pp. 203, 229, 289–90, 371, 378.

73. *LP 1546*, I, p. 275.

74. *LP 1546*, I, pp. 371, 373; *APC 1542–47*, pp. 363–4, 383, 386, 402–3.

75. *APC 1542–47*, pp. 427–30; HCA 1/34, ff. 19–22; A.K. Longfield, *Anglo–Irish Trade in the Sixteenth Century* (London, 1929), pp. 157–8, 179.

76. *LP 1546*, I, p. 360; *APC 1542–47*, p. 398.

77. *LP 1546*, I, pp. 363, 471, 490, 519, 539, 662, 697–8; II, p. 55; *APC 1542–47*, pp. 438–9, 441; *NAW*, I, pp. 207–15 for Hore.

78. *LP 1546*, I, pp. 454, 667; *APC 1542–47*, pp. 431–2, 452, 455–6.

79. *Calendar*, pp. 3–4; Connell–Smith, *Forerunners*, pp. 165–8; G.V. Scammell, 'War at Sea under the Early Tudors– Part II', *Archaeologia Aeliana*, 39 (1961), pp. 180–1 for a description of a small man–of–war.

80. *LP 1546*, I, p. 698.

81. *LP 1546*, I, p. 497; *APC 1542–47*, p. 446; Connell–Smith, *Forerunners*, pp. 158–63.

82. *Select Pleas*, I, pp. 141, 236–7.

Chapter 2: Pirates and Rebellious Rovers during the 1540s and 1550s

1. *APC 1547–50*, pp. 130–1, 254; Rodger, *Safeguard of the Sea*, p. 195.

2. *APC 1547–50*, p. 155.

3. *APC 1547–50*, p. 131.

4. *APC 1547–50*, pp. 363–4, 448, 465, 467–8, 489; *CSPD Edward*, p. 45; Oppenheim, *Administration*, pp. 101–8.

5. *CSPD Edward*, pp. 59–61.

6. *CSPD Edward*, p. 59.

7. *CSPD Edward*, p. 60.

8. M.J.G. Stanford, 'The Raleghs take to the Sea', *MM*, 48 (1962), pp. 22–4; J. Youings (ed.), *Raleigh in Exeter 1985: Privateering and Colonisation in the Reign of Elizabeth I* (Exeter, 1985), pp. 94–5.

9. *Calendar*, pp. 7–8; *Tudor Proclamations*, I, pp. 444–5; *CSPI 1509–73*, p. 90; Stanford, 'Raleghs take to the Sea', pp. 24–5. According to a report of September 1549 at least 300 ships were taken, Byrne (ed.), *Lisle Letters*, I, p. 696.

10. *Calendar*, pp. 6–7; *CPR 1549–51*, pp. 296–8. For the Flemish response see also B.L. Beer and S.M. Jack (eds.), 'The Letters of William, Lord Paget of Beaudesert, 1547–63', *Camden Miscellany XXV* (Camden Society, Fourth Series, 13, 1974), pp. 42–3, 49, 68.

11. *Calendar*, p. 11; HCA 13/5, ff. 248–50; HCA 1/34, ff. 73–4, 80–1.

12. *Calendar*, p. 5.

13. *CSPI 1509–73*, pp. 80, 86; SP 61/1/29.

14. *CSPI 1509–73*, p. 81.

15. *CSPI 1509–73*, pp. 80, 83, 86–7, 90, 99–100.

16. *CSPI 1509–73*, pp. 92, 96, 100; HCA 1/34, ff. 19–22; *Tudor Proclamations*, I, p. 438.

According to a report of April 1549, 'a horde of pirates some 20 sail strong, composed of lawless men of all nations' were ranging the coast of Ireland, *CSPF 1547–53*, p. 31.

17. *CSPI 1509–73*, pp. 100, 103.

18. *CSPI 1509–73*, pp. 92, 100, 107.

19. *CSPI 1509–73*, pp. 83, 105; *CSPD Edward*, p. 151.

20. *APC 1547–50*, p. 253; L.B. Smith, *Treason in Tudor England: Politics and Paranoia* (London, 1986), pp. 27–8.

21. *APC 1547–50*, pp. 253–4

22. *APC 1550–52*, pp. 29, 31, 53, 98, 112–3, 157.

23. *APC 1550–52*, pp. 79, 113, 148–9, 233, 354, 442, 467; *Tudor Proclamations*, I, p. 497.

24. *APC 1550–52*, pp. 149–50, 197.

25. *APC 1550–52*, pp. 369, 464; *APC 1552–54*, pp. 8, 10, 22, 76, 254–5 for the rest of the paragraph. D. Loades, *England's Maritime Empire: Seapower, Commerce and Policy 1490–1690* (Harlow, 2000), p. 63.

26. *APC 1550–52*, pp. 370–1, 377, 467; *APC 1552–54*, pp. 57–8, 81, 174, 197, 273. J.G. Nichols (ed.), *The Diary of Henry Machyn, Citizen and Merchant–Taylor of London* (Camden Society, 42, 1848), p. 25 for the *Bark Aucher*.

27. *Calendar*, pp. 13–4; *Select Pleas*, II, pp. 99–100.

28. *Calendar*, pp. 13–4; *CSPF 1553–58*, p. 231.

29. Nichols (ed.), *Diary*, p. 4.

30. *CSPD Edward*, pp. 254, 283, 293.

31. *APC 1554–56*, pp. 52, 55–6, 58, 60–1, 100–4, 109, 126–7.

32. *APC 1554–56*, p. 151.

33. *APC 1554–56*, pp. 168, 183–4, 215; Oppenheim, *Administration*, pp. 110–4.

34. *CSPD Mary*, pp. 31, 40–1.

35. *CSPD Mary*, pp. 40–1 and for the rest of the paragraph.

36. D.M. Loades, *Two Tudor Conspiracies* (Cambridge, 1965), pp. 21–40; *CSPD Mary*, pp. 21, 40, 163–4.

37. Loades, *Tudor Conspiracies*, pp. 161–3, 165, 204; Rowse, *Tudor Cornwall*, pp. 317–9.

38. *CSPD Mary*, pp. 157, 159, 187. They were proclaimed traitors in April 1556, *Tudor Proclamations*, II, pp. 64–7.

39. *CSPD Mary*, p. 235; Loades, *Tudor Navy*, pp. 164–5.

40. *CSPD Mary*, p. 235. Though one of Killigrew's company claimed that he was forced to serve, Ibid., p. 236.

41. *CSPD Mary*, p. 224.

42. *APC 1552–54*, pp. 230, 236, 417–8; *APC 1554–56*, p. 52.

43. *CSPD Mary*, pp. 232–4.

44. Loades, *Tudor Conspiracies*, pp. 162–5; *CSPD Mary*, p. 235.

45. *CSPD Mary*, p. 236.

46. Loades, *Tudor Conspiracies*, p. 233; *CSPF 1547–53*, pp. 242, 245.

47. *APC 1554–56*, pp. 227–8, 236, 282, 288, 290, 294, 307–8.

48. *APC 1554–56*, pp. 308–9.

49. *APC 1554–56*, pp. 316–7, 335; Loades, *Tudor Conspiracies*, p. 225.

50. *APC 1554–56*, pp. 336, 358–9, 362–3.

51. *CSPV 1534–54*, p. 352.

52. Nichols (ed.), *Diary*, pp. 111, 131.

53. A.L. Merson (ed.), *The Third Book of Remembrance of Southampton 1514–1602*, 3 vols.

(Southampton Record Series, 2, 3 & 8, n. s., 1952–65), II, pp. 55–6. The chain cost three shillings to make.

54. *APC 1556–58*, pp. 54, 65, 70.

55. *Calendar*, pp. 16–9. Paget's ship also took a French vessel which seems to have been returned, Beer and Jack (eds.), 'Letters of William, Lord Paget', p. 121.

56. *CSPD Mary*, p. 279; Loades, *Tudor Navy*, pp. 173–4.

57. *APC 1556–58*, pp. 135–6, 139–40.

58. *CSPD Mary*, p. 282.

59. *CSPD Mary*, p. 283.

60. *CSPD Mary*, pp. 286–7.

61. *APC 1556–58*, pp. 291–3, 298, 319, 323; *CSPD Mary*, pp. 287, 298.

62. *CSPD Mary*, p. 286; *Tudor Proclamations*, II, pp. 79–82; M. Oppenheim, *The Maritime History of Devon* (Exeter, 1968), p. 31. By the 1550s many of the practices of Elizabethan privateering were evident, G.V. Scammell, 'Shipowning in the Economy and Politics of Early Modern England', *The Historical Journal*, 15 (1972), p. 402, reprinted in *Ships, Oceans and Empire*.

63. *CSPD Mary*, p. 355.

64. Stanford, 'Raleghs take to the Sea', pp. 25–7; *Select Pleas*, II, pp. 31–4; Williamson, *Hawkins*, pp. 68–9.

65. *APC 1556–58*, pp. 126–7, 135–6, 140–1, 212, 214, 221.

66. *APC 1556–58*, pp. 268–9, 291–3, 298, 319, 323.

67. *CSPD Mary*, p. 343.

68. *APC 1556–58*, pp. 279–80, 300, 320, 340, 385.

69. Stanford, 'Raleghs take to the Sea', pp. 28–9.

70. *CSPI 1509–73*, p. 100; *APC 1552–54*, pp. 203, 222, 236, 245; *Select Pleas*, II, pp. 84–6, 109–10.

71. F.J. Levy, 'The Strange Life and Death of Captain Henry Stranguishe', *MM*, 48 (1962), pp. 133–7; *CSPD Mary*, pp. 163–4, 179; *CPR 1553–54*, p. 412; *CSPF 1547–53*, p. 242; J.G. Nichols (ed.), *The Chronicle of Queen Jane, and of the Two Years of Queen Mary* (Camden Society, 48, 1850), p. 68; Williamson, *Hawkins*, p. 50. On the portrait see National Portrait Gallery Collection, 6353, www.npg.org/live/search/a–z

72. Levy, 'Strange Life and Death', p. 135.

73. HCA 1/38, f. 95v.

Chapter 3: Pirates, Privateers and Slave Traders from the later 1550s to the later 1560s

1. *CSPI 1509–73*, p. 151; *APC 1558–70*, p. 23; *CSPS 1558–67*, pp. 24–5; G.D. Ramsay, *The City of London in International Politics at the Accession of Elizabeth Tudor* (Manchester, 1975), pp. 113–4, 125–6; *Tudor Proclamations*, II, p. 101.

2. *CSPD 1547–80*, p. 136; J.H. Burton (ed.), *The Register of the Privy Council of Scotland, 1545–1569* (Edinburgh, 1877), pp. 430–2.

3. *APC 1558–70*, pp. 97–8; *CSPS 1558–67*, p. 61; *CSPF 1558–59*, pp. 228, 233, 585–6; *CSPF 1559–60*, p. 251.

4. *CSPF 1558–59*, p. 388; *Pays–Bas*, I, pp. 604–5; II, pp. 138, 635; HCA 1/38, ff. 94–5v.

5. *CSPS 1558–67*, p. 92.

6. Nichols (ed.), *Diary*, pp. 212–3; *CSPF 1559 60*, p. 4; HCA 1/38, f. 95v.

7. *CSPD 1547–80*, p. 144; Levy, 'Strange Life and Death', pp. 135–6.

8. *Calendar*, pp. 25–6 for Fobbe; *Pays–Bas*, I, p. 601; II, pp. 180–1, 415, 501–2, 569–75, 589–90.

9. *CSPS 1558–67*, pp. 150, 207; *Pays–Bas*, II, pp. 406–7; *Calendar*, p. 24.

10. *CSPF 1560–61*, p. 558; *CSPS 1558–67*, pp. 24–5, 37.

11. *CSPF 1560–61*, p. 558.

12. *CSPF 1560–61*, p. 559. J.D. Tracy, 'Herring Wars: The Habsburg Netherlands and the Struggle for Control of the North Sea, c. 1520–1560', *The Sixteenth Century Journal*, 24 (1993), pp. 256–66.

13. *CSPF 1560–61*, p. 56; *CSPF 1561–62*, pp. 134, 191–2, 276–7.

14. *CSPF 1561–62*, pp. 133, 149, 193.

15. *CSPF 1561–62*, pp. 134–5, 137, 193.

16. *CSPF 1561–62*, pp. 134–5.

17. *CSPF 1561–62*, pp. 143–4, 150; *CSPF 1560–61*, pp. 557–60.

18. *CSPF 1561–62*, pp. 133, 192.

19. *CSPF 1561–62*, pp. 192–3, 276–7; *CSPS 1558–67*, pp. 207, 211–2; *Tudor Proclamations*, I, pp. 171–2.

20. *CSPF 1562*, p. 162. Phetiplace or Fetiplace was also known as Petit-Pas, *Pays–Bas*, III, p. 626. Marychurch was pardoned in 1562, *CPR 1563–66*, p. 327.

21. *CSPF 1562*, p. 89.

22. *CSPF 1562*, pp. 162, 590–1.

23. *CSPF 1563*, pp. 61, 232, 259; *CPR 1560–63*, p. 502; J. Bain et al. (eds.), *Calendar of the State Papers relating to Scotland and Mary, Queen of Scots 1547–1603*, 13 vols. (Edinburgh, 1898–1969), II, p. 1.

24. *CSPF 1563*, p. 619. By January 1566 he was in Milford Haven, E.A. Lewis (ed.), *The Welsh Port Books (1550–1603)* (London, 1927), p. 315.

25. *CSPI 1509–73*, pp. 230–1; *CSPF 1564–65*, pp. 27, 79–80, 174. Phetiplace's declaration presented his actions in northern Spain as a legitimate response to Spanish hostility, SP 63/10/22. In 1563 Cecil noted that piracy was 'detestable and can not last', R.H. Tawney and E. Power (eds.), *Tudor Economic Documents*, 3 vols. (London, 1924), II, p. 106.

26. Nichols (ed.), *Diary*, pp. 256, 281. A report of 1563 claimed there were at least 400 known pirates operating in the waters around the British Isles, Oppenheim, *Administration*, p. 177.

27. *Tudor Proclamations*, II, pp. 206–9; R.B. Wernham, *Before the Armada: The Growth of English Foreign Policy 1485–1588* (London, 1966), pp. 281–2.

28. *APC 1558–70*, pp. 136, 141; *CSPS 1558–67*, pp. 276, 299, 300, 322–3; Ramsay, *London*, pp. 134–5. William Hawkins was part–owner of a man–of–war with Stukely, Williamson, *Hawkins*, pp. 96–7.

29. J.A. Twemlow (ed.), *Liverpool Town Books*, 2 vols. (Liverpool, 1918–35), I, pp. 224–5; *CSPD 1547–80*, pp. 224, 228, 239; *CSPF 1563*, p. 431; *Tudor Proclamations*, II, pp. 228, 232; Rodger, *Safeguard of the Sea*, pp. 197–200.

30. *CSPS 1558–67*, pp. 349–51; *Tudor Proclamations*, II, pp. 235–6.

31. *CSPF 1563*, p. 132; *Pays–Bas*, III, pp. 384–5, 538, 540, 585–6.

32. *CSPS 1558–67*, pp. 345–6; *CSPF 1563*, pp. 414, 429. Trading vessels from Bristol were seized in Spanish ports as pirate ships during the early 1560s, J. Vanes (ed.), *Documents illustrating the Overseas Trade of Bristol in the Sixteenth Century* (Bristol Record Society, 31, 1979), pp. 154–6.

33. *CSPS 1558–67*, pp. 349–55; *CSPF 1563*, pp. 611–2, 619; *CSPF 1564–65*, pp. 9, 19, 27, 46, 79, 158–9, 174, 199–200.

34. *CSPS 1558–67*, pp. 376, 536, 572–3; *CSPF 1563*, pp. 598, 631; *CSPF 1564–65*, pp. 192, 201, 224; Ramsay, *London*, pp. 138–9.

35. *CSPF 1564–65*, p. 39. Phetiplace noted thirty English men–of–war off Belle Isle in October 1563, SP 63/10/22.

36. *CSPF 1564–65*, pp. 80, 158–9, 199–201, 224, 415; *Pays–Bas*, III, pp. 668–9.

37. *Tudor Proclamations*, II, pp. 245–6; *HMC Salisbury*, I, pp. 286–7; *Pays–Bas*, III, pp. 585–6, 645–6.

38. *CSPF 1564–65*, p. 46; *APC 1558–70*, pp. 186, 202–3, 212–3; *Pays–Bas*, III, p. 665; Ramsay, *London*, pp. 201–3.

39. *CSPD 1547–80*, pp. 244–6, 251; *APC 1558–70*, pp. 146–8, 151, 184, 202; *HMC Salisbury*, I, p. 299.

40. *CSPS 1558–67*, p. 376.

41. *APC 1558–70*, pp. 153–4, 164, 182, 186, 229–30.

42. *CSPS 1558–67*, pp. 402–3; *APC 1558–70*, pp. 175, 179.

43. *CSPD 1547–80*, p. 251; *APC 1558–70*, pp. 206–7, 209, 211, 215–6, 235–6.

44. *CSPF 1564–65*, p. 350; *Tudor Proclamations*, II, p. 252.

45. *CSPS 1558–67*, pp. 359–60, 397; *CSPF 1563*, p. 619; *Pays–Bas*, III, p. 514; D.B. Quinn, *Explorers and Colonies: America, 1500–1625* (London, 1990), pp. 260–2; *NAW*, II, p. 285; *ODNB*, 'Thomas Stukely'.

46. *CSPF 1564–65*, p. 46; *CSPS 1558–67*, pp. 354–5.

47. *CSPS 1558–67*, pp. 359, 373–9.

48. *CSPS 1558–67*, pp. 373, 376, 440.

49. *CSPS 1558–67*, pp. 440–1, 449–50, 454–5, 472–3.

50. *CSPS 1558–67*, pp. 450, 454–5; *CSPS 1558–67*, p. 450.

51. *CSPS 1558–67*, pp. 454–5, 472–3. It has been argued that there is no evidence that benefit of clergy was allowed during the sixteenth century (M.J. Prichard and D.E.C. Yale (eds.), *Hale and Fleetwood on Admiralty Jurisdiction* (Selden Society, 108, 1992), pp. ccviii–ccx), though Marsden accepted that Cobham appeared to evade punishment by these means, R.G. Marsden, 'Thomas Cobham and the Capture of the "St. Katherine"', *EHR*, 23 (1908), pp. 290–1.

52. *CSPI 1509–73*, pp. 275, 341–2, 408, 466–72.

53. *CSPS 1558–67*, pp. 539, 552.

54. *APC 1558–70*, pp. 229–30, 240–1, 244–45, 251; *Calendar*, p. 25.

55. *APC 1558–70*, pp. 252–4, 256, 260, 273.

56. *CSPS 1558–67*, p. 496; *APC 1558–70*, pp. 260, 267, 272–3, 298.

57. *APC 1558–70*, pp. 273, 275, 293.

58. *CSPS 1558–67*, p. 496. Cobham remained at sea, *Calendar*, pp. 27–8.

59. *APC 1558–70*, pp. 278–90; Tawney and Power (eds.), *Tudor Economic Documents*, II, pp. 117–22.

60. *APC 1558–70*, pp. 278–90; P. Williams, *The Tudor Regime* (Oxford, 1979), pp. 190, 416–7.

61. *APC 1558–70*, pp. 278–90; N. Williams, *The Sea Dogs: Privateers, Plunder and Piracy in the Elizabethan Age* (London, 1975), pp. 149–50.

62. *APC 1558–70*, p. 307.

63. *CSPD 1547–80*, p. 267; *APC 1558–70*, p. 325.

64. *APC 1558–70*, pp. 292–5, 312.

65. *CSPS 1558–67*, pp. 539, 552, 688.

66. J. McDermott, *Martin Frobisher: Elizabethan Privateer* (New Haven, 2001), pp. 50–66;

R.G. Marsden, 'The Early Career of Sir Martin Frobisher', *EHR*, 21 (1906), pp. 538–44.

67. *APC 1558–70*, p. 317.

68. *APC 1558–70*, pp. 320–1; *CSPD 1547–80*, p. 276.

69. *CSPF 1566–68*, pp. 388, 450, 578, 583, 588, 592; *APC 1558–70*, p. 334, 348; Williamson, *Hawkins*, pp. 99–100; Hammer, *Elizabeth's Wars*, pp. 80–1. Overseas retaliation included the arrest of Bristol shipping in Spain, evidently in response to the continued activities of Cobham, Vanes (ed.), *Overseas Trade of Bristol*, pp. 131–2.

70. K.R. Andrews, *Trade, Plunder and Settlement: Maritime Enterprise and the Genesis of the British Empire, 1480–1630* (Cambridge, 1984), pp. 102–15.

71. *PN*, VI, pp. 225, 229, 232–4.

72. *PN*, VI, pp. 235–52.

73. *PN*, VI, pp. 250–1.

74. Andrews, *Trade, Plunder and Settlement*, pp. 103–4, 122–3.

75. *PN*, VI, pp. 266–84. For an earlier venture which ran into trouble off the coast of Spain see K.R. Andrews, 'Thomas Fenner and the Guinea Trade, 1564', *MM*, 38 (1952), pp. 312–4.

76. Andrews, *Trade, Plunder and Settlement*, pp. 121–8; K.R. Andrews, *The Spanish Caribbean: Trade and Plunder 1530–1630* (New Haven, 1978), pp. 108–33; *CSPS 1558–67*, pp. 470, 502–4; *PN*, VI, pp. 235–6; H. Kelsey, *Sir John Hawkins: Queen Elizabeth's Slave Trader* (New Haven, 2003), chaps. 3 & 4.

77. I.A. Wright (ed.), *Spanish Documents concerning English Voyages to the Caribbean 1527–1568* (Hakluyt Society, Second Series, 57, 1929), pp. 78, 82, 117–8, 121.

78. Ibid., pp. 119, 123, 127; *CSPS 1568–79*, pp. 1, 68; *NAW*, II, pp. 406, 567–8.

79. The bullion was owned by Genoese bankers. P. Croft, '"The State of the World is Marvellously Changed": England, Spain and Europe, 1558–1604' in S. Doran and G. Richardson (eds.), *Tudor England and its Neighbours* (Basingstoke, 2005), pp. 183–5.

80. McDermott, *Frobisher*, pp. 70–2; R.G. Marsden, 'The Early Career of Sir Martin Frobisher', *EHR*, 21 (1906), pp. 538–44; *CSPD 1547–80*, pp. 273–4.

81. *CSPS 1568–79*, pp. 79, 82–3; Andrews, 'Expansion of English Privateering and Piracy', pp. 205–10; J. Marx, *Pirates and Privateers of the Caribbean* (Malabar, Fl., 1992), pp. 61 ff.

82. *CSPS 1568–79*, pp. 83–4, 88, 94–5; B. Dietz, 'The Huguenot and English Corsairs during the Third Civil War in France, 1568 to 1570', *Proceedings of the Huguenot Society of London*, 19 (1952–58), pp. 278–94.

83. *CSPS 1568–79*, pp. 73, 75, 99–104; *Tudor Proclamations*, II, pp. 301–5; Williamson, *Hawkins*, pp. 218–20, 225–6.

84. He claimed that booty valued at 200,000 ducats was taken by pirates, *CSPS 1568–79*, pp. 107, 135–7.

85. *Tudor Proclamations*, II, pp. 313–5.

86. *Tudor Proclamations*, II, pp. 315–6. Plundering under French commissions continued, HCA 14/9, nos. 22, 137–8. 176.

87. *CSPS 1568–79*, pp. 107, 112, 135–9, 154–6, 176.

88. *CSPS 1568–79*, pp. 188, 201, 212–3, 232; Dietz, 'Huguenot and English Corsairs', pp. 287–90.

89. *CSPS 1568–79*, pp. 218, 230–1, 234, 240; *CSPV 1558–80*, pp. 444–7.

90. *CSPS 1568–79*, pp. 216, 219–20.

Chapter 4: *Piracy, Plunder and Undeclared War during the 1570s*

1. *APC 1558–70*, pp. 337–8, 366–7; *Tudor Proclamations*, II, pp. 339–41.
2. *CSPS 1568–79*, pp. 235, 245–6, 250.
3. *CSPS 1568–79*, p. 245.
4. *CSPS 1568–79*, p. 482.
5. *CSPS 1568–79*, p. 329.
6. *CSPS 1568–79*, pp. 288–9, 325.
7. Dietz, 'Huguenot and English Corsairs', pp. 284–5; *CSPS 1568–79*, pp. 75–6, 253; Quinn, *Explorers and Colonies*, pp. 130, 258–9.
8. *CSPS 1568–79*, pp. 235, 242–3, 250, 258.
9. *CSPS 1568–79*, pp. 243, 263.
10. *CSPS 1568–79*, pp. 263, 267.
11. *CSPS 1568–79*, p. 290.
12. *APC 1558–70*, pp. 386, 395; *CSPF 1569–71*, p. 471; *CSPS 1568–79*, p. 361.
13. *CSPS 1568–79*, pp. 231, 243, 245; *Calendar*, p. 33.
14. *CSPS 1568–79*, p. 277; *APC 1558–70*, p. 389.
15. *CSPS 1568–79*, pp. 283, 288–9.
16. *APC 1558–70*, p. 409; A. Spicer, *The French–Speaking Reformed Community and their Church in Southampton 1567–c.1620* (Southampton Record Series, 39, 1997), p. 131.
17. *CSPS 1568–79*, pp. 351–2, 399; D.B. Quinn and A.N. Ryan, *England's Sea Empire, 1550–1642* (London, 1983), pp. 41–2.
18. *CSPS 1568–79*, p. 329.
19. *CSPS 1568–79*, pp. 283, 338, 347.
20. *CSPS 1568–79*, p. 286; *APC 1558–70*, pp. 368–9, 385–6, 391–2. For the loss to customs referred to in this paragraph see C. Wilson, *Queen Elizabeth and the Revolt of the Netherlands* (London, 1970), p. 25.
21. *CSPS 1568–79*, pp. 291, 292, 305, 364.
22. *CSPS 1568–79*, pp. 296, 341, 347, 376; *Tudor Proclamations*, II, pp. 357–8.
23. *CSPS 1568–79*, pp. 385, 490; V. von Klarwill (ed.), *The Fugger News-Letters 1568–1605* (London, 1926), pp. 13–4.
24. *CSPS 1568–79*, p. 457.
25. *CSPF 1572–74*, p. 259; *CSPS 1568–79*, pp. 456, 459, 470–1, 476.
26. *CSPS 1568–79*, pp. 459, 465.
27. *CSPS 1568–79*, p. 476.
28. *CSPS 1568–79*, pp. 429–30, 464.
29. *APC 1571–75*, pp. 64–5, 77–9; *Select Pleas*, II, pp. 149–50. A fleet was also despatched to scour the Channel for pirates, Williamson, *Hawkins*, pp. 273–5.
30. *APC 1571–75*, pp. 85, 107, 110, 114, 256.
31. *CSPF 1572–74*, p. 454.
32. *APC 1571–75*, p. 187.
33. *APC 1571–75*, pp. 191, 230; *CSPS 1568–79*, pp. 482, 486; *Calendar*, pp. 39–41. Dutch rebel rovers also remained based in English ports, such as captain David of Flushing who was based in Dover for at least four years, *Pays–Bas*, VII, pp. 40–1, 50, 146–7, 161–2, 451.
34. *APC 1571–75*, pp. 102–3, 110, 113, 116–7 301. And for Ireland see M. O'Dowd (ed.), *Calendar of State Papers Ireland: Tudor Period 1571–1575* (Dublin, 2000), pp. 11, 292, 296, 298.

35. *CSPF 1572–74*, p. 454. V. W. Lunsford, *Piracy and Privateering in the Golden Age Netherlands* (New York, 2005), p. 115.

36. *APC 1571–75*, pp. 150, 160, 176, 213, 222–3, 333; *CSPF 1575–77*, p. 151; *CSPF 1572–74*, pp. 511, 515, 520.

37. *APC 1571–75*, pp. 253, 275–6; *CSPF 1572–74*, p. 537.

38. *CSPF 1572–74*, pp. 511, 531. Clashes with the French persisted along the coast of Spain, Andrews, 'Thomas Fenner', pp. 313–4.

39. *CSPF 1572–74*, pp. 522, 525–7, 530–3; Bain et al. (eds.), *Calendar of State Papers relating to Scotland*, V, pp. 8–10, 14–5, 24–8.

40. *CSPF 1572–74*, pp. 522–3, 536–7, 540–1, 544; *APC 1571–75*, p. 293.

41. *CSPS 1568–79*, p. 477.

42. *CSPS 1568–79*, pp. 480–2.

43. K. R. Andrews, *Drake's Voyages: A Re-assessment of their Place in Elizabethan Maritime Expansion* (London, 1967), pp. 29–42; K. E. Lane, *Pillaging the Empire: Piracy in the Americas 1500–1750* (Armonk, 1998), pp. 39, 44–6.

44. Andrews, *Spanish Caribbean*, pp. 134–46; *NAW*, II, pp. 575–84.

45. I. A. Wright (ed.), *Documents concerning English Voyages to the Spanish Main 1569–80* (Hakluyt Society, Second Series, 71, 1932), pp. xviii–xxii, 16–7; Lane, *Pillaging*, pp. 33–4; Wernham, *Before the Armada*, pp. 349–50. On the lack of experienced English pilots for the Caribbean see Rodger, *Safeguard of the Sea*, p. 244.

46. Andrews, *Drake's Voyages*, pp. 32–5. The most comprehensive treatment of Drake remains J. S. Corbett, *Drake and the Tudor Navy*, 2 vols. (London, 1898, repr. Aldershot, 1988). Recent studies include H. Kelsey, *Sir Francis Drake: The Queen's Pirate* (New Haven, 1998).

47. Wright (ed.), *Voyages*, pp. 40, 46.

48. Ibid., p. 265; *PN*, X, p. 76.

49. Wright (ed.), *Voyages*, p. 298.

50. Wright (ed.), *Voyages*, p. 298.

51. Ibid., pp. 71, 73, 326. The actual amount of plunder from the voyage is unknowable.

52. Ibid., p. 62.

53. Ibid., p. 72.

54. Ibid., pp. 93–4, 96, 98; Williamson, *Hawkins*, pp. 297–9.

55. Wright (ed.), *Voyages*, pp. 100, 123.

56. And for the rest of this paragraph, *PN*, X, pp. 82, 84, 87–8.

57. Wright (ed.), *Voyages*, pp. liii, 110–11, 171–2.

58. Ibid., p. 121.

59. Ibid., pp. 152, 166–7, 176, 187–8.

60. Ibid., pp. 174–5. On defence see Andrews, *Spanish Caribbean*, pp. 99–107, 151–6 and H. Kamen, *Spain's Road to Empire: The Making of a World Power 1492–1763* (London, 2002), pp. 257–64.

61. Wright (ed.), *Voyages*, pp. 13, 61; Quinn and Ryan, *England's Sea Empire*, pp. 30–2.

62. Wright (ed.), *Voyages*, p. 7.

63. Ibid., p. 68.

64. Ibid., p. 50.

65. Ibid., pp. 101, 117, 120, 187.

66. Ibid., pp. lxiii, 217, 235, 240.

67. These crude estimates are based on figures in Wright (ed.), *Voyages*, pp. 7, 36, 48, 100, 172, 196–7, 253, 327.

68. Wright (ed.), *Voyages*, pp. 172, 254.

69. Ibid., pp. xlix, 112–3, 203–6, 213, 228.

70. Ibid., pp. 174, 254.

71. Ibid., pp. 102–5.

72. *PN*, X, p. 86; Wright (ed.), *Voyages*, p. 105.

73. Ibid., p. 118.

74. Ibid., p. 265.

75. *PN*, X, p. 81.

76. *CSPF 1575–77*, pp. 1–2, 67–8, 134–5. On Rogers' mission see also *Pays–Bas*, VII, pp. 526–9, 531–4, 575–8.

77. *CSPF 1575–77*, pp. 72–4; *CSPD 1547–80*, pp. 502–4.

78. *CSPF 1575–77*, pp. 215–6.

79. *Tudor Proclamations*, II, p. 395.

80. *CSPF 1575–77*, pp. 57, 168, 190; *Pays–Bas*, VII, pp. 505–6.

81. *Tudor Proclamations*, II, pp. 396–7.

82. *CSPF 1575–77*, pp. 128, 227–8, 309, 400–1, 491–2, 501, 518, 607–8; *CSPF 1577–78*, p. 3.

83. *CSPF 1575–77*, pp. 259, 263–6, 269–70, 305, 310–1, 336–7, 341–2, 352–3, 370–1.

84. *CSPF 1575–77*, pp. 414, 432–5, 468.

85. *APC 1575–77*, pp. 172, 174, 181–3, 189.

86. *APC 1575–77*, pp. 200–1, 204, 231.

87. *CSPF 1575–77*, pp. 386, 388–9, 406, 408.

88. *CSPF 1577–78*, p. 72.

89. *CSPF 1577–78*, pp. 123, 135, 147.

90. *CSPF 1577–78*, p. 457.

91. *CSPF 1577–78*, pp. 468, 472, 507, 532–3.

92. *CSPF 1577–78*, p. 519.

93. *CSPF 1577–78*, pp. 517–20; *CSPF 1579–80*, pp. 13–4.

94. *CSPD 1547–80*, p. 523.

Chapter 5: The Profession of Piracy from the mid–1570s to 1585

1. *CSPF 1585–86*, pp. 409, 411–2.

2. SP 12/103/61; 12/75/19; 12/135/11–12, 28–33. On good fellowship, Robin Hood and the spread and use of stories see J.C. Holt, *Robin Hood* (London, 1982), pp. 38–9, 140–2, 147 and A.J. Pollard, *Imagining Robin Hood: Late–Medieval Stories in Historical Context* (London, 2004), pp. 206–22. For a vivid overview of piracy during the 1570s see Williams, *The Sea Dogs*, pp. 152–65.

3. These estimates should be interpreted cautiously. They are based on a wide range of evidence which is used in this chapter. Evidently more than 900 men were tried for piracy during 1578, though only three were executed, Williams, *The Sea Dogs*, p. 150. For the later period see M. Rediker, *Between the Devil and the Deep Blue Sea: Merchant Seamen, Pirates, and the Anglo–American Maritime World, 1700–1750* (Cambridge, 1987), pp. 256–7.

4. *CSPD Addenda 1566–79*, p. 563; *CSPI 1574–85*, p. 157.

5. H. Doh (ed.), *A Critical Edition of Fortune by Land and Sea by Thomas Heywood and William Rowley* (New York, 1980), pp. 225, 277 (for the jubilee). D. Mathew, *The Celtic Peoples and Renaissance Europe* (London, 1933), pp. 296–304 for the links between England, Wales and Ireland. For evidence of richer pickings from piracy see Scammell, 'Shipowning in the Economy and Politics of Early Modern England', pp. 401–2.

6. *APC 1576–77*, pp. 73–4, 89, 127–30; C. L'Estrange Ewen, *The Golden Chalice: A Documented Narrative of an Elizabethan Pirate* (Paignton, 1939); HCA 1/40, ff. 22–5.

7. *APC 1576–77*, pp. 209, 219, 240, 267–8, 293–4; HCA 13/21, ff. 29v–30.

8. *APC 1576–77*, pp. 337, 351, 357, 365; *APC 1577–78*, pp. 57–8, 106, 146; *CSPF 1577–78*, p. 275; HCA 1/40, ff. 17–20.

9. *CPR 1575–78*, p. 537; Bain et al. (eds.), *Calendar of the State Papers relating to Scotland*, V, p. 308. On Gilbert see *NAW*, III, pp. 181–257.

10. SP 15/25/60, I–III.

11. And for the rest of the paragraph SP 15/25/60, III.

12. SP 15/25/60, II; SP 12/135/167; HCA 1/40, f. 36v; *APC 1575–77*, p. 357; *APC 1578–80*, pp. 300–1.

13. Andrews, *Trade, Plunder and Settlement*, pp. 188–9; D.B. Quinn, *England and the Discovery of America, 1481–1620* (London, 1974), pp. 248–51 on Fernandes. D.B. Quinn (ed.), *The Voyages and Colonising Enterprises of Sir Humphrey Gilbert*, 2 vols. (Hakluyt Society, Second Series, 83 & 84, 1938–39), I, pp. 33–46, 198, 201–4, 222–3.

14. *CSPF 1579–80*, p. 67; Quinn (ed.), *Voyages*, I, pp. 225–9; II, pp. 498–509. A plan c. 1580 for taking control of the Straits of Magellan envisaged using Clarke, the pirate. E.P. Cheyney, *A History of England from the Defeat of the Armada to the Death of Elizabeth*, 2 vols. (London, 1914–26, repr. New York, 1948), I, p. 430.

15. Bain et al. (eds.), *Calendar of the State Papers relating to Scotland*, V, p. 449; *CSPF 1582*, p. 130; *CSPF 1584–85*, p. 522; *CSPF 1585–86*, pp. 3–4.

16. E.S. Donno (ed.), *An Elizabethan in 1582: The Diary of Richard Madox, Fellow of All Souls* (Hakluyt Society, Second Series, 147, 1976), p. 192; Rowse, *Tudor Cornwall*, pp. 390–2.

17. *APC 1577–78*, pp. 48–9.

18. *APC 1575–77*, p. 377; *APC 1577–78*, pp. 18, 33, 36–7, 71, 141; SP 12/135/83, 89.

19. *CSPI 1574–85*, pp. 130, 150, 162, 167–9; *Calendar*, pp. 41–3.

20. *APC 1577–78*, p. 14; HCA 13/23, ff. 239–9v.

21. SP 15/25/54, I. Other pirates were active along the east coast of Yorkshire, *CPR 1575–78*, p. 429.

22. SP 15/25/54, I; SP 12/135/15. BL, Additional MS 12505, f. 352.

23. *APC 1577–78*, pp. 28, 36–7, 156, 260; *HMC Salisbury*, II, p. 150; SP 12/135/28–33.

24. *APC 1577–78*, pp. 26–7, 89–90, 102; *APC 1578–80*, pp. 65, 68–9, 90–1; SP 12/135/20.

25. *APC 1577–78*, pp. 22, 156.

26. *APC 1577–78*, pp. 59, 221, 263, 271, 273, 276, 279; *APC 1578–80*, p. 109.

27. Bain et al. (eds.), *Calendar of the State Papers relating to Scotland*, V, pp. 375–6; *APC 1577–78*, pp. 193–4, 277–80.

28. *APC 1577–78*, pp. 318, 332, 361–2, 429.

29. SP 12/122/6; Williams, *Tudor Regime*, pp. 245–6; A. Hassell Smith et al. (eds.) *The Papers of Nathaniel Bacon of Stiffkey* (Norwich, 1979), pp. 229–30, 247–8; A. L. Rowse, *Sir Richard Grenville of the 'Revenge'* (London, 1937), pp. 146–7, 165–8.

30. SP 12/123/24, 38, 40.

31. SP 12/122/59; Hassell Smith et al. (eds.), *Papers*, pp. 267–8, 271.

32. SP 12/123/44.

33. O. Ogle (ed.), *Copy–Book of Sir Amias Paulet's Letters Written during his Embassy to France* (Roxburghe Club, London, 1866), p. 82; *CSPF 1577–78*, pp. 468, 517–20.

34. Ogle (ed.), *Copy–Book*, pp. 83, 94–5, 137, 213. For Bristol losses see Vanes (ed.), *Overseas Trade of Bristol*, p. 113.

35. SP 12/122/47, 60; 12/123/36; Lloyd, *Gentry of South–West Wales*, pp. 156–9.

36. SP 12/122/22; Ewen, 'Organized Piracy', pp. 34–9.

37. SP 12/103/3; 12/135/153, 165–7.

38. And for the rest of the paragraph, SP 12/103/3.

39. SP 12/111/36; Lloyd, *Gentry of South–West Wales*, pp. 162–4.

40. J.H. Matthews (ed.), *Cardiff Records*, 6 vols. (Cardiff, 1898–1911), I, p. 349.

41. Ibid., pp. 349–50.

42. Ibid., pp. 355–6; SP 12/122/2.

43. Matthews (ed.), *Cardiff Records*, I, pp. 353–5.

44. *APC 1575–77*, pp. 267–8; *APC 1577–78*, pp. 57–8, 67, 179–81, 193–4, 296; *APC 1580–81*, pp. 16, 73, 93–4, 107, 144.

45. *APC 1578–80*, pp. 6–9, 13, 35–6, 44, 47, 65, 76, 99–100, 173–4, 259; *Calendar*, p. 62; *EPV*, pp. 143, 159; S. Maxwell, 'Henry Seckford: Sixteenth–Century Merchant, Courtier and Privateer', *MM*, 82 (1996), pp. 387–97

46. *APC 1578–80*, pp. 13, 34, 38–9, 84–5, 98.

47. SP 12/123/37; *CSPD 1547–80*, p. 656.

48. Andrews, *Drake's Voyages*, p. 50.

49. Ibid., p. 48; BL, Cotton MS Otho E VIII, f. 65.

50. Andrews, *Drake's Voyages*, pp. 41–7, 54.

51. Ibid., p. 52; G.V. Scammell, *The World Encompassed: The First European Maritime Empires c. 800–1650* (London, 1981), pp. 465–7.

52. Andrews, *Drake's Voyages*, p. 67.

53. *CSPF 1578–79*, pp. 45–60; BL, Cotton MS Otho E VIII, ff. 59–60. The booty included 90 pounds in gold, 26 tons in silver and 13 chests of plate. Plunder was accompanied by damage to churches. Z. Nuttall (ed.), *New Light on Drake* (Hakluyt Society, Second Series, 34, 1914), pp. 214, 331, 341–4.

54. Andrews, *Drake's Voyages*, p. 80; Nuttall (ed.), *New Light*, pp. 50–1. The booty has been estimated at £1.5 million, D.M. Palliser, *The Age of Elizabeth: England under the Later Tudors 1547–1603* (2nd edition, London, 1992), pp. 170–1. It was comparable to royal revenue for 1579 or 1581, Hammer, *Elizabeth's Wars*, pp. 110–1. On the Northwest Passage see S. Bawlf, *The Secret Voyage of Sir Francis Drake 1577–1580* (New York, 2003).

55. Andrews, *Drake's Voyages*, pp. 81–2; *CSPD 1581–90*, p. 54. Spanish authorities were alarmed that the Pacific (or South Sea) would fill up with corsairs 'who would devastate it', Nuttall (ed.), *New Light*, p. 122.

56. Andrews, *Drake's Voyages*, pp. 87–8; P. Williams, *The Later Tudors 1547–1603* (Oxford, 1995), pp. 287–90.

57. R. Hakluyt, *Discourse of Western Planting*, eds. D.B. and A.M. Quinn (Hakluyt Society, Extra Series, 45, 1993), pp. 119–20.

58. Andrews, *Drake's Voyages*, p. 88; *CSPF 1580–81*, pp. 338–40, 411–12.

59. *CSPF 1580–81*, pp. 385–6, 418–9, 433–4; Williamson, *Hawkins*, p. 407.

60. *CSPF 1580–81*, pp. 423–4, 625–6.

61. *CSPF 1582*, pp. 134, 378; HCA 13/24, ff. 320–20v.

62. *CSPF 1583–84*, pp. 342, 452, 491; *CSPF 1584–85*, pp. 63, 116.

63. *CSPF 1583*, pp. 93–4.

64. *CSPF 1582*, pp. 440–1, 456–7; *NAW*, IV, pp. 2–3, 13–9. One vessel involved in the raid was owned by Sir John Perrot.

65. E.G.R. Taylor (ed.), *The Troublesome Voyage of Captain Edward Fenton 1582–1583* (Hakluyt

Society, Second Series, 113, 1959), pp. xxx–xxxi; Donno (ed.), *Diary of Madox*, pp. 17–8; BL, Cotton MS Otho E VIII, ff. 85v–6v.

66. Taylor (ed.), *Troublesome Voyage*, p. 202; Donno (ed.), *Diary of Madox*, p. 302; Quinn, *England and the Discovery of America*, pp. 253–4.

67. Taylor (ed.), *Troublesome Voyage*, p. 55.

68. Ibid., pp. 46, 65–6; Donno (ed.), *Diary of Madox*, p. 280

69. Taylor (ed.), *Troublesome Voyage*, p. 284.

70. Ibid., pp. 74, 284; Donno (ed.), *Diary of Madox*, pp. 141, 174.

71. Ibid., pp. 168, 264–5.

72. Ibid., pp. 144, 188.

73. Ibid., p. 184.

74. Ibid., p. 200.

75. Ibid., pp. 255–6.

76. Taylor (ed.), *Troublesome Voyage*, p. 142.

77. Donno (ed.), *Diary of Madox*, pp. 273–4.

78. Ibid., p. 274.

79. *CSPD 1581–90*, pp. 11, 14.

80. *APC 1581–82*, pp. 92, 128–9, 171; *CSPD 1581–90*, pp. 19, 21.

81. BL, Lansdowne MS 33, ff. 184–4v.

82. Ibid., ff. 185–5v.

83. *CSPD 1581–90*, pp. 21, 23, 28–9, 124, 247. The council also investigated the mayor and gaoler in Exeter, who were suspected of allowing a pirate to escape, though the outcome was inconclusive, W.T. MacCaffrey, *Exeter, 1540–1640: The Growth of an English County Town* (Cambridge, Mass., 1958), pp. 232–3.

84. *APC 1581–82*, pp. 315, 356–7, 397, 415; *HMC Salisbury*, II, p. 522; V, p. 520; *Calendar*, pp. 47–9.

85. *CSPD 1581–90*, p. 64.

86. SP 12/156/7; Ewen, 'Organized Piracy', pp. 38–42; C. L'Estrange Ewen, 'The Pirates of Purbeck', *Proceedings of the Dorset Natural History & Archaeological Society*, 71 (1949), pp. 88–109.

87. *APC 1580–81*, pp. 342–3; *CSPD 1581–90*, pp. 11–2, 16, 25, 28–9, 56, 201; *CSPS 1580–86*, pp. 410, 432.

88. SP 12/156/43; Spicer, *The French–Speaking Reformed Community*, pp. 50–1, 131.

89. *CSPD 1581–90*, pp. 186, 201, 214–5, 217, 238.

90. BL, Lansdowne MS 162, ff. 59–60v.

91. *CSPF 1582*, pp. 42, 271–3; *CSPD 1581–90*, p. 121.

92. Donno (ed.), *Diary of Madox*, pp. 111–3.

93. *CSPI 1574–85*, pp. 433, 436, 438, 447, 473–5, 487.

94. *CSPI 1574–85*, p. 350.

95. *CSPD 1581–90*, pp. 186, 192, 208; HCA 13/25, ff. 243–3v; Williams, *The Sea Dogs*, pp. 150–1.

96. *EPV*, pp. 153–4.

97. And for the rest of the paragraph SP 12/172/90. On recruitment see C.A. Fury, *Tides in the Affairs of Men: The Social History of Elizabethan Seamen, 1580–1603* (Westport, CT, 2002), pp. 22–3. From 1581 to 1583 forty vessels seized by pirates and rovers were brought into Studland Bay, Ewen, 'The Pirates of Purbeck', pp. 92, 100–3.

98. SP 12/172/90–1, 94.

99. BL, Lansdowne MS 33, f. 184.

100. Donno (ed.), *Diary of Madox*, p. 131.

101. BL, Lansdowne MS 26, ff. 71–1v.

102. BL, Lansdowne MS 33, ff. 183–4. According to the same report, Piers had been pardoned twice for such offences.

103. Clinton had already given to his friends a velvet coat with gold lace, 'apparell too sumptuous for sea rovers which he had worne at the seas'. J. Stow, *The Annales of England* (London, 1605), p. 1175; *A True Relation of the Lives and Deaths of the two most Famous English Pyrats, Purser and Clinton* (London, 1639), chap. 4; Williams, *The Sea Dogs*, p. 152 on the growing use of fine clothes.

104. C. Jowitt, 'Scaffold Performances: The Politics of Pirate Execution' in C. Jowitt (ed.), *Pirates? The Politics of Plunder, 1550–1650* (Basingstoke, 2007), pp. 152–9; Fury, *Tides*, pp. 24–6.

105. Andrews, *Drake's Voyages*, pp. 92–3; Oppenheim, *Maritime History of Devon*, p. 44.

106. SP 12/177/46.

107. SP 12/177/46. Fenner was back at sea, sailing with letters of reprisal, in 1586, despite charges of piracy for which his uncle was not pardoned until 1598, K.R. Andrews, *Elizabethan Privateering: English Privateering during the Spanish War, 1585–1603* (Cambridge, 1966), p. 91.

Chapter 6: *War, Reprisals and Piracy from 1585 to 1603*

1. The war created a myth of naval power in which English sea power was expressed as the 'nation in arms'. N.A.M. Rodger, 'Queen Elizabeth and the Myth of Sea–Power in English History', *Transactions of the Royal Historical Society*, Sixth Series, 14 (2004), pp. 156–7; Loades, *England's Maritime Empire*, pp. 122–31.

2. J.S. Corbett (ed.), *Papers relating to the Navy during the Spanish War 1585–1587* (Navy Records Society, 11, 1898), p. 36; *Law and Custom*, I, pp. 236–41.

3. Andrews, *Elizabethan Privateering*, pp. 22–31; *Law and Custom*, I, p. 251; R.W. Kenny, *Elizabeth's Admiral: The Political Career of Charles Howard Earl of Nottingham 1536–1624* (Baltimore, 1970), pp. 44–8, 67–71.

4. Corbett (ed.), *Spanish War*, p. 35. Flood or Fludd was sailing with a commission from Don Antonio in 1584, *Calendar*, pp. 50–2.

5. Andrews, *Elizabethan Privateering*, pp. 96–7; D.B. Quinn (ed.), *The Roanoke Voyages 1584–1590*, 2 vols. (Hakluyt Society, Second Series, 104 & 105, 1955), I, pp. Ix, 24–32; I.A. Wright (ed.), *Further English Voyages to Spanish America 1583–1594* (Hakluyt Society, Second Series, 94, 1951), pp. 46, 195; G.T. Cell, *English Enterprise in Newfoundland 1577–1660* (Toronto, 1969), pp. 24–5, 47–8; *NAW*, IV, pp. 47–55.

6. M.F. Keeler (ed.), *Sir Francis Drake's West Indian Voyage 1585–1586* (Hakluyt Society, Second Series, 148, 1981), pp. 141–6, 150.

7. Ibid., pp. 76–108; Wright (ed.), *Further English Voyages*, p. 134.

8. Keeler (ed.), *Drake's West Indian Voyage*, p. 197. Drake expected a ransom of 500,000 ducats, Corbett (ed.), *Spanish War*, p. 71.

9. *Monson's Tracts*, I, p. 130.

10. Keeler (ed.), *Drake's West Indian Voyage*, pp. 200–2; *NAW*, V, pp. 39–52. A ransom of 1 million ducats was expected, Corbett (ed.), *Spanish War*, p. 71.

11. Quinn (ed.), *Roanoke Voyages*, I, pp. 480–8; II, pp. 497–8, 555–6, 580–98; Keeler (ed.), *Drake's West Indian Voyage*, p. 171.

12. Wright (ed.), *Further English Voyages*, pp. 179, 213, 217–8; *CSPF 1586–88*, pp. 1, 42, 341.

13. Wright (ed.), *Further English Voyages*, p. 122; Keeler (ed.), *Drake's West Indian Voyage*, pp. 275–6.

14. Corbett (ed.), *Spanish War*, p. xv.

15. Keeler (ed.), *Drake's West Indian Voyage*, p. 212. The voyage was widely reported, *CSPF 1586–88*, pp. 1, 42.

16. Corbett (ed.), *Spanish War*, p. 102. The expedition has been described as 'privateering writ large', Andrews, *Elizabethan Privateering*, p. 94.

17. C. Hopper (ed.), 'Sir Francis Drake's Memorable Service done against the Spaniards in 1587. Written by Robert Long, gentleman', *Camden Miscellany, V* (Camden Society, 87, 1864), pp. 12, 15–6, 19, 22; *PN*, VI, pp. 438–41; *CSPF 1586–88*, pp. 280, 286.

18. Hopper (ed.), 'Drake's Memorable Service', pp. 21–2.

19. And for the following quote, Corbett (ed.), *Spanish War*, pp. 109, 112, 194–5. Drake had written to Foxe during the circumnavigation, Nuttall (ed.), *New Light*, p. 357.

20. In their absence, Boroughs and the ringleaders were sentenced to death by a court held aboard the *Elizabeth Bonaventure*, BL, Additional MS 12505, ff. 241–6v. As Corbett commented, for some, Drake was little better than a 'pardoned pirate', *Spanish War*, p. xlvi.

21. One of the best studies of the Armada campaign, among a rich selection, is C. Martin and G. Parker, *The Spanish Armada* (2nd edition, Manchester, 2002) and on strategy G. Parker, *The Grand Strategy of Philip II* (New Haven, 1998), pp. 179–268.

22. J.K. Laughton (ed.), *State Papers relating to the Defeat of the Spanish Armada*, 2 vols. (Navy Records Society, 1 & 2, 1894), I, pp. 59–61; II, p. 214; Andrews, *Drake's Voyages*, p. 127.

23. Laughton (ed.), *State Papers*, I, p. 94. There was a demand for open war in the parliament of 1589, Cheyney, *History of England*, II, pp. 212–3, 227–8.

24. Laughton (ed.), *State Papers*, I, pp. 124–5, 147–9, 165–7.

25. Ibid., I, pp. 130, 135–6, 143–5, 151–3, 160–1.

26. According to one tradition the Armada was first sighted by the pirate, captain Flemyng, *Monson's Tracts*, I, p. 170. Laughton (ed.), *State Papers*, I, pp. 255, 283–4, 321 for supply problems. A Spanish report claimed that Elizabeth could send out 200 ships against the Armada, but 'most part of them are more fit for piracy than to fight a real battle', *CSPF 1586–88*, p. 342.

27. Laughton (ed.), *State Papers*, II, pp. 102–3; Andrews, *Drake's Voyages*, pp. 130–1; McDermott, *Frobisher*, pp. 353–5, 363–6.

28. Laughton (ed.), *State Papers*, II, pp. 11, 54; Rodger, *Safeguard of the Sea*, pp. 261–71; G. Parker, 'The *Dreadnought* Revolution of Tudor England', *MM*, 82 (1996), pp. 273–4. On rate of fire see also N.A.M. Rodger, 'The Development of Broadside Gunnery, 1450–1650', *MM*, 82 (1996), pp. 313–6.

29. Laughton (ed.), *State Papers*, II, p. 95.

30. Ibid., II, pp. 163–5, 183–4, 239, 261–2, 272–3; Loades, *Tudor Navy*, pp. 253–4.

31. R.B. Wernham (ed.), *The Expedition of Sir John Norris and Sir Francis Drake to Spain and Portugal, 1589* (Navy Records Society, 127, 1988), pp. 27–31; Andrews, *Drake's Voyages*, pp. 136–8.

32. Wernham (ed.), *Expedition*, p. 83.

33. Ibid., pp. 56–7, 133–8, 343–52.

34. Ibid., pp. 141–54, 162.

35. Ibid., pp. 177, 179.

36. Ibid., pp. 222–4, 248–9, 285, 296–9; Andrews, *Drake's Voyages*, pp. 143–6.

37. Rodger, *Safeguard of the Sea*, pp. 278–81.

38. Andrews, 'The Expansion of English Privateering and Piracy', pp. 210–7.

39. Andrews, *Elizabethan Privateering*, pp. 100–2, 225–30; R. Brenner, *Merchants and Revolution: Commercial Change, Political Conflict, and London's Overseas Traders, 1550–1653* (Cambridge, 1993), pp. 19–20, 47–9.

40. *EPV*, pp. 40–2; Andrews, *Elizabethan Privateering*, pp. 76–7, 104–9; R.T. Spence, *The Privateering Earl: George Clifford, 3rd Earl of Cumberland, 1558–1605* (Stroud, 1995), pp. 146–70.

41. Andrews, *Spanish Caribbean*, pp. 162–3; Andrews, *Elizabethan Privateering*, pp. 185–6, 219–24.

42. Ibid., pp. 70, 75–9; G.C. Williamson, *George, Third Earl of Cumberland (1585–1603): His Life and His Voyages* (Cambridge, 1920), pp. 240–3; *Law and Custom*, I, pp. 278–80.

43. Andrews, *Elizabethan Privateering*, pp. 32–4; Fury, *Tides in the Affairs of Men*, pp. 102–8. English men–of–war also sailed with French or Dutch commissions, including those issued by Leicester when he was in the Low Countries, *CSPF 1586–88*, p. 297.

44. Andrews, *Elizabethan Privateering*, pp. 30–5.

45. Ibid., pp. 76–8, 107, 218, 252.

46. *Fugger News–Letters*, pp. 219–20; *CSPF 1586–88*, pp. 503, 560; *CSPF 1588–89*, p. 66.

47. Andrews, *Spanish Caribbean*, p. 156; *EPV*, p. 173.

48. Andrews, *Elizabethan Privateering*, pp. 164–8; *EPV*, p. 95; BL, Additional MS 12505, ff. 467–9.

49. *EPV*, pp. 44–8, 59–67, 107–12.

50. Rodger, *Safeguard of the Sea*, p. 259; Andrews, *Elizabethan Privateering*, pp. 124–49.

51. BL, Additional MS 12505, ff 351–1v. In 1589 Sir William Herbert complained that Munster 'is made a receptacle of pirates', *CSPI 1588–92*, pp. 190–2.

52. Andrews, *Elizabethan Privateering*, pp. 73, 127–8, 131–2; *Monson's Tracts*, I, pp. 290–5; A. Latham and J. Youings (eds.), *The Letters of Sir Walter Raleigh* (Exeter, 1999), pp. 76–80, 87–8.

53. Andrews, *Elizabethan Privateering*, pp. 68, 147–9.

54. *CSPF 1586–88*, pp. 28–30; *Monson's Tracts*, I, pp. 269–74; Cheyney, *History of England*, I, pp. 463–5, 477–9, 482–6.

55. *CSPF 1586–88*, pp. 89, 114–5, 169, 280, 654.

56. Ibid., p. 214.

57. And for the rest of the paragraph, *CSPF 1586–88*, pp. 483, 556, 565–6, 613, 632–3.

58. *CSPF 1586–88*, pp. 57–8, 90, 295–6, 300–1.

59. *CSPF 1586–88*, pp. 295–6, 357–8, 371.

60. *CSPF 1586–88*, pp. 494, 568–9.

61. *Select Pleas*, II, pp. 163–5.

62. Hatfield House, CP 16/2. I am grateful to Mr Robin Harcourt Williams for a copy of this document.

63. Laughton (ed.), *State Papers*, II, pp. 172–3.

64. *APC 1586–87*, pp. 143–4, 168, 203.

65. *APC 1586–87*, pp. 167, 198–9, 212, 215, 255–6; *Calendar*, p. 57.

66. *HMC Salisbury*, III, pp. 193–6, 200–3, 222–3, 288, 372, 378–9; XIII, p. 322.

67. *CSPF 1588–89*, p. 149; *APC 1587–88*, pp. 59–60, 236–7, 309, 316. Leveson was involved in various disorderly ventures. In 1590 he was imprisoned for debt; he escaped, was re–captured and later died in prison. *Tudor Proclamations*, III, p. 59; N.E. McClure (ed.), *The Letters of John Chamberlain*, 2 vols. (Philadelphia, 1939), I, pp. 56–7, 169.

68. *APC 1586–87*, pp. 236–7, 331; *APC 1588*, pp. 12–3, 365–6, 371–2; *CSPD 1581–90*, p. 635.

69. Laughton (ed.), *State Papers*, II, p. 172: *Calendar*, pp. 61–2.

70. *APC 1588*, pp. 228–9, 236, 254, 268, 385–6, 414–5.

71. On this phase of the sea war see R.B. Wernham, *After the Armada: Elizabethan England and the Struggle for Western Europe 1588–1595* (Oxford, 1984), pp. 235–60; Andrews, *Trade, Plunder and Settlement*, pp. 241–55.

72. *CSPF 1588*, p. 227.

73. *List and Analysis 1590–91*, pp. 321–2; *List and Analysis 1591–92*, p. 338; *Calendar*, p. 62; *APC 1588–89*, pp. 260–1; *APC 1589–90*, pp. 28–9; *APC 1591–92*, pp. 22, 35–6, 65–6.

74. *List and Analysis 1591–92*, pp. 351, 360, 369–70, 372–3; *List and Analysis 1592–93*, pp. 300–4, 325–6, 329–32.

75. *List and Analysis 1589–90*, pp. 419–20, 423–30, 434; BL, Cotton MS Nero B III, ff. 294–5.

76. *List and Analysis 1589–90*, pp. 195–7, 214–5, 227–8, 232; Wilson, *Queen Elizabeth and the Revolt of the Netherlands*, p. 115.

77. *List and Analysis 1591–92*, pp. 6–11, 158–62; *List and Analysis 1590–91*, pp. 119, 177–81; *Law and Custom*, I, pp. 262–5.

78. *List and Analysis 1590–91*, pp. 199–203, 207–12; *List and Analysis 1591–92*, pp. 162–3; *List and Analysis 1592–93*, pp. 141–2; *Tudor Proclamations*, III, pp. 83–6; HCA 1/45, ff. 4–5.

79. *APC 1588–89*, pp. 352, 358–60, 370–410 *passim* on the hulks; *Calendar*, p. 63; *Fugger News–Letters*, pp. 207–8.

80. *APC 1592–93*, pp. 356–7, 385–93; *Tudor Proclamations*, III, pp. 71–4; *Fugger News–Letters*, pp. 222–3, 255–6. Seckford's ships were also involved in attacks on Venetian vessels, Maxwell, 'Henry Seckford', pp. 392–5.

81. *APC 1588–89*, pp. 48–9; *APC 1589–90*, pp. 66, 209–10, 433; *APC 1590*, p. 104; *APC 1592–93*, pp. 469–70; *HMC Salisbury*, XIII, pp. 386, 435.

82. *APC 1589–90*, pp. 367–8.

83. *HMC Salisbury*, IV, p. 72; XIII, p. 434; *APC 1590*, p. 367.

84. *APC 1591*, pp. 226, 302–3, 341–2; *APC 1592*, p. 230; *APC 1592–93*, pp. 312–3, 481–2.

85. Proclamations issued during 1591, 1592 and 1594 tried to regulate the war at sea, *Tudor Proclamations*, III, pp. 99–101, 109–10, 137–8.

86. The most comprehensive treatment of the sea war after 1595 remains J.S. Corbett, *The Successors of Drake* (London, 1900).

87. *List and Analysis 1591–92*, p. 118. About 1580 merchants of Chester claimed to have suffered losses of about £12,000 to piracy since 1570, D.M. Woodward, *The Trade of Elizabethan Chester* (Hull, 1970), pp. 45–6, 87–8.

88. *List and Analysis 1590–91*, pp. 380, 389; *List and Analysis 1592–93*, pp. 359–60.

89. *CSPD 1595–97*, pp. 21, 34, 40, 51. There may have been as many as fifty privateering vessels operating from the port between 1584 and 1586, V.W. Lunsford, *Piracy and Privateering in the Golden Age Netherlands* (New York, 2005), p. 31.

90. Ibid., pp. 130–3; P. E.J. Hammer, *The Polarisation of Elizabethan Politics: The Political Career of Robert Devereux, 2nd Earl of Essex, 1585–1597* (Cambridge, 1999), pp. 212–4, 241–2; Rodger, *Safeguard of the Sea*, pp. 282–5.

91. K.R. Andrews (ed.), *The Last Voyage of Drake & Hawkins* (Hakluyt Society, Second Series, 142, 1972), pp. 23–4.

92. Ibid., pp. 29, 76–8.

93. Ibid., p. 106.

94. Ibid., pp. 158–9.

95. Ibid., pp. 93–5.

96. Ibid., pp. 98–100.

97. Ibid., pp. 100–2 and ensuing quote.

98. Ibid., p. 246; Rodger, *Safeguard of the Sea*, pp. 283–4; Rodger, 'Development of Broadside Gunnery', p. 310.

99. Andrews (ed.), *Last Voyage*, pp. 106, 257–8. It is doubtful, as Rodger points out, whether a base in the Caribbean could have been maintained by the English, *Safeguard of the Sea*, p. 284.

100. HCA 1/45, ff. 80–1.

101. *CSPD 1595–97*, pp. 533–4; Hammer, *Polarisation*, pp. 257–60.

102. *CSPD 1595–97*, pp. 232–4; G.F. Warner (ed.), *The Voyage of Robert Dudley to the West Indies, 1594–1595* (Hakluyt Society, Second Series, 3, 1899), p. 25.

103. Rodger, *Safeguard of the Sea*, pp. 282–5; Hammer, *Elizabeth's Wars*, pp. 196–9. BL, Cotton MS Otho E IX, ff. 336–8 for Essex's apology for proceedings at Cadiz.

104. Rodger, *Safeguard of the Sea*, pp. 282–3, 288; McClure (ed.), *Letters of Chamberlain*, I, pp. 30–1.

105. Ibid., p. 106. Wood was in command of an abortive voyage to China. It is not clear if the survivors at Puerto Rico were of his company, Sir W. Foster, *England's Quest of Eastern Trade* (London, 1933), pp. 138–43. On Hawkins, *List and Analysis 1593–94*, pp. 453–4.

106. *CSPD 1598–1601*, pp. 3, 37, 41, 43; *CSPV 1592–1603*, pp. 230, 313, 318–9, 331–3.

107. McClure (ed.), *Letters of Chamberlain*, I, p. 47; Williamson, *George, Third Earl*, pp. 175–203; *Fugger News–Letters*, pp. 201, 226–7, 269, 304–7, 310–11.

108. Fury, *Tides in the Affairs of Men*, pp. 168–9 on rising violence.

109. The problem was exacerbated by a proclamation of September 1597 authorizing the arrest of ships from northern Europe and the Low Countries carrying grain and munitions to Spain and Portugal, *Tudor Proclamations*, III, pp. 183–5. On the continuing problem over the spoil of Dutch and neutral shipping, *List and Analysis 1595*, pp. 99–101, 160, 177, 257–9.

110. *CSPI 1596–97*, pp. 238, 253; *Calendar*, pp. 98–9; HCA 1/45, ff. 63v–4.

111. *APC 1595–96*, pp. 318–9, 334–5, 354–5, 399–400; *Calendar*, pp. 64–8, 71–3, 88–103; *HMC Salisbury*, VIII, p. 104.

112. *APC 1595–96*, pp. 466–7; Andrews, *Elizabethan Privateering*, p. 116.

113. *APC 1597*, pp. 19–20; *APC 1597–98*, pp. 171–2; *APC 1599–1600*, pp. 173, 320, 660–2; *APC 1601–3*, p. 95; Latham and Youings (ed.), *Letters*, pp. 192–4, 223–4.

114. *HMC Salisbury*, VII, pp. 82, 124; L. Stone, 'The Fruits of Office: The Case of Robert Cecil, first earl of Salisbury, 1596–1612' in F.J. Fisher (ed.), *Essays in the Economic and Social History of Tudor and Stuart England* (Cambridge, 1961), pp. 91–4; K.R. Andrews, 'Sir Robert Cecil and Mediterranean Plunder', *EHR*, 87 (1972), pp. 520–2; Kenny, *Elizabeth's Admiral*, pp. 104–5.

115. On the use of Barbary see Sir G. Fisher, *Barbary Legend: War, Trade and Piracy in North Africa 1415–1830* (Oxford, 1957), pp. 122–3, 131–2.

116. *APC 1596–97*, pp. 126–7, 414–5; *APC 1597–98*, pp. 247–8; *APC 1598–99*, pp. 223, 451–2, 493–4; *APC 1599–1600*, pp. 157, 283; Andrews, *Elizabethan Privateering*, p. 68; *ODNB*, 'Edward Glemham'.

117. *CSPV 1592–1603*, pp. 301–2, 319, 378.

118. The number may have varied from seven to seventeen, Andrews, 'Cecil and Mediterranean Plunder', p. 517; *CSPV 1592–1603*, pp. 412–21, 516. For the damage to Venice see A. Tenenti, *Piracy and the Decline of Venice 1580–1615* (London, 1967).

119. HCA 1/45, ff. 7–25; Tenenti, *Piracy*, p. 66.

120. HCA 1/45, f. 13v. The merchants were of Portuguese origin, but resident in Leghorn.

121. HCA 1/45, ff. 9v–10v, 15, 18.

122. Ibid., f. 14.

123. *Tudor Proclamations*, III, pp. 198–9; McClure (ed.), *Letters of Chamberlain*, I, p. 68; *CSPV 1592–1603*, p. 334; *APC 1597–98*, pp. 324–6, 382–6, 397–9, 454, 492–3, 604.

124. *CSPV 1592–1603*, pp. 364–5, 398–9, 401–3, 433.

125. *CSPV 1592–1603*, pp. 440, 446, 481–2; *Fugger News–Letters*, pp. 323–5; McClure (ed.), *Letters of Chamberlain*, I, p. 63.

126. *APC 1599–1600*, p. 745; *CSPV 1592–1603*, p. 460; *HMC Salisbury*, XV, pp. 225–6. The regent of Algiers reportedly received one–eighth of prizes brought in by the English, HCA 1/45, ff. 182–3v.

127. *CSPV 1592–1603*, pp. 537, 550–2; Fisher, *Barbary Legend*, pp. 130–1.

128. *CSPV 1592–1603*, pp. 515–6, 521–2, 542, 559, 567–8; *CSPV 1603–7*, pp. 28, 31–4; *HMC Salisbury*, XV, pp. 225–6. English rovers included William Hull and Philip Ward of Exeter, who plundered a Venetian vessel off Sardinia during the closing months of the war, HCA 1/5, ff. 11, 150; 1/45, ff. 24v–26v.

129. Andrews, *Elizabethan Privateering*, pp. 53–60, 67; *CSPV 1592–1603*, pp. 537–9, 544–7, 550; *ODNB*, 'Sir Thomas Sherley'.

130. And following quote, *HMC Salisbury*, XV, p. 127.

131. *APC 1595–96*, pp. 204–5. The lords of Orkney were also accused of being involved in piracy, H.D. Smith, *Shetland Life and Trade 1550–1914* (Edinburgh, 1984), pp. 43, 267.

132. *APC 1596–97*, p. 507; *APC 1597*, pp. 132–3, 354; *APC 1597–98*, pp. 282–3.

133. *CSPI 1600–1*, p. 437; *APC 1599–1600*, p. 724.

134. *APC 1601–4*, p. 361; *Calendar*, p. 97.

135. *CSPD 1598–1601*, p. 154.

136. The raids of the Dunkirkers provoked complaints in parliament and projects for the reorganization of the war: McClure (ed.), *Letters of Chamberlain*, I, p. 182; T.E. Hartley (ed.), *Proceedings in the Parliaments of Elizabeth*, 3 vols. (London, 1981–95), III, pp. 429–31.

137. BL, Lansdowne MS 142, ff. 159–61, 165–78; McClure (ed.), *Letters of Chamberlain*, I, p. 188; *Select Pleas*, II, pp. 203–5; C. L'Estrange Ewen, *Captain John Ward, 'Arch–Pirate'* (Paignton, 1939), pp. 1–3.

Epilogue

1. W.B. Rye (ed.), *England as seen by Foreigners in the Days of Elizabeth and James the First* (London, 1865), p. 110.

2. *HMC Salisbury*, XV, pp. 151, 168, 170, 202–3, 253; G.V. Scammell, 'The Sinews of War: Manning and Provisioning English Fighting Ships, c. 1550–1650', *Mariner's Mirror*, 73 (1985), pp. 360–1 reprinted in *Ships, Oceans and Empire*.

3. *HMC Salisbury*, XV, p. 151.

4. For a recent study of Ward see G. Bak, *Barbary Pirate: The Life and Crimes of John Ward* (Stroud, 2006), and on Jacobean piracy see C.M. Senior, *A Nation of Pirates: English Piracy in its Heyday* (Newton Abbot, 1976).

5. Rediker, *Villains of All Nations*, pp. 19–37.

Bibliography

Manuscript Sources

The National Archives, Kew
    SP 12 (State Papers, Elizabeth I)
    SP 63 (State Papers, Ireland)
    HCA 1/33, 34, 37, 38, 40, 44, 45, 48 (High Court of Admiralty, oyer and terminer records)
    HCA 13/2-36 (High Court of Admiralty, examinations)
    HCA 14/9 (High Court of Admiralty, exemplifications)
The British Library, London
    Additional MS 12505
    Lansdowne MS 26, 33, 142, 162
    Cotton MS Nero B III
    Cotton MS Otho E VIII, IX

Printed Sources

A True Relation of the Lives and Deaths of the two most Famous Pyrats, Purser and Clinton
    (London, 1639, repr. Amsterdam, 1971)

K.R. Andrews (ed.), *English Privateering Voyages to the West Indies 1588-1595* (Hakluyt Society,
    Second Series, 111, 1959)

—, *The Last Voyage of Drake & Hawkins* (Hakluyt Society, Second Series, 142, 1972)

J.C. Appleby (ed.), *A Calendar of Material relating to Ireland from the High Court of Admiralty
    Examinations 1536-1641* (Irish Manuscripts Commission, Dublin, 1992)

J. Bain et al. (eds.), *Calendar of the State Papers relating to Scotland and Mary, Queen of Scots
    1547-1603*, 13 vols. (Edinburgh, 1898-1969)

B.L. Beer and S.M. Jack (eds.), 'The Letters of William, Lord Paget of Beaudesert, 1547-63',
    Camden Miscellany XXV (Camden Society, Fourth Series, 13, 1974)

G.A. Bergenroth et al. (eds.), *Calendar of Letters, Despatches, and State Papers, relating to the
    Negotiations between England and Spain, 1485-1558*, 13 vols. (London, 1862-1954)

J.S. Brewer et al. (eds.), *Calendar of the Carew Manuscripts 1515-1603*, 4 vols. (London, 1867-70)

J.S. Brewer et al. (eds.), *Letters and Papers, Foreign and Domestic, of the Reign of Henry VIII & Addenda*, 22 vols. (2nd edition, London, 1920-32)

R. Brown et al. (eds.), *Calendar of State Papers and Manuscripts, relating to English Affairs, existing in the Archives and Collections of Venice, 1558-1603*, 9 vols. (London, 1890-1603)

J.H. Burton (ed.), *The Register of the Privy Council of Scotland, 1545-1569* (Edinburgh, 1877)

M. St Clair Byrne (ed.), *The Lisle Letters*, 6 vols. (London, 1981)

Calendar of Patent Rolls preserved in the Public Record Office 1461-1582, 24 vols. (London, 1897-1986)

Calendar of the Manuscripts of the Most Hon. the Marquis of Salisbury, 23 vols. (Historical Manuscripts Commission, London, 1883-1973)

J. Payne Collier (ed.), *Illustrations of Early English Popular Literature*, 3 vols. (London, 1863-64)

J.S. Corbett (ed.), *Papers relating to the Navy during the Spanish War 1585-1587* (Navy Records Society, 11, 1898)

J.R. Dasent (ed.), *Acts of the Privy Council of England 1542-1604*, 31 vols. (London, 1890-1907)

E.S. Donno (ed.), *An Elizabethan in 1581: The Diary of Richard Madox, Fellow of All Souls* (Hakluyt Society, Second Series, 147, 1976)

G.R. Elton (ed.), *The Tudor Constitution* (2nd edition, Cambridge, 1982)

R. Hakluyt, *The Principal Navigations Voyages Traffiques & Discoveries of the English Nation*, 12 vols. (3rd edition, Glasgow, 1903-5, repr. New York, 1969)

R. Hakluyt, *Discourse of Western Planting*, eds. D.B and A.M. Quinn (Hakluyt Society, Extra Series, 45, 1993)

F.E. Halliday (ed.), *Richard Carew of Antony: The Survey of Cornwall* (London, 1953)

H.C. Hamilton et al. (eds.), *Calendar of State Papers relating to Ireland 1509-1603*, 11 vols. (London, 1860-1912)

R.K. Hannay (ed.), *The Letters of James V* (Edinburgh, 1954)

T.E. Hartley (ed.), *Proceedings in the Parliaments of Elizabeth I*, 3 vols. (London, 1981-95)

C. Hopper (ed.), 'Sir Francis Drake's Memorable Service done against the Spaniards in 1587. Written by Robert Long, gentleman', *Camden Miscellany V* (Camden Society, 87, 1864)

P.L. Hughes and J.F. Larkin (eds.), *Tudor Royal Proclamations*, 3 vols. (New Haven, 1964-69)

M. Hume et al. (eds.), *Calendar of Letters and State Papers relating to English Affairs, preserved principally in the Archives of Simancas, 1558-1603*, 4 vols. (London, 1892-99)

M.F. Keeler (ed.), *Sir Francis Drake's West Indian Voyage 1585-1586* (Hakluyt Society, Second Series, 148, 1981)

V. von Klarwill (ed.), *The Fugger News-Letters 1568-1605* (London, 1926)

C.S. Knighton (ed.), *Calendar of State Papers Domestic Series of the Reign of Edward VI 1547-1553* (London, 1992)

—, *Calendar of State Papers Domestic Series of the Reign of Mary I 1553-1558* (London, 1998)

C.S. Knighton and D. Loades (eds.), *Letters from the Mary Rose* (Stroud, 2002)

A. Latham and J. Youings (eds.), *The Letters of Sir Walter Raleigh* (Exeter, 1999)

J.K. Laughton (ed.), *State Papers relating to the Defeat of the Spanish Armada*, 2 vols. (Navy Records Society, 1 & 2, 1894)

R. Lemon et al. (eds.), *Calendar of State Papers Domestic, 1547-1603 & Addenda*, 7 vols. (London, 1856-71)

K. de Lettenhove (ed.), *Relations Politiques des Pays-Bas et de l'Angleterre sous Le Règne de Philippe II*, 11 vols. (Brussels, 1888-1900)

E.A. Lewis (ed.), *The Welsh Port Books (1550-1603)* (Cymmrodorion Record Series, 12, 1927)

R.G. Marsden (ed.), *Select Pleas in the Court of Admiralty*, 2 vols. (Selden Society, 6 & 11, 1894-97)

—, 'Voyage of the Barbara to Brazil, A.D. 1540', *Naval Miscellany II* (Navy Records Society, 40, 1912), pp. 3-66

—, *Documents relating to the Law and Custom of the Sea*, 2 vols. (Navy Records Society, 49 & 50, 1915-16)

J.H. Matthews (ed.), *Cardiff Records*, 6 vols. (Cardiff, 1898-1911)

N.E. Mc Clure (ed.), *The Letters of John Chamberlain*, 2 vols. (Philadelphia, 1939)

A.L. Merson (ed.), *The Third Book of Remembrance of Southampton 1514-1602*, 3 vols. (Southampton Record Series, 2, 3 & 8, n. s., 1952-65)

J.G. Nichols (ed.), *The Diary of Henry Machyn, Citizen and Merchant-Taylor of London* (Camden Society, 42, 1848)

Z. Nuttall (ed.), *New Light on Drake* (Hakluyt Society, Second Series, 34, 1914)

M. O'Dowd (ed.), *Calendar of State Papers Ireland: Tudor Period 1571-1575* (London & Dublin, 2000)

O. Ogle (ed.), *Copy-Book of Sir Amias Paulet's Letters Written during his Embassy to France* (Roxburghe Club, London, 1866)

M. Oppenheim (ed.), *The Naval Tracts of Sir William Monson*, 5 vols. (Navy Records Society, 22, 23, 43, 45, 47, 1902-14)

D.B. Quinn (ed.), *The Voyages and Colonising Enterprises of Sir Humphrey Gilbert*, 2 vols. (Hakluyt Society, Second Series, 83 & 84, 1938-39)

—, *The Roanoke Voyages 1584-1590*, 2 vols. (Hakluyt Society, Second Series, 104 & 105, 1955)

—, *New American World: A Documentary History of North America to 1612*, 5 vols. (London, 1979)

W.B. Rye (ed.), *England as seen by Foreigners in the Days of Elizabeth and James the First* (London, 1865)

A. Hassell Smith et al. (eds.), *The Papers of Nathaniel Bacon of Stiffkey* (Norwich, 1979)

A. Spont (ed.), *Letters and Papers relating to the War with France 1512-1513* (Navy Records Society, 10, 1897)

J. Stow, *The Annales of England* (London, 1605)

R.H. Tawney and E. Power (eds.), *Tudor Economic Documents*, 3 vols. (London, 1924)

E.G.R. Taylor (ed.), *The Troublesome Voyage of Captain Edward Fenton* (Hakluyt Society, Second Series, 113, 1959)

W.B. Turnbull et al. (eds.), *Calendar of State Papers, Foreign Series, 1547-89*, 23 vols. (London, 1861-1950)

J.A. Twemlow (ed.), *Liverpool Town Books*, 2 vols. (Liverpool, 1918-35)

S. and E. Usherwood (eds.), *The Counter-Armada, 1596: The Journall of the 'Mary Rose'* (London, 1983)

J. Vanes (ed.), *Documents illustrating the Overseas Trade of Bristol in the Sixteenth Century* (Bristol Record Society, 31, 1979)

G.F. Warner (ed.), *The Voyage of Robert Dudley to the West Indies, 1594-1595* (Hakluyt Society, Second Series, 3, 1899)

Sir G. Warner (ed.), *The Libelle of Englyshe Polycye: A Poem on the Use of Sea-Power 1436* (Oxford, 1926)

R.B. Wernham (ed.), *List and Analysis of State Papers Foreign Series Elizabeth I 1589-1596*, 7 vols. (London, 1964-2000)

—, *The Expedition of Sir John Norris and Sir Francis Drake to Spain and Portugal, 1589* (Navy Records Society, 127, 1988)

I.A Wright (ed.), *Spanish Documents concerning English Voyages to the Caribbean 1527-1568*

(Hakluyt Society, Second Series, 57, 1929)

—, *Documents concerning English Voyages to the Spanish Main 1569-80* (Hakluyt Society, Second Series, 71, 1932)

—, *Further English Voyages to Spanish America 1583-1594* (Hakluyt Society, Second Series, 94, 1951)

3 Secondary works

K.R. Andrews, *Elizabethan Privateering: English Privateering during the Spanish War 1585-1603* (Cambridge, 1966)

—, *Drake's Voyages: A Re-assessment of their Place in Elizabethan Maritime Expansion* (London, 1967)

—, 'The Aims of Drake's Expedition of 1577-1580', *American Historical Review*, 73 (1968), pp. 724-41

—, 'Sir Robert Cecil and Mediterranean Plunder', *English Historical Review*, 87 (1972), pp. 513-32

—, *The Spanish Caribbean: Trade and Plunder 1530-1630* (New Haven, 1978)

—, 'Beyond the Equinoctial: England and South America in the Sixteenth Century', *Journal of Imperial and Commonwealth History*, 10 (1981), pp. 4-24

—, 'The Elizabethan Seaman', *Mariner's Mirror*, 68 (1982), pp. 245-62

—, *Trade, Plunder and Settlement: Maritime Enterprise and the Genesis of the British Empire, 1480-1630* (Cambridge, 1984)

J. Baer, *Pirates of the British Isles* (Stroud, 2005)

S. Bawlf, *The Secret Voyage of Sir Francis Drake 1577-1580* (New York, 2003)

S.T. Bindoff et al. (eds.), *Elizabethan Government and Society* (London, 1961)

F. Braudel, *The Mediterranean and the Mediterranean World in the Age of Philip II* (2nd edition, London, 1972)

R. Brenner, *Merchants and Revolution: Commercial Change, Political Conflict, and London's Overseas Traders, 1550-1653* (Cambridge, 1993)

D. Burwash, *English Merchant Shipping 1460-1540* (Toronto, 1947)

G.T. Cell, *English Enterprise in Newfoundland 1577-1660* (Toronto, 1969)

A. Chambers, *Granuaile: The Life and Times of Grace O'Malley c. 1530-1603* (Dublin, 1979)

E.P. Cheyney, *A History of England from the Defeat of the Armada to the Death of Elizabeth*, 2 vols. (London, 1914, repr. New York, 1948)

D. Childs, *The Warship Mary Rose: The Life and Times of King Henry VIII's Flagship* (London, 2007)

P. Clark (ed.), *The European Crisis of the 1590s* (London, 1985)

G. Connell-Smith, *Forerunners of Drake: A Study of English Trade with Spain in the early Tudor Period* (London, 1954, repr. Westport, CT, 1975)

J. Corbett, *Drake and the Tudor Navy*, 2 vols. (London, 1898, repr. Aldershot, 1988)

—, *The Successors of Drake* (London, 1900)

D. Cordingly, *Life among the Pirates: The Romance and the Reality* (London, 1995)

P. Croft, 'English Mariners trading to Spain and Portugal, 1558-1625', *Mariner's Mirror*, 69 (1983), pp. 251-66

—, 'Trading with the Enemy 1585-1604', *The Historical Journal*, 32 (1989), pp. 281-302

S. Cunningham, *Henry VII* (London, 2006)

R. Davis, *The Rise of the Atlantic Economies* (London, 1973)

R.C. Davis, *Christian Slaves, Muslim Masters: White Slavery in the Mediterranean, the Barbary Coast, and Italy, 1500-1800* (Basingstoke, 2003)

B. Dietz, 'The Huguenot and English Corsairs during the Third Civil War in France, 1568 to 1570', *Proceedings of the Huguenot Society of London,* 19 (1952-58), pp. 278-94

S. Doran and G. Richardson (eds.), *Tudor England and its Neighbours* (Basingstoke, 2005)

M. Duffy et al. (eds.), *The New Maritime History of Devon,* 2 vols. (Exeter, 1992-94)

P. Earle, *Corsairs of Malta and Barbary* (London, 1970)

—, *The Last Fight of the Revenge* (London, 1992)

—, *The Pirate Wars* (London, 2003)

J.H. Elliott, *Imperial Spain 1469-1716* (London, 1963)

—, *Empires of the Atlantic World: Britain and Spain in America 1492-1830* (New Haven, 2006)

C. L'Estrange Ewen, *Captain John Ward, 'Arch-Pirate'* (Paignton, 1939)

—, *The Golden Chalice: A Documented Narrative of an Elizabethan Pirate* (Paignton, 1939)

—, 'Organized Piracy round Britain in the Sixteenth Century', *Mariner's Mirror,* 35 (1949), pp. 29-42

—, 'The Pirates of Purbeck', *Proceedings of the Dorset Natural History & Archaeological Society,* 71 (1949), pp. 88-109

F.J. Fisher (ed.), *Essays in the Economic and Social History of Tudor and Stuart England* (Cambridge, 1961)

Sir G. Fisher, *Barbary Legend: War, Trade and Piracy in North Africa 1415-1830* (Oxford, 1957)

Sir W. Foster, *England's Quest of Eastern Trade* (London, 1933)

E.W. Fowler, *English Sea Power in the Early Tudor Period 1485-1558* (Ithaca, 1965)

M. Franks, *The Basingstoke Admiral: A Life of Sir James Lancaster* (Salisbury, 2006)

M.F. French, 'Privateering and the Revolt of the Netherlands: The *Watergeuzen* or Sea Beggars in Portsmouth, Gosport and the Isle of Wight, 1570-71', *Proceedings of the Hampshire Field Club & Archaeological Society,* 47 (1991), pp. 171–80

C.A. Fury, *Tides in the Affairs of Men: The Social History of Elizabethan Seamen, 1580-1603* (Westport, CT, 2002)

P. Gerhard, *Pirates of the Pacific, 1575-1742* (Lincoln, Nebraska, 1960)

T. Glasgow, 'The Royal Navy at the Start of the Reign of Elizabeth I', *Mariner's Mirror,* 51 (1965), pp. 73-6

—, 'The Navy in Philip and Mary's War, 1557-1558', *Mariner's Mirror,* 53 (1967), pp. 321-42

—, 'The Navy in the first Elizabethan Undeclared War, 1559-1560', *Mariner's Mirror,* 54 (1968), pp. 23-37

J. Glete, *Warfare at Sea, 1500-1650: Maritime Conflicts and the Transformation of Europe* (London, 2000)

P. Gosse, *The History of Piracy* (London, 1932)

I.F. Grant, *The Social and Economic Development of Scotland before 1603* (Edinburgh, 1930)

J. Guy, *Tudor England* (Oxford, 1988)

P.E.J. Hammer, *The Polarisation of Elizabethan Politics: The Political Career of Robert Devereux, 2nd Earl of Essex, 1585-1597* (Cambridge, 1999)

—, *Elizabeth's Wars: War, Government and Society in Tudor England, 1544-1604* (Basingstoke, 2003)

P.E.H. Hair, 'Protestants as Pirates, Slavers and Proto-Missionaries: Sierra Leone 1568 and 1582', *Journal of Ecclesiastical History,* 21 (1970), pp. 203-24

R. Harding, *The Evolution of the Sailing Navy, 1509-1815* (Basingstoke, 1995)

J. Heers, *The Barbary Corsairs: Warfare in the Mediterranean, 1480-1580* (London, 2003)

W.G. Hoskins, *The Age of Plunder: The England of Henry VIII 1509-1547* (London, 1976)

C.E. Hughes, 'Wales and Piracy: A Study in Tudor Administration 1500-1640' (University of Wales, MA thesis, 1937)

D.G.E. Hurd, 'Some Aspects of the Attempts of the Government to Suppress Piracy during the Reign of Elizabeth I' (University of London, MA thesis, 1961)

A. G. Jamieson (ed.), *A People of the Sea: The Maritime History of the Channel Islands* (London, 1986)

C. Jowitt (ed.), *Pirates? The Politics of Plunder, 1550-1650* (Basingstoke, 2001)

R.W. Kenny, *Elizabeth's Admiral: The Political Career of Charles Howard Earl of Nottingham 1536-1624* (Baltimore, 1970)

C.L. Kingsford, *Prejudice and Promise in Fifteenth-Century England* (Oxford, 1925, repr. London, 1962)

H. Kamen, *Philip of Spain* (New Haven, 1997)

—, *Spain's Road to Empire: The Making of a World Power, 1492-1763* (London, 2003)

H. Kelsey, *Sir Francis Drake: The Queen's Pirate* (New Haven, 1998)

—, *Sir John Hawkins: Queen Elizabeth's Slave Trader* (New Haven, 2003)

P. Kemp and C. Lloyd, *The Brethren of the Coast: The British and French Buccaneers in the South Seas* (London, 1960)

P. M. Kennedy, *The Rise and Fall of British Naval Mastery* (London, 1976)

R.J. Knecht, *The Rise and Fall of Renaissance France 1483-1610* (London, 1996)

K. Kupperman, *Roanoke: The Abandoned Colony* (2nd edition, Lanham, 2007)

K.E. Lane, *Pillaging the Empire: Piracy in the Americas 1500-1750* (Armonk, 1998)

H.A. Lloyd, *The Gentry of South-West Wales, 1540-1640* (Cardiff, 1968)

J. Loach and R. Tittler (eds.), *The Mid-Tudor Polity c. 1540-1560* (London, 1980)

D. Loades, *Two Tudor Conspiracies* (Cambridge, 1965)

—, *The Reign of Mary Tudor* (2nd edition, London, 1991)

—, *The Tudor Navy: An Administrative, Political and Military History* (Aldershot, 1992)

—, *England's Maritime Empire: Seapower, Commerce and Policy, 1490-1690* (Harlow, 2000)

A.K. Longfield, *Anglo-Irish Trade in the Sixteenth Century* (London, 1929)

V.W. Lunsford, *Piracy and Privateering in the Golden Age Netherlands* (New York, 2005)

W.T. MacCaffrey, *Exeter, 1540-1640: The Growth of an English County Town* (Cambridge, Mass., 1985)

—, *The Shaping of the Elizabethan Regime* (Princeton, 1968)

—, *Queen Elizabeth and the Making of Policy, 1572-1588* (Princeton, 1981)

—, *Elizabeth I, War and Politics 1588-1603* (Princeton, 1992)

A.I. Macinnes, *Clanship, Commerce and the House of Stuart, 1603-1788* (East Linton, 1996)

Rev. J. MacInnes, 'West Highland Sea-Power in the Middle Ages', *Transactions of the Gaelic Society of Inverness*, 48 (1972-74), pp. 518-56

R.G. Marsden, 'The Early Career of Sir Martin Frobisher', *English Historical Review*, 21 (1906), pp. 538-44

C. Martin and G. Parker, *The Spanish Armada* (2nd edition, Manchester, 2002)

D. Mathew, *The Celtic Peoples and Renaissance Europe* (London, 1933)

S. Maxwell, 'Henry Seckford: Sixteenth-Century Merchant, Courtier and Privateer', *Mariner's Mirror*, 82 (1996), pp. 387-97

J. McDermott, *Martin Frobisher: Elizabethan Privateer* (New Haven, 2001)

—, *England and the Spanish Armada: The Necessary Quarrel* (New Haven, 2005)

M. Mollat (ed.), *Course et Piraterie*, 2 vols. (Paris, 1975)

G. Moorhouse, *Great Harry's Navy: How Henry VIII gave England Sea Power* (London, 2004)

M. Oppenheim, *A History of the Administration of the Royal Navy and of Merchant Shipping in relation to the Navy from 1509 to 1660* (London, 1896, repr. Aldershot, 1988)

—, *The Maritime History of Devon* (Exeter, 1968)

G.D. Owen, *Elizabethan Wales: The Social Scene* (Cardiff, 1964)

D.M. Palliser, *The Age of Elizabeth: England under the Later Tudors 1547-1603* (2nd edition, London, 1992)

G. Parker, *The Dutch Revolt* (London, 1977)

—, 'The *Dreadnought* Revolution of Tudor England', *Mariner's Mirror*, 82 (1996), pp. 269-300

—, *The Grand Strategy of Philip II* (New Haven, 1998)

J.H. Parry, *The Spanish Seaborne Empire* (London, 1966)

C.R. Pennell (ed.), *Bandits at Sea: A Pirates Reader* (New York, 2001)

D.B. Quinn, *Ralegh and the British Empire* (London, 1947)

—, *England and the Discovery of America, 1481-1620* (London, 1994)

—, *Explorers and Colonies: America, 1500-1625* (London, 1990)

D.B. Quinn and A.N. Ryan, *England's Sea Empire, 1550-1642* (London, 1983)

G.D. Ramsay, *English Overseas Trade in the Centuries of Emergence* (London, 1957)

—, *The City of London in International Politics at the Accession of Elizabeth Tudor* (Manchester, 1975)

M. Rediker, *Between the Devil and the Deep Blue Sea: Merchant Seamen, Pirates, and the Anglo-American Maritime World, 1700-1750* (Cambridge, 1987)

—, *Villains of All Nations: Atlantic Pirates in the Golden Age* (London, 2004)

C.F. Richmond, 'The Earl of Warwick's Domination of the Channel and the Naval Dimension to the Wars of the Roses, 1456-1460', *Southern History*, 20-21 (1998-99), pp. 1-19

R.C. Ritchie, *Captain Kidd and the War against the Pirates* (Cambridge, Mass., 1986)

N.A.M. Rodger, 'A Pirate's Log', *Mariner's Mirror*, 67 (1981), pp. 201-4

—, 'The Development of Broadside Gunnery, 1450-1650', *Mariner's Mirror*, 82 (1996), pp. 301-24

—, *The Safeguard of the Sea: A Naval History of Britain 660-1649* (London, 1997)

—, 'The New Atlantic: Naval Warfare in the Sixteenth Century' in J.B. Hattendorf and R.W. Unger (eds.), *War at Sea in the Middle Ages and the Renaissance* (Woodbridge, 2003)

—, 'Queen Elizabeth and the Myth of Sea-Power in English History', *Transactions of the Royal Historical Society*, Sixth Series, 14 (2004), pp. 153-74

M.J. Rodriguez-Salgado and S. Adams (eds.), *England, Spain and the Gran Armada 1585-1604* (Edinburgh, 1991)

S. Ronald, *The Pirate Queen: Queen Elizabeth I, her Pirate Adventurers, and the Dawn of Empire* (Stroud, 2007)

S. Rose, *The Medieval Sea* (London, 2007)

C. Ross, *Edward IV* (London, 1974)

A.L. Rowse, *Sir Richard Grenville of the 'Revenge'* (London, 1937)

—, *Tudor Cornwall: Portrait of a Society* (London, 1941)

R. Saunders, *If a Pirate I must be … The True Story of Bartholomew Roberts, King of the Caribbean* (London, 2007)

G.V. Scammell, 'War at Sea under the Early Tudors: Some Newcastle upon Tyne Evidence', *Archaeologia Aeliana*, Fourth Series, 38 (1960), pp. 73-97 and 39 (1961), pp. 179-205

—, *The World Encompassed: The First European Maritime Empires, c. 800-1650* (London, 1981)

—, *The First Imperial Age: European Overseas Expansion c. 1400-1715* (London, 1989)

—, *Ships, Oceans and Empire: Studies in European Maritime and Colonial History, 1400-1750* (Aldershot, 1995)

C.M. Senior, *A Nation of Pirates: English Piracy in its Heyday* (Newton Abbot, 1976)

L. Sicking, *Neptune and the Netherlands: State, Economy, and War at Sea in the Renaissance* (Brill, 2004)

R.T. Spence, *The Privateering Earl: George Clifford, 3rd Earl of Cumberland, 1558-1605* (Stroud, 1995)

L. Stone, *An Elizabethan: Sir Horatio Palavicino* (Oxford, 1956)

D. Studnicki-Gizbert, *A Nation upon the Sea: Portugal's Atlantic Diaspora and the Crisis of the Spanish Empire, 1492-1640* (Oxford, 2007)

A. Tenenti, *Piracy and the Decline of Venice 1580-1615* (London, 1967)

J.E. Thomson, *Mercenaries, Pirates and Sovereigns: State-Building and Extraterritorial Violence in Early Modern Europe* (Princeton, 1994)

R. Thrower, *The Pirate Picture* (London, 1980)

J. Tracy, 'Herring Wars: The Habsburg Netherlands and the Struggle for the Control of the North Sea, *c*.1520-1560', *The Sixteenth Century Journal*, 24 (1993), pp. 249-72

T. Travers, *Pirates: A History* (Stroud, 2007)

R. Trevelyan, *Sir Walter Raleigh* (London, 2002)

R.M.S. Tugwood, 'Piracy and Privateering from Dartmouth and Kingswear, 1540-1558' (University of London, MA thesis, 1953)

R.B. Wernham, *Before the Armada: The Growth of English Foreign Policy 1485-1588* (London, 1966)

—, *After the Armada: Elizabethan England and the Struggle for Western Europe 1588-1595* (Oxford, 1984)

—, *The Return of the Armadas: The Last Years of the Elizabethan War against Spain 1595-1603* (Oxford, 1994)

N. Williams, *The Sea Dogs: Privateers, Plunder and Piracy in the Elizabethan Age* (London, 1975)

P. Williams, *The Tudor Regime* (Oxford, 1979)

—, *The Later Tudors: England 1547-1603* (Oxford, 1995)

G.C. Williamson, *George, Third Earl of Cumberland (1558-1603): His Life and His Voyages* (Cambridge, 1920)

J.A. Williamson, *Maritime Enterprise 1485-1558* (Oxford, 1913)

—, *Sir John Hawkins: The Time and the Man* (Oxford, 1926)

—, *Hawkins of Plymouth* (2nd edition, London, 1969)

T.S. Willan, *Studies in Elizabethan Foreign Trade* (Manchester, 1959)

C. Wilson, *Queen Elizabeth and the Revolt of the Netherlands* (London, 1970)

P.L. Wilson, *Pirate Utopias: Moorish Corsairs & European Renegadoes* (New York, 1995)

D.M. Woodward, *The Trade of Elizabethan Chester* (Hull, 1970)

G. Wycherley, *Buccaneers of the Pacific* (Indianapolis, 1928)

Index